FAXTON

Excavations in a deserted Northamptonshire village 1966–68

by

Lawrence Butler (†)

and

Christopher Gerrard

with contributions from

Paul Blinkhorn, Peter Brown, Geoff Egan,
Louisa Gidney, Ian Goodall, David Hall, Brian Hartley,
Richard Kelleher, Ronan O'Donnell, Paul Stamper,
Eleanor Standley and Stuart Wrathmell

THE SOCIETY FOR MEDIEVAL ARCHAEOLOGY
MONOGRAPH 42

First published 2021
by Routledge
2 Park Square, Milton Park, Abingdon, Oxon OX14 4RN

and by Routledge
52 Vanderbilt Avenue, New York, NY 10017

Routledge is an imprint of the Taylor & Francis Group, an informa business

British Library Cataloguing-in-Publication Data
A catalogue record for this book is available from the British Library

Library of Congress Cataloging-in-Publication Data
A catalog record has been requested for this book

ISSN: 0583-9106
ISBN: 978-0-367-51772-4 (hbk)
ISBN: 978-0-367-51771-7 (pbk)
ISBN: 978-1-003-05515-0 (ebk)

Typeset in Bembo
by A. Gutiérrez

Publisher's Note
This book has been prepared from camera-ready copy provided by the author.

Series editor: Gabor Thomas

The Society for Medieval Archaeology is grateful to Historic England and the Medieval Settlement Research Group for a grant towards this publication

The Society for Medieval Archaeology
www.medievalarchaeology.co.uk

Cover: *Excavations at Faxton in 1967*

CONTENTS

iv

Appendices

LIST OF FIGURES

COLOUR PLATES

ACKNOWLEDGEMENTS

LAWRENCE BUTLER'S 1996 ACKNOWLEDGEMENTS

The excavations at Faxton would not have been possible without the co-operation of the landowners Mr and Mrs Frank Beers of Scaldwell and of their son Gerald. The ready assistance of Mr and Mrs Geoffrey Hayward of Old Lodge made life more comfortable than twenty weeks of camping sometimes can be. The local knowledge of these families, of Mr and Mrs Hayward senior of Kites Hall, of Mr Jack Knight of Old and of Mrs Bamford, formerly of Faxton, illuminated the recent history of Faxton. Discussions with Sir Gyles Isham of Lamport Hall and with Dr Joan Wake assisted on many themes from Faxton's past; the extended loan of his historical notes by Mr P I King of Northamptonshire Record Office was an undeserved kindness. Recent residents, notably Miss Bamford, conveyed a vivid picture of village life from the end of Victoria's reign to the time that excavations began. Mr John Steane shared his knowledge of local pottery and housing at Lyveden, and encouraged his senior pupils at Kettering Grammar School to participate in the excavation.

The three seasons of excavation were funded by generous grants from the Ancient Monuments Inspectorate of the (then) Ministry of Works on the recommendation of the Deserted Medieval Village Research Group. The officers of the Group, particularly Professor W F Grimes and Mr J G Hurst, were always prepared to discuss the problems arising from the work. Support from Leeds University in the use of equipment and the provision of storage space must be acknowledged. The efforts and enthusiasm of supervisors, volunteer excavators and paid workmen in hot summers and dank autumns made this excavation possible; particular thanks are due to the three assistant directors, Kenneth Wilson and his wife Peggy Wilson, and Mrs Gwen Brown, to site supervisors Bob Carr and Steven Taylor and to finds assistant Mrs Isobel Butler. The authors of other contributions to the work are acknowledged during the text.

The post-excavation programme was funded by English Heritage and housed at the Department of Archaeology, Leeds University. The conservation of metalwork was undertaken in the Department's Laboratory by Jim Black and later by Mrs Julie Jones. The conservation of coins and tokens was by Robert Janaway. The initial sorting of the excavation archive was by Dave Evans, who also commenced work on the pottery, advised by Mr M J McCarthy. For the pottery, the authors wish to thank Stephen Moorhouse for guiding them through the methodology of studying medieval pottery, and Terry Pearson who gave the benefit of his expert knowledge of the pottery of Northamptonshire. Two evening classes were enlisted to help with the washing and sorting of the pottery; in particular Stephen Fairclough, Lynne Hick and Dorothy Wharram should all be warmly thanked. Advice on the coins was given by Jeffrey North and on the corn drier by Robert Rickett. The principal study of the pottery was completed in 1984–85 by Dr Julian Richards and Mrs Linda Bamber. The drawings which illustrate this monograph are all the work of Malcolm Stroud; photographs are individually acknowledged.

CHRISTOPHER GERRARD'S 2017 ACKNOWLEDGEMENTS

My first thanks go to Paul Stamper, Lawrence Butler's literary executor, for acting with his customary efficiency and good sense in gathering what remains of the Faxton archive together and for his support throughout the writing up process. We have laughed together, wondered, and often been left not a little bewildered by what we discovered there.

This final publication and the additional post-excavation work on the animal bones and pottery were funded largely by Historic England, without whom this publication would not have been possible. I would particularly like to thank Caroline Howarth and Barney Sloane for their support. A grant was also generously given by the Medieval Settlement Research Group for the re-drawing of some figures, travel and copying costs, and I am grateful to Bob Silvester for his encouragement and efficiency. The writing up of Faxton was completed during a period of research leave for me in 2017 granted by the University of Durham. As anyone who has committed themselves to an exercise of this type will know, without a concentrated period of time it is simply impossible to undertake. Very probably it was exactly that lack of time which prevented Lawrence from doing the job for himself.

There are particular people I would like to acknowledge; Alejandra Gutiérrez for reviving the illustrations and creating so many new ones; Stuart Wrathmell for all his advice on the Faxton buildings; Bob Croft and Beverley Nenk for hunting down references to Faxton in John Hurst's diaries; Neil Lyon at the Lamport Estate Office for his help in tracking down fragments of Faxton's lost church; Janice Morris for all her work in tracing Faxton's history; Cassandra Hodgkiss for making the best of Lawrence Butler's handwriting and for transcribing the 'Faxton broadcast'; Vedita Ramdoss at the British Library for trying to track down the lost 1967 radio broadcast for me, and Matthew Chipping at the BBC Written Archives Centre for searching related correspondence; Douglas Brown who performed miracles in converting the magnetic recording tape to a digital format and brought long-lost voices to life again; Rhona Huggins who provided extensive comments to Lawrence Butler in correspondence (26 November 1996) which I hope have been attended to in this newly finalised version; staff at the Northamptonshire HER and the NMR in Swindon and at SPAB in London; Sarah Bridges and Matt Bazley at Northampton Record Office.

In particular, I would like to thank Julian Richards for his comments on the post-excavation process generally and to thank Linda Bamber and Julian Richards for their work on the original medieval pottery report at the Centre for Archaeological Studies, University of Leeds. Judith Hodgkinson and Geoffrey Starmer provided additional details on the Faxton windmill for me and Bruce Bailey helped to tie down some of the stray references.

Paul Blinkhorn, Peter Brown, Christopher Dyer, Louisa Gidney, David Hall, Richard Kelleher, Ronan O'Donnell, Steve Rippon, Eleanor Standley and Stuart Wrathmell all patiently answered my queries and between them they have vastly improved the quality of this volume. The anonymous referee made very valuable comments which have also been fully incorporated. Above all, Paul Stamper offered insights, suggestions and corrections throughout and I am enormously grateful to him for his endless encouragement during this project. The index to the volume was prepared by Nicola King, and the French and Italian summaries by Nicolas Mias and Maria de Falco respectively.

FOREWORD

Between 1966 and 1968 Lawrence Butler (1934–2014), then a lecturer at the University of Leeds and later at York, directed one of the most important medieval excavations of its day at the deserted village site of Faxton, 10 miles north of Northampton (UK). Subsequently the site was regularly cited in the archaeological literature but the results were only partly written up and the final text was never fully published. Fifty years on, this volume draws together the archive to produce the first coherent account of the excavations.

It is perhaps important at the outset to enunciate some general principles behind this finalised text. No Faxton volume can ever be what Lawrence Butler might have published in the 1980s or before, partly because there were so many gaps in his surviving manuscript and partly because the result would be deemed hopelessly out of date and irrelevant. In an ideal world the entire excavation, including the documentary evidence and all the excavated materials, might have been re-evaluated, but that was judged to be neither cost-effective nor desirable, particularly given the state of the Faxton on-site archive. This volume is therefore a compromise — one which needs to work as an historical account of thinking in the 1960s and 1980s when the excavation and post-excavation were completed, but also as a reflection of current understanding.

To achieve this, Lawrence Butler's surviving manuscript has been comprehensively edited; everything has been done to respect his writing and give voice to the original excavator. Figures have been added in, errors corrected and blocks of text restructured and inserted for greater clarity and readability. Butler's core text is then complemented by modern specialists currently working in the same field. Entirely new sections now address some of the gaps in the original report such as those for post-medieval pottery and faunal remains, neither of which were originally analysed. There are also three entirely new chapters: Chapter 1 sets out background to Faxton, the circumstances of the site's discovery, as well as the excavation and the post-excavation process; Chapter 11 re-interprets the evidence for Faxton's medieval buildings; and Chapter 12 draws together a new conclusion. Essentially, more recent thinking book-ends an edited and re-ordered Butler text with an opening chapter setting out the context and the final few chapters reflecting more recent thinking. This combination of 'new' and 'old' highlights many of the advances in methodology and knowledge in later medieval archaeology over the past 30 years. Elsewhere, there are some important differences of interpretation and debates around the archaeological evidence from Faxton; we strongly suspect that Lawrence would have approved of this and would have been delighted to find that Faxton still had a role to play in medieval settlement studies. The final result, we hope, is not merely a 'period piece' but one that makes a distinctive contribution to our understanding of village formation and desertion.

Christopher Gerrard
Durham

SUMMARY

The village of Faxton in Northamptonshire was only finally deserted in the second half of the 20th century. Shortly afterwards, between 1966 and 1968, its medieval crofts were investigated under the direction of archaeologist Lawrence Butler. At the time this was one of the most ambitious excavations of a deserted medieval settlement to have been conducted and, although the results were only published as interim reports and summaries, Butler's observations at Faxton were to have significant influence on the growing academic and popular literature about village origins and desertion and the nature of medieval peasant crofts and buildings. In contrast to regions with abundant building stone, Faxton revealed archaeological evidence of a long tradition of earthen architecture in which so-called 'mud-walling' was successfully combined with other structural materials.

The 'rescue' excavations at Faxton were originally promoted by the Deserted Medieval Village Research Group and funded by the Ministry of Public Buildings and Works after the extensive earthworks at the site came under threat from agriculture. Three areas were excavated covering seven crofts. In 1966 Croft 29 at the south-east corner of the village green revealed a single croft in detail with its barns, yards and corn driers; in 1967 four crofts were examined together in the north-west corner of the village in an area badly damaged by recent ploughing and, finally, an area immediately east of the church was opened up in 1968. In all, some 4000m² were investigated in 140 days over three seasons.

The post-excavation process for Faxton was beset by delay. Of the 12 chapters presented in this monograph, only two were substantially complete at the time of the director's death in 2014. The others have had to be pieced together from interim summaries, partial manuscripts, sound recordings, handwritten notes and on-site records. Building on this evidence, a new team of scholars have re-considered the findings in order to set the excavations at Faxton into the wider context of modern research. Their texts reflect on the settlement's disputed pre-Conquest origins, probable later re-planning and expansion, the reasons behind the decline and abandonment of the village, the extraordinary story behind the destruction of its church, the development of the open fields and the enclosure process, as well as new evidence about Faxton's buildings and the finds discovered there. Once lauded, then forgotten, the excavations at Faxton now make a new contribution to our knowledge of medieval life and landscape in the East Midlands.

RÉSUMÉ

Le village de Faxton, dans le Northamptonshire, n'a été définitivement déserté que dans la seconde moitié du XXe siècle. Peu de temps après, entre 1966 et 1968, ses fermes médiévales ont été étudiées sous la direction de l'archéologue Lawrence Butler. À l'époque, il s'agissait de l'une des fouilles les plus ambitieuses jamais menées sur un village médiéval déserté. Bien que les résultats n'aient été publiés que sous forme de rapports et de résumés provisoires, les observations de Butler à Faxton allaient avoir une influence significative, tant dans les travaux universitaires que sur la littérature populaire, lesquels portaient sur la question des origines du village et de sa désertion, ainsi que sur la nature des cultures agricoles et des bâtiments paysans médiévaux. Contrairement aux régions où la pierre de construction est abondante, Faxton a fourni les évidences archéologiques d'une longue tradition d'architecture en terre crue, dans laquelle les élévations de terre (*mud walling*) étaient associés avec succès à d'autres matériaux de construction.

Au départ, les fouilles de sauvetage à Faxton ont été encouragées par le *Deserted Medieval Village Research Group* et financées par le *Ministry of Public Buildings and Works*, alors que les importants travaux de terrassement mis en œuvre sur le site étaient mis en péril par le développement agricole. Trois secteurs, dont sept exploitations, ont été fouillés. En 1966, la fouille de la ferme 29 (*Croft 29*), au sud-est du village, a permis la documentation détaillée d'une unité de production agricole avec ses granges, enclos et séchoirs à grain. En 1967, un ensemble de quatre fermes a été étudié à l'angle nord-ouest du village, dans une zone très affectée par les labours contemporains, puis enfin, en 1968, à été ouvert un sondage situé immédiatement à l'est de l'église. Au total, en 140 jours répartis sur trois campagnes de fouille, quelque 4000m² ont été examinés.

Les travaux de post-fouille de Faxton ont été retardés. En 2014, au moment du décès du directeur des fouilles, seuls deux des chapitres de la présente monographie étaient quasiment achevés. Les données manquantes ont dû être reconstituées à partir de résumés provisoires, de manuscrits partiels, d'enregistrements sonores, de notes manuscrites et de relevés de terrain. A partir de ces informations, une nouvelle équipe d'universitaires a réexaminé les résultats afin de replacer les fouilles de Faxton dans le contexte plus large de la recherche contemporaine. Leurs textes abordent la question débattue de l'éventuelle origine du village avant la conquête normande, son probable réaménagement et développement ultérieur, les raisons de son déclin et de son abandon, l'étonnante histoire de la destruction de son église, le développement des champs ouverts (*open field*) et le mouvement des enclosures, mais aussi les nouvelles données concernant les bâtiments et le mobilier archéologique découvert à Faxton. Autrefois admirées, puis oubliées, les fouilles de Faxton apportent aujourd'hui une nouvelle contribution à notre connaissance de la vie quotidienne et du paysage des East Midlands à l'époque médiévale.

RIASSUNTO

Il Villaggio di Faxton nel Northamptonshire fu abbandonato definitivamente solo alla fine del XX secolo. Poco tempo dopo, tra il 1966 e il 1968, le sue piccole fattorie medievali furono scavate sotto la direzione dell'archeologo Lawrence Butler. Al tempo, lo scavo di Faxton era uno degli scavi più ambiziosi di un villaggio medievale abbandonato e, sebbene i risultati furono pubblicati solo sottoforma di brevi report e riassunti, le osservazioni di Butler su Faxton avrebbero avuto una grande influenza nella letteratura accademica e popolare riguardante le origini e l'abbandono dei villaggi e la natura delle fattorie e degli edifici contadini medievali. A differenza di regioni caratterizzate dall'abbondante presenza di pietra adatta alla costruzione, Faxton ha restituito un'evidenza archeologica testimoniante una lunga tradizione di architettura in terra in cui la muratura in fango era sapientemente combinata con altri materiali di costruzione.

Gli scavi preventivi condotti a Faxton furono originariamente promossi dal *Deserted Medieval Village Research Group* e finanziati dal *Ministry of Public Buildings and Works* nel momento in cui il sito divenne a rischio a causa degli estensivi lavori per lo sfruttamento agricolo. In questa occasione furono scavate tre aree che restituirono sette fattorie. Nel 1966, la *Croft 29*, localizzata nell'angolo sud-est dei giardinetti pubblici, rivelò in dettaglio una singola fattoria con granaio, cortile ed essiccato per mais. Nel 1967 altre quattro fattorie furono esaminate nell'angolo nord-ovest del villaggio, in un'area fortemente danneggiata dalle recenti arature. Un'ulteriore fronte di scavo fu infine aperto nel 1968 immediatamente ad est della chiesa. In totale, furono investigati circa 4000m² in 140 giorni, durante tre campagne di scavo.

Il processo di analisi post scavo è stato sottoposto ad un forte ritardo. Solo due dei 12 capitoli presentati in questa monografia erano stati sostanzialmente completati nel 2014, al momento del decesso del direttore degli scavi. Gli altri sono stati realizzati mettendo insieme riassunti preliminari, parziali manoscritti, registrazioni audio, note scritte a mano e sopralluoghi sul campo. A partire da queste evidenze, un nuovo gruppo di ricercatori ha riconsiderato i ritrovamenti in modo da inserire gli scavi di Faxton nel più ampio contesto di ricerca moderna. I loro contributi analizzano diverse evidenze: la contestata origine pre-Conquista dell'insediamento, la probabile successiva ripianificazione ed espansione, le ragioni alla base del declino e dell'abbandono del villaggio, la straordinaria storia della distruzione della sua chiesa, lo sviluppo del sistema a campi aperti e recinzioni, così come anche nuove evidenze sugli edifici di Faxton e sui reperti restituiti. Gli scavi di Faxton, un tempo esaltati e poi dimenticati, tornano ora a dare un nuovo contributo alla nostra conoscenza della vita e del paesaggio medievale nelle East Midlands.

ABBREVIATIONS

DMV	Deserted medieval village
DMVRG	The Deserted Medieval Village Research Group
HER	Historic Environment Record
HMSO	Her Majesty's Stationery Office
JHC	Journals of the House of Commons
MOLA	Museum of London Archaeology
NRO	Northamptonshire Record Office
ODNB	Oxford Dictionary of National Biography
OS	Ordnance Survey
PRO	Public Record Office
RCHME	Royal Commission for Historical Monuments of England
SMA	The Society for Medieval Archaeology
SPAB	The Society for the Protection of Ancient Buildings
VCH	Victoria County History

I first came across [Faxton] whilst walking from the edge of Rugby... and was astonished to find it absented and cottages empty (their windows sometimes stuffed with 1937 newspapers). Calling at a farm near the Old road, a woman explained its emptiness by 'Wasn't there a plague sometime or other?'.

(From notes by J L Carr, *c*.1953, appended to the bottom of his pen and oil sketch reproduced at Figure 1.1)

The rumour has it that the 'Old Peddler' came down from London and brought the Black Death and the people living at Faxton and the village of Mawsley got the plague and that's how the two villages were wiped out.

(Anonymous local inhabitant recorded by a film crew in 1966)

Well, I lived there when I was 30 and there was 25 people there then and the reason why it died was there was no industry and no road. That's my version of Faxton but I understand now they are digging up there aren't they, yes, but I've never been up there since they pulled the church down, because they never had authority to pull the church down, they never approached people like myself who had the monuments up there to their forebears and it was all done just the simple reason that they thought that somebody was gonna steal something I think.

(Anonymous local inhabitant recorded by a film crew in 1966)

1

PURPOSE AND PAST

Christopher Gerrard

Faxton is unusual among the deserted villages of Midlands England because it still had an active farming community at the end of the Second World War; its cottages, almshouses and a church were all in occupation or at least capable of use. In 1947 Faxton was even proposed as the site for a Northamptonshire new town. That plan was rejected and, 20 years on, in the spring of 1966, the last inhabitant moved out of the village and her cottage quickly became derelict. The taking down of the village almshouses and most especially the church during the previous decade resonated, as it still does today, as a depressing chapter in the history of historic buildings preservation. By the year that excavations began in Faxton, in 1966, only their fences and gates were still visible, together with a pair of red-brick farm-workers' cottages, though they too were abandoned and windowless. Around the village green, the unmistakable earthworks of the medieval village were still readily traced among the sheep pastures.

Faxton was of little interest to Northamptonshire antiquarians (Bridges 1791, II, 92–96), but the village's later decline attracted considerable comment. 'Anyone of a neurotic or morbid temperament would not be able to endure living at Faxton for a day', ominously predicted the *Northampton Independent* on 7 October 1911. Nor was the paper alone in its pessimism. Two decades later, writing under the unlikely pseudonym Wakeling Dry, the Reverend R L P Jowitt found Faxton to be a 'sequestered, roadless hamlet' with a church and almshouses 'long untenanted and desolate' (Dry 1932, 121). This desolation was soon to fill *The Countryman's Bedside Book* (Watkins Pitchford 1941) with 'vivid uneasiness, almost fear'. Its author, Denys Watkins Pitchford, was the son of Faxton's rector and knew the place well. 'Not far from the church', he observed, 'were some low green mounds, all that remained of the once great manor house that stood on this spot. What was the story of this forsaken place? Why had the manor house crumbled beneath the turf and the almshouses fallen down?'. Writing in 1947, the Northamptonshire author Jim Carr noted that:

> the name was on the map but the village had almost gone. Of seven cottages sprinkled along the grass tracks, four were collapsing and a fifth unoccupied... the lead from the [church] roof had

been officially stripped and sold. The two bells lay cracked in a nettle patch, beneath their turret. The furniture smashed, the font and monument gone (Carr 1993, Foreword).

Carr was to return to paint the by-then unroofed church in about 1953 (Figure 1.1).

While Carr and many others visited on foot to picnic and to paint, landscape historian William Hoskins name-checked Faxton in an early essay on deserted villages (Hoskins 1950, 71) and archaeological attention was also being drawn to Faxton from the air. A 1947 vertical RAF aerial photograph of the village earthworks attracted the interest of Leeds economic historian Maurice Beresford who used it to illustrate *The lost villages of England,* published in 1954 (Figure 1.2). Further sorties were later undertaken by Cambridge flyer Kenneth St Joseph. To Beresford this was a prime example of a shrunken village, and the caption for Figure 12 in *Lost villages* duly reads: 'some houses remain, but surrounding them are earthworks similar to those of the depopulate villages, showing that the settlements were once much more extensive'. Although there was in fact still a community of sorts living there in 1954, Beresford nevertheless included Faxton in his accompanying gazetteer of 'lost villages' (Beresford 1954, 367), and in June of the same year it was listed as one of the 81 deserted villages which had been newly designated as an archaeological site of national importance (entry 1003899; DMVRG 1954, 9). This new status was felt to be merited not only because of Faxton's well preserved earthworks with its manorial centre, church and the crofts and tofts around the green, but also due to the quality of its associated historical documentation. As Lawrence Butler explained in one of the many handwritten notes 'to self' found in the archive: 'Faxton is in many ways a typical village of the Northamptonshire uplands. It first appears in the Domesday Book, its growth can be plotted through successive surveys in the medieval and later periods and its buildings (church, farms, almshouses) provide a mute commentary on that growth and replenishment'.

In fact, Maurice Beresford was not the only historian delving into the Faxton documentation in the early 1950s. Patrick King, curator of the Northamptonshire Record Society and later archivist at Northamptonshire Record Office, was

FIGURE 1.1

Pen and oil painting of Faxton church c.1953 by Northamptonshire author Joseph Lloyd Carr (1912–94) (reproduced by kind permission). Below the picture are several lines of handwritten notes (see PLATE 1), the uppermost of which reads:

> *Alas Faxton! The Diocese took off its roof 'for safety'. Its twin bells gloriously*
> *inscribed 1704 (Blenheim) were left in the yard for target practice. Cattle wandered*
> *into the nave. Bicycle gangs took up where the Church left off. Skulls were gouged*
> *from the chancel. Authority finished it off. The monument to a Tudor judge was*
> *clubbed from its walls and lay in pieces for years in Lamport Rectory. (It is now one*
> *of the glories of the V&A). Headstones were laid face down and earthed over. Sir*
> *Gyles Isham had [a] cairn put up on the spot where once the altar stood and this too*
> *was viciously attacked and had to be parcelled in barbed wire. Quite astonishing!*

FIGURE 1.2

RAF vertical air photograph of Faxton and its surrounding landscape taken in January 1947 (CPE/UK 1925. JAN 16. '47. F/20"/MULTI(4)58SQDN). Historic England Archive. RAF Photography.

This photograph was included by Maurice Beresford in his ground-breaking volume 'The lost villages of England', first published in 1954. North toward bottom. The church and rectory lie at the centre of the photograph, the Old Brook stream to the east is picked out by the tree line with Shortwood to the north-east (bottom right). The ridge and furrow visible here is plotted on Figure 2.5

also drawing together what he could find from the many historical documents to which he had access locally. King had come to live in the county in 1948 and soon afterwards happened upon a footnote in the *Place-names of Northamptonshire* volume which referred to Mawsley as 'a decayed parish, now united with Faxton' (Gover *et al.* 1933, 128). According to King's handwritten notes, which seem at one time to have been intended for publication, this 'intrigued' him. As he explains:

> I was rather curious, got out a map and a directory but could find nothing about it... it was not very long before I had heard about the plague. It was not very long either before I found out Faxton was a favourite picnicking place on a Saturday afternoon in high summer. It was not very long before I went there (Patrick King notes).

On the basis of what he had learnt, King went on to deliver lectures locally about Faxton in the early 1950s. By this time, Faxton had developed something of a reputation as a 'ghost village', as one local resident explained during interviews for a film crew in 1966 (Faxton tape 2):

> Well, we heard that the people that lived there... they said there was always a window open whether [or not] if they closed it at night, even nailed it up... it'd still be open the next morning. In the church, they used to have leper windows. I expect they were for the sick or for the ones that were the Lepers to stand outside and watch the service... And the bells, they hung outside, and there is a story of some boys one evening, tying a bundle of hay on the ropes and the cows went and pulled the hay and rung the bells and that, I think, is how this story of the ghost started.
>
> *Is your house haunted?*
>
> I've lived there 27 years and come in at all hours of the night... I've been all round the buildings, all over everywhere and I've never seen anything.
>
> *So you haven't got a ghost?*
>
> Well, I don't think so. I should like one, it'd be company sometimes.

Stories around the desertion of the village were undoubtedly one of the reasons people visited the site. It was a place, to use Patrick King's word, whose 'mysteries' had earned it 'notoriety in the public mind'. As he investigated further, King's historical research was to provide excavator Lawrence Butler with an essential starting point and his work underpins much of the historical detail presented in Chapter 2 of this volume. Nor was it King's only contribution to medieval settlement studies in the county; in 1953 he drew John Hurst's attention to the site at Wythemail where stone and pottery had been turned up by the plough. Subsequent excavation there was to prove influential for interpretations at Faxton (Hurst and Hurst 1969, 169).

1.1 THREATS AND RESPONSES

By 1965 some 2,000 deserted medieval villages (DMVs) had been identified in England, of which about 250 survived in good condition (DMVRG 1965a). But while their numbers grew with each passing year, the tempo of their destruction had increased markedly since the end of the Second World War in 1945. Sites were constantly being threatened, particularly by ploughing but also by house building, quarrying and road schemes. As a category of archaeological monument, DMVs tended to be vulnerable because they were extensive. Not only that, they often lay on grassland which had become inconvenient to retain under the latest mono-productive farming regimes which were dominated by crops rather than by stock. 'Specialisation' and 'intensification', the watchwords of British farming in the 1960s and 1970s under the Common Agricultural Policy, had by then begun to take their toll on the British landscape (Gerrard 2003, 126–128; 2009). With prices for cereals guaranteed and land prices rising ever higher, the logic for the farmer was irresistible: deep plough what you could and take the cheque. Ever more powerful agricultural machinery was on hand to help so that tasks once completed over many weeks could now be tackled in a matter of hours. The inevitable consequence for the countryside was the erasure of hedge boundaries, the creation of ever-larger fields, the bulldozing of fox coverts and the infilling of field ponds: all across the East Midlands the earthworks of medieval open-field landscapes recorded on RAF verticals in the late 1940s were being lost.

By the 1960s this arable 'prairie farming', as it became known, was having its impact on Northamptonshire and several deserted settlements were completely levelled, among them Downton, Elkington, Finedon, Lower Catesby, Upper Catesby, Newbold in Catesby, Papley, and Silsworth (RCHME 1981). In 1965, Faxton duly made its debut as a site 'under threat' in the pages of the 13th annual report of the Deserted Medieval Village Research Group (DMVRG 1965a, 17). That entry is worth quoting in full:

> This important scheduled site has been threatened for some years by a new owner who wishes to level and cultivate the site. The first field to go was a fine area of ridge and furrow. Another field containing six crofts was levelled before the site was scheduled [as being of national importance]. As the site was not intact it was not felt that a stand could be made on this site although there are very few sites left in Northamptonshire of 'A' quality. Agreement was therefore made for about six more crofts to be released in 1965. It was hoped to excavate beforehand but a supervisor was not available, so the site was watched by Mrs G Brown and remains of a stone building were

recorded. Two further fields will be released in 1966 and this site will be the DMVRG's main Midland excavation under the direction of Dr L A S Butler.

It may be a puzzle to some readers to find that the Faxton earthworks were actively being levelled 'for agricultural improvement' even though the DMVRG had previously classified the site as a DMV with earthworks of high quality ('A', 'very good'). These sites were defined as having 'excellent visual quality, a clear pattern of earthworks recognisable as roads and croft-boundaries'. Of course, it was precisely because of these qualities that Faxton had been scheduled more than a decade before. The answer as to why destruction was nevertheless in progress is that State designation did not ensure protection. Under the terms of the *Ancient Monuments Consolidation Act and Amendment Act 1913* and the *Ancient Monuments Act 1931* the owner was only required to give notice of any intention to damage or remove the monument. This then created a fleeting opportunity for negotiation, usually of a few months only, often less, during which the owner might be persuaded as to the importance of the site and desist of their own accord (as at Argan, Yorkshire, in 1967, for example; DMVRG 1967, 9). Owners, however, were not always so easily convinced and did not always comply; partly because they objected to interference from the Ministry as a matter of principle and partly for fear of any perpetual restrictions which might be placed on their land (for example at Sulby, Northamptonshire; DMVRG 1967, 8). Where opinions were entrenched, the ensuing negotiations might be conducted under what was blandly described as 'very difficult conditions' (DMVRG 1965b). Alternatively, they might lead to some form of compensation being paid to try to preserve the site, or at least part of it, either in perpetuity or temporarily, or they might lever an opportunity for an archaeologist to watch and record while the destruction was underway, usually with appropriate costs being borne by the State (then in the form of the Ministry of Public Buildings and Works) and limited compensation being paid to the farmer. Archaeological interventions typically took the form of a watching brief (as at Babingley, Norfolk) or sometimes something on a much larger scale (as at Hangleton, Sussex), the general feeling being that small-scale work generally obtained few useful findings and that 'it is the "persistent" excavations, such as Wharram Percy, Hound Tor, Faxton, Gomeldon, West Whelpington and Upton which have produced significant results, and then only after several seasons' (DMVRG 1967, 1). If, however, the site was deemed to be of the very highest value then another, more drastic option was available. The responsibility for its upkeep could be transferred to the State through a process known as

'guardianship'. In 1965 the six deserted village sites nominated in this category were Wharram Percy (Yorkshire), Gainsthorpe (Lincolnshire), Broadstone (Oxfordshire), Hound Tor (Devon), Godwick or Pudding Norton (Norfolk), all in England, and Runston and Rossall (Sutherland) in Wales and Scotland respectively (DMVRG 1965b). Faxton, being already damaged, could not by then be argued to be in that highest bracket of merit; indeed by 1965 its 'A' rating had already been removed.

The elliptical phrasing in the DMVRG 1965 entry to the effect that 'it was not felt that a stand could be made on this site' should also be explained. When a site such as Faxton came under threat it was customary for the Ministry of Public Buildings and Works through its Ancient Monuments Inspectorate to consult the archaeological community. The DMVRG, to which John Hurst was secretary while also a Ministry man, fulfilled that advisory capacity attentively. What the DMVRG entry implies is that the fate of Faxton would now become a process of negotiation between State and landowner as parts of the site, year on year, came under threat. Although there were some hiccups along the way (see Chapter 4), this is subsequently what happened. As the entry mentions, the excavation of one house in Croft 50, then newly ploughed, was undertaken in that year by Gwen Brown of Wellingborough who also watched the bulldozing of Crofts 44–49 (for location of crofts, see Figure 3.6) (Wilson and Hurst 1966, 214). On the basis of her observations of interior paved areas, wall footings and exterior cobbling, the scale of the threat to high-quality remains led the Inspectorate of Ancient Monuments to arrange for further crofts to be fully excavated in advance of destruction on the recommendation of the DMVRG. Work on site was then financed for three seasons from 1966 to 1968—but it was entirely coincidental that large-scale excavation got underway in the very same year that Faxton's last inhabitant moved out.

There is some hint in the correspondence that at one time more ambitious plans were being hatched for Faxton. In one letter, Butler talks of Hurst's idea to have Faxton 'as a showplace' (letter Butler to Hurst, 20 September 1966), but this evidently came to nothing once the site had been so badly damaged (Figure 1.3). In 1966 the DMVRG noted only that 'the village site had been released for levelling' (DMVRG 1966, 16). Entries on Faxton come to a sad end with this note in 1968, again quoted here in full:

> It was hoped that the green area of the village would remain under grass although the rest of the village was destroyed. Early in 1968 the owner gave notice of his intention to level the rest of the site, leaving only the manor site intact. Now that all the surroundings are under the plough there was no point in objecting further
> (DMVRG 1968, 10).

FIGURE 1.3

Oblique air photograph of Faxton in February 1969 after the village and many of the earthworks of the open-field landscape had been ploughed out (AWV4 SP7875/44/02.02.1969 SP784751). Looking north. Crossroads Farm and Ladyholme can be seen still standing on the north side of The Green. The demolished church and churchyard are the pale ungrassed area centre left, the south-east quadrant of the village earthworks is especially clear (see Figure 3.5). Cambridge University Collection of Aerial Photography © Copyright reserved.

1.2 THE EXCAVATION AND ITS DIRECTOR

The director of the three seasons of excavation at Faxton was Lawrence Butler (Figure 1.4). Looking back on his life after he died in December 2014, Lawrence's colleagues rightly highlighted the variety of his academic interests through the course of a long career. There were regional commitments to Welsh and Yorkshire archaeology and a formative role in the Society for Post-Medieval Archaeology, but above all Lawrence is remembered for his work on churches and cathedrals (he was Consultant Archaeologist at Lincoln, Wakefield and Sheffield Cathedrals and York Minster) and medieval castles, among them Sandal Castle in Wakefield in Yorkshire

(Mayes and Butler 1983) and Dolforwyn Castle in Wales (Barnwell 2015; Mytum 2015). In 1966, however, all this was before him.

In 1965, by now in his early 30s, Butler made the move into academic life and joined the University of Leeds (where Maurice Beresford was based) as a lecturer in medieval archaeology. Having previously been employed with the Welsh Royal Commission for Historic Monuments in Aberystwyth, he now had a little more time to spare during the summer vacations. He had acquired the necessary familiarity with archaeological practice, the experience and know-how of excavation techniques on medieval rural settlement sites, and he knew John Hurst personally as well as other members of the DMVRG,

FIGURE 1.4
Lawrence Butler at Faxton, ridge and furrow behind, and Ministry hut to left

having dug at Wharram Percy in Yorkshire and having recently co-directed an excavation of his own at Thuxton in Norfolk in 1964, another deserted medieval site (Butler and Wade-Martins 1989).

In deciding how to dig and record the archaeology at Faxton, it was perhaps inevitable that Wharram Percy would provide the lead and, as is well documented, many of the techniques developed there were, in turn, derived from Axel Steensberg's excavations at Store Valby in Denmark; Jack Golson being the common link between the two sites (Hurst 1956, 271–272; Bentz 2012; Smith 2006). Butler's system for recording finds, for example, followed the lead of Wharram Percy with small finds being bagged according to level and grid square. By 1966 it was also well understood that deserted medieval settlements under excavation typically had virtually no archaeological stratigraphy. Buildings might only be defined by the cobbled surfaces that once surrounded them, walls could be robbed of their stone and, when weather and light conditions were not optimal, distinguishing the clay floors of buildings from the natural clays beneath could be a test for even the most experienced excavator. To help overcome this, Faxton adopted the principle of alpha-numerical coding of layers (A, B, etc.) used at Wharram in which the buildings were dug in a series of spits rather than stratigraphically. Butler, however, was not quite so consistent in its application; the timber buildings at Faxton were not all given C numbers as they were at Wharram, for example (Hurst 1956, 272). In other respects, Butler drew on his own experience from the excavations at Thuxton, digging long trenches perpendicular to the village street and revealing successive phases of road surfaces. He also focused resources and time on the farm yard and its buildings as well as the croft boundary ditches, something which was not always the case in excavations in the 1960s.

In several important respects, however, Butler departed from accepted methodology on site. As Chapter 4 describes, through all three years at Faxton, Butler used a 10ft (3m) grid and, once the turf and topsoil had been dug away, the baulks were removed and the site was then excavated as an open area. This differed from the 1964 season at Thuxton when an open area 30 by 23m was opened up 'to see far more of one toft' (Butler and Wade-Martins 1989, 22) and 'control sections' were left in place in two places and excavated one layer 'behind' the main excavation. This was the same system which had operated at Wharram Percy since 1961 in Area 6 (Beresford and Hurst 1971, 88) which had the benefit of leaving a series of temporary sections which could then be recorded before being removed to reveal the whole open area in its entirety. At Faxton, in 1966, the topsoil was around 30cm deep, with yard surfaces, walls and the floors of buildings directly beneath, but Butler left no sections across the site, permanent or temporary.

One person who remembers Lawrence Butler well is Bob Carr. Bob dug in the first season at Faxton in 1966, in the year before he went to Southampton University to read Archaeology, and had previously worked with Lawrence Butler and Peter Wade-Martins at Thuxton. He writes (pers. comm. 2018):

> My impression, then as now, is that Lawrence was not an enthusiastic excavator; in retrospect this isn't really surprising—archaeology was then a process largely carried out by university staff and students in the long vacation, none of the staff had much practical experience and digging 28 days in a year was never going to provide it (a massive contrast to the succeeding era when simple diggers with no responsibilities could easily accumulate three years full-time labour). I don't think the actual process of 'digging' excited him—only the final interpretation and conclusion: he didn't haunt the site as a hands-on director.

Whatever the reasons, it seems likely that Lawrence Butler's decision in 1966 to leave no temporary sections left him short of stratigraphical information, and when he returned to Faxton to dig again in 1967 he left 2ft (61cm) baulks in place in the topsoil for much longer, removing them only as became convenient and necessary (see Chapter 5). This enabled him to have sections drawn right across the site in a way he had not been able to do the previous year. Quite possibly he was anxious about how to approach a ploughed site with no clear stratification and wished to monitor the stratigraphy more carefully. Either way, the approach was very different from that at Wharram and other medieval excavations of its day and somewhat against perceived wisdom. John Hurst, for example, had been very clear on his views stating a decade earlier that 'vital evidence which might have rendered more intelligible the work in progress [on House 6] lay under each of these baulks, thus confirming Dr Steensberg's contention that trenches and cut vertical sections on a medieval peasant settlement site are more of a nuisance than a help' (Hurst 1956, 272, Plate XLV shows this system in use). Hurst insisted that medieval peasant houses could not be understood 'by digging the grids and trenches of the Mortimer Wheeler school' (Bentz 2012, 20) and by 1952 he was already persuasive in his views, suggesting to Ernest Greenfield and Philip Rahtz that they should dig a moated site and the earthworks of a shrunken medieval village in the Chew Valley in Somerset in open areas and abandon the grid method (Rahtz 2003). In some ways, it seems extraordinary that John Hurst would acquiesce to the approach taken by Butler at Faxton 15 years later and so long after the open-area method had been refined and tested at Wharram. However, this was not so much a rejection of Hurst's methodology as an experiment of Butler's own devising in which the topsoil was dug using the grid method in boxes, and then the baulks were cleared away over areas where the site proved most interesting. So we have a sense of innovation in Butler's digging in which he is responding to the nature of the site at Faxton by adopting different methodologies. In 1968 *Current Archaeology* called his excavation technique 'brilliant'.

Although he received praise for his digging techniques, Butler's frustrations with the Faxton project are only too evident. By 1969 he had, as he himself said, come to question 'the organisation required to approach village excavation and the solutions to be expected from the various types of investigation' (Butler 1969a). These were strong words, expressed as they are in the muted codes of academic language of the time. Although he was full of praise for his workforce—if somewhat less complimentary about the Northamptonshire drizzle—he felt emboldened to speculate openly in print under the provocative heading 'Should medieval village excavation be abandoned?' (Butler 1969a, 147). He clearly felt that the model of the 'traditional summer vacation excavation' was 'unsuitable' for complex sites like Faxton. As we now know from correspondence (see Chapters 4 and 5), Butler twice threatened to throw in the towel, once after the 1966 season at Faxton had concluded and then again after the even less satisfactory experience of 1967. After exploring alternative sites, he only returned to Faxton because he was unable to identify a suitable candidate for excavation elsewhere which might yield better results.

'The only excuse', Butler wrote, 'for undertaking a village excavation would be that the sequence of documents enabled the excavator to know the status of the occupant of one particular house at a number of fixed points in the medieval period. Since England possesses such a wealth of royal, ecclesiastical and manorial documents this requirement should not impose such an intolerable burden on medieval archaeologists' (Butler 1969a, 147). Without doubt, the Faxton experience had forced Butler to reflect on the merits of excavations under what were less than ideal conditions. When he spoke of the 'intolerable burden' he was probably referring, at least in part, to his own experience. At the beginning of the excavations in 1966, Butler was happy to stress that his work at Faxton was 'a rescue dig, though with research questions uppermost' which had to be undertaken in under three years, the threat being 'the needs of agriculture, the deep ploughing over the village area, will soon obliterate the very slight earthwork remains which are visible from aerial photography and which can be seen on the ground before any ploughing takes place' (Faxton tape 1). It was this constraint on time which meant that houses could only be sampled in the hope that 'the information we get from those areas will be typical of the village as a whole and can also relate to other sites within the Midlands' (Faxton tape 1). However,

if Butler really believed this in 1967, he did not by 1969. By that point he had come to question the most effective distribution of resources, firmly favouring long term research-based excavations such as Wharram Percy and West Whelpington over short duration 'rescue-stimulated' excavations such as Faxton, Grenstein, Hangleton or Thuxton. In that sense, Faxton may be considered formative, not only for the excavation, but for medieval archaeology as a whole.

1.3 ON SITE AT FAXTON

The workforce on an archaeological site in Britain in the 1960s, even one with the financial sponsorship of the Ministry of Works, was a hybrid of the paid and unpaid, the experienced and novice. One group did not necessarily equate with the other. Thus, for all three years of excavation, the workforce on site at Faxton consisted of paid labour (usually about three workmen for a period of a few weeks only), volunteers from Kettering and students from Leeds and Exeter Universities, and others attracted by advertisement or through the American Archaeology Association for Cultural Exchange and seeking practical experience. Schoolboys also attended from Kettering Grammar School, several of them from its archaeological society having already accumulated significant experience at other sites. The excavation was advertised as providing training with payment to volunteers of between 10 shillings a day and £1 a day depending upon their accommodation. The following guidelines were offered:

> Volunteers should come prepared for all extremes of climate (wind, sun, rain, mud) and stout footwear is advisable (Wellington boots but not nailed or studded boots)...Those wishing to obtain their own trowel should buy a 4 or 5 inch mason's pointing trowel with a comfortable handle with a well founded end. The tang and blade should be cast in one piece. A cheap trowel with a riveted blade will snap easily and a gardener's trowel with a curved blade is quite useless... Food supplies can be obtained from Broughton (including fish-and-chips) and Kettering. Water has to be brought from Old.

As John Stapleton, then a schoolboy of 16–17 years of age (in theory those under 16 were not to be accepted on site), recalls (pers. comm. 2018):

> I remember seeing an advert for help at the annual summer Faxton excavations in the local evening paper and applied to Old Village Post Office! Having previous experience with [the Northamptonshire archaeologist] Dennis Jackson helped my application, leading to me being 'a local' on the teams of 1968/69... So began my involvement with Faxton during the school holidays, earning a small amount to help run my

motorbike and gaining experience of working on a large excavation site. I would ride out each day from Wellingborough, park the motorbike at the farm and walk with everyone else down the track which led to the two shells of houses left with intact roofs, being the site office/tool store/pot-washing area. Toilet facilities were a single Elsan toilet inside a tin hut... On rainy days we would all abandon the site and go into Rothwell and spend time together inside the Rothwell House Hotel waiting for the weather to clear. The majority of the student team lodged at the hotel.

Trowelling the Northamptonshire Boulder Clay was a nightmare. Often it became rock hard during the heat of the day, and no amount of water sprinkled on top seemed to make it any easier to work with. At the end of each afternoon we would cover areas over with plastic sheeting to trap the overnight moisture... ready to work on the following day. Kneeling down to trowel became painful... and the intense heat of a high summer sun... could become quite blinding. Health and safety was never mentioned, those excavating wore practical working clothes and (especially the girls) big floppy 'hippy' style hats. The students were deliberately separated to stop endless chatter but we were employed to work, not to gossip. [Among my working colleagues on site] were Isobel Butler, who wore a 1950s style anorak, a 'beatnik' student called Martin from Oxford with beard and heavy plastic-framed glasses, Ken Wilson who specialised in cleaning sites up ready for photography and always carried all his tools in a metal toolbox, Peggy Wilson who wore a turban-style headscarf, an ex-hospital nurse, the son of a sea captain, the students and Lawrence Butler, who always seemed to wear a bobble hat and with his blond beard appeared a very sombre character, looking rather sad.

As the funding for Faxton ran out, everyone was 'laid off'—we packed our kit away for a final time, said our goodbyes, went on our way... yet in a strange way this Northamptonshire DMV still lives on in the hearts and minds of those who served there.

One undated newspaper report describes 'borstal boys providing the heavy digging force and volunteers doing the lighter trowelling' but it appears they were 'confined to their institutions on account of prison escapes' and did not in the end attend (letter Butler, 4 July 1966). The excavation supervisors were often very experienced on sites of different periods. Guy Beresford applied in 1966 but then wrote to say he could not attend because the weather at his Cornish Tresmorn site was delaying him (letter Beresford to Butler, 4 September 1966). In 1968, Ken and Peggy Wilson, already mentioned above, had travelled from Alderney to take up their roles; they had previously worked on Bronze Age barrow sites in Yorkshire (John Stapleton notes, February 2017). Bob Carr recalls (pers. comm. 2018):

The conduct of the excavation was true to the period: the entire excavation kit was delivered by the regional MPBW [Ministry of Public Buildings and Works] depot; the principal soil shifting was done by a team of builder's general labourers delivered by open lorry each morning (building at this time included the excavation of foundation trenches and utility trenches by hand); the archaeologists were LB's Leeds students who had never dug before, and were mostly there because it was a course requirement; the director, having briefed his site supervisor in the morning, disappeared to hut or caravan until the cool of the day (LB had hay-fever). Remaining memories of the dig and digging are less centred on the archaeology, but rather the stresses (as the 19-year-old site supervisor) of overseeing a wayward group of builder's labourers, probably from Raunds or Rushden and without the archaeological spark, who found management by a schoolboy entertaining; and teaching a group of forward students how to dig.

A sense of the organisational anxieties of the dig director can be got from surviving correspondence. There were demanding letters from volunteer diggers ('it would be possible to change my dates... but we don't all have four months' holiday'; 'I have to tell you that I am aged 14 and I have had a fair amount of experience on other archaeological excavation'; 'I hope all is well and that Mrs Butler has washed all of the pottery'; 'Hope you have an interesting site, otherwise I'll wish I had gone to West Stow') to each of whom Butler replied politely with details of suitable accommodation. In the end many were sorry to leave Faxton, but not displeased to escape the Northamptonshire weather which flooded the trenches on more than one occasion: 'we snuggled down in bed with the rain beating on the van roof, and sorrowed for you and the men at 8am on Tuesday! And again on Wednesday!' (letter 17 August 1968). Lawrence had gamely offered a 'retreat to the [windowless] cottages... if camping under canvas becomes too dreary' (letter Butler, 7 July 1966). Isobel, Lawrence's wife, seems to have done most of the driving, endlessly ferrying volunteers to and from Kettering and shopping in Wellingborough. Such was the merry-go-round of movement that Lawrence declared in an entry for 30 August 1966: 'No-one went anywhere, it RAINED'; the final of the World Cup attracted no comment whatsoever.

Everything had to be accounted for. In the archive there are orders of stationery on Ministry of Works paper for everything from elastic bands to bottles of ink and 'official paid adhesive labels' to be sent c/o Post Office in Old; invoices for trowels and mattocks; articles in the *Kettering Leader* (9 September 1966) describing the Faxton 'dig... before bulldozers move in'; invitations to lecture on the site (fee £5 5s), and a day-book recording costs. From these we can track Lawrence Butler's movements from the moment he spent £1 2s 6d on petrol in Leeds on 22 July 1966 to his arrival in Faxton for an 'evening cider'. Thereafter cider, papers, milk, meat and groceries make up the bulk of recorded expenditure together with occasional treats such as wine, 'shaggy rug', 'sweeties' and socks.

The greatest expense by far was the workmen, almost half of the total cost of the 1967 excavations, some £1,952, was used up on their wages. But it was the promised help in-kind which frayed the director's temper far more. Internal papers in the Ministry of Public Buildings and Works reveal that Butler's requests for hutting and equipment were not received with any enthusiasm partly because the Ministry felt under no obligation to act in instances of 'grants case' excavation, and partly because of the short notice given. When the huts finally did arrive they were not weather-proof and one roof blew off. 'Fortunately', wrote Butler to Hurst (letter 18 October 1966), 'this did not cause any injury, the first-aid box would have been unable to deal with it'. Buckets arrived from the Ministry with rusty bottoms, hand brushes were tattered, the forks had splayed tines, pick hafts were worn, and the sickles too blunt. When, at the end of the 1966 season, the Ministry claimed that one spade, one shovel and six hand shovels were missing from the equipment it had loaned, there followed an exhausting correspondence with Butler about what had been supplied and what had not ('where is Elsan?', reads one note). Butler was sometimes late with his accounts, causing John Hurst to worry that his colleagues at the Ministry were 'getting so cross that [they] may refuse to take on [the] job which would be disastrous' (letter Hurst to Butler, 10 June 1969). When Butler complained that the necessary clerical forms had not been supplied to him, the Ministry man replied to say that 'perhaps a phone rang and distracted my attention'. Butler himself preferred a more tried and tested admission of guilt: 'I must apologise for the long delay in replying to your letter but it slipped behind a file cabinet and has only been unearthed in the vacation cleaning' (letter Butler to Ministry, 23 April 1974). As experienced excavators will not be surprised to hear, there is higher word count on this and other similar matters than there is on the results of the excavations themselves. John Hurst noted testily at the time in a memo, 'we have all wasted a great deal of time we can ill afford' (Hurst memo, 1 November 1966).

1.4   THE POST-EXCAVATION PROGRAMME

Once excavation on the site was completed in 1968, the post-excavation work, always intended to be rounded off by a major publication, was funded by English Heritage and housed with Lawrence Butler at the Department of Archaeology, University of Leeds. From time to time there were questions about progress. One American reviewer of Christopher Taylor's *Village and farmstead*, in whose pages Faxton had featured to good effect, was led to comment: 'As far as I have been able to determine, Faxton has not been published anywhere', but clearly there was some doubt (Cheyette 1984, 958); '[Taylor] has drawn on his considerable wealth of local knowledge, much of it apparently still in his (or his colleagues?) desk drawers and file cabinets'. This much was true, for although summary reports of each of the three seasons' reports had been submitted to the DMVRG and short accounts did appear in *Current Archaeology* (Butler 1968a; 1968b; 1969a) and *Medieval Archaeology* (Wilson and Hurst 1967, 307–308; 1968, 203; 1969, 279) as well as more locally (Butler 1967; 1969b), nothing more substantial about Faxton was ever forthcoming. Even so, the Royal Commission did survey and publish the earthworks on the site (RCHME 1981), and it was widely known that draft sections of an excavation report had been readied. A monograph was said to be 'in preparation' as early as 1969 when further details were promised (Butler 1969b) and an incomplete draft of a volume was offered for consideration to the Society for Medieval Archaeology monograph series in late 1985 (letter Butler, 4 November 1985). The standard format for the volume had been set by Wharram I, Goltho, and Barton Blount, all previous volumes in the SMA monograph series, and by Grenstein and Thuxton reports, published by East Anglian Archaeology. Historical sources would be described, the geographical evidence reviewed and the archaeological record pithily explained with an accompanying illustrated catalogue of the finds. Finally, conclusions would be drawn about the specific characteristics of the site and possible lines of further research.

In the absence of either financial or institutional support even these modest ambitions foundered. It is clear that Butler knew just how much remained to be done and the archive is littered with evidence of his frustrations: broken Xeroxes, missing figures, figures yet to be drawn, scales to be added, alterations needed, floppy discs and processors to be battled with, footnotes to be finished, bibliography to be checked, conclusions unwritten. Much of the text was first written up by hand on the back of examination papers and old lecture notes on the abbeys of northern England, and later (largely) transferred to computer (the floppy discs themselves are lost), before being printed out on a dot matrix printer in multiple hand-corrected, unpaginated editions. Also in the archive is correspondence relating to an hour-long BBC Home Service radio programme about DMVs produced by Roger Laughton. Broadcast at 3.30pm on 10 September 1967 as the fifth programme in the series 'On Site', its title was the Oliver Goldsmith verse 'Amidst thy desert walks, the lapwing flies'. The programme featured interviews with Maurice Beresford and John Hurst on Wharram Percy, Philip Rahtz on

FIGURE 1.5
Part of the Faxton archive in 2017

Upton (Gloucestershire), Marie Minter talking about Hound Tor (Devon) and Lawrence Butler on Faxton. Lawrence was paid a fee of ten guineas for his part. The 'narrator's script' (for Vincent Waite), which does survive, shows how the programme was structured, although the final broadcast cannot itself now be traced in the BBC archives at the British Library. This is a sad loss to anyone with an interest in medieval settlement studies, but there is at least a useful transcript of the interview with Lawrence Butler (referred to here as 'Faxton tape 1'). In addition, there is a tape of a second sound recording, referred to here as 'Faxton tape 2', which has been salvaged as a digital copy. The provenance of this tape is uncertain but it may be associated with correspondence in the archive with Michael J Holding, the director of a freelance narrow gauge filming unit (8mm and 16mm) from Kettering. The name of the company is never stated but the film was to be on the subject of the 'facts, legends and mysteries relating to the deserted medieval village of Faxton, known locally as "the ghost village"'. The sound documentary for this film, recorded in August 1966, was sent to Lawrence Butler and it may well be a copy of this which is in the Faxton archive, the intention being to post-dub this soundtrack onto an 8mm colour film (letters Holding to Butler, 6 April 1966, 3 January 1967, 20

July 1967). The final product has not been located and it is not known if the programme was ever completed. Both transcript and sound recording are nevertheless valuable testimonies to the practice of later medieval archaeology at an important moment in its development and to public beliefs around village desertion (see frontispiece quotes). The latter, as might be expected, focused on plague and ghost stories. As one interviewee concisely explained: 'all we know is there's nothing there now, that's all we know' (Faxton tape 2).

For Lawrence Butler, the question of final publication was greatly complicated by the increasing delay between the excavations of 1966–68 and the completion of the finds reports which would enable more detailed interpretation of the sites. Once more, at the very time when Butler was supposed to be wrapping up his commitments to Faxton, he became heavily involved in administrative duties as head of the Leeds Department of Archaeology after 1981 and the fraught negotiations which eventually closed it in 1989. In January 1990 the Society for Medieval Archaeology had written back with comments on his draft manuscript, to which he responded a year later with what he referred to as a 'lack of progress report'. The pottery drawings were being 'done to a better standard'. By August 1991 the Society's monographs editor had written to Butler with some urgency: 'Monograph is getting desperate! Can you bring the final parts with you to the meeting which I shall attend—please'. Even Northamptonshire County Council also wrote in a formal fashion to ask for information about 'progress or completion of the report for publication' (letter 1 December 1992). It seems likely that many of the original inked drawings from the site were lost when the director moved to the University of York or perhaps subsequently when he retired in 2001. Either way, other projects certainly crowded in: Butler's work as a consultant archaeologist for four cathedrals, his presidency of societies such as Church Archaeology and the Yorkshire Archaeological Society and, above all, his responsibilities to his other excavations. It is perhaps telling that Butler was driven to sketch the facade of his own filing cabinet as an 'aide memoire' with details of the paperwork within: 'subscriptions to pay', 'books for review', 'extramural, new material', 'Sandal guide', 'current letters to answer', 'Fx 66', 'Fx 67', 'St K 64', 'Monks Wood work to follow up' and so on. In the end, most of the Faxton finds were removed to Northampton Museum in 1995 and later transferred to a store at Daventry (accession number 1995.339); other finds were given to the landowner and cannot, for most part, be located. When Lawrence Butler became ill in March 2014 he left notes on the whereabouts of the archive ('Faxton letters are on front room under table; Faxton report is in bedroom under dressing table') and all these materials were then gathered together by Paul Stamper (then President of the Medieval Settlement Research Group and Butler's literary executor) and shortly afterwards passed to this author with the intention of assessing what remained to be done to bring the site to publication (Figure 1.5). Lawrence was fully aware of this and gave the revived project his blessing before he died on 10 December 2014.

1.5 THE VALUE OF FAXTON

The formation of the DMVRG in 1952 and the publication of Maurice Beresford's *The lost villages of England* (1954) had prompted not only the research excavations at Wharram Percy in Yorkshire, but also the publication of county monographs by the University of Leicester Press for Oxfordshire (Allison *et al.* 1965) and Northamptonshire (Allison *et al.* 1966). These two Midland counties lay at the heart of medieval depopulation and desertion, and the kinds of questions then being asked of settlements both there and elsewhere are clearly set out in Beresford and Hurst's *Deserted medieval villages*. Although it was not published until 1971, the narrative of the first edition of this volume is based on a survey of the known archaeology of medieval settlement as it was understood to be in 1968–69, the same year that the Faxton excavations were drawing to a close; in

other words, the text for *Deserted medieval villages* was being developed at exactly the time when Lawrence Butler was on site. As stated there, the research agenda in the mind of John Hurst and others in the DMVRG centred around the origins of the village, the components of the 'village economy', the nature of peasant housing, and the date and progress of desertion as well as the relationship of the deserted village to its neighbouring surviving settlements.

A decade of excavation at Wharram Percy had shown one sequence of house development and a timescale for desertion (Andrews and Milne 1979, 138–141). The work at Gomeldon (Wiltshire) had given another structural sequence of long-house to farmstead (Algar and Musty 1969; later published as Musty and Algar 1986). Other contemporary work at Upton (Gloucestershire) (Hilton and Rahtz 1966; Rahtz 1969, 88, 74–126) and West Whelpington (Northumberland) (Jarrett 1962; 1970, 4, 48; Evans and Jarrett 1987; Evans *et al.* 1988; Jarrett and Wrathmell 1977) offered some alternative lines of enquiry (see Figure 11.1 for all sites mentioned in this chapter). Together with Hound Tor in Devon (Beresford 1979), Tresmorn in Cornwall (Beresford 1971), Broadfield in Hertfordshire (Klingelhofer 1974), Caldecote (now identified as Bedgrove, Buckinghamshire; MacDonald and Gowing 1989) and West Hartburn in Durham (Pallister and Wrathmell 1990), these were the main campaigns at medieval village sites as Butler was setting out for Faxton in 1966. In selecting all these sites, there was a deliberate design on the part of John Hurst to sponsor a broader campaign of excavation at one village with (formerly) well preserved earthworks, rather than to dissipate endeavour and skills on a number of small-scale rescue trenches or watching briefs which did little more than confirm that it was a medieval house that had just been bulldozed (Hurst 1971, 78–79, 84–89, 95–96; 1986; Butler 1969a; DMVRG 1970, 8–10).

The rationale behind excavations at Faxton has to be seen in this broader context of the DMVRG's wish to widen the range of its understanding of village formation, development and desertion. Every effort was made by the Group to spread the geographical range of excavation to embrace different regions with varying tenurial patterns, agrarian regimes and building resources, although little intensive work had hitherto been conducted on any 'clayland' site. The general perception was that there was less potential there for good results. As John Hurst commented to the British Association for the Advancement of Science in September 1960: 'in the clay lands where there is no building stone, the peasant houses were built only of wood and therefore have left no earthworks as all the wood has decayed' (DMVRG 1960, Appendix E). Early excavations on sites of this type had not been promising but, rather than give up on them, a series of sites was chosen by the DMVRG for the

Ministry of Works for more detailed examination. These were Thuxton (Butler and Wade-Martins 1989) and Grenstein (Wade-Martins 1980, 93–161), both in Norfolk, Faxton in Northamptonshire, and Barton Blount in Derbyshire (Beresford 1975)—the first three of these sites all being directed or co-directed by Lawrence Butler. In the event what was excavated at Faxton confounded expectation. Rather than a complex sequence of timber buildings with no evidence of stone buildings, the excavations at Faxton seemingly uncovered timber and earthen houses built on a dwarf stone foundation of which no traces were visible on the surface. As Hurst commented ruefully: 'this makes it very difficult to classify sites by examining the earthworks alone' (Hurst 1971, 96). Nevertheless, the observation was an important one because, as things stood in the late 1960s, there was a tendency to devise schemes of classification and argue for protective measures (for example, through Guardianship by the State, see above) on the basis of what were typically well preserved surface remains.

The local context to the excavations at Faxton was also important. In the late 1950s and 1960s there had been a steady growth of interest in archaeology locally centred around the archaeological section of the Northamptonshire Natural History Society and the archaeology staff at Northampton Museum. The Northamptonshire Federation of Archaeological Societies was established in 1965 (Moore 2015) and large-scale work had been undertaken at nearby Draughton on the Iron Age settlement site there (May 1973) as well as at Great Weldon Roman villa (1953–56) and Northampton Castle (1961–64) (Moore 2015, 17). The East Midlands region already had some experience of deserted village excavations, for example at Snarford in 1957 (West 1969), Somerby in 1957 (Mynard 1969a), Kettleby Thorpe in 1964 (Russell 1974), all in the adjacent county of Lincolnshire, and at Martinsthorpe in Rutland in 1960 (Wacher 1960; May 1973, 15). All of these were founded by the Ministry and generally in advance of, or following, heavy ploughing. More locally, David Hall had completed fieldwork on medieval field systems at Strixton by 1966 and begun parish surveys (e.g. Hall and Nickerson 1966), while the archaeological evidence for late medieval desertion in the county of Northamptonshire had already been established to some extent by three major excavations and a number of minor ones (Allison et al. 1966, 27–29). At Wythemail, 6.5km south-east of Faxton, Gillian Hurst had excavated a single croft in 1954. The main building there was identified as a 'long-house' of stone and half-timber approached over a cobbled yard with an outhouse beyond (Hurst and Hurst 1969). Another excavation was at Muscott, 21km south-west of Faxton and set in a stream valley. An aerial photograph of this settlement had appeared in John Hurst's early summary of fieldwork on deserted medieval villages (Hurst

1956, Plate XLVI) and, in 1958, P Savage excavated a farm-complex of three buildings there, consisting of a long-house, barn and shed. Only the long-house was stone-built, though it did not have a byre and Hurst thought it was probably used to store grain (Hurst 1965, 192). A third substantial excavation was also underway at Lyveden near Oundle, 22.5km north-east of Faxton, under the direction of John Steane and Geoffrey Bryant (1964–75). This site revealed a forest-edge potters' settlement in which house, kiln and drying shed were combined within the same croft. The stone-based houses at Lyveden were smaller than the farm houses at Wythemail and Muscott, and also showed greater changes in relation to the use of their yards (Steane 1967; Bryant and Steane 1969; 1971; Steane and Bryant 1975).

Elsewhere in the county, minor excavations and watching briefs, mostly by Gwen Brown in the mid-1960s, were usually only sufficient to establish the presence of houses at deserted or shrunken sites. At Great Harrowden, masonry foundations, clay floors, and a circular structure with walls 1.22m thick were identified (Wilson and Hurst 1967, 308), at Silsworth there was medieval occupation and road surfaces (Wilson and Hurst 1965, 214), and at Thorpe Waterville where medieval houses were destroyed by road widening, there was evidence for burnt thatch and the use of wattle and daub (Wilson and Hurst 1968, 203). Some of the sites in question were substantial in size and, in the case of Kelmarsh, a deserted settlement within and around the park of Kelmarsh Hall, judged to be of national importance and therefore subsequently protected through scheduling. Kelmarsh consists of house platforms, crofts, a back lane, enclosures and prominent earthworks of hollow-ways, and while the excavations in 1961 were able to confirm the presence of 'post-built timber structures' and also recover pottery of 11th-century and later date, the trench was simply not large enough to show sequences of occupation, or the relationships between structures identified within a single croft (Kelmarsh is omitted from Beresford and Hurst 1971, but see RCHME 1981, 109–112). Faxton was an altogether larger and more ambitious project, and for many years to come, it remained the fullest excavation of any medieval village site in the county.

His mission, so Butler informed the BBC audience for a 1967 radio broadcast, would be 'to find out information about village life in the clay belt of Midland England' (Faxton tape 1), but Faxton was always much more than a local case study. It was a pioneering venture which influenced methods and interpretations at better known sites which were more promptly published, Wharram Percy among them. The main aim of work on site was to provide 'an example of a typical house in the medieval period' (Butler 1968a, 48) and Butler would observe how buildings inside medieval crofts could change their alignments and construction materials. This was to be one of the first occasions in which construction in cob or 'mud' was documented archaeologically and it is perhaps no coincidence that the academic interests of the director spanned not just excavation but also standing buildings and documentary study. Even fieldwalking was undertaken over the ploughed areas during the winters, both by the director and by John Steane from nearby Kettering Grammar School whose articulate and experienced pupils attended the Faxton excavations (Steane 1971, and above). With this information to hand, Butler hoped to compare the medieval archaeological record in different parts of the village, to examine house planning, periods of occupation and levels of prosperity through objects.

Above all, it was at Faxton that the difficulties of reconciling the written evidence of Domesday Book and the archaeological record were first spelt out. Although the place-name with its –*tūn* ending and an entry in Domesday Book recording six serfs, six villeins and nine bordars (and therefore a population of as many as 80 people) were apparently convincing evidence that Faxton was flourishing in the Late Saxon period and was certainly present in the late 11th century, Lawrence Butler's excavations appeared to show convincingly that the village had only come into being later, in the late 12th century.

Faxton, or at least the place called Faxton until recently, therefore did not exist at Domesday and must, on that basis, have been located somewhere else, perhaps nearby. Christopher Taylor, in his highly regarded volume *Village and farmstead*, used Faxton to underline the point that Domesday Book does not list the names of villages but holdings or manors (Taylor 1983, 126–128). He illustrated this argument with the aerial photographs which had first set Faxton on its archaeological journey. Geographer and historian Norman Pounds (2000, 27) later repeated the claim that Faxton did not come into existence until at least a century after the Conquest, and Faxton has since become the classic illustration of a Domesday place-name where the name is seemingly much older than the village itself; Richard Muir (1992, 48–50) saw Faxton as a demonstration of the 'misleading nature of place-name evidence'. Most recently, Jones and Lewis (2012, 199) have reiterated the same point; 'extensive excavation', they write, 'found no evidence anywhere in this large complex settlement, for any occupation pre-dating *c.* AD 1150, and it showed how part of the village was not laid out until *c.* AD 1200'. We will return to these claims about origins and reasons for the desertion of the settlement later in this volume but, as we shall see, there is much else at Faxton which still merits our attention 50 years on.

2

PLACE AND LANDSCAPE

Lawrence Butler

with contributions by Ronan O'Donnell, David Hall and Paul Stamper

This chapter remains largely as Lawrence Butler intended. His text was based in turn on handwritten notes (c.1957) provided by Patrick King, the first Northamptonshire County Archivist. Any changes are mostly corrections of fact, minor enhancements of bibliography and the filling of spaces left blank in the original text where further work was clearly intended by Butler but never completed. Figures have been added in and corrected as necessary. Further discoveries may await the medieval historian but for now a complementary section on Faxton's landscape context has been added by Ronan O'Donnell which updates Butler's original text. David Hall kindly contributed to this section while Paul Stamper wrote the paragraphs on RAF Harrington.

2.1 GEOGRAPHICAL BACKGROUND

The village (SP785752) lies in the township of Faxton within the modern parish of Lamport on a south-facing spur of the Northamptonshire uplands, 16km north of Northampton and 10km south-west of Kettering (Figure 2.1). In northern Northamptonshire, the Jurassic limestone series provides varied building stone ranging from beds of high quality at Barnack and Weldon to poorer utilitarian stones suitable for rubble walling and infilling behind ashlar faces. The Jurassic belt has a northern scarp edge above the broad valley of the Welland, with a steep profile near Rockingham, but more generally has been smoothed by glaciation. To the south the belt decreases in height gradually towards the Nene and is cut by a number of stream valleys. Two such valleys lie east and west of Faxton draining into the Pitsford Brook and joining the Nene at Northampton. Faxton, at 135m OD, Draughton and Maidwell are the most northerly of the villages set above southward-draining streams. To their north-east lies a watershed ridge beyond which the streams flow eastwards into the River Ise, a more substantial tributary of the Nene, joining it near Wellingborough. The soils within Faxton township are derived from the Lias clays but both elevation and aspect affects their usefulness for arable cultivation.

One interpretation of the place-name Faxton gives the meaning 'the farm where the coarse grass grows' (Gover *et al.* 1933, 124; Ekwall 1960, 176). The other interpretation derives from a personal name *Fakr*, meaning 'the settlement or farm of Fakr', a Norse name given in the 9th or 10th century; an alternative, derived from an Old English personal name *Faecce* might suggest an even earlier origin for the village. Place-names ending in 'ton' are the commonest settlement element in this area of Northamptonshire, though woodland clearance names such as Cransley and Pytchley also occur. On the northern and western fringes of Faxton parish there is substantial ancient woodland at Shortwood and Mawsley.

The parish is a geographical entity in many ways similar to Old and Scaldwell further south. Indeed, its eastern and western boundaries extend southwards to form the eastern and western boundaries of Scaldwell suggesting that Faxton was carved out of a larger territorial unit combining the two parishes, while the eight parishes of Mawsley Hundred may represent the northern arc of villages dependent on an Anglo-Saxon minster at Brixworth. After the Norman Conquest, however, Faxton seems to have been linked tenurially most frequently to Old and Mawsley, but for ecclesiastical purposes it was a member of Lamport parish as was another small settlement at Hanging Houghton, 1km south of Lamport.

2.2 HISTORICAL BACKGROUND

Medieval Faxton

The first mention of the settlement at Faxton is in Domesday Book where the manor was held by the king. A charter of *c.*1175 then mentions a 'messuage' in Faxton which belonged to Walter de Balliol (Stenton 1961, 159 note 1, Appendix 32; British Library Harley Charters 49.F.53; this information is extracted from Patrick King's notes). Throughout the 12th century the Balliol family was the main tenant and four knights' fees were owed to the king from Faxton and from the two other members of the same fee, Old and Walgrave (1.6km south-east

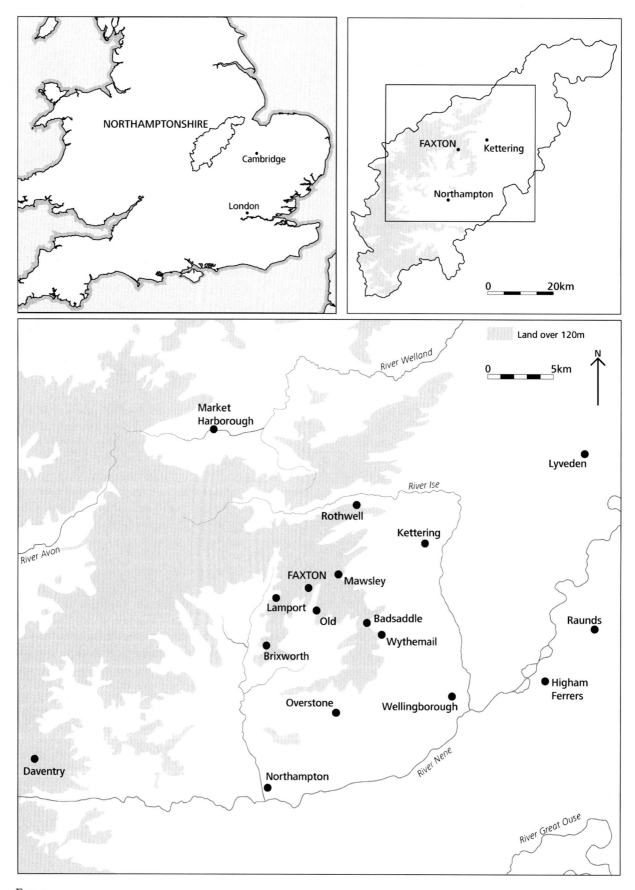

FIGURE 2.1

Location maps showing main places mentioned in the text

of Old). The most detailed account of this manor is given in the Victoria County History (VCH 1937, 169–172; Loyd and Stenton 1950, 208–209) and only those episodes which have a direct bearing on the nature of settlement are emphasised here. The superior lords were successively the Balliols (later the kings of Scotland), the earls of Richmond, the countess of Pembroke and the dukes of York.

The manor of two hides and two knights' fees was held during the mid-13th century by Adam de Periton ('Adam of Faxton'). Between 1280 and 1314 this manor, with its lands in Mawsley and Walgrave, was held by Adam's daughter Isabel who married first Robert de Welles and secondly William de Vescy. On her death the manor was divided between the Welles and Vescy/Vessy families (two-thirds and one-third respectively) of whom various family members are documented (e.g. Welles 1876; PRO 1906). When Robert de Welles died in 1320, his estate included a chief messuage with its buildings in ruins and two parts of a windmill (VCH 1937). In 1344 the divided holding was re-united under Adam de Welles. In 1389 it was held by his grandson John, a notable warrior who was knighted in 1373 and ennobled by Richard II. Faxton remained in the hands of Lord Welles and his descendants until 1507. The family had risen in social class through military and political endeavour and a succession of marriage alliances. This rise, however, brought disasters during the Wars of the Roses when adherence to the Lancastrian cause resulted in the death of Lionel, Lord Welles, at Towton in 1461, the execution of Richard Lord Welles in 1469 and the death of his son and heir Sir Robert in the same year. The Welles' direct possession of Faxton was therefore lost between 1461 and 1485, only being regained when the acts of attainder were reversed. The death of John, Viscount Welles, in 1499 and of his widow Cecily in 1507 meant that the manor was subsequently subdivided into thirds or ninths throughout the 16th century.

Medieval Faxton was therefore the centre of a manor which usually included Mawsley and at times parts of Old, Walgrave and Moulton (8km south of Faxton). The tenure by Adam de Periton in the mid-13th century is a likely period when the moated homestead was created (see Chapter 3), and the two centuries of tenure by the Welles family would have given the village a resident landowner, despite political upheavals and the temporary loss of the property. To some extent, Faxton was resilient. Neighbouring settlements at Mawsley, Wythemail and Badsaddle all seem to be examples of late 14th-century desertion with both Wythemail and Badsaddle being incorporated into parks. They were very much smaller than Faxton and had very little catchment for water. Further north, five other small settlements in the drainage catchment of the River Ise were converted into sheep-walks and at one of

these the Montagu family built their mansion at Boughton House. Yet Faxton remained. Its recorded Domesday population of 21 puts it in the top 8% of Northamptonshire villages subsequently deserted; it was those with less than 20 people and more often those with less than ten recorded persons (or heads of households) that became the principal candidates for desertion. Similarly, in the 1334 Taxation 60% of the desertions came in those villages assessed at less than 40 shillings, and the average quota levied in each deserted vill was 36s 5d. Faxton's quota stood at 38s 8d and so above the danger line. Later in the 14th century it was those villages with fewer than 60 taxpayers in the Poll Tax of 1377 who were most at risk, but Faxton and Mawsley, with 94 paying tax, again lay outside the jeopardy zone. On these criteria at least Faxton was not an obvious candidate for desertion and it survived the critical period of 1450 to 1600 unscathed, though it did absorb the lesser settlement of Mawsley (Allison et al. 1966, 7–21, 39–40).

Post-medieval history and archaeology

In one sense its divided inheritance may have proved beneficial to Faxton. There was no concentration of power into the hands of a single owner who could depopulate the village in favour of sheep husbandry as the Knightleys did at Fawsley or the Spencers did at Althorp. It was difficult too to re-assemble the divided manor and it may be that Edward Bullen was the only holder actually resident in the parish. Not until 1596 were the nine portions of the manor concentrated in one holder, Thomas Morgan, though Edward Saunders and Richard Purefoy had attempted to do something similar in the previous decade. The Morgans, whose main interest was in Aynho, held Faxton until 1606 in which year Anthony sold it to Augustine Nicols, a Justice of Common Pleas. The manor remained in the Nicolls family for four generations until the death of Sir Edward in 1717. This marks another peak in the fortunes of Faxton. The Nicolls family rebuilt the manor house and cared for the church; houses and cottages around the village green were built during their period as landlords. Some flavour of the local life of the gentry class at this time (perfecting lawns, eliminating rabbits, cock-fighting and much else) is given by the colourful diaries of Thomas Isham of Lamport (Isham 1971; Fletcher 2010). The Faxton almshouses were directly a result of the generosity of Sir Edward's sister Susannah Danvers (d'Anvers) in her will (1730; Susannah having died without issue after an unhappy marriage; Macnamara 1895), being erected by her surviving sister Jane in 1736. From the Nicolls, the village passed to Jane's grandson John Nicolls Raynsford of Brixworth, who held the manor at the time of the Enclosure Award (1745–46). However, although Hester, the mother of John Nicolls Raynsford, may have lived at

Faxton where she was buried in 1763, her nephew and his wife subsequently put the 'manor of Faxton and Mawsley' up for auction on 29 March 1784. Its tenants were described then as 'very respectable' and the income as £1,723 10s per year (Patrick King notes). The purchaser was James Langham of Cottesbrooke in whose family it descended until much of their estate was sold in 1911. Memorials to Augustine Nicolls, Edward Nicolls, Susannah Danvers, John Nicolls Raynsford and Hester Raynsford were all once among those to be found in Faxton church (see Appendix 2 and Chapter 3).

Population figures during the post-medieval period, wherever it is possible to obtain them, show a generally steady pattern of families and occupied houses. In the Muster Rolls, Faxton played its full part, though ranked in the lowest of three categories of village size: only Brixworth in Orlingbury Hundred is in the highest category, nine villages are in the middle category, and six are in the lowest category (Wake 1935, 11, 30, 61, 76, 77; Mellows 1927, 114, where Lamport and Faxton together supply 10 men). Faxton was always able to provide two or three trained men, and Justice Nicolls or Sir Francis provided a light horse[-man]. A maximum of 16 men were available for service. In 1674, 34 householders paid the Hearth Tax, perhaps representing a population of about 144. In the Compton Census of religious attendance the number given for Faxton in 1676 was 180 persons (though this may be a misreading for 130 persons). When the county historian John Bridges described Faxton in about 1720 there were 32 families or houses, including the manor house, in addition to two cottages at Mawsley (Bridges 1791, II, 95). In the churchwardens' accounts of 1737–46 there were 24 holdings liable for tithe which corresponds with the Hearth Tax returns which show 23 taxable hearths (NRO 126P/11). At the 1746 Enclosure Act there are 19 buildings shown around The Green together with two farms in the fields at Faxton Lodge and Shortwood; in addition there were the two cottages at Mawsley (NRO 702).

Taken together, this documentary and cartographic evidence demonstrates some major changes in the village between c.1720 and 1746; the manor house had gone and only the Rectory Farm now stood to the east of the church together with the single row of almshouses built in 1736. On the north side of the village there were three farms and at least 10 cottages. Some of these 19 buildings might have been in multiple occupancy, but by 1790 when the estate map was altered, there were only 12 homesteads by The Green. Very similar information is provided by militia lists for 1777 when seven males are listed (Hatley 1973, 149) for the village levies raised to meet the needs of Lamport church when only 13 holdings are taxed (1789–1830), dropping to 11 through the amalgamation of holdings during the Napoleonic Wars. The 1801 Census records 15

families at Faxton totalling 54 persons: 12 families in the village and 3 outside it at Faxton Lodge, Shortwood and Foxhall.

Another indicator of population fluctuation is the number of families being baptised, married and buried at Faxton between 1570 and 1836. This may not be an entirely satisfactory guide in so far as Faxton males could marry non-local brides in their home village before bringing them back to Faxton, while the local females would then live outside the parish after marriage unless their husband was also local; this was the case in about 50% of recorded marriages (Phillimore *et al.* 1908, 143–148; 1909, 101–122). Nevertheless, there is a striking pattern of marriages which falls into three distinct phases: between 1570 and 1640 there was an average of 15 marriages per decade in the range from 12 to 20; between 1660 and 1730 there was an average of 3 per decade with a maximum of 5 and with two decades when no marriages of Faxton inhabitants took place at either Faxton or Lamport; between 1730 and 1836 there was an average of 5 per decade in the range 2 to 8.

As far as local industry is concerned, Faxton windmill is marked on the estate map of 1746 (NRO 702) and for the preceding century it gave its name to the common field in which it stood. It is marked on the map as a post-mill as is the mill in the neighbouring parish of Old. A windmill was mentioned as one of the manorial possessions in the Inquisition of 1320 (VCH 1937, 171). In 1612 the Faxton millwright Edward Jones was employed to keep the bell frame and woodwork of Draughton church in good repair for an annual payment. At a later date it is likely that the post-mills at Faxton and Old were provided with roughly coursed stone basements since stone scatters show on the air photographs and in the plough soil. In this they would be similar to surviving or recently destroyed mills at Fen Stanton near St Ives or Easton-on-the-Hill (Wailes 1954; Posnansky 1956; RCHME 1979, 116; Hall 1973). The Faxton mill was to be sold at auction and 'taken away at the first opportunity' in 1761 (Geoffrey Starmer pers. comm.).

The recent past

The process of desertion at Faxton extended throughout the late 19th and early 20th centuries, punctuated by a number of incidents, singly sustainable in a vigorous village but cumulatively disastrous in a declining or dispirited community. The rector himself wrote of 'forlorn Faxton' (*Northampton Mercury*, 23 April 1909, 6) and the first major contributory factor to this malaise was the absence of a resident squire. The Langhams were absentee landlords and for much of the late 19th century the estate remained in the hands of the trustees or guardians; there was therefore no benevolent personal interest on the part of the landowner to provide for the welfare of the villagers in times of agrarian depression, or to provide employment as domestic and estate servants in the village. Secondly, the absence of a resident clergyman closely involved in the village education and spiritual teaching meant that this task devolved upon a rapid succession of poorly paid curates who usually lived in the 'Rectory House'. In the later 19th century curates of Faxton occasionally lived at Old from which Faxton is much easier of access than Lamport (Patrick King notes); they frequently sought other curacies or teaching posts in order to make an adequate living. Often the rector was a member of the Isham family who resided at Lamport, so there was some sporadic and often benevolent contact with Faxton. Thirdly, there was no resident schoolmaster so Faxton children had to travel daily the 3km across the meadow paths to school in Old. The absence of a shop and any locally conducted trades meant that apprentices had to travel to the market towns and the village was dependent on travelling salesmen, hawkers and cheapjacks. For a time before the 1914–18 War there was an alehouse at the north-east corner of the village green, remembered by pre-War inhabitants who could point out its location. No alehouse, however, is mentioned in trade directories and it may be that it was serving home-brewed ale for harvest feasts and 'church ales'; it was certainly not a licensed establishment. The fate of the village was effectively dependent on the fortunes of agriculture. The Langham estate did build a pair of farm-workers' cottages in the 1880s but that was the only new building in the 19th century and the most modern house in the village.

The population censuses show a rise in the early 19th century and a steady fall in the latter half. The numbers are:

1801: 54 persons,
1831: 103,
1841: 108,
1851: 95,
1871: 73,
1891: 46,
1901: 35,
1921: 37.

In 1801 there were 13 major holdings; by 1901 there were only 10 holdings and the 11 houses occupied. The most significant fall in population took place in 1851–91 during which time the population halved; by 1921 just 37 people lived in the parish. The reasons for this rise and fall are not entirely straight forward, but the rise may be influenced by an increased need for agricultural labour on the larger farms, the tendency towards larger families (with less infant mortality) and the transient needs of canal and railway labour in the local area. The fall is probably to be associated with the decline of minor trades within the village (a butcher, shepherd, carpenter, servant, shoemaker, a 'leaber' (labourer?) with 'one ie' and a constable

were all recorded in 1777 but not later; Hatley 1973, 149; Whellan 1849), not to mention the greater attractions of industrial towns such as Kettering, Rothwell, Desborough, Wellingborough and above all Northampton. Some Faxton families also travelled much further afield, such as the two newly wed brothers of the Craxford family who emigrated to South Australia in the 1840s.[1]

New cottages were also built on the northern margin of the parish when a short-lived brickworks, known as the Faxton Brickworks, was opened by the Langham estate at Fackley near Bullocks Penn Spinney. In 1966, kiln debris and bricketage lay in the fields next to the Spinney and the clay pit was still visible. It was reported locally then that the workers at the brickworks lived in the cottages east of Foxhall Inn (demolished around 1942 to make way for Harrington aerodrome). In 1929, the kiln itself was photographed and recorded as a round brick structure with a conical top adjacent to a quarry pit for clay (Thompson and Markham 1929; Holden 2008, 74). The kiln was destroyed in 1935–36 and the quarry pit, first recorded on the 6 inch Ordnance Survey map of 1885, had also been filled by 1984 when a small excavation took place. This revealed the base of a brick-built updraught kiln some 4m high and an internal diameter of 3m with its fire-holes and flue channels. The kiln would have been coal-fired and mainly used to produce bricks, tiles and drainage pipes; complete examples of bricks were recovered with the initials JHL, the 19th-century landowner James Hay Langham of Cottesbrooke Hall. A reference in the *Northampton Mercury* of 23 April 1909, taken together with materials from the site, suggests that an attempt was also made to fire pottery there (Bellamy 1985) and some possible products, a salt cellar glazed in chocolate brown and blue, together with a cup in white and yellow with raised brown bands, were described.

A second brickworks was also opened east of Faxton Lodge late in the 19th century, operated by Joseph Bonsor, of an established family of brick and tile makers from Naseby. His operations in Lamport and Faxton began in the 1870s and ran until he died between 1894 and 1903; by the latter date his executers were supervising. The brickworks had apparently closed by 1914, after about 40 years' brick and tile production (Kelly's Directories 1877–1910). The 1885 6 inch OS map shows an L-plan range of buildings with one square kiln surveyed in 1884 off the road running south-east from Lamport.[2] Its kiln bank and the clay pit were still visible among undergrowth in 1966. It is likely that its main products were also bricks, roof tiles and field drainage pipes for local farm use.

---

1 www.craxford-family.co.uk/themepurple/craufaxton.php, accessed February 2017.

2 This information is kindly supplied by Paul Stamper.

The second period when the village was pushed further into decline occurred during the agricultural depression of the 1930s. The highway authority, Brixworth Rural District Council, did not consider it necessary to provide a metalled road to Faxton. This was not a major problem just so long as horse-drawn carts were the normal means of transport; field tracks radiated out from the village north to Rothwell, east to Old Lodge, south to the Lamport-Old road and west to Shortwood Lodge, but no tarmac-surfaced road ran within the parish though two surfaced roads formed its boundaries to south and north. The smallholders then living within the parish were reluctant to petition for roads which they were too poor to maintain. Other services too were not provided: there was no piped water, no electricity and no telephones.

After the Second World War, the absence of such advantages of civilisation was acutely felt by those returning from war service or factory work in Northampton, or even from civilian work at RAF Draughton. Faxton was a backwater in many senses, particularly when compared to the flourishing village of Old. At Old could be found all the amenities that Faxton lacked: in particular there was a post office and postal collection there and, at a time when the welfare state had increased villagers' financial dependence upon maternity benefits, family allowances and state pensions; this was a significant influence upon the quality of life. Old flourished as a village while Faxton continued on a downward spiral of deprivation. From 1945 to 1966 there was a gradual exodus of families until the last inhabitant left in the spring of that year.

This same period, 1945–66, had also seen increased problems over access to compulsory schooling, to medical care and to shops, as well as limited employment possibilities at a time when farming was rapidly becoming mechanised and residents had to drive or cycle over dusty or muddy unmade roads for the first kilometre from the village. Motorised travelling shops or delivery vans were reluctant to visit Faxton on the un-metalled road surfaces; indeed, a baker's rounds-man using a pony and trap still visited Faxton until about 1950. Such families as did make Faxton their home were increasingly non-locals who were prepared to tolerate a lack of amenities for a short time in order to obtain cheap housing. Even these new settlers found the irregular water supply to be a major disadvantage. As the aquifers were tapped by deeper wells and boreholes to supply the increased needs of Northampton, so the shallow wells in Faxton became more unreliable in dry summers. Perhaps symbolically, the church was demolished in 1958/9 and the almshouses had already fallen into disrepair during the 1939–45 War. In the 1970s the pair of farm-workers' cottages in brick and Welsh slate were re-occupied as a single dwelling, now known as 'Ladyholme' after a field-name on the

1746 estate map. This house now stands amid the plough land and new plantations which obscure the former village layout (see also Chapter 12).

2.3 THE OPEN FIELDS AND THEIR ENCLOSURE

Throughout the Middle Ages Faxton parish (1,760 acres) was divided between arable, pasture, meadow and woodland (Figure 2.2). The eastern parish boundary is predominantly natural, following the Old Brook stream in the valley between Faxton and Old from a point near its source southwards to Old village. The northern boundary is the watershed along the highest ground between Faxton on the south and the three parishes of Cransley, Loddington and Orton to the north-east (Figure 2.3). For most of this boundary, a road runs between wide grass margins or freeboards; it has been suggested that this represents an important prehistoric routeway, the 'Jurassic Way' (Steane 1974, 6, 35–36; Northamptonshire HER 195), which dates from at least the Early Bronze Age and may be significantly older. At Foxhall, this track turns north joining with another road from Lamport. The western boundary of Faxton parish has a sinuous line suggesting woodland clearance between Faxton and Draughton. Only south of Shortwood does the parish boundary follow a fairly straight north–south track leading to Lamport, running between long-established arable fields. The southern boundary is shared with Scaldwell and follows the road between Lamport and Old; it has an artificial character, similar to the south-west sector dividing Faxton from Lamport.

Although much of north-eastern Northamptonshire was technically within the forest of Rockingham during the Middle Ages, there is little evidence for the woodland character of Faxton. The Market Harborough to Northampton road formed approximately the western boundary of the forest until 1291 and this ancient definition of the land subject to forest law was briefly revived between 1637 and 1641 (Pettit 1968, 203, Table XXIV). Long before 1291 the real forest margin had retreated northwards. Relict stretches were left, however, and Mawsley Wood was described in 1249 as being in Rockingham Forest and Mawsley in 1246 or 1249. It is likely that the small settlement there (RCHME 1979, 106 and Plate 16) represents clearance within a greater area of woodland originally extending to over 500 acres. The moated homestead in the western extremity of Loddington parish may mark another woodland clearance (RCHME 1979, 107). It is probable that Shortwood is also ancient and formerly extended to a total of 120 acres through the western part of the two fields known as Jamesgore in 1746 to reach the northern extremity of the parish at Foxhall; it

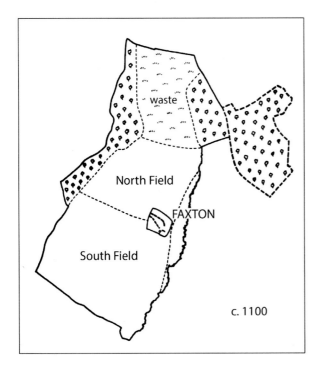

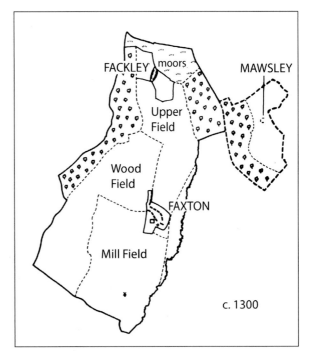

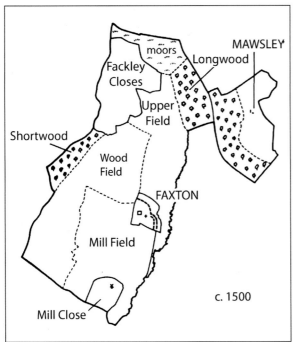

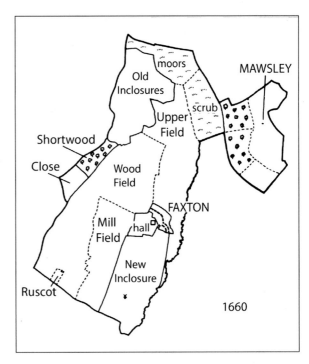

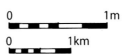

FIGURE 2.2

Reconstruction of Faxton fields c.1100–1660

FIGURE 2.3
Faxton in 1746 as shown on the estate map

may also have extended southwards across Short-wood Close to Symark (Figure 2.3; for detailed location, see Figures 2.4A and 2.4B). All the other woodlands in the parish (10 acres) are spinneys of recent origin planted on poor ground or on the steep slopes, to which have been added fox coverts of late 18th- or 19th-century date, such as Claridge Spinney.

Relatively little of the parish was maintained as permanent meadow. Only the Holmes' along the Old Brook to the south-east of the parish seems to have been retained, subject to annual re-allotment into 'swapes' or swathes between the different landholders. The ten fields (73 acres) are all small, being two acres or multiples of that acreage up to eight acres, apart from the three largest which have taken in former crofts and previously ploughed paddocks (Ladyholme: 14 acres; *Parklays*: 10 acres;

and *Honey Holme*: 13 acres). In 1966 all these were still under meadow grass as was the streamside portion of Ladyholme, Park Leys and Honeyholme, but in 1969–70 the stream was straightened by the Water Board to hasten the run-off flow into Pitsford Reservoir and its meadow flora was lost. Elsewhere, there are other parts of the former open fields which carry 'meadow' names, perhaps referring to their normal usage when under fallow as well as to their present occupation. They occur in the valley of the western stream between Faxton and Shortwood (Broad meadow: 7.5 acres; Bowling Lays meadow: 7.5 acres; Oxlay meadow: 8 acres) and all are located in the mid-17th-century enclosures south of the village (for detailed location, see Figure 2.4C).

By 1300 there were three medieval open fields: Mill Field, Wood Field and Upper. The main enclosure of the open fields took place in 1745–46

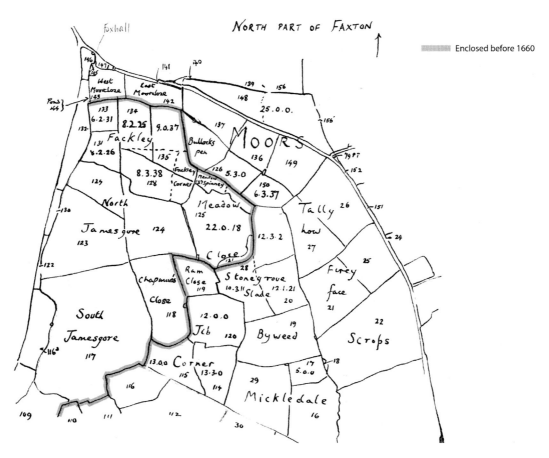

FIGURE 2.4A

1746. North part of estate map (as transcribed by Patrick King)

FIGURE 2.4B

1746. Middle part of estate map (as transcribed by Patrick King). This map may be compared with the aerial photograph Figure 1.2

Enclosed before 1660

FIGURE 2.4C
1746. South part of estate map (as transcribed by Patrick King). This map may be compared with the aerial photograph Figure 1.2

when 1,140 acres in the three main fields were allocated between the tenants of John Nicolls Raynsford (Figures 2.3, 2.4A, 2.4B, 2.4C). However, there had been two previous episodes of enclosure totalling 453 acres. The first is not precisely recorded but is likely to have occurred in the 16th century when Fackley along with Jamesgore adjoining it to the south were taken out of common cultivation (for a detailed location, see Figure 2.4A). This enclosure of 214 acres may have included not only arable, but also, possibly, former woodland on the western margin of Jamesgore, former rough grazing in Meadow Close, former waste at Fackley Corner and the former settlement at Fackley (it should be noted here that Butler's claim for a medieval settlement at Fackley is speculative and most of the area has since been mapped as open field by David Hall; Partida *et al.* 2013, maps 22M and 35M). North of Fackley was an area of poor ground (115 acres), enclosed in 1746, known as the Moors and the Moor Closes. The capping of Boulder Clay ensured that all these fields served only as poor quality grazing land.

The second enclosure was undertaken in 1659 by Sir Edward Nicolls; it enclosed a group of furlongs at

the south-east end of the parish totalling 239 acres. It was conventionally regarded as of 230 or 226 acres (NRO IL 5345; NRO LFM 44 of 23/11/1663). These were the 'New Enclosures' taken out of Mill Field but kept in cultivation (Figure 2.2): they comprised three large closes (Bowling Lays: 63 acres; Bringhursts Close: 58 acres; Mill Close: 56 acres), two smaller fields (Red Roods: 23 acres; Hall Lays: 17 acres) and three meadows of 78 acres, already mentioned (for detailed location, see Figure 2.4C). This enclosure took out of the Mill Field all the arable land lying between the two streams south of Faxton. The new field divisions were arbitrary and crossed within furlongs and across interlocking strips. An annual compensation of £60 was paid in lieu of tithes of corn.

This enclosure virtually halved the Mill Field leaving only 194 acres to be divided into hedged fields at the 1745–46 enclosure. This action produced three large closes and two small ones (Rockley Hill: 52 acres; Burrow: 43 acres; Crossway: 36 acres; Long Doles: 15 acres; Rye Croft: 8 acres) (for location, see Figure 2.4C). The field-name Burrow may refer to a lost Bronze Age barrow; another barrow was situated in Shortwood Lays (RCHME 1981, 115). The enclosures generally respected furlong boundaries and ran with the lie of the land.

The second main open field in the medieval period was Wood Field (Figure 2.2). It was an irregular shape, and had two divisions of almost equal size: South Wood Field or Nether Field (208 acres) situated south of the Faxton to Shortwood track, and North Wood Field or Middle Field (207 acres) situated in the centre of the parish north-west of the village. Two closes, probably early enclosures, separated the two divisions: Banscroft and Shortwood Close, both of 29 acres (for locations, see Figure 2.4B). The first of the two divisions of Wood Field, South Wood Field, was divided into three large closes (Debdale [glebe]: 40 acres; Rye Hill: 36 acres; and Spring Close: 29 acres), five medium-sized closes (Thorney Lays: 21 acres; Deadmans Headland: 20 acres; Breckhill: 17 acres; Catacre: 16 acres; Cow Muck Slade: 16 acres) and two small ones (John Green's Slade: 9 acres; Ruscot: 4 acres). A feature of these new closes was the varied direction of small bundles of interlocking strips. The second of the two divisions of Wood Field, Middle Field, was a roughly square field at the head of the western stream valley. Here the presence of this stream and the desire to respect furlong groupings make the close sizes much more varied. In descending order of size they were: Shortwood Lays: 37 acres; Washpit Hill: 36 acres; Pensham: 28 acres; Sandpit Close: 27 acres; Hill Croft: 24 acres; Nofield: 20 acres; Hall Headland: 13 acres; Spinney Lays: 13 acres; Great Green Close: 6 acres; and Little Green Close: 3 acres. South of the Green Closes lay the paddocks and then the former house Crofts 6–9, already clear of housing by 1746 and probably periodically ploughed to be sown with grass. The eastern border of this field was a track leading from Faxton northwards to Orton. Two later features in Woodfield were a dam and pond near Shortwood, apparently used to fill the ice house in winter and to provide snipe shooting, and a dam and pond intended for a sheep dip indicated by the adjacent field-name Washpit Hill; both were noted as earthworks (RCHME 1981, 124).

The third major field, Upper Field, was an elongated tract of land (386 acres) extending from the village up the western flank of the Old Brook as far as the high ground on the north-eastern boundary of the parish. Apart from the irregularly shaped Jib Corner (and possible gibbet location), all the post-enclosure closes in Upper Field were east of the ridge road to Orton. Three large closes, on poor soil, were east of the Old Brook (Tally How: 36 acres; Firey Face: 34 acres; Scrops: 43 acres); their regular sizes and boundaries suggest recent intakes from waste or scrubland (for location, see Figure 2.4A). The eight closes further to the south range in size between 46 and 20 acres: Mickledale: 46 acres; Cliffesdale: 41 acres; Jib Corner: 39 acres; Stonegrove Slade: 35 acres; Claridge: 31 acres; Littledale Syke: 27 acres;

Burn'd Pool: 26 acres; Byweed: 21 acres. The three 'dale' names together with Debdale in Wood Field, suggest a Norse influence which the *Fakr* personal name interpretation supports (similar names occur in Draughton, e.g. Clippindale). The remaining field was much smaller (Ram Close: 7 acres) and may represent an old enclosure since it lies between two closes, Meadow Close to the north and Chapman's Close to the west, in the area of ancient enclosures.

By 1790 the closes created in 1746 had typically been subdivided into more manageable units of about 10 acres, only to be returned again to their 1746 boundaries early in the 20th century. In the south of the parish there has been more drastic removal of hedge boundaries to create Hundred Acre; perhaps this is nearer to the medieval hedge-less appearance, but the single-direction ploughing has eradicated headlands, the paths or slades and the sensitive intimacy of the strips to the contours and the natural drainage of the land. In the north of the parish, on the poorer land there, late 20th-century ploughing has respected the enclosure field boundaries and has not totally eliminated the evidence of ridge and furrow, which in places remains visible in the permanent pasture (and see Chapter 12 for the 21st-century picture). Figure 2.5 takes the evidence from aerial photographs to reconstruct the cultivated arable land in medieval Faxton. The limited information mapped by Butler has been supplemented here by more recent and remarkable evidence published by Partida, Hall and Foard in their *Atlas of Northamptonshire* (Partida et al. 2013, 22M, 34M, 35M).

To some extent this process of enclosure, the creation of consolidated holdings at the periphery of the parish and the declining population within the village itself are all linked together. At Old, enclosure did not take place until 1767 and it is likely that the outlying farms of Old Lodge and the Kites Hall, both in the north of the parish, were constructed after that. At Faxton (as noted above) an enclosure by agreement was made in 1659 by which 239 acres were taken out of open-field cultivation in the Mill Field, and it is possible that all three outlying farmsteads in this part of the parish were constructed between then and the 1746 enclosure.

The first farmstead, noted in the parish register in 1723, stands north-east of the modern Faxton Lodge farmhouse. It is stone-built and two-storey with a central chimney stack; by 1985 it had been converted into two farm cottages. It may originally have been called Faxton Lodge farmhouse, the name perhaps being transferred to the modern Faxton Lodge farmhouse after its construction in 1849 (datestone).

The second, Shortwood Lodge, is a prominent house on the western margin of the parish alongside a substantial wood (described in 1966 as 'ancient woodland') of the same name. The house shown on the 1746 estate map is a three-unit building

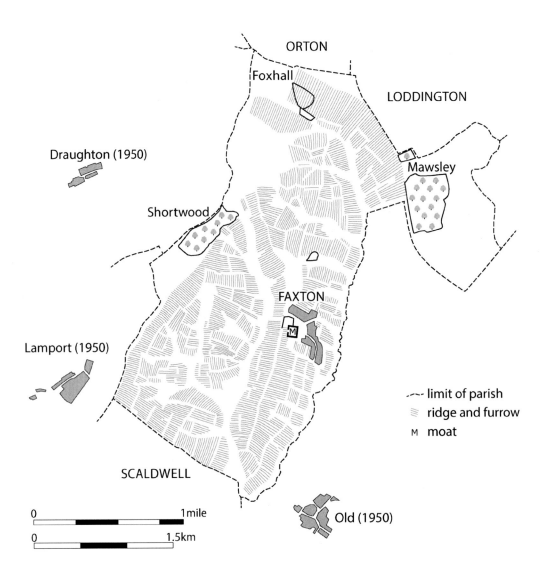

FIGURE 2.5
Faxton. Ridge and furrow transcribed from aerial photographs by Lawrence Butler, with more recent additions from Partida et al. 2013, maps 22M, 34M, 35M

with its axis east–west. The surviving house has its main axis north–south with a central three-storey tower topped by a balustrade parapet (Figures 2.6A and 2.6B). Prominent on the east face of the octagonal top storey is an arch, said to be part of a fireplace brought from Pytchley Hall (demolished 1828–29; Heward and Taylor 1996, 288–289). The side wings are normal two-storey domestic ranges with chimneys in the gables, but with pedimented windows and chamfered pilasters of ashlar-faced ironstone at the angles with some Weldon stone. A three-storey staircase block is attached to the rear of the house. The plaque on the front of the tower is now illegible but may once have carried a date. The description of this house as a 'Hawking Tower' carries echoes of others in the county such as the mid-18th-century example at Boughton Park to the north of Northampton, and the early 17th-century one at Althorp. A late 18th-century remodelling of

a simpler farmhouse is possible, perhaps by Sir James Langham of Cottesbrooke.

Finally, a third farm called 'Foxhall' stood at the northern extremity of the parish (SP779780). In the 19th century, this was an inn and a regular meeting place for the Pytchley Hunt because of its location at the junction of metalled roads and bridle tracks. It is marked on the 1746 map and was probably built earlier in that century, although the first farmer to live there is not recorded until 1754. It was demolished in about 1942 when the war-time airfield at Draughton was constructed.

2.4 OTHER ASSOCIATED SETTLEMENTS

Mawsley was a small settlement on the ridge at the head of a northward flowing stream (SP805763) which, for much of the post-Conquest period, was

FIGURE 2.6A
The Hawking Tower, Lamport, Northamptonshire. Photo taken in 1966 by Lawrence Butler

FIGURE 2.6B
The Hawking Tower, Lamport, Northamptonshire. Photo taken in 1966 by Lawrence Butler

linked tenurially with Faxton (Figures 2.3 and 2.5). The place-name means 'the clearing on the stony ridge'; the place-name element *malure* being the same as that encountered in Wythemail (Gover *et al.* 1933, 122, 128–129). The first mention of the settlement is as a hundredal name (for example in 1076), possibly a half-hundred of eight townships within the larger unit of Orlingbury. This hundred was attached to Orlingbury during the mid-13th century, but had disappeared as a separate entity by 1275. A memory of the Mawsley Hundred court may occur in the permission granted by John de Grey of Rotherfield, steward of King Edward III, in 1353 to John de Welles, Lord of Faxton, to hold his hundred courts and courts leet in the vill of Faxton (Loyd and Stenton 1950, 251–252).

Although the settlement name does not occur in Domesday Book, references to tofts and crofts at Mawsley are found in the late 12th century and early 13th century. Mention of Mawsley Wood first occurs in 1249. The hamlet was regarded as a separate vill in 1316 and held by Robert de Welles (*Nomina Villarum* 1316; PRO 1906). In the 1334 survey it was included within Faxton and from that date seems to have had little separate existence. In the 1439 division of tithe responsibilities, Mawsley was judged to be a part of Faxton and contributed with it to the support of Lamport church. In 1486, Mawsley Field was held by the Lord of Loddington from the Lord of Faxton for a rent of 2s and the division of Mawsley hamlet between Faxton and Loddington may stem from this tenure (Mawsley field 1486). The division had certainly occurred by 1609 when Maurice Kinsman mortgaged the land, which he later (1612) sold to Augustine Nicolls.

By the time of the 1745 Enclosure Act there were 238 acres of Mawsley parish regarded as part of Faxton, both wood (55 acres) and pasture, and 187 acres reckoned part of Loddington. There are maps of Mawsley for 1727 (NRO T228, Map 702), 1839 and 1843. In terms of its general location, Mawsley has a far better claim to be part of Loddington: it lies to the north-east of the ridge-top road, its boundary forms a tongue into Loddington parish and its isolation gave rise to claims that it was an extra-parochial civil parish, free of tithes and parish rates and not to be assessed for the support of its poor or the maintenance of its highways. This claim for exemption from tithes was strongly argued in the period 1824–32 by the then owner of Mawsley Lodge, Mr T C Higgins of Turvey, Bedfordshire (NRO LJM 27, LJM 32.39). His claim failed on three counts: firstly, that documents showed that Faxton tithes had included Mawsley lands since 1439; secondly, a widow of Mawsley had been married in Faxton as her parish church in 1803; and thirdly, the poor of Mawsley had been given poor relief from Faxton parish funds. This evidence throws interesting light on local memory and on the nature of the settlement there.

Throughout the 18th century Mawsley was a hamlet with just two cottages, both occupied by shepherds: one served the landowner in Faxton lordship and the other the landowner of the Loddington portion. This accords with the description by Bridges in 1720 of Mawsley as a 'decayed' village with only one or two cottages (Bridges 1791, II, 96). At the Parliamentary Survey in about 1655 it was considered that the 'tithes arising out of Moseley, a decayed village member of the same parish [of Faxton, belonged to Lamport and] we conceive it fit that Faxton and Moseley may be divided from Lamport and made a distinct parish'. Faxton was considered to be a separate parish from 1660 to 1935. In the 1841 census there were 18 inhabitants recorded under Mawsley, most living at Mawsley Lodge, by then a prominent Victorian farmhouse, a mile south-west of Loddington. There was still one cottage in Mawsley on the 1884 Ordnance Survey map. The ruins of this cottage (at SP802766) were still visible in 1966 as a rectangular building with a central doorway, two rooms on the ground floor each with a gable chimney and a staircase to lofts under the eaves, presumably with dormer windows under the thatched roof. There was a hint of former enclosure west of the cottage, but only post-medieval pottery was found in the field. A large modern farm, 'Mawsley Wood', was built near the site of the cottage in 1988. Intriguingly, during the Tithe Case in 1830, a labourer called Banhan Norton who had lived at Foxhall from 1755 to 1815 claimed that pieces of stone and marble were once to be found in Mawsley Wood and that these were the remains of a church at Mawsley. In about 1790 these pieces were in the house of a Thomas Errington at Old, but there is no documentary evidence to support the existence of any church. The stone fragments were more likely found in the enclosure noted by RCHME (1979, 106) at SP79867646 and should be identified as belonging to a post-medieval farmhouse.

A second habitative field-name, Fackley, is located on the ridge at the north-western edge of the parish (SP781775) (Figure 2.3). It appears to indicate a secondary settlement from Faxton and contains the same personal element *Fakr* linked to a clearing name. It occurs in the late 12th century as a place-name attributed to a soke or liberty, and is included within its territory Draughton to the west of Fackley (Loyd and Stenton 1950, 143–144, 159–160; Ekwall 1960, 172). There is no further mention of the name in the Middle Ages, which next occurs on the 1746 map attached to a group of fields already enclosed on the edge of the moors. In 1966 the area had been altered considerably by the construction of a wartime airfield, but there was no obvious evidence there of early settlement although there is a regular pattern of ridge and furrow.

Finally, the name Rockley or Rocklay is attached to a hill and group of fields 800m south-west of Faxton (SP775747) on a corresponding spur of a similar elevation (Figures 2.3 and 2.4C). The name, meaning 'a stony clearing', might refer to a settlement but equally may be no more than a field clearance name. The area has long been under plough and shows no sign of earlier habitation. David Hall comments (2019) that in his opinion there is no evidence for settlement at either Fackley or Rockley, the latter a furlong name. Both, he considers, are evidence of Late Saxon woodland clearance; if created after 1066 these might well have been termed 'assarts' or 'sarts'.

2.5 THE LANDSCAPE CONTEXT
by Ronan O'Donnell

Landscape history was a relatively new discipline when Butler wrote the core of the text above. Over the 40 years since it was written, research has revealed much of which he would have been unaware. In this new section, some comments are made on his discussion of the Faxton landscape as well as some additions which are intended to place his findings within the context of modern research. This is especially important for the archaeology of the deserted village at Faxton because, as we shall see, changes to the landscape and land use are fully implicated in the process of village desertion, while the landscape of the parish provided the setting for many generations of Faxton inhabitants.

Open fields

By virtue of its Midland location, the parish of Faxton lies within one of the best understood regions of the medieval and early modern landscape. The Midlands form part of the open-field province as defined by Gray in one of the earliest academic examinations of English field systems (Gray 1915), but also reflects an earlier antiquarian understanding of contrasting woodland and champion countrysides (Rackham 2000, 5). By the time Butler was excavating at Faxton, many writers had followed Gray in viewing this region as that in which the most developed and advanced open-field systems were to be found (Orwin and Orwin 1938; Homans 1941; Thirsk 1964; 1966). More recently, Roberts and Wrathmell (2003) have refined the definition of this region through close analysis of historic maps, naming it the 'Central Province' and identifying a number of sub-regions. Their work forms part of a re-assessment over the last two decades of our understanding of the English landscape which, for instance, has identified a great variety and complexity within the field systems outside the Central Province, overturning notions that these areas were less developed or more 'ancient' (Bailey 2009; Rippon 2008). At the same time, a great deal of research has been carried out within the county of Northamptonshire and several important landscape studies have shed new light on

aspects of the landscape local to Faxton (e.g. Foard et al. 2009; Jones and Page 2006; Parry 2006).

It is unfortunate that Faxton is without surviving manorial documents, as this restricts discussion of its open fields to their physical form; most details of their cultivation, common grazing rights, rotation etc. are now beyond recovery. Lawrence Butler describes three fields with small amounts of meadow, and while he does not discuss woodland and pasture in detail in his text, small pieces are marked on Figures 2.2 and 2.3. This is typical of the Midlands and similar to field systems described at Whittlewood and Laxton (Jones and Page 2006; Orwin and Orwin 1938). It also conforms to the model of Midland field systems recently described by Hall (2014, 35–44). We can probably assume that Faxton's fields were used for intensive arable agriculture (Hall 2014, 35–44) and this is further suggested by the lack of pasture land. We may also assume, by comparison with other Midland parishes, that grazing was permitted after harvest and on the fallow. It is not, however, possible to speculate beyond this based on present evidence.

Butler examined ridge-and-furrow earthworks visible on 1940s RAF aerial photographs (Figure 1.2 and plotted on Figure 2.5). From this, he observed that the ridge and furrow of Woodfield had more varied orientations than that of the rest of the parish. The ridge and furrow of Middlefield and Upper Field has a much more regular alignment, largely running north-west to south-east. Since the Faxton excavations were carried out, analyses by Hall (Foard et al. 2009, 31; Hall and Wilson 1978, 31) and Harvey (1980; 1982; 1983; 1984) have discovered similar forms in Cambridgeshire, Northamptonshire and Yorkshire, showing that they are a significant national phenomenon. This was first observed by Harvey in Holderness; she argued initially that it represented the planning of open-field systems following the Harrying of the North, or at the time of the 9th-century Danish invasions. This claim was based on the fact that the area had been under the control of only a few lords at Domesday, which would have facilitated large-scale planning (Harvey 1980). Subsequently, she expanded the distribution of this feature throughout Yorkshire (Harvey 1982; 1983; 1984), while Hall observed similar evidence in Northamptonshire and Cambridgeshire, albeit obscured by later changes (Hall 1995, 133–135; Hall and Wilson 1978). The fact that regular furlong patterns occur throughout the Midland province means that a Middle Saxon date has become more probable, partly because fieldwalking data from Raunds has suggested that re-planning may have occurred at the same time as settlement nucleation (Parry 2006, 275), although a model based on the tenurial division of Holderness can no longer be supported. While Hall (1995, 125–139; 2014, 175–214) argues that such patterns result from deliberate planning, others have argued that they stem from the re-use of prehistoric land divisions within open-field systems (Oosthuizen 2006). Regardless of whether this is true or not, there does appear to be sufficient evidence to suggest that, at an early phase, Faxton's open fields consisted of regular furlongs.

These regular furlongs were obscured by later changes to the furlong pattern. Recent detailed reconstructions of the open fields of Faxton by Hall (recorded in Partida *et al.* 2013), show evidence for these changes which was not available to Lawrence Butler in the 1960s and 70s. The forms of some of the open-field furlongs shown in these reconstructions imply that some furlongs were created later than others as some appear to 'cut' into those adjacent (Figure 2.5). This has been examined in detail in Leicestershire, where such changes were shown to be part of a long process between the Anglo-Saxon and Early Modern periods (O'Donnell 2011). In the specific case of Faxton, the furlongs seem to be concentrated outside the areas of early enclosure in the south-east of the parish and around the area of Fackley. In the case of Fackley, this may simply be because there is little ridge and furrow there, but this cannot be the case in the south-east corner. At the same time the south-east corner is the area with the most regular furlongs. This may imply that the majority of alterations to Faxton's furlong pattern occurred *after* the early enclosures of the 16th and 17th centuries, although this can be no more than speculation without further dating evidence.

Butler's text does not describe a sequence of development for Faxton's open fields though he does illustrate it. Figure 2.2 shows four phases, the first two of which deal with the development of the open fields while the second two show the first stages of its enclosure. Without a textual commentary it is difficult to know the basis of his reconstruction. The first phase is dated to about 1100 and shows two fields and relatively large areas of waste and woods. The fields are named North and South fields, and the boundary between them is particularly straight. As there are few documents relating to Faxton from this period it is unclear how this mapping has been arrived at; very likely it is entirely conjectural. The second phase shows three fields: Mill, Wood and Upper, which are the three fields discussed in the text above. The creation and addition by arrangement of a third field to a two-field system is common in the area. Hall (2014, 40–42), using a sample of Northamptonshire townships, found no three-field systems in the 12th century while 74 per cent of his sample had three-course rotations by the 18th century. By rearranging to form another field, the inhabitants would have increased the area under cultivation each year to two-thirds rather than one half. Gray (1915) suggested that the three-field system, as a type, had been created from the two-field system during a period of intensive change between 1250 and 1350 under population pressure.

This proposal has since been criticised and it now seems more likely that the change was gradual and completed when convenient rather than being the result of population pressure (Fox 1986; Hall 2014, 41), indeed Fox (1986) suggests that some three-field systems already existed during the Anglo-Saxon period. Gray's model was still current at the time that the fieldwork at Faxton was being carried out and it is possible, likely even, that the timing of the change, and even the earlier existence of two fields, was assumed on this basis.

The map of the second phase on Figure 2.2 also marks two conjectured minor settlements, Fackley and Mawsley, in the woods and moors of the earlier phase. The names of these settlements do not appear in Domesday Book, but Fackley is mentioned in the late 11th century and the Mawsley hundredal name in the 12th century. In both cases the -ley element of the name indicates woodland clearance, which when combined with the earliest date of their names has been taken to imply an 11th- to 13th-century phase of woodland clearance. Again, this is typical of the county. For instance, West Cotton near Raunds had reached its final form by 1150 when alluvium covered some of its ridge and furrow (Chapman 2010, 217). Similarly at Whittlewood new settlements were created called Cattle End, Elm Green and Heybarne during the 12th and 13th centuries (Jones and Page 2006, 131) although it should be noted that this is a woodland edge area where 'assart' names abound. Assarting may have created severalty fields around Faxton and Mawsley, although this was not the only possible outcome of such clearance. For instance, in Leicestershire some open-field land appears to have been formed by intakes from meadow and waste, although the dating of this is rarely clear (O'Donnell 2011, 68–72). Alternatively, the two settlements may have had their own open-field systems, essentially forming new townships within Faxton parish. This is rare in the Midlands, though not unheard of, as West Cotton appears to have had a field system which was only merged with Raunds in the 14th century (Chapman 2010, 24). It should be noted, however, that this was not an assart; it lies on the finest soil of an area previously used for prehistoric settlement and was an early township (information from David Hall). If the two settlements did have their own open-field systems then it would have facilitated the early enclosure of the fields around Fackley, which probably occurred in the 16th century, as we shall see in the following section.

Enclosure

The enclosure of Faxton is not straight forward. Its earliest phases may date to the medieval assarting discussed above. Without medieval manorial documents, however, this cannot be demonstrated conclusively. At the same time, some small enclosures in Wood Field may be the result of piecemeal enclosure during the medieval or early modern periods, but again there is little evidence to confirm this. During the early modern period, enclosure proceeded via two small agreements and concluded with an Act of Parliament in 1745 (JHC 1803, vol. 24, 18 & 19 Geo 2 1744–45, page 829b). Faxton's division between several owners may well have precluded swifter and more comprehensive enclosure.

The first enclosure, presumably by agreement, was at Fackley; Lawrence Butler dated this to the 16th century (Figure 2.2). Possibly Fackley had had a separate open-field system which made enclosure relatively simple in tenurial terms. A second agreement was made in 1659 (Figure 2.2). It is possible that this area of enclosure was partly a block demesne. Such demesnes are known in Northamptonshire but are less common there than they are in other parts of the country (Hall 2014, 99–103). This would have made enclosure of a section of the open fields easier than otherwise, and there is little other reason for the area to have been enclosed on its own, as it is of a similar quality and topography to the rest of the parish. However, at least part of it was glebe rather than demesne as the rectory was compensated for its loss.

Early modern enclosure is common in the Midlands. Following a lull in enclosure activity in the mid-16th century, enclosure agreements became common. This phase of enclosure was different in character to the depopulating enclosures of the 15th to early 16th centuries. By now enclosures usually had greater freeholder involvement, created mixed agriculture rather than pasture and did not lead to depopulation in most cases (Yelling 1977, 52–53). Even so, the process could be controversial and provoke unrest, though it failed to do so in the case of Faxton. This violent context for the peaceful Faxton enclosures included the Midland Rising of 1607, the Western Rising of 1626–32 and the Fenland Riots throughout most of the 17th century (Lindley 1982; Sharp 2010). These riots were mostly quite organised and restrained and were probably a last resort for villagers, though the government often over-reacted to them (Wrightson 2003, 177). By this time the government had stopped opposing enclosure as it had during the Tudor period, and had begun to allow it or even to become involved in the activity itself. This was because fears of rising grain prices as a result of increased pasture had abated, so much so that enclosure was more often associated with the improved use of land (Beresford 1961, 45–47, 54).

The Parliamentary Enclosure at Faxton is more unusual. The Act was passed in 1745 (above; and see Adkins and Serjeantson 1902), and the award made in 1746 was on the usual grounds that 'several common fields and common grounds' lay 'intermixed and dispersed in small parcels' and were 'inconvenient and detrimental' and 'incapable of improvement'. Frustratingly, the award document itself has not survived and so our analysis of the enclosure is severely limited (Tate 1978, 191). In passing, it should be noted that the 1746 map of Faxton is not an enclosure map as has sometimes been stated (and as Butler believed it to be), but rather an estate map drawn up immediately after enclosure for the principal landowner, Sir John Nicolls Raynford. While some Parliamentary Enclosures are much older than this, it was around 15 years before the Parliamentary process became common and well before the explosion of Parliamentary Enclosure during the Napoleonic Wars (Turner 1980, 63–93). A similar chronological pattern has been identified locally in Rockingham Forest, where there were peaks in Parliamentary Enclosure in 1770–1780 and 1800–1820 (Foard et al. 2009, 41). Faxton's enclosure by Act in 1745–46 was thus an outlier both nationally and locally, its early date very probably because it represented a formalisation of changes which had already occurred.

There are a number of reasons for believing this. Firstly, the enclosure made little change to Faxton's pattern of outlying farms. The 1746 estate map of Faxton shows three farmsteads: Faxton Lodge in the south, Shortwood Lodge on the western edge, and Fox Hall in the north. These are the same farms depicted on the 1841 tithe plan and all subsequent maps of the parish. Of these three, only Shortwood Lodge is in an area of pre-1746 enclosure. This is in contrast to findings made elsewhere, where dispersed farmsteads usually developed following enclosure or agrarian improvement (Brown 1999; O'Donnell 2015). Butler himself was unable to explain the presence of outlying farms prior to Parliamentary Enclosure, and attempted to link them to pre-Parliamentary Enclosure. This is unconvincing, firstly because only one of them is actually placed on a piece of pre-Parliamentary Enclosure. Secondly, the field boundaries created by the Parliamentary Enclosure appear to reproduce the furlong boundaries which are preserved in ridge and furrow (Figure 2.5). While not common, this did occur elsewhere, for instance in Northamptonshire at Ashby St Ledgers and in Warwickshire at Willoughby. Finally, the Enclosure Act shows that John Nicolls Raynsford, the lord of the manor, then owned 1,135 acres, virtually the whole township. Thus the open-field system appears to have been significantly engrossed (in the sense of belonging to one owner) prior to enclosure itself, although it will have continued to be farmed in the traditional way with the yardlands let out to tenants as they always had been in the past. It is also notable that the allotment made for the glebe (36 acres) is exactly the same size as the glebe holding in the open fields. This is unusual because enclosure commissioners were normally required to take into account the quality of the land that was allotted, and to allot larger holdings where good land was exchanged for poor and vice versa, though in this Act this is not stated. Cases in which Parliamentary Enclosure made little change to the farming of a parish are not uncommon. For instance, while pre-Napoleonic War Parliamentary Enclosure was usually intended to create pasture (Partida *et al.* 2013, 62; Turner 1980, 75), Partida notes that the conversion of arable open fields to pasture in Northamptonshire often began well before enclosure and this is also likely at Faxton.

As Parliamentary Enclosure was unlikely to have been motivated by a desire to change the farming of the parish significantly, its main motivation was probably the abolition of the tithes. The Enclosure Act provided for the lands allotted to John Nicolls Raynsford to be changed with an annual rent charge of £80 to the rector in lieu of tithes. The abolition of tithes was considered strongly desirable by some (but by no means all) landowners at this period. That was because tithes were often seen as a barrier to improvement because they were a payment of ten per cent of produce, meaning that if a farmer improved his or her husbandry practices they would have to increase the amount of tithe that they had to pay. This may explain why an Act of Parliament was used. It has been argued that Acts of Parliament were only used for enclosure where the particular legal circumstances made them necessary, as cheaper methods were preferred for the simplest enclosures (O'Donnell 2014). Apart from the tithe abolition the enclosure of Faxton is too simple to require an Act of Parliament.

As the Parliamentary Enclosure of Faxton may have had little landscape or agricultural impact we may speculate about its social effect. The social context of enclosure during the Parliamentary Enclosure period is perhaps less well understood than that of the Early Modern period. The traditional position is that the Parliamentary process necessarily disenfranchised the smallholder and commoner because it required only the consent of a majority of the community by land area owned, so that a few large landowners could bring about enclosure against the will of smallholders (Hammond and Hammond 1987, 49–50). This perspective has come under criticism in recent years. For instance, Shaw-Taylor (2001a), using case studies from south-east England, has found that some common rights were not in the hands of the labouring poor at the time of Parliamentary Enclosure; they had been engrossed by farmers who had bought common right cottages. Similar results were obtained by French (2000) at Clitheroe in Lancashire. The implication is that the rural poor had been reliant on wage labour prior to Parliamentary Enclosure. Shaw-Taylor (2001b) also found that when contemporary writers made quantifiable comments about the effect of enclosure this effect was usually minor. Against this we may weigh the evidence of the riots which resulted from

some enclosures such as that at Otmoor, Oxfordshire (Eastwood 1996), which show that whatever the economic impact of enclosures, opinions against them could be strongly held. However, none of these examples is directly applicable to Faxton's Parliamentary Enclosure which dealt nearly entirely with arable open fields. It is likely that the enclosure of open fields was less damaging to the poor than was the enclosure of commons because rights to the former were more easily defined. Nonetheless, McDonagh and Daniels (2012) found that reactions were quite mixed across the county of Northamptonshire. Famously, John Clare, who came from a labouring family, wrote poetry against enclosure. Similarly, George Clarke, a member of the gentry, thought that enclosure in Northamptonshire had spoilt the riding in the county. Direct action such as hedge breaking was taken against some Parliamentary Enclosures and was used in conjunction with legal proceedings. Interestingly, however, McDonagh and Daniels (2012, 112–113) did not find very much evidence for changes to parish life resulting from enclosure outside the sphere of agriculture, such as in administration or worship, suggesting that much of life may have remained unchanged by the process. If, as has been argued above, Faxton's enclosure had little effect on land-holding in the parish, and because it enclosed no common waste, it is likely to have been similar to the examples examined by French and Shaw-Taylor, in which Parliamentary Enclosure resulted in little social change. However, as the enclosure itself is clearly unusual we cannot safely generalise from this example to the regional or national situation.

Post-enclosure

After enclosure, Faxton's landscape continued to develop gradually, and there was no major rearrangement after 1746. Lists of tenant farmers were originally compiled from the churchwardens' accounts by Patrick King, the Northamptonshire County Archivist, but they were laid aside for Butler's text above. They cover the period between 1789 and 1892 and show how tenant farms were periodically merged together under one tenant and, less frequently, split apart again at the end of a tenancy. Overall, there was a slight reduction in the number of farms from 13 to 11 across the period in question.

The 1839 tithe plan (NRO T228) is the first opportunity we have to assess changes to the Faxton landscape made after the 1746 estate map. This shows a few significant changes. Firstly, by 1839 the mill had been demolished and some of the roads and field boundaries surrounding it moved to create a more convenient field pattern. A stream had been diverted to run along a field boundary and straightened to improve drainage. Significant changes were made over the period to the buildings at Faxton Lodge (which gained an ornamental garden) and Smallwood Lodge, both being rebuilt around square courtyards. Some field boundaries around these farmsteads were rearranged.

More generally, across the field system as a whole, a few new boundaries were made which reduced the size of some fields. In one field, called Hart's Hill, a pond was dug out and field boundaries shifted to accommodate it. Some quite significant changes were made to the roads in the parish; two running south-west to north-east between the village and the Lamport Road and another to the north-east of the village were removed, while a new one running north from the village was created. It appears that this was designed to remove roads which cut diagonally through fields.

This reduction in the size of some fields and the removal of roads cutting across them may suggest a phase of increased arable agriculture at some time after enclosure, possibly during the era of high grain prices during the Napoleonic War. By 1839, however, the vast majority of the fields were listed as 'meadow', perhaps improved pasture rather than hay-meadow. By then the arable land itself was mostly near the farmsteads, with clusters of ploughland around Fox Hall, Smallwood, Mawsley Lodge and quite an extensive area at Faxton Lodge. Little apparent relationship between geology and land use is visible, so land use was presumably determined by proximity to the farmsteads.

Between 1839 and the publication of the first six inch to the mile edition of the Ordnance Survey in the late 1880s change continued with further removal of field boundaries. In Faxton, this was in the areas of old enclosure near the site of Fackley and to the south of the village, although in Mawsley some hedges seem to have been removed in areas of later enclosure. It is possible that this represents a response to agricultural mechanisation and the introduction of steam ploughs (Whetham and Orwin 1964, 104–106). However, the fact that some hedgerow trees were left as standards in one field to the south of Faxton village implies that, at least in this case, the field had been pasture since the removal of the boundary. Similarly, a section of road running diagonally across a field to the north of the village was probably removed to clear an obstruction to ploughing. Further evidence for agricultural improvement includes the straightening of a stream to the south of the village to improve drainage, while the farmsteads at Mawsley, Faxton Lodge and Fox Hall were all rebuilt. In all cases the new farms included yards. In the case of Faxton Lodge, an E-shaped plan was used which was of the general type advocated by improvers (Harvey 1970, 77–79, Fig. 5).

By the time of the next Ordnance Survey revision in 1901, ironstone pits served by light railway lines had been opened in Mawsley. After 1901 there was no full Ordnance Survey revision until 1952. The 1952 plan shows continued enlargement

of fields in the south of the parish near Faxton Lodge, presumably reflecting further agricultural mechanisation following the introduction of the petrol-driven tractor (Williamson 2013, 183–187; and see Chapter 1). The closure of a footpath in the same area presumably preceded the National Parks and Access to the Countryside Act 1949. This, a result of increasing pressure upon government from a diverse range of groups who wished to use the countryside for leisure (Blunden and Curry 1989, 21–36), compelled local government to make definitive maps of public rights of way. After 1949 the re-routing of footpaths was far more difficult.

The greatest change to the parish's landscape in the 20th century came with the construction, starting in 1942, of what became generally known as RAF Harrington (Smith 1998, 131–142). It had a complex, and notable, operational history. Initially it was a Class A USAAF airfield, built by the American army for B-17 Flying Fortress bombers. In November 1943, however, before flying began, the airfield was handed over to the RAF as a satellite training station for the 84th Operational Training Unit stationed at nearby Desborough, flying Wellington bombers. Then, in May 1944, the station passed to the 8th USAAF Special Operations Group for 'Carpetbagger' operations, delivering agents and supplies to Resistance Units in occupied Europe. In the latter stages of the war, planes from Harrington transported fuel and equipment to the advancing allied armies, as well as carrying out further Carpetbagger deployments. Overall, some 2,800 sorties were made from the airfield, with 1,040 persons delivered behind enemy lines. Harrington was returned to the RAF in October 1945, and then became a storage depot.

Military activity resumed at RAF Harrington in 1959, when it opened as a satellite Thor Missile site under the control of RAF North Luffenham in Leicestershire (Historic England List Entry 1400809). Thor missiles—with a range of 1,500 nautical miles—were the first operational Intermediate-range Ballistic Missile (IRBM) system deployed by the West during the Cold War. In all, 60 missiles were deployed at 20 sites in the east of England; these could be brought to operational readiness in 15 minutes after receiving the order to launch. Strict understandings about the operational control of the missile included an agreed British and US launch protocol through a dual key system and a veto for each government. Although Thor deployment in Britain was an interim measure, 59 of the 60 including the three at Harrington were placed at readiness in the Cuban Missile Crisis of October 1962, the most tense period of the Cold War.

With the deactivation of the Thor missiles in mid-1963, RAF Harrington was decommissioned and returned to agricultural use. Almost all the concreted areas of the airfield were dug up, although the Thor Missile launch pads survive. All three were listed at Grade II in 2011 because of their national special interest.

The final major changes to the parish landscape took place between 1958 and 1965/6 in Faxton, and between 1958 and 1972 in Mawsley (the re-mapping of these areas was revised at two different dates). In both parishes, as across much of England, still more field boundaries were removed during what was a period of agricultural intensification in response to new and larger farm machinery, government subsidies and periods of high grain prices (Rowley 2006, 261–268; and see Chapter 1). In addition, some river improvement occurred in Mawsley in order to reduce flooding. The routes of several footpaths were changed, both in the wood at Shortwood and to the north of Faxton, perhaps as

leisure use of the countryside increased. Finally, at some point between 1958 and 1972, the ironstone pits closed as demand from ironworks at Corby and elsewhere declined.

Today, all the historic farms in Faxton and Mawsley remain in occupation, and two new houses have been built since the 1960s. A major change to the local settlement pattern came in 2001 when construction of a large new village, Mawsley, began just to the south of the township boundary in what historically was part of Cransley parish. By the time of the 2011 census, this had a population of over 2,300. The site of Faxton remains, however, isolated: still a 'blank patch' on the Ordnance Survey map, which for Hoskins (1950, 68), in the earliest days of deserted village investigation, was so indicative of a 'lost village'.

3

FIELD SURVEY, STANDING BUILDINGS AND THE CHURCH AT FAXTON

Lawrence Butler and Christopher Gerrard

Lawrence Butler always envisaged a discussion of the earthworks at Faxton as they were before much of the evidence was bulldozed away. His texts on the earthworks and the standing buildings are combined here and edited, with corrected bibliography and the insertion of matching figures. Lengthy notes have been re-incorporated into the main text.

The writing of this chapter presented some challenges of which Lawrence Butler was fully aware, not least because his text was superseded in 1981 by the publication of the Royal Commission's earthwork survey of the village. The content below brings together both sets of observations with additional evidence about the church, about which Lawrence Butler wrote very little in spite of his evident interests in church archaeology. He was apparently unaware of the existence of an archive on the church's final years held by the Society for the Protection of Ancient Buildings.

There are several sources of information to help understand the development of the layout of the village at Faxton from the mid-18th century onwards. The most useful of these are the historic maps mentioned in Chapter 1, namely the estate map of 1746 (Figure 3.1), the tithe map of 1839 (Figure 3.2) and a succession of Ordnance Survey plans (Figure 3.3) which show changes to housing in the late 19th and early 20th centuries. As a starting point for discussion, these cartographic sources have been transcribed onto a modern basemap at the same scale and orientation, and are accompanied by an enlarged version of the vertical RAF aerial photograph taken in 1947 and used by Maurice Beresford (Figure 3.4) (RAF/CPE/UK/1925 3223–4, 4367–8; also CUAP AKP74, AWVI-6, BAP87).

Taken in sequence like this, the evidence shows a significant reduction in the number of buildings over time and, in particular, along the track fringing the north side of The Green. At no point are any of the crofts later excavated by Lawrence Butler occupied by structures. Figure 3.5 reproduces the plan by the Royal Commission for Historical Monuments of England (RCHME) as originally published in 1981 (RCHME 1981, Fig. 93) and this adds a significant new dimension by showing all the earthworks surviving *at that time*, some of the detail having being taken from aerial photographs with enhancements made possible by field observation on the ground. The sites of the manor house, almshouses, church, Rectory Farm and 'green' are all depicted, together with a number of buildings numbered *i* to *vii* transcribed from the 1746 estate map (Figure 3.1). The RCHME plan does not, however, incorporate the observations of Lawrence Butler who had seen for himself the slow eradication of the buildings and

the village earthworks over a number of years. For example, on 20 September 1966 Butler wrote to Hurst to say:

> The bulldozing of all the house sites in the two available fields has been done but it is unlikely that more than three out of the twenty will produce satisfactory plans because of considerable later disturbance and robbing. I will do what I can here and will hope to return to inspect the ploughing which seems to provide a better indication of house plans...

Butler clearly felt aggrieved that these and other observations were not taken into account by the Royal Commission and noted that:

> the [RCHME] survey was only undertaken after destruction was complete and when it was impossible to verify on the ground most of the information provided by the air photographs. The investigators of the RCHME did not consult the author about his fieldwork but relied only on his published work.

The Commission itself was well aware of this and warned in its own text that the plan it had produced was 'not necessarily either complete or wholly accurate' (RCHME 1981). Figure 3.6 is a re-drawn version of Lawrence Butler's own interpretative plan which restores all the different components for the later medieval period to create what he referred to as his 'village plan' for Faxton. It was on the basis of this plan, with its 53 numbered crofts, that Butler made his own descriptions of the earthworks, adding in information gathered from the recollections of former inhabitants and their local knowledge, as

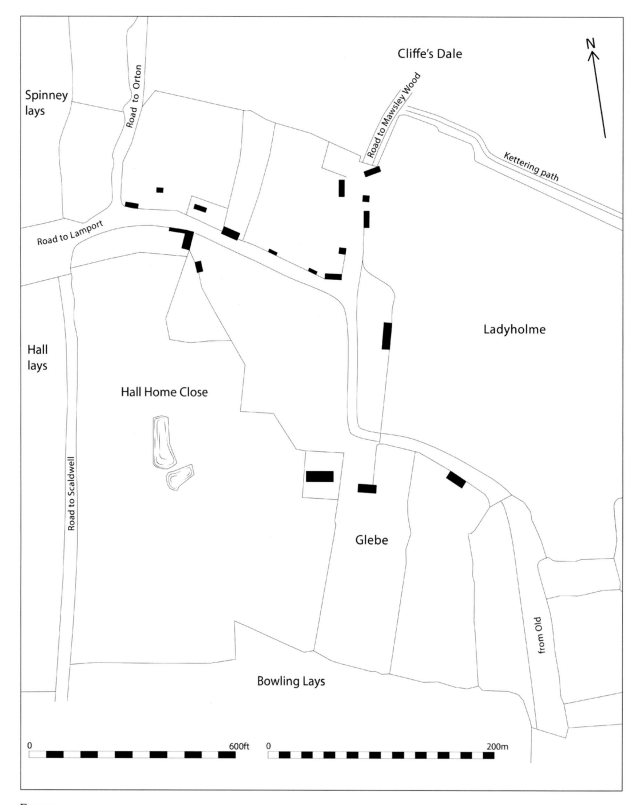

FIGURE 3.1

Detail of Faxton village from the 1746 estate map transcribed onto a modern basemap. Hall Home Close became The Green; the church is to the west of the rectory, here in the plot marked 'Glebe'. Some of the ditches of the moat still retain water. Note the convergence of roads at The Green

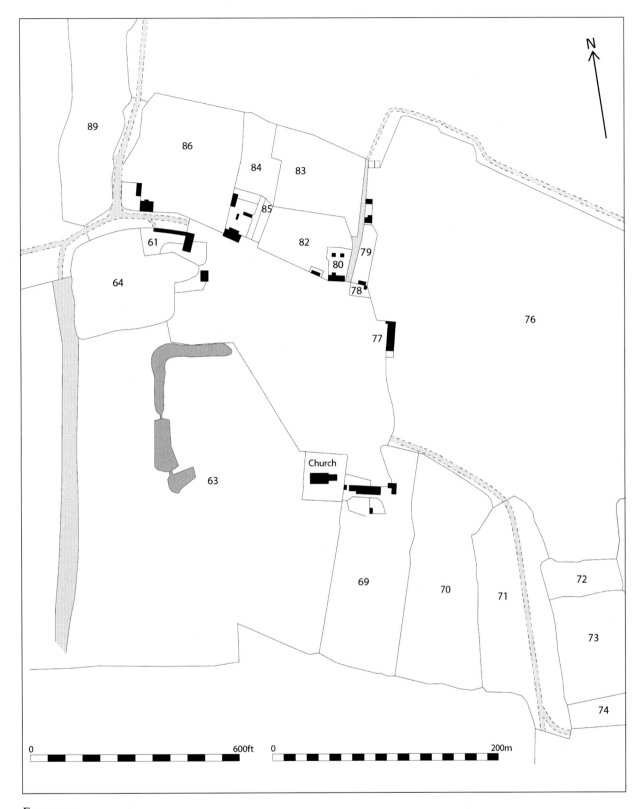

FIGURE 3.2

The 1839 tithe map of Faxton, showing detail of the village, transcribed onto a modern basemap. The church is now marked and the moated site is depicted in greater detail

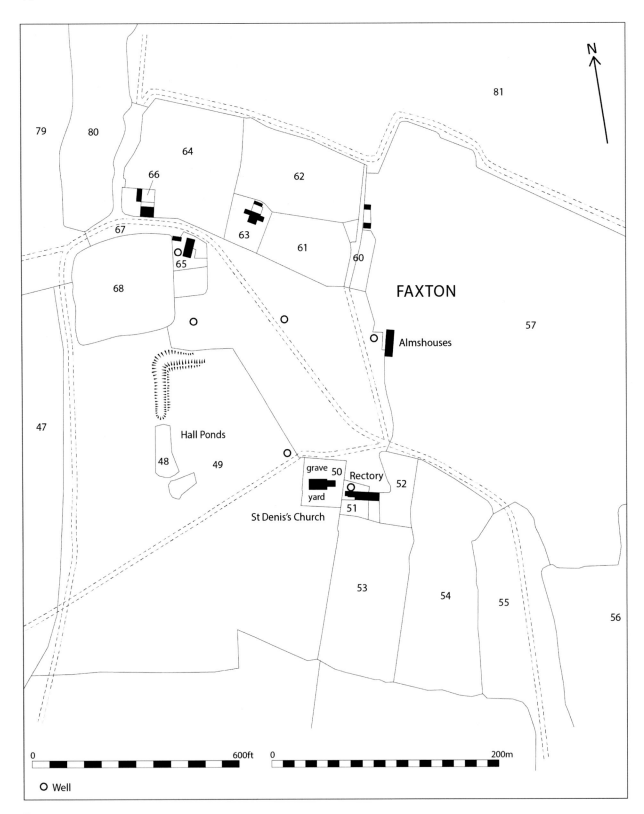

Figure 3.3

The 1900 Ordnance Survey map showing detail of the village, re-drawn and transcribed onto a modern basemap. Compare this map with Figures 3.1 and 3.2. Church, rectory and almshouses are named here as are the village wells. For a plot-by-plot biography, see Figure 3.21

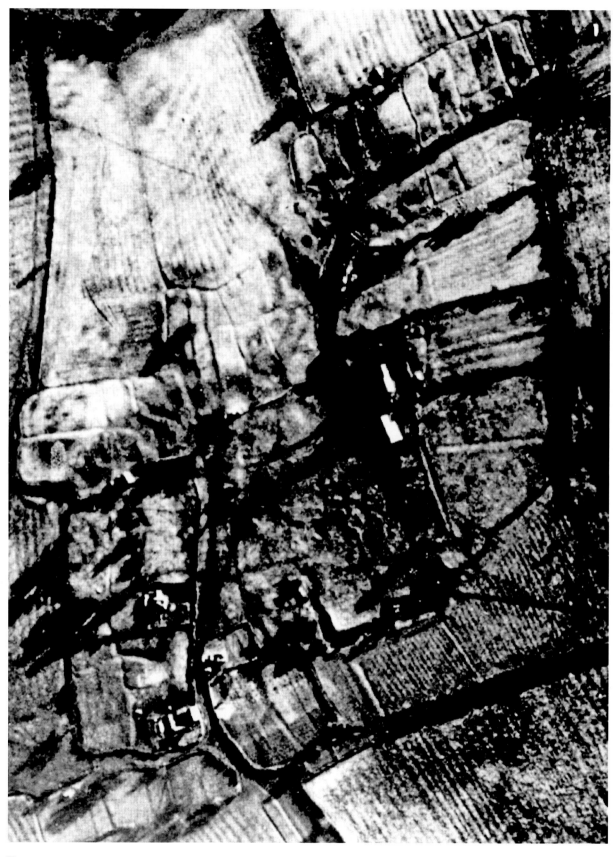

FIGURE 3.4

Enlargement of RAF vertical air photograph of Faxton in Figure 1.2 taken in January 1947 (RAF/CPE/UK/1925 JAN 16.1947. F/20"/MULTI(4)58SQDN). Historic England Archive. RAF Photography.

North is to the left. The church and adjacent rectory are clearly visible.

FIGURE 3.5
RCHME earthwork plan of Faxton (from RCHME 1981, Figure 93) © Crown copyright. Historic England Archive

well as planning and describing some of the standing buildings. Below, Butler's text is allowed to 'lead' the discussion of the village plan with comments interjected from the Royal Commission survey text (RCHME 1981).

3.1 THE OVERALL PLAN OF THE VILLAGE

The village green at Faxton was a roughly triangular enclosure into which the manor house had encroached on its south-west side. Known as 'The Green' by former inhabitants, it is so named on an early-19th century map. It was crossed diagonally by a grass track with rough metalling under the turf: other tracks ran down the east and north sides of The Green but their surfaces were not exposed. On The Green there was a shallow pond with an artificial clay base, which was drained in 1967, together with a number of wells. Two wells are shown on the 1900 Ordnance Survey on The Green together with three others which served the almshouses, rectory and church (Figure 3.3). These wells were still serviceable in the late 1960s and during the three seasons of excavations provided ample water for washing of humans and excavated finds. Most of the wells had a brick shaft of four or five courses supporting a wooden lid; below this was a further 50–100cm of coursed stone before the natural clay was exposed. The water level usually remained close to the ground surface except in periods of prolonged drought (another factor influencing desertion mentioned by the former cottage inhabitants). The wells filled up rapidly after rainfall. Only the two large farms had deeper wells with proper winding mechanisms.

3.2 THE WEST SIDE OF THE GREEN

Crofts 1–5

Five narrow crofts lay on the western side of The Green (see Figure 3.6). Croft 1 was partly encroached upon by the northern arm of the moated homestead. It was omitted by the RCHME who regarded it as part of the close to the south, and its investigators show five later gardens encroaching on The Green. In 1966 all five were under grass with their dividing banks still visible as shallow baulks; by 1968 they were ploughed. Although the backs of the crofts bounded by the bridle track to Scaldwell were distinct, their fronts were disturbed by later housing which seems to be an encroachment onto The Green (i.e. the crofts south of *vi* on the RCHME plan, Figure 3.5). The RCHME (1981) concluded much the same, adding that this encroachment must pre-date 1746 since the Well Farm is shown at that time and noting also a further building in one of the crofts immediately to the south which was present in 1746 but gone by 1839 (Figures 3.1 and 3.2).

At the north-west angle of The Green, the **Well Farm** stood at the front of Croft 4. It was already present in 1746 (Figure 3.1), is clearly visible in the 1947 aerial photograph (Figure 3.4) and only demolished in about 1960, having then been unoccupied for five years. Parts of its wall foundations were visible in the undergrowth in 1966. Air photographs and local memories suggest that this was a large building similar to the larger farms of 17th-century date in Old. It was built of roughly coursed local stone but without any finer details; originally thatched but latterly slated, it had low ceilings and large beams on the ground floor. It was served by a well within the croft plot (Figure 3.3). To the west, backing on the road, was a range of barns and sheds with a boundary alongside the surfaced track which led out of the north-west corner of The Green and towards the roads to Orton (north) and Lamport (west). This is the layout depicted on the 1839 tithe map (Figure 3.2). Further west, this boundary had a field ditch separating Croft 5 from the field track. The west boundary of these five crofts was also marked by a shallow ditch and a hedge bank. Immediately south of Well Farm on the 1746 map is a cottage, noted on Figure 3.1, which was demolished soon after 1900 (RCHME 1981). This area was fieldwalked by John Steane in February 1971 (Steane 1971; letter Steane to Butler, 26 May 1962) when an iron barrel padlock, quernstone (both from Crofts 4 and 5) and pottery sherds (from Crofts 1–5 and 25) were all recovered.

3.3 THE NORTH SIDE OF THE GREEN

Crofts 6–9

These four small crofts at the north-west margin of the village were the target of excavation in 1967 (see Chapter 4). They were bounded on the south by a field track that dropped sharply down into a stream valley before climbing to Shortwood; a sinuous boundary on the east was provided by the track to Rothwell and Orton. The western boundary of the crofts was the hedge separating the level platform of the crofts from a drop onto the lower ground of Spinney Lays. The clay ridge on which these four crofts were situated continued northwards, being divided into two small closes. The RCHME survey shows six crofts in this area with the comment that in 1947 the southernmost croft had a narrow rig running east–west. There was no convincing evidence that further houses extended the village in this direction and on the 1746 estate map this area is not named, though a little medieval pottery was collected from fieldwalking after ploughing. The boundaries noted by Butler and the RCHME are very different in this area and elsewhere and sometimes present plots of completely different dimensions.

Crofts 10–12

Three small crofts flanked the track leading out of the north-west corner of The Green at a point where Croft 5 formed the southern boundary of that track. In 1966 a local authority signpost here marked the junction of the four bridle tracks converging on Crofts 5, 6 and 10. According to Lawrence Butler, on many occasions mystified ramblers searching for Faxton could be seen consulting this signpost and were puzzled when they failed to find the village name mentioned on any of its four arms (Palmer 1947).

Crossroads Farm had occupied the front portion of Croft 10, facing southwards, and destroyed any medieval house platform preceding it (*v* on Figure 3.5). It was a roughly coursed stone-built house with a central doorway leading into a hall with stairs up and two rooms either side of the hallway. There was a dairy at the rear and three bedrooms on the first floor. It was slated, but may once have been thatched. At the back of the house around a concreted yard were three ranges of sheds, brick-built and open-fronted on the north, stone built to west and east. One range is shown in 1839 (Figure 3.2). Two of these sheds remained in use when visited in 1989 by Butler. The farmhouse was demolished in about 1960 (*contra* the 1966 date given by the RCHME 1981), having stood vacant since the end of the Second World War. A farm had stood on this spot since at least 1746.

Crofts 11 and 12 were under grass and a variety of banks and hollows were visible. A contour survey was made but no clear pattern of medieval housing could be discerned. It is likely that the earthwork pattern reflects, firstly, an 18th-century house and, secondly, clay digging and rubble dumping from adjacent properties. In all these three crofts the inner area closest to The Green was extended northwards beyond a boundary bank into one or two further paddocks. A back lane ran east–west along the northern boundary of Crofts 10–12 (clearly shown on Figure 3.5) and the four crofts (13–16) further to the east. North of Croft 10 was a disturbed area which was said to be rubble dumped from the destruction of the farms around The Green, ready for use as metalling to fill in deep ruts at field gates. Their function is recorded as 'unknown' by the RCHME (1981). The Royal Commission survey also recorded a hollow-way running east–west to the rear of Crofts 10–16 towards Mawsley Wood (Figure 3.5; see also Figure 12.5 for the earthworks today).

Crofts 13–16

These four crofts on the north side of The Green are the most difficult to describe because of later disturbance. Croft 13 is a double croft and may well have had two boundary divisions removed; there is also no indication of a division into an inner toft and outer croft but an outer paddock survives. On this croft stood the third large farm, shown on the 1746 estate map and the 1839 Tithe Award Map (and remained there until just after 1874; RCHME 1981), with a smaller house to the east (Figures 3.1 and 3.2). In 1966 this area was occupied by a pair of typical estate-workers' cottages erected in the 1880s in red brick and roofed with Welsh slate. In 1970–72 these cottages were converted and combined into a single dwelling called 'Ladyholme' which was subsequently extended further.

Crofts 14–16 are similar to one another with an inner toft, an outer croft and a paddock beyond; all three are of similar size. In 1966 the areas of Crofts 14 to 16 fronting The Green showed an uneven ground surface, probably marking the rubble of three post-medieval cottages, while the eastern part of Croft 13 had hollows which suggested the removal of house debris or the position of a stack yard, its surface being deepened by cart traffic. All three had buildings standing at their southern ends in 1746, two of which were gone by the time of the tithe map in 1839 (Figure 3.2), the third surviving until the late 19th century (RCHME 1981). This group of crofts was bounded on the east by a narrow overgrown grassy lane which led past Cliffdale Cottage to reach Cliffesdale field (this lane is shown on Figure 3.5).

Crofts 17–22

These crofts occupied the north-east corner of The Green around Cliffdale Cottage (identified as *iv* on the RCHME plan, Figure 3.5; Cliffdale also appears as Cliffe Dale and Cliffe's Dale). This cottage, dated by the RCHME (1981) to the 19th century, stands on the site of earlier buildings shown from 1746 onwards and opposite other buildings which had already been demolished by 1839 (Figures 3.1 and 3.2). In its latest form, this was a roughly coursed stone-built cottage with a central doorway leading into an eastern room which had a large fireplace with a side-oven to the left. A western room, also with a fireplace, was reached from within the house. There were two bedrooms on the first floor under a low ceiling. The roof was of ceramic pantiles. The back door led to a modern lean-to kitchen and there was a stone-built privy shed down the garden which was walled along the eastern boundary. The cottage was lived in until spring 1966, when Mrs Bamford moved to Old (Lawrence Butler thereafter used it as his headquarters); it became derelict during 1966–70 and in 1989 (when Lawrence visited) it was found to be very ruinous although its east gable wall with the protruding semi-circular side-oven was still visible.

The pattern of holdings was not easy to discern in this area; Croft 17, which was a recently occupied cottage and garden, was clearly a later feature imposed upon and carved out of Crofts 18 and 19. Either Crofts 18–20 represent an inner toft 18, an outer Croft 19 and a paddock 20, or else there was a small Croft 18 and a larger Croft 19 with its paddock 20. Both 18 and 19 occupied the higher ground around The Green while beyond it the paddock 20 sloped gently away towards the stream valley. At a lower level were the Croft 22 and its paddock 21. When ploughing took place 'early medieval shelly wares' were collected from this area, but there were no later Lyveden or Stanion wares. The stone scatters close to The Green probably represent some of the houses depicted on the 1746 estate map (and demolished before 1874; RCHME 1981). The earthworks running north here were identified by the RCHME as the main medieval road running north-east out of the village which make their way out to an impressive hollow-way identified as 'the road to Mawsley Wood 1746' (Figure 3.1). Curving banks flanking a hollow-way were clearly visible, both on the ground and from air photographs, forming the eastern boundary of this block of crofts. The RCHME omits this boundary because it had been ploughed away and bulldozed by the time of their visit. It may, however, be that Crofts 18 and 23 at one time were united in one croft because this block of land shares similar boundaries to the north and east, distinct from the crofts further west and further south. There was also evidence, clearest from air photographs, of post-medieval ploughing inside the paddock areas.

3.4 THE EAST SIDE OF THE GREEN

Crofts 23–30

These represent a group of surface features long under pasture, but with the majority of the closes sharing a frontage to the east side of The Green. Crofts 24–27 were tofts on higher ground but the back of the crofts sloped towards Ladyholme (the field of that name) and the stream called Old Brook. Crofts 29–30 were on lower ground alongside a curving dry valley utilised by the track from Faxton to Old. Croft 28 did not have a street frontage and is more probably a paddock attached to Croft 27 or to 30.

This whole block shows greater variety in dimensions and divisions; the surface features may indicate the final late medieval stage in a long process of amalgamation and re-alignment which only excavation could disentangle. In particular, Crofts 23 and 30 have irregular outlines and may point to squatter origins in abandoned crofts. Similarly, Crofts 24–26 may show expansion from an inner toft and an outer croft to absorb land from strips in the former common field at Ladyholme (Figure 3.6). Croft 29 was excavated in 1966 (see Chapter 4).

The almshouses

A range of four almshouses stood on the east side of the village green (Figures 3.7A and B). Their origin lay in the generosity of Susannah (née Nicols), wife of Sir John Danvers and daughter of Sir Edward Nicols; she gave 10 shillings each year to maintain four poor widows or widowers, charged on Pitsford Bridge Close in Brixworth. The gift was made in 1730 and her sister Jane, widow of John Raynsford of Mears Ashby and later wife of William Kemsey of Hill Hampton in Worcestershire, caused the almshouses to be erected before her own death in 1736. Letters survive concerning the welfare of the occupants of the almshouses in the early 19th century (Holden 2008, 46–47). In 1831, the Charity Commissioners reported that a sum of £100 was formerly given for the use of the occupants by Jane Kemsey (see Chapter 1), but that this fund was now exhausted 'having been placed in the hands of a former lord of the manor who died several years ago in embarrassed circumstances' (Charity Commissioners 1831, 166). Nevertheless, the almshouses were occupied at that time. The site chosen for the almshouses overlay Croft 26, a former medieval enclosure (see Figure 3.6 for croft numbering), indicating that this area must then have been empty of houses.

The almshouses were built in rough-coursed ironstone and formed a single block of housing with two rooms at ground level and one bedroom above it for each occupant. A tablet on the west wall recorded the donor's charitable intention. A garden wall enclosed the block and there were privies in two pairs as outhouses by the back doors. The almshouses were clearly fully functioning in 1877 (when one pauper was in residence; Patrick King notes) and in 1900 (Figure 3.3) and continued to be occupied until the Second World War though with only one or two old women in the last decade. During the war they fell into ruins and were roofless by 1947, though still clearly visible on aerial photographs (Figure 3.4). By 1966 only a part of the front wall and the base of the garden wall to the south still remained.

Crofts 34–49

All these crofts, either side of the track to Old, were sited on low ground in relation to the rest of the village. They were similar in width and in possessing an inner toft and an outer croft and they show up particularly well on aerial photographs (Figure 3.4, and ploughed out in Figure 1.3). Fieldwalking also demonstrated that they were similar in the composition of their pottery scatters, these being exclusively of late medieval wares of the 13th and 14th centuries. The interpretation placed upon this by the RCHME (1981) is that this part of the village might have been developed at a later date than the rest. House areas were marked by charcoal patches

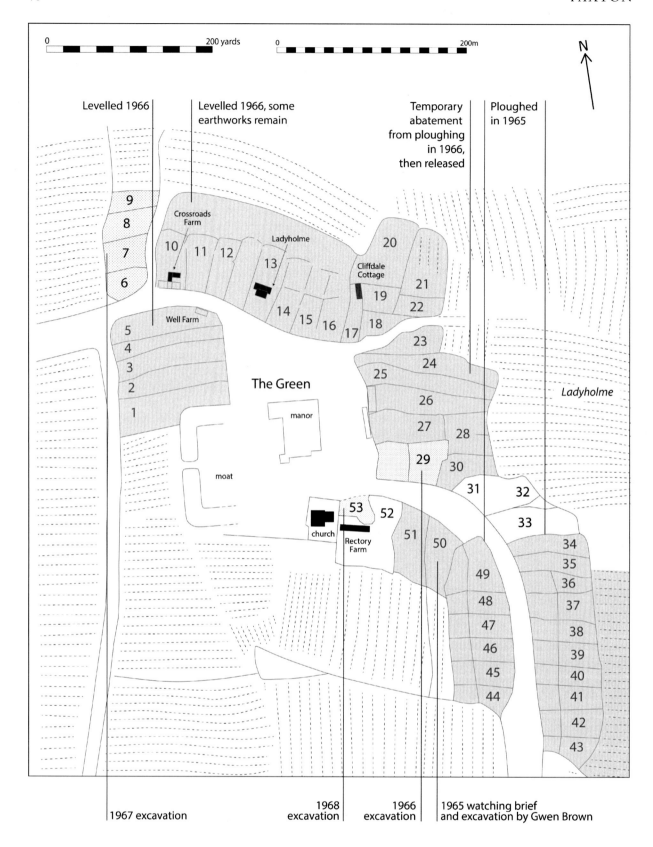

FIGURE 3.6

Faxton. Medieval village plan as reconstructed by Lawrence Butler from the 1746 enclosure plan and observation of earthworks

FIGURE 3.7A

The almshouses, Faxton. The photograph was a gift from Sir Gyles Isham, 10 February 1967

FIGURE 3.7B

The almshouses, Faxton. The photograph was a gift from Sir Gyles Isham, 10 February 1967

with only a few pieces of sandstone; there was insufficient material to suggest that any substantial stone houses had been built on these crofts (though stone robbing may have occurred soon after desertion took place). Crofts 43 and 44 were not fully developed and may have been no more than grazing land at the southern margin of the village.

3.5   THE SOUTH SIDE OF THE GREEN, INCLUDING THE CHURCH

The manor house

The manor house at Faxton was located on the south side of the village green and shows clear evidence of two main phases of occupation. The first is a moated homestead associated with the families of Periton and Welles; the second is an Elizabethan stone-built mansion erected by the Nicols family and lived in by them for more than a century (see Chapter 1).

The evidence for the moated homestead in 1966–68 was an enclosure measuring 90 by 80m north–south. The moat is clearly depicted in 1746 (Figure 3.1), on the 1839 tithe (Figure 3.2) and again on the 1900 Ordnance Survey (Figure 3.3) where it is labelled as 'Hall Ponds'. In 1966 it was still defined by a broad water-filled moat on the north and west of maximum width 17m and maximum depth 3m, now partly water-filled by the 'hall ponds'. This moat was set between inner and outer banks up to 1.5m high and had a causeway or gap at the mid-point on the west (shown by the RCHME on Figure 3.5). An infilled depression continued along part of the northern boundary. The eastern boundary had been infilled, being overlain by the later mansion which had also disturbed the interior of the platform. The topographical evidence therefore indicates a small single moated enclosure which appears to be typical of others in the area such as Thrupp (Norton), for example (RCHME 1981).

In 1966 the remains of the Elizabethan mansion showed as prominent earthworks close to the church. These were traces of the house described by Bridges in 1724 as 'an ancient manor-house' (Bridges 1791, II, 92). Latin inscriptions under a stone dial over the gateway once referred to the completion of the house in 1625 and indicate that the work had extended over three periods of ownership, those of Elizabeth, James and family, Anne, Augustine (her son) and Francis (his nephew) (Green 1805).

It is certain that this house was lived in by the Nicols family until 1717, possibly by members of the Raynsford family whose main property was at Brixworth until the sale of the estate in 1785 and perhaps by Elizabeth Raynsford up to her death in 1810, although the house is not shown in 1746. It is not known whether any materials from the Hall were incorporated into buildings at Brixworth Hall, at Cottesbrooke or at Shortwood Lodge.

The remains of this mansion on the ground in 1966–68 were difficult to interpret but the hollows seemed to represent cellars and the higher lines indicated walls. This showed a house of T-plan with garden walls and a square gatehouse facing The Green to the east of the house (see Figure 3.5, where a rectangular feature is depicted). To the west of the house were lines of terrace walks and a prominent garden wall on the south. No archaeological work was undertaken on this site by Lawrence Butler nor subsequently; terraces and ponds, however, are typical of gardens of the mid-16th to 18th century. Other examples have been recorded locally for example at Lamport (RCHME 1981).

The church

The church which served Faxton was located on The Green immediately adjacent to the manor house and its moated enclosure (see Figure 3.6 for location and also Figure 3.8). There are good reasons for regarding the origins of the church as a manorial chapel both from its location and from the relatively few items of documentation about its medieval history. The structure mirrored the rise and stability of the medieval village; in it were displayed the tombs of the 17th-century squires (see below and Appendix 2).

The status of the church and responsibility for its upkeep was a continuing sore which was never resolved right up to the point of the church's demolition. In the 19th century a case reached the High Court of Chancery brought by the rector of Lamport who sought the tithes he believed to be owed to him from the chapelry of Faxton which lay within his parish. The village claimed itself to be a separate parish, stating that the inhabitants of Faxton had 'for a great length of time, christened and buried there, and not in Lamport'. In response, the plaintiff stated that this permission had been granted by a Faculty in 1613, the original being lost in the Great Fire of London in 1666 (Simons 1834).

Faxton church with its lands and tithes was given by Guy de Balliol to the Priory of Lewes in Sussex. This event must be dated to the second quarter of the 12th century. In about 1180 the prior complained that Thomas, rector of Lamport, with the support of Simon Malesaures, caused bodies of dead parishioners of Faxton to be buried at Lamport. In his defence Thomas asserted that the 'burial belonged to his church at Lamport by parochial right from ancient times'. The dispute was settled by the priory giving up all its rights in Faxton in return for an annual payment of 40s from the rector of Lamport. About 40 years later, payment of this sum, then said to be for two parts of the tithe of sheaves from the demesne of Ingeram de Dumart, was enforced against William de Walda, then rector (VCH 1937, 171–172; Salzman 1943, 126–127; Maxwell Lyte 1902, 234: A.7896). This suggests

FIGURE 3.8

St Denys, Faxton, in 1945, looking east. Historic England Archive

that from its foundation the church of Faxton was a parochial chapel dependent upon Lamport, as it most clearly became after 1208, though the implication of the 1180 complaint is that the bodies should be buried in some burial ground which was not Lamport (either Faxton, Old or Scaldwell).

In 1429 the Commissary General of the Bishop of Lincoln, in whose diocese Faxton was situated until 1540, delivered a judgement whereby he decreed that every yardland in Lamport was to pay towards the repair of the church at Lamport, its belfry and its churchyard 12d, every yardland in Hanging Houghton 6d and every yardland in Faxton and Mawsley 4d (NRO LFM 42). It is impossible to know how many yardlands lay in Faxton at that date but the Faxton Enclosure Act of 1745 states that John Nicolls Raynsford, then lord of the manor, owned 22 and a half yardlands (about 1135 acres) in the open fields (NRO LFM 211, 18 Geo. II, cap. 27). About 450 acres had already been enclosed before this Act and represent a further 9 yardlands. Payments from Faxton towards the repair of Lamport church were certainly made in the post-medieval period. In the late 16th century the opinion of Dr William Lewyn (died 1598) was obtained on this very point, namely the legality of the levies made on Hanging Houghton, Faxton and Mawsley for the repair of Lamport church (ODNB sub Lewin, William; NRO LFM 53). It appears from the case then stated that instead of every yardland

contributing a fixed sum, the total sum required by the Lamport churchwardens to defray their expenses was annually divided between the three villages in the proportion of 12d, 6d, and 4d as determined in 1439. Entries in the 18th-century churchwarden's accounts of Lamport and of Faxton confirm that this was the usual practice.

Extracts from wills relating to Faxton church throw some light on the internal arrangements of the building. In 1521 Simon Smyth left 12d 'to the gylting [gilding of the monument] of Nycolas Water in Faxton Chapel' and in 1557 Humfrey Garryte left 'to the sepulchre light in the chapel of Faxton my best ewe with her lame' (Serjeantson and Longden 1913). Other early 16th-century wills use the description 'church' or 'chapel' interchangeably. No early wills mention the dedication which is to St Denys, a saint popular in the 12th century. No Edwardian inventory of church plate and other valuables has survived.

The presence of the Nicols family in the manor house from 1606, and probably earlier, meant that the church received more attention both legally and structurally at that time. In 1613 the burial ground was consecrated on the initiative of Sir Augustine Nicolls and with the consent of Sir John Isham, patron, and the Reverend D Baxter, rector (NRO I(L)/5342). This fact was also commemorated by an inscription in the glass of the east window (Bridges 1791, II, 95), the first person to be buried there being Edward Bringest on 23 February 1613–14. The Rectory House was newly built and the curates served for longer periods than the customary year as a deacon or two years awaiting an incumbency: Robert Edmonds (1590–1610) and Thomas Bunning (1610–29). The register begun in 1570 was kept assiduously until 1640, but afterwards only the activities of the Nicols and Raynsford families were recorded until 1753. Sir Augustine Nicolls had also acquired a lease of the tithes of Faxton and Mawsley, the parsonage house of Faxton, the parson's close and the glebe lands for £700 on 30 September 1607 (NRO I(L)/5314). The Ishams bought the patronage of Lamport in 1560, but only leased the temporalities of the rectory (on a 99-year lease from John White the rector) on 9 November 1568 for £48 p.a. (1568 lease, NRO I(L)/2279/2284). In Faxton, John Isham leased all the glebe, tithes and the parson's close to Andrew Dennis, yeoman, for 10 years at £50 p.a. (8 February 1583) and then for 3 years (19 March 1606) in both cases excepting two houses, one of which was occupied by the curate. The Nicols family enjoyed the Faxton glebe lands and tithes until 1667, in which year the lands reverted to the rector of Lamport (1583 lease, NRO I(L)/5339; 1606 lease, NRO I(L)/5340).

Although church plate was purchased during the curacy of Benjamin Resbury (1669–71) and the bells were cast (or perhaps recast) in 1703 by Henry Penn of Peterborough, there was no major change to the legal status of the church or to its structure. The churchwardens' accounts survive from 1737 to 1828 (see Chapter 1). They indicate the regular items of maintenance but no major expense. They do conceal, however, a major crisis in 1796 when it was intended to pull down the entire church and rebuild it in classical taste. The contractor was to be S Brampton who submitted an estimate for £339 6s 7½d; presumably the instigator of the project was Sir William Langham who had beautified Cottesbrooke church and hall. The rector Euseby Isham would need to have given his approval. In the event, the drastic rebuilding was not carried through and instead a substantial repair of walls, copings, roofs and porch together with internal plastering was undertaken for an estimated £163 15s 6d (NRO I(L)3079/BB/1 & 1a). The nave roof carried the inscription W★A★I★H-1796-T★B on the third truss from the west and these initials were probably those of the carpenters; they do not correspond to any known curate or wardens. The churchwardens' accounts show that £203 8s had been spent by 14 August 1797 and further sums were spent during the course of the next century when the chancel was rebuilt and a fire damaged the interior in 1899 (see Appendix 1). That restoration was supervised by a noted local architect and architectural historian, John Alfred Gotch of Kettering (1852–1942) who was also a Vice-President of the Society of Antiquaries (Hargrave 2013).

The Reverend Robert Isham had acted as curate at Faxton (1829–33) before becoming rector of Lamport (1845–90), and it became the custom for those members of the Isham family who became ordained to preach their first sermon or the Christmas sermon at Faxton. When the patron Sir Charles Isham sold the right of the next presentation in 1897 this link was broken but the memoirs of Reverend Henry Isham Longden refers to his Christmas in 1882 as continuing the tradition preaching there 'as everyone had' at a time when 'the hamlet pulsed if feebly with life' (Longden 1943, xv–xvii). In the late 19th century curates of Faxton occasionally lived at Old from which there was much easier access from Lamport. The Reverend Walter Watkins Pitchford, rector of Lamport (1903–44), used to employ a clergyman from Old to conduct services at a guinea a month since he was concerned that if no services were held at all he might not be entitled to draw that part of his income which derived from the glebe land in Faxton parish. This deputy only acted when the rector was too infirm to ride his own horse over the bridle paths to Faxton and former residents remember his visits continuing until about 1935. Faxton ceased to be a separate parish in that year.

The appearance and plan of the church at Faxton can be reconstructed from drawings and photographs and a description is available in the Victoria County History. The only known plan of the church was found recently (2018) in the archives of the Society for the Protection of Ancient Buildings (SPAB) and is re-drawn and reproduced here as Figure 3.9. The earliest depiction is 1805 (Green 1805, 793) and there is a mid-19th century drawing of the leper window by N A Hartshorne. In particular, the church was the subject of a famous watercolour by John Piper (1903–92) in 1940, now in the Victoria and Albert Museum, London (Accession number E.1973-1949) (Figure 3.10). It shows an architectural study of the church with a double bell-cote illuminated against a dark grey sky. This work is from a collection called 'Recording the Changing Face of Britain' which was commissioned in the early 1940s from well known artists by the Director of the National Gallery, Sir Kenneth Clark, to record places which captured a sense of national identity. Clark, who had launched the scheme in 1939, was keen to document a 'vanishing' Britain triggered by the outbreak of war and new agricultural practices. Piper also took two photographs of the church and sketched the interior (reproduced in Holden 2008, 56; the project is the subject of Saunders 2011).

The main components of St Denys were a chancel, a nave of four bays with a handsome oak roof (Figure 3.11) and a south aisle, all built of the local orange-brown sandstone with lead and Welsh slate roofs (Figure 3.12) (letter and report, Martin to SPAB, 19 July 1950). Over the west gable was a bell-cote of two openings. There was formerly a south

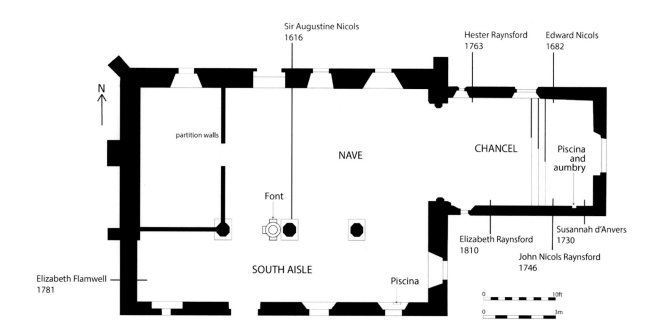

FIGURE 3.9

St Denys, Faxton. Ground plan drawn by David Martin in July 1950, re-drawn here from the SPAB archives with minor corrections. For further details on memorials, see Appendix 2. For interior views, see Figures 3.13 and 3.14

FIGURE 3.10

Watercolour by John Piper of the exterior of the church of St Denis or Denys, Faxton, 1940. From the north-west © Victoria and Albert Museum, London

FIGURE 3.11

St Denys, Faxton, in 1945. Interior oak roof, from the west. Mainly 15th century with minor late 18th-century repairs. From NMR AA46/867. Historic England Archive

FIGURE 3.12

St Denys church, Faxton, in 1945. Historic England Archive.

From the south-east and showing the chancel (right), nave with clerestory and south aisle with four windows. Note the low side window beneath the lancet window in the chancel, said to be a 'leper's window' (NMR AA46/859). For plan, see Figure 3.9

porch which was removed in a 19th-century repair. The north door arch and the jambs of the south door indicated a 12th-century structure, perhaps of the same length as the nave, the 12th-century door jambs being re-set in a new position when the aisle was inserted. The un-buttressed chancel was basically 13th century, indicated by its surviving original windows, the low side window and the combined piscina and aumbry. The chancel arch was rebuilt in the 14th century at the same time as the erection of the south aisle. In the south wall of the aisle there was a piscina confirming its use as a chapel ('St Nicholas altar'). This is visible in Figure 3.13. The clerestory windows, the roof and probably the double-gables bell-cote were of 15th-century date as was a large window on the nave north wall. The font, lined with lead, was a 12th-century bowl set on a later stem and base.

The overall impression is of a church which expanded steadily until about 1500 and then received little further structural attention apart from the rebuilt chancel. In 1831, Faxton still had a population of 103 and seating in the church for 120, so there was little incentive to reduce the structure. There was occasional friction over the need for Faxton pa-

rishioners to pay levies for the upkeep of Lamport church when they already paid for repairs to their own church, and this was particularly acute in 1860 to 1870 when Lamport needed extensive repairs. Nevertheless, Faxton did retain its south aisle unlike Hardwick (1795) and Great Harrowden (c.1710), or Little Harrowden which lost its north aisle.

By 1909, Faxton church already had a 'patient outworn air' (*Northampton Mercury*, 23 April 1909) and by 1924 'the plaster [was] coming away like fur from a mangy animal' (*Northampton Independent*, 1924). Records now with the Society for the Protection of Ancient Buildings show that the church was reported to be in a poor condition in 1926. 'Worm eaten, mildewed and rotting' was the architect's verdict on the pews and floors and he had 'no hesitation is stating that it would be a waste of money to attempt any restoration... the Church is uninteresting and superfluous, and... the village will be extinct in a few years time' (letter Gotch, 1926, in SPAB archive). Two years later a different architect saw only 'a charming little building... worth careful repairing' (letter Pearce, June 1928 in SPAB archive). A local appeal was subsequently successful in raising money to repair the roof and foundations

FIGURE 3.13

St Denys Church, Faxton, in 1945. Historic England Archive.

Interior. Looking south-east into the chancel (left) and the south aisle (right). From NMR AA46/864. It is one of the drums of these aisle columns which stands today at the site of the altar

FIGURE 3.14

St Denys Church, Faxton, in 1945. Interior. Taken from chancel, looking west. Historic England Archive.

In the nave, beyond the chancel arch, the monument to Judge Nicolls (1616) can be seen over the arcade in the south aisle and the memorials to Elizabeth Raynsford (1810), now in the Victoria and Albert Museum, London, and Hester Raynsford (1763), now in Lamport church, to left and right. Note the stove and flue

FIGURE 3.15

St Denys Church, Faxton. Wall paintings from the National Monuments Record. Historic England Archive.

FIGURE 3.16

St Denys Church, Faxton, in 1945. Historic England Archive.

Monument to Judge Nicolls 1616 on the south wall of the nave. This monument, in alabaster and white marble, can now be seen in the Victoria and Albert Museum, London. The artist, Nicholas Stone, was the foremost English sculptor of the first half of the 17th century. From NMR AA46/868

FIGURE 3.17

John Piper preparatory sketch of Faxton church interior, 1940. Compare with Figure 3.14 for a view from chancel into nave and south aisle beyond © Victoria and Albert Museum, London

(Morris 2016). In 1940 the visiting writer Arnold Palmer described St Denys as 'remarkable as one of the very few unrestored churches in this part of the country… a certain amount of simple repair is now needed if the church is to be saved from the opposing dangers of decay and restoration' (Palmer 1947). Clearly, all was not lost.

With the decline of the village, the church was closed for public worship in 1939 under the war-time National Emergency Regulations and it is alleged to have been used for war-time training exercises during the Second World War (Holden 2008, 53). It may have opened briefly after the war but was soon closed again and in 1946 fears were expressed about the condition of the building (letter Amos to SPAB, 1946) (Figure 3.14). By July 1950, the rector and the Church Council of Lamport were being urged to consider the church's future and were seeking advice. Reporting for SPAB, architect David Martin noted the 'dilapidated condition' of the church, the lack of 'normal maintenance repairs', the 'wanton destruction', the peeling plaster, the rotting floors, woodworm, leaks, the cracks and the bulges. He suggested, as had more than one person before him, that the church be left as a ruin with the roof removed, the wall tops strengthened, the graveyard enclosed, and thereby allow the structure to become 'a natural and decent ruin' (letter Martin, 19 July 1950). SPAB agreed with this course of action, given that other uses for the chapel could not then be found (letter SPAB to Anderson, 6 August 1950). During the course of the next few years, however, monuments were damaged, windows smashed and ornaments taken (*Northamptonshire Evening Telegraph*, 17 July 1952; *The Mercury*, 10 April 1953). There were still influential voices who wished to see the church saved and intact, among them the historian Joan Wake, but this rescue plan failed and the roof was finally removed as Martin had suggested in 1953. Then, in June 1957, a local councillor wrote to a local newspaper to protest that 'the interior of the church was one mass of filth'; evidently gravestones had been tampered with and the cows were inside (letter Wake to SPAB, 20 March 1958). Joan Wake again protested ('the time for tact is passed'), feeling the ecclesiastical authorities had neglected their duty of care by neither capping the walls with slates and slabs once the roof was removed nor erecting railings to keep the cows out (letter Wake to Archdeacon of Northampton, 17 February 1958 in the SPAB archive). Subsequent correspondence with the Bishop of Peterborough was to no avail. Even with the sale of the lead from the roof, the estimated cost of capping the walls was considered too high a price to pay, not least because of the history of vandalism and the fact that only one inhabitant now remained in the village; any future costs would likely fall on Lamport, a small village in 1958, and this too was thought unacceptable. The church was finally totally demolished as an unsafe structure in 1958/9.

As the Bishop commented at the time: 'The whole business of Faxton is an object lesson in how not to do things' (letter from Bishop Robert Stopford, quoted in Holden 2008, 58). For her part, Joan Wake felt the seven-year saga to be 'a huge pile of correspondence and a devastating waste of time… the end of Faxton church… will be repeated elsewhere unless determined steps on a national level are taken to prevent it' (Wake 1959, 301).

Drawings of the wall paintings and details of the commissioning of these scale drawings (signed by Maurice Keevil) in November 1953 can be found at The National Archives in Kew (NRA WORK/13154; 31/1229–1230); the National Monuments Record at Swindon also hold six coloured measured drawings by the Ministry of Works dating to November 1958 based on those at Kew (NMR MD59/00185-00190; Redundant Churches Fund 1990, ix–x) (Figure 3.15). Attention was first drawn to these mural paintings by Ministry architect H G R Frost on a visit in May 1953. He identified at least four different phases of painting around the chancel arch and on the wall above the arcade as well as on the east and west walls (letter Frost to Bishop of Peterborough, 17 May 1953).

The most imposing monument in the church, to Sir Augustine Nicols (sometimes 'Nicolls'), erected after his death in 1616 and then 'new adorned' by his great grandson Sir Edward in 1705, was finally transferred to the Victoria and Albert Museum in 1965 (Figure 3.16); it had been damaged during its removal from the church and kept in a potting shed at Lamport Rectory (Figure 3.17). Other monuments to Sir Edward Nicols, John Nicols Raynsford and Elizabeth Raynsford were also brought to the Museum by curator Terence Hodgkinson (Wake 1962; Hodgkinson 1971–72; Bilbey with Trusted 2002). The Hestor Raynsford monument is in the Isham chapel in Lamport church (see Appendix 2). The church plate was removed to Lamport church. There was formerly funeral armour hanging above the memorial of Sir Augustine Nicols, Jacobean altar rails, two coffin stools in the vestry and a clock which was installed in the 18th century. Their whereabouts is unknown, as is the monument to Susannah Danvers (National Buildings Record photograph AA46/873; Morris 2016).

The graves in the churchyard were not lifted and once contained more than 60 headstones of the 18th and 19th centuries, mainly located on the north side of the yard closest to The Green. In 1966 a rough stone wall enclosed the rectangular churchyard. The timeline for repairs and the final demolition of Faxton church are presented in Figure 3.18.

Crofts 50–53

These crofts lay on rising ground to the south of the track to Old at the south-east corner of The

Date	Nature of work	Details	Contractor	Comment
1125–50		Parochial chapel first constructed, dependent on Lamport. 12th-century date also indicated by architecture and font bowl		See text
13thC		Chancel added		See text
14thC		Chancel arch rebuilt and south aisle added which had its own altar		See text
15thC		Clerestory, roof and bell-cote with added fenestration		See text
1613		Burial ground consecrated at request of Augustine Nicholls		See text
1600s	Major work	Several good monuments added inside the church		See Appendix 2
1730	Major work	Building of churchyard wall		Revd Henry Isham Longden collection (NRO L17)
1737	Minor repairs	For mending church 'dore'	¼d	
1738	Minor repairs	Repairs to roof, mending windows	£1 10s 5d and 7d	
1762	Minor repairs	Repairs to roof	13⁄6d	
1783	Minor repairs	700 plain tiles, lime and ridge tiles, fetching lime from Kettering, fetching stone and mortar	various small payments	
1788	Minor repairs	Mason paid for 7 days work	Mr Kiteley	
1796	Major repairs (NRO IL 307/ DD/1 and 1e), also churchwardens' accounts	An estimate for pulling down the church is prepared (see Appendix 1). Instead, repairs are made to roofs of the north and south aisle and the porch, new doors, plastering and whitewashing	£203 8s to Samuel Brampton, William Cook, John Ball, William Corby and John Davis	Inscribed roof timber dated 1796; the porch mentioned was not present by 1966
1804	Minor repairs	New coping stone	£16 10s 6d	
1855	Minor repairs	Unknown, costs detailed in the churchwardens' accounts	£14 16s 2d, Mr Brown of Scaldwell	
1862	Major repairs	Walls of chancel taken down and rebuilt, putting in 2-light new window, enlarging and fixing east window	£76 4s 1d, Mr Cosford	Later noted as 'a poor addition, disfigured by some rascally mason' (Northampton Mercury 23 April 1909)
1862	Minor repairs	Unknown, costs detailed in the churchwardens' accounts	£17 4s 9d, Mr Gammage	
1863	Minor repairs	Unknown, costs detailed in the churchwardens' accounts	£15 10s 0d, Mr Brown	
1863	Major repairs	Not specified	£36 9s 2d, Mr Woods	
1899	Fire damages pews	Old square pews replaced with some new stone flooring	£8 4s 6d work undertaken by F J Kirby for architect J A Gotch	Some panelling bought by Gotch. Whereabouts now unknown
1909		Church said to be 'outworn'		*Northampton Mercury*
1924		Holes in the roof, plaster coming away, holes in floorboards, east window boarded up, mildew on hymn books and Bibles		*Northampton Independent*
1926		'We have no hesitation in stating that it would be a waste of money to attempt any restoration of the fabric as the church is uninteresting and superfluous'		Report by architect Gotch, held in SPAB archive
1930s		Appeals leaflets, £74 raised for repairs		Morris 2016
1939	Church closed	Notice erected: 'National Emergency Measure 1939. By direction of the Bishop of the diocese given in pursuance of the above measure, the Chapel of Faxton is closed for Public Worship until further notice'		

FIGURE 3.18A

St Denys, Faxton. Repairs and demolition 1796–1958/9 (details from Patrick King handwritten notes, churchwardens' accounts; Holden 2008; with additions from the SPAB archive and Morris 2016). The earliest extant Faxton churchwardens' accounts cover the years 1737–1828 and were studied by King

Date	Nature of work	Details	Contractor	Comment
1939–45	Used for war-time manoeuvres	Some damage implied, details unknown		John Piper paints the church in 1940 (Figures 3.10 and 3.17); writer Arnold Palmer visits
1942		'The high altar was desecrated, its tapestries hanging in shreds. The broken plain glass leaded windows hung crazily in their frames... choirboys' cassocks and surplices hung green with mould'		Memoir recorded in Holden 2008, 109
1946		Fears expressed about condition of the fabric		
1950		Future of church under consideration. Condition report prepared by David Martin, architect, on behalf of SPAB		SPAB archives
1950s	Vandalism	Monuments damaged, windows smashed, ornaments stolen, 'isolated, crumbling and defenceless against vandals'		Joan Wake's seven-year campaign to save the church begins
1953		Wall paintings discovered, the church is un-roofed but upper walls are not consolidated and the site remains unfenced. Interior monuments removed to Lamport		Figure 3.15
1958		Church described as 'one mass of filth'; further vandalism when floorboards ripped up and lath and plaster wall destroyed		Holden 2008, 57; continuing correspondence with SPAB
1958/9	Churchyard deconsecrated; demolition of the church	One stone to garden of contractor in Kettering. Other items to Lamport Hall and Rectory where 12th-century north door is re-erected		Holden 2008, 102
1965		Several Faxton church monuments are given to the Victoria and Albert Museum, London		Appendix 2; Figure 3.16
		Site of church is marked by stone column		Figure 12.6

FIGURE 3.18B

St Denys, Faxton. Repairs and demolition 1796–1958/9 (details from Patrick King handwritten notes, churchwardens' accounts; Holden 2008; with additions from the SPAB archive and Morris 2016). The earliest extant Faxton churchwardens' accounts cover the years 1737–1828 and were studied by King

FIGURE 3.19

The Rectory Farm, Faxton, from the north-west. A curate lived here and was employed to take services in the church until the early 20th century. Lawrence Butler excavated at the front of this property (Croft 52–53), to the east of the church. From NMR Northants XXVI 2 (18). Historic England Archive.

Green. A watching brief in Croft 50 by Gwen Brown in 1965 revealed a rectangular house 20ft (6m) wide with stone flagging within the house and cobbling outside (Wilson and Hurst 1966, 214). No further details of this watching brief/excavation survive. This house was set across the slope with an entrance at the lower end. Pottery indicated a late medieval period of occupation. The 1746 map shows a small building at the front of Croft 51 (Figure 3.1; *vii* on Figure 3.5). Only Croft 53 actually fronted onto The Green. These crofts were larger and wider than was normal at Faxton and showed no clear evidence of a division between an inner toft and an outer croft.

The **Rectory Farm** stood immediately east of the church, set well back from The Green in Croft 53 (Figure 3.19). Here lived a curate who was employed by the rector of Lamport to take services. A good many of their names can be recovered from receipts signed by them for their stipends; few stayed for long (Patrick King notes; NRO IC 1657, 26 June 1703/4). It was stone-built and roughly coursed but with fine stone quoins, gables and chimneys; its windows were ovolo-moulded and one doorway was of good quality stone. Holden (2008, 64, 102, 109) has the two known photographs of the intact building. Its original roof had been of thatch. The ground floor was divided into three rooms; the upper floor contained fine stone fireplaces with depressed arches (Figure 3.20). On the south wall was a stone tablet which had held a sundial, but no inscription was visible. It was flanked by single-storey sheds, both formerly thatched but one now (in 1966) covered in corrugated iron. Ruins of another shed parallel to the house stood on the southern boundary.

The toft in which the Rectory Farm stood was marked 'Glebe' on the 1746 estate map and on the 1839 Tithe Award Map (see Figures 3.1 and 3.2). It

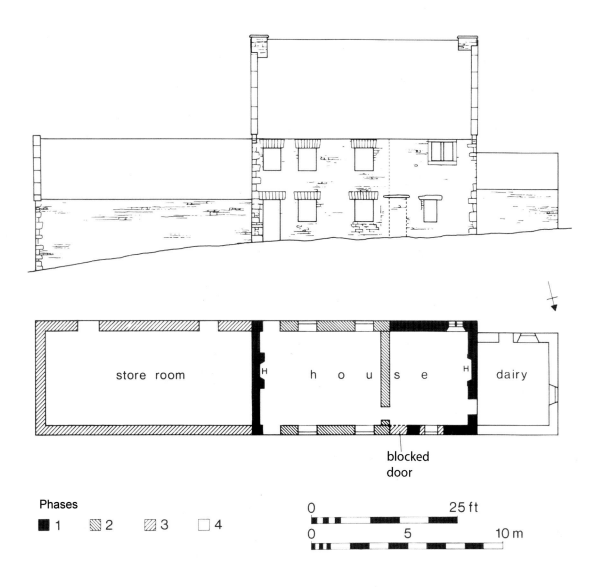

Phases

■ 1   ▨ 2   ▨ 3   ☐ 4

FIGURE 3.20

The Rectory, Faxton. Facade and ground floor plan, drawn by Lawrence Butler. The original roof would have been thatched

		1746	1790	1839	1884	1930	1966
Croft 2	House	Plot 3	-	-	-	-	-
Croft 3	House	Plot 4	House	House	House	-	-
Croft 4	House	Plot 5	House	House	House	-	-
Croft 5	Farm	Plot 6	Farm	Farm	Farm	Farm	-
Croft 10 & 11	Farm	Plot 7	Farm	Farm	Farm	Farm	Sheds
Croft 12	House	Plot 12	House	-	-	-	-
Croft 13	Farm	Plot 13	Farm	Farm	Pair	Pair	Pair
Croft 14	House	Plot 17	-	-	-	-	-
Croft 15 & 16	Houses	Plot 18	Houses	Houses	Houses	-	-
Back of 16	House	Plot 16	-	-	-	-	-
Paddock of 16	House	Plot 15	House	-	-	-	-
Croft 17	House	Plot 20	House	House	House	House	House
Back of 17	House	Plot 19	House	House	-	-	-
Croft 18	Hut?	-	-	-	-	-	-
Croft 19	House	-	-	-	-	-	-
Croft 20	House	Plot 40	-	-	-	-	-
Road	Hut?	-	-	-	-	-	-
East of Green	Almshouses	Almshouses	Almshouses	Almshouses	Almshouses	Almshouses	-
Croft 43	Hut?	-	-	-	-	-	-
Croft 50	Farm	Plot 37	Farm	-	-	-	-
Croft 53	Rectory	Rectory	Rectory	Rectory	Rectory	Rectory	Ruin

FIGURE 3.21

Comparison between the 1746 estate map, the 1839 Tithe Award Map and the 1884 Ordnance Survey Map shows the location of houses and their gradual desertion over 200 years

was described in the 1761 Glebe Terrier as a house of three rooms on a floor, two barns and a stable all thatched. It possessed a Home Close of three acres and the three Glebe Closes of 42 acres situated adjoining Lamport Field. A parsonage house is mentioned in leases of 1583, 1606 and 1607 and occurs in the various glebe terriers. At the 1831 visitation it was described as 'unfit for residence'; in 1877 the house and its dairy were in need of a new roof (Reverend Henry Isham Longden collection L25; Patrick King notes). The date of the house surviving in 1966–68 is unclear. Excavation in Crofts 52–53 in 1968 suggested that the dumping of pottery and the occasional coin started in about 1560 while architecturally the house could date between 1550 and 1600. It had incorporated into one window jamb a portion of 14th-century sculpture (see Chapter 9 and Figures 9.1 and 9.2) which was presumably part of a tomb thrown out of the church at the Reformation or during the Nicols family's re-ordering of the chancel.

On the 1746 estate map a house was situated at the front of this croft, along the slope and parallel to the track. Part of the house wall still survived in 1966 forming the back wall of a cattle byre

alongside the track; it was open-fronted and roofed with corrugated iron. In 1746 the garden of this croft was elongated southwards to run along the rear boundary of Crofts 44–49. It seems likely that this garden had absorbed a strip or headland from the coming field to the south. In similar fashion Croft 51 had extended to include a close on its south, and Rectory Farm (Crofts 52–53) had also extended to its south with the 'Glebe Close' or 'Rectory Home Close'. All these enlarged crofts showed evidence of narrow rig ploughing in them.

In conclusion, comparison between the 1746 estate map, the 1839 Tithe Award Map and the 1884 Ordnance Survey Map shows the location of houses and their gradual desertion over 140 years (Figure 3.21). The greatest period of loss was in the period 1790 to 1839 when six cottages were demolished. Paradoxically, however, this was also the time of greatest recorded population growth in Faxton.

This apparent contradiction may be explained by two factors: the first is that the farms on the periphery of the parish were expanding, and the second is that the cottages were abandoned by poorer inhabitants who had moved into the existing farms as servants and labourers.

4

EXCAVATIONS IN THE SOUTH-EAST OF THE VILLAGE IN 1966 (CROFT 29)

Lawrence Butler and Christopher Gerrard

The first season of excavations at Faxton in 1966 was never fully written up by the excavator and no finalised descriptions of contexts or the minimal stratigraphy on the site now exist. At one time there were large inked-up versions of the excavations plans on linen but today only a selection of bromides survives in greatly reduced sizes together with on-site drawings, in some cases with features sketched in. The excavation account below is therefore frustratingly brief. To assemble it, the chapter is introduced by re-casting some handwritten notes by Lawrence Butler followed by a short description of the excavation recording system which has been amalgamated from four different drafts. Fortunately, an interim report on the 1966 excavations was provided to the Deserted Medieval Village Research Group and then re-cycled, with some minor additional interpretation, for a short article published in Current Archaeology in 1967 (Butler 1968a). The excavation text below integrates these two sources to create a new account which is as faithful to the excavator's own observations as is now possible. Unfortunately the on-site notebook for 1966 amounts to just 6 short pages but, more happily, there is good photographic coverage. A new analysis of the faunal remains from this site is presented in Chapter 10 while further detail and interpretation of the buildings found in 1966 can be found in Chapter 11.

When Lawrence Butler first visited the fine earthworks at Faxton in July 1965 ploughing had already taken place in the area south-east of the village, levelling Crofts 34–43 on the east side of the street and Crofts 44–49 on the west side (see Figure 3.6 for location of these crofts). Ploughing had also begun in Crofts 50–51 and in Croft 50 Gwen Brown had excavated a single house set east–west across the slope and found evidence for late medieval occupation. This was recorded in a note for *Medieval Archaeology* as follows:

> Bulldozing of the village site watched by Mrs Gwen Brown disclosed a 13th-century paved area enclosed on two sides by narrow walls and on the third by substantial 3ft-wide footings. On the other side of the walls, which appear to be 13th century, was ironstone cobbling
>
> (Wilson and Hurst 1966, 214).

In 1965, ploughing was also being proposed for the area east of the village green in Crofts 23–33. Negotiations by the Ancient Monuments Inspectorate obtained a temporary abatement of the ploughing so that those portions of Crofts 23–27 nearest The Green were left unploughed as were Crofts 29 and part of 30 (for context and role of the Ancient Monuments Inspectorate, see Chapter 1). After further consideration of the earthworks, however, it was realised that the almshouses stood in Croft 26 and that there had

been post-medieval housing on the western margin of Crofts 23–24. On that basis a decision was made in the winter of 1965 to excavate Croft 29 in the following July (for locations of these and all excavations, see Figure 4.1). This had not been the original intention as Hurst recorded in an internal Ministry memo (Hurst to Hamilton, 23 June 1966), but by that date some 26 crofts had already been levelled and both Hurst and Butler were persuaded that Croft 29 might be typical of the crofts east of The Green even though it was slightly larger than the rest. There was no surface indication to show whether its housing had been aligned westwards towards The Green or southwards towards the village street leading to Old. Indeed, there were no firm indications that any house at all lay within the Croft 29. Consequently, turf was also stripped from part of Croft 30 so that full-scale excavation could be transferred to that area should Croft 29 prove to be empty (as had occurred previously at Muscott, another DMV in Northamptonshire). In the event, Croft 29 provided an extremely interesting sequence of housing: ten weeks (July to September 1966) were spent there and on sectioning the road between Croft 29 and Croft 51.

Another 20 crofts were levelled during September 1966 and this was closely observed by Lawrence Butler. By this point, only the village green, the churchyard and moated manor site and four crofts flanking the north side of The Green remained under pasture. Throughout the periods of

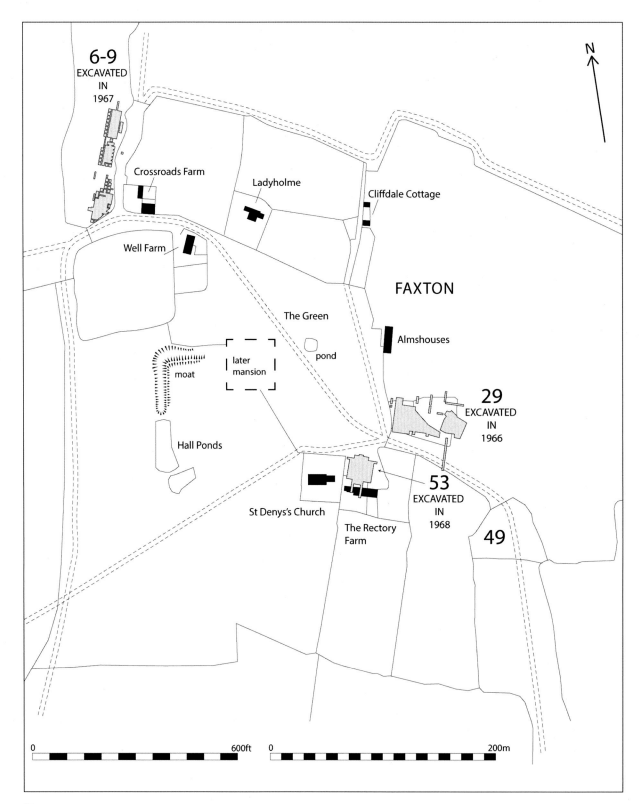

FIGURE 4.1
Main features of Faxton village in 1966 with excavation areas indicated

autumn and spring ploughing in the years 1965 to 1970 all the former crofts were searched by Butler for evidence of pottery concentrations and other occupation debris; stony areas and burnt material were noted. Fieldwalking was undertaken by a team from Kettering Grammar School led by John Steane from 1971 onwards (Steane 1971).

4.1 RECORDING SYSTEM ON SITE

The same procedures operated for all three years of excavation at Faxton. The area was first divided into a grid of 10ft squares (3m) with alphabetical lettering on the east–west axis and a numerical notation on the north–south axis (for an example, see Figure 7.32). Initially, an 8ft square (2.43m) was opened up, removing the turf and topsoil. When the Victorian garden soil had been removed and any post-medieval features recorded, then the baulks between the squares were taken out and open-area excavation commenced at the level of the highest observable medieval features. A few major north–south baulks were retained to facilitate the removal of soil by bucket and barrow; minor baulks were left one layer in retard of the area excavation when the information they contained might prove useful to refer back to during the next phase of excavation. Ditches and large post-holes were sectioned during their excavation. All the major baulks were removed towards the end of the excavation period (Figure 4.2).

Bob Carr, a supervisor on the site in 1966, remembers (pers. comm. 2018):

I recall only that on my first day LB and I laid out a main grid line at his direction; that it was a very long line set out by sighting along ranging-poles, and that at the end of the season, following at least one extension, it was curiously curved. The recording itself was entirely imperial and the use of 10ft square trenches may seem slightly anomalous in retrospect, but this was still the standard methodology at the time on anything other than deserted medieval villages. I remember Thuxton (which Lawrence Butler had dug in 1964) as being dug largely with smallish but nonetheless open-area trenches which were shallow and machine dug, I would guess this was probably largely down to Peter Wade-Martins who was subsequently one of the first (along with Phil Mayes) to use machine-stripped open-areas. Lawrence must have been aware of the use of open-area excavations because he had gained his main experience of DMV excavation from Wharram, which was very targeted and done on house-platform scale, if I remember rightly; but this was only possible because the platforms and boundaries had shallow chalk subsoil and dwarf walls to enhance definition and were readily distinguishable as earthworks, aided by successive years of good aerial photographs.

I don't recall such helpful earthworks at Faxton, and I'm fairly sure the ground was well covered with rank pasture in the summer of 66, which would have made any definition very poor. I think this may be why it was dug in trenches—Lawrence will have been able to locate the sunken roadways but he possibly didn't have enough detailed information to know quite where he was in relation to croft boundaries and house

FIGURE 4.2
Croft 29 1966. General shot of the excavations looking east. Note the shallow stratigraphy and tape laid out for planning

platforms. As it turned out, the site was significantly deeper than either Wharram or Thuxton, and consequently would have been more difficult to excavate as an open area. Whether an intended strategy, or simply a reversion to old and familiar methodologies, the 10ft square trenches may well have been the best technique.

The Faxton recording system on site recognised two independent numerical sequences for 'layers' and 'features'. Cuts and fills were not recognised. Layers were designated by soil change:
— turf, layer A: topsoil;
— layer B: destruction and collapse of housing;
— layer C: latest period of occupation;
and thus downwards, with features identified numerically throughout the site (and re-numbered after excavation finished). The soil was removed within the excavated area in a series of spits, typically the topsoil 0–6 inches or 9 inches (16–23cm), layer A1 a further 3 inches down (23–30cm), layer A2 a further 3 inches (usually to 33–38cm) and according to Butler's on-site notebook 'the scrape which removes any intrusive material and shows the medieval features' (entry for 1966 Week 5), layer A3 to 16 inches (41cm), layer A4 to 18 inches (46cm), layer B1 to 12–18 inches (max. 46cm) is 'the general clearance of the medieval features ready for plotting and levelling', layer B2, 18–22 or 24 inches (56–61cm) is the 'scrape over the house floor and cleaning of tumble to E & W', layer B3, 22–27 inches (56–69cm), usually yellow and chalky then natural yellow or blue-grey clay at 24–30 inches (60–76cm). Ditches were given layer numbers C–N which were individual to each ditch but sometimes correlated across the site where the sequence was found to be similar; deeper sections within ditches could be up to 26 inches or 30 inches deep or more (66 or 76cm). Material was recorded by 5ft (1.52m) squares using letters from west to east and numbers from south to north. All pottery and finds were recorded by these layers; small finds such as coins, worked bone and worked stone were recorded by precise location three-dimensionally and triangulated onto field plans (which have not survived). Additionally, the progress of excavation was recorded in a 'day book' ('personnel and finance'), a 'trench book', a 'small finds' book and a 'survey level' book. These formed the basic excavation record but most are now lost. This recording system forms the basis of the area descriptions and the finds discussion which follow. No attempt was made to use Harris matrix analysis either at the time or subsequently, though the principles by which such analysis operates are inherent in the Faxton recording system.

Together with these grid co-ordinates and the layer 'numbers' given on site, both explained by Lawrence Butler above, a third wholly numerical system of 'bags' of finds was also in place. These 'bag' numbers were allotted on site at the time of the excavation and can be related to both grid co-ordinates and layers. However, the bag numbers for all three years of excavation all begin at 1 and so there was (and still is) considerable potential for confusion. In the 1980s, when some of the material was found to be mixed (pottery with bone etc.) and in some cases unwashed, all the materials were re-bagged and labelled with these bag numbers. There were some gaps in the numerical sequence where numbers were not used, and a number of bags could not be located in the 1980s (those numbered 900 onwards). These 'bag' numbers are effectively context numbers but, unfortunately, it is only for the 1967 excavations that there are any descriptions to accompany them. Pottery sherds were marked with the bag numbers and where they were illustrated these are also given a 'pot number'.

Further complications then arose late in the preparations for publication in the 1980s when an entirely new numerical sequence was introduced for features, so that, for example, Figure 4.4 has contexts 38, 39, 59–69 marked. No sense can now be made of these numbered features and any details of them (such as dimensions, dating, etc.) are now lost; they bear no relation to the 'bag sequence' described above and there are no correspondence tables in the archive. The numbers have been left on the plans in case they can be interpreted at some time in the future and serve to highlight the features Butler though important enough for comment. Five (of the 11) bromides which survive for the 1966 excavations now indicate numbered features which were not mentioned in the original summary text and plan. In addition, there are also four un-labelled sections on bromide which have now been located on the plans and inserted into the text below. They have no context numbers but they do at least indicate the depth of the stratigraphy and the morphology of some of the features.

4.2 EXCAVATIONS IN CROFT 29

The excavations in 1966 took place between 25 July and 1 October 1966, a ten-week period. The selected croft stood on sloping ground at the south-east angle of The Green, north of 'East Street' leading to the neighbouring village of Old, 2km to the south-east (Figures 4.3A and B). An area measuring roughly 150ft east–west by 100ft (240 x 160m) was excavated (Figure 4.1); the majority of the house and its yards were stripped of topsoil by bulldozer while the boundary banks and the adjacent village street were sectioned by hand. As far as is known, no description of the work in 1966 was ever fully written up by the excavator. The most complete account is that provided as an interim for the DMVRG Newsletter in October 1966, shortly after the excavations that year were completed.

FIGURE 4.3A

March 1956. Ten years before excavations began at Faxton, this oblique aerial photograph shows the location of the 1966 excavations in Croft 29 very clearly (SD79 SP7875/30/06.04.1956 SP 784750 CAP). Looking west. The Rectory and the church lie beyond with The Green and the earthworks of the moated site to the north (right). Reproduced with permission of the Cambridge University Collection of Aerial Photography © Copyright reserved.

FIGURE 4.3B

Aerial shot looking west, showing the location of Croft 29 1966 in the south-east corner of The Green with the ruined rectory building to the west (left), and three sets of buildings along the north end of The Green. They are the house now known as 'Ladyholme' (right) and the barns of Crossroads Farm (left)

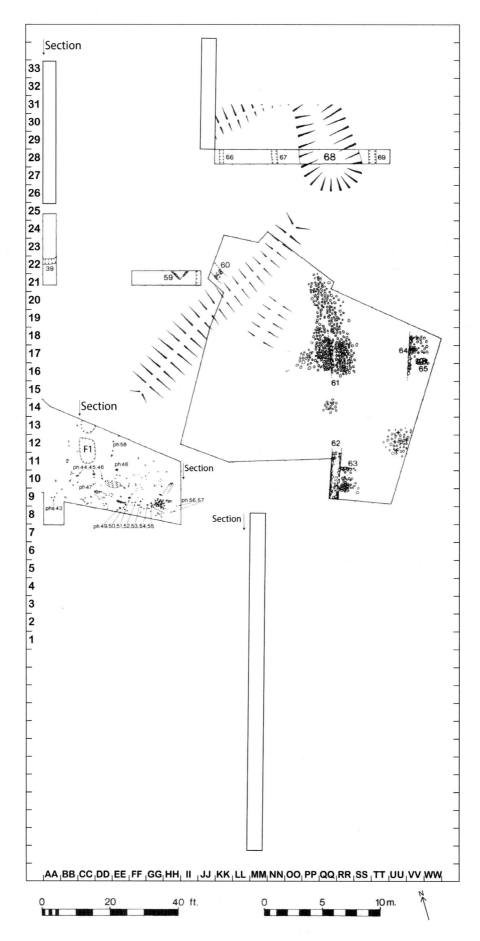

FIGURE 4.4

Croft 29 1966. Early features in Phase 0

The account below is taken from that interim and the article in *Current Archaeology* in May 1967 which describes 'a long and comparatively wealthy occupation between 1200 and 1400' (Butler 1968a).

Phase 0: Prehistory, Roman and Anglo-Saxon

Evidence of earlier occupation in the area (Figure 4.4) included worked flints, a hammer stone and a stone axe fragment and a scatter of 2nd/3rd century Romano-British pottery. The most significant feature was a ?Neolithic infant burial (F1) in an oblong pit recorded on site as 3ft deep and 4ft wide (0.91 x 1.20m) (Figure 4.5) immediately east of section CC 8-12 (Figure 4.6). No photograph exists of the burial and the rationale behind the date suggested by Butler is not now known. Any future interventions at Faxton, however, should take into account the possibility of underlying prehistoric and Roman features. Early medieval pottery is also noted from this site in Chapter 8, but is not discussed by the excavator in this text.

Phases 1–5: Later medieval

At the time of excavation four main phases of later medieval occupation were apparent. These are detailed below. Phase 5 marks the desertion of the croft.

Phase 1 (c.1200–1250)

A clay platform was built slightly above the level of the surrounding clay and a building (A1), 14 by ?30ft (4.24 x ?9.14m), running east–west, constructed with mud or cob walls and timber post-holes (211 and 212) (Figure 4.7). Butler describes this as a 'living house', and originally identified it in his 1967 text as a 'long-house' (Butler 1968a; repeated by the RCHME 1981), an interpretation he later rejected. No end walls were identified and its construction Butler found to be 'crude'. Contemporary with this was a Barn B (tentatively located only on Figure 4.7) on the northern boundary of the croft. Shallow ditches (not indicated) marked the boundary on all sides except the south. The southern ditch (D5, 202) was up to 3ft (0.91m) deep and 10ft (3.05m) wide and was replaced by a ditch (D6) of lesser dimensions further south. It should be noted that the pottery report in Chapter 8 suggests occupation 'by the 12th century' and therefore earlier than the phasing suggested here.

Phase 2 (c.1250–1300)

Some 50 years later, the first house was replaced by a larger building (A2) further down the slope (Figure 4.8). This measured 36ft 9in by 15ft 9in (11.2 x 4.8m) internally with its main axis north–south. In other words, the change was made from a

building sited *parallel* to the contours to one sited *perpendicular* to the slope. The walls of this building, also interpreted as a dwelling, are numbered on Figure 4.8 as 10, 23, 22 and 12. They are described in Butler's on-site notebook as 'stone walls of ironstone and other pebble and tumble, mainly medieval material between' (entry for 28 July 1966). Photographically, this structure is among the best documented at Faxton (Figures 4.9–4.12). At its southern end, it overlay ditches D5 and D6 documented in Phase 1. The first phase of its construction was mud or cob walls laterally with stone sleeper walls at the gable ends, but during the second phase the lateral walls were placed on stone footings with mud or cob walls above. According to Butler's account, the internal arrangements suggest a clean sleeping end at the upper (north) end and a working area with heat supplied by braziers—not an internal hearth—and opposing doors on the long walls near the lower end. However, a hearth is clearly marked on the plan (labelled H) of the building more or less in the centre of the interior space (the RCHME 1981 refer to this as a 'long-house') and this hearth is also marked on the on-site plans.

To the west, Barn D lay at right angles to the lower end (22) of Building A2. The east end of Barn D was constructed up against the west wall of Building A2 but the west wall of Barn D was not identified so the dimensions of the barn are uncertain. To the east of the house was a circular structure (F8) on the south of the inner yard (Figures 4.13–4.18). This was originally interpreted by Butler as a 'bake-oven' with an internal diameter of 5ft (1.5m) standing three courses high and an encircling wall two stones thick of c.12 inches (30cm). An alternative function is suggested in Chapter 11. The fill was of reddened earth, ash and yellow clay and contained many fire burnt stones. On excavation (Figure 4.17) the floor of the oven was found to contain a paving of two large stones, one 20 inches (50cm) square in the centre, the other 10 inches (25cm) square near the entrance (Figure 4.18). Stratigraphically, the oven sat on dark brown earth over the Phase 1 south and centre ditch. There was also a clay-lined water trough (F4) sunk into the centre of the yard (Figures 4.19 and 4.20 for section), and another barn, Barn E, again of unknown dimensions, stood to the north (Figure 4.21). The principal evidence for this structure seems to be the presence of drip gully (31). The rubbish area to the east of these structures was gradually filled and new ditches were cut along the southern margin of the inner yard and garden area. Section HH 8-11 shows the layering and build up being described (Figure 4.22).

Phase 3 (c.1300–1350)

Another 50 years later and the second house (by now 'shabby' according to Butler 1967) was replaced

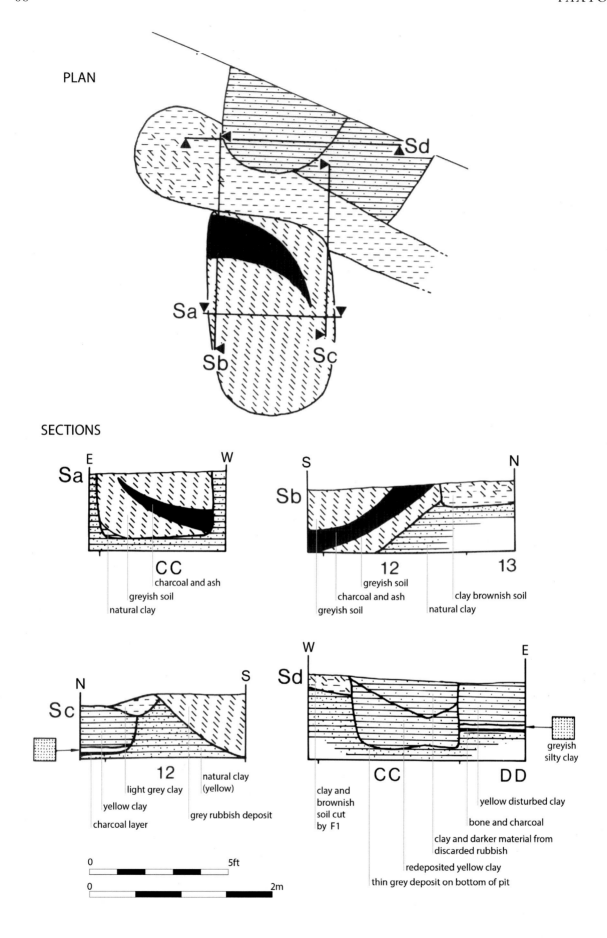

FIGURE 4.5

Croft 29 1966. Prehistoric burial F1. Pit and sections. Details of the stratigraphy are taken from site notes. For location, see Figure 4.4

CC 8-12

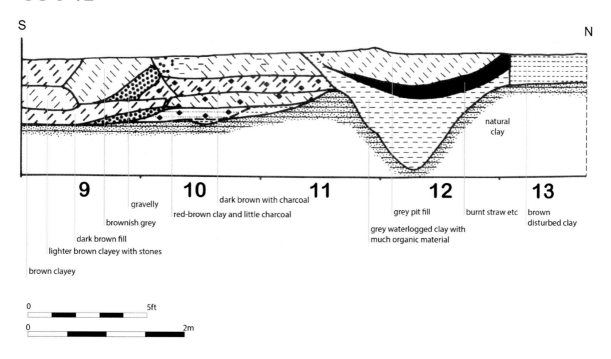

S   N

natural clay

9   **10**   **11**   **12**   **13**

gravelly
brownish grey

dark brown with charcoal
red-brown clay and little charcoal

grey pit fill   burnt straw etc   brown
disturbed clay

grey waterlogged clay with
much organic material

dark brown fill

lighter brown clayey with stones

brown clayey

0   5ft

0   2m

FIGURE 4.6

Croft 29 1966. Prehistoric burial at south-west corner of site. Details of the stratigraphy are taken from site notes. To locate this section, see Figure 4.4

upslope and partly overlying A1 by building A3, another domestic building, measuring 47ft 9in by 14ft 9in internally (14.5 x 4.5m) (Figure 4.23); it lay on the same north–south axis as house A2 and made use of the north wall of house A2 (12) as its south wall. The walls of this house were (14), (12), (16) and an unnumbered north wall. A cross wall is indicated on the original plans (Figures 4.24–4.27). Building A2 probably still remained in use for storage during this phase since Barns D and E seem to have been abandoned by this time. Building A3 was very similar in plan to the previous house. The walls of the house were interpreted as 'sleeper trenches' by Lawrence Butler—packed with clay with large boulders and rubble and faced with ironstone blocks which we might today interpret as 'stone footings'; on this would have been placed a timber or mud-wall building with a thatched roof (Butler, it might be noted, used the term 'sleeper' trench to imply any horizontal cut, whether filled by timber or not, a misuse of the term as we would regard it today). At one stage the thatched roof caught fire and the smouldering remains were dumped in the garden, where the excavators found the evidence (though this is nowhere described). The central fire-pit (Figure 4.27; labelled H in Figure 4.23) was later replaced by a paved hearth area in the corner of the central room (Figure 4.28; labelled H9 in Figure 4.23). Barn F (to the north of wall 19), a replacement of E (to the north of drip gully 31),

but likewise of unknown dimensions, stood at the north of the east yard, a second water trough (F7) was sunk (Figure 4.19 for plan and sections), and several sheds indicated only by post-settings of stone and clay were erected in the rubbish area.

According to the excavator, the boundary ditches were re-cut to their final limits on the north, and it is this northern boundary which is recorded in the long AA 21-33 section (Figure 4.29). This is potentially one of the most informative sections recorded at Faxton and shows a collapsed mud/cob wall with adjacent ditch to the north over occupation surfaces. The description of the contexts is taken from the on-site notebooks. Possibly it is a north boundary wall although this northern limit remains confusing because, as Figure 4.23 shows, there is a boundary wall north of Building A4 (originally labelled in this phase) and a sizeable ditch, labelled the North Ditch, immediately to the east. This ditch was caught in Section JJ 29-34 (Figure 4.30) where it is depicted as a shallow ditch 1m wide containing bluish silt with an internal bank and a more substantial external bank.

Phase 4 (c.1350–1400)

Building A4 was a slight enlargement or rebuilding of House A3 (wall 13) though retaining the same limits on the south (wall 12) and east (wall 14) (Figure 4.31). This building, measuring 15.25 by

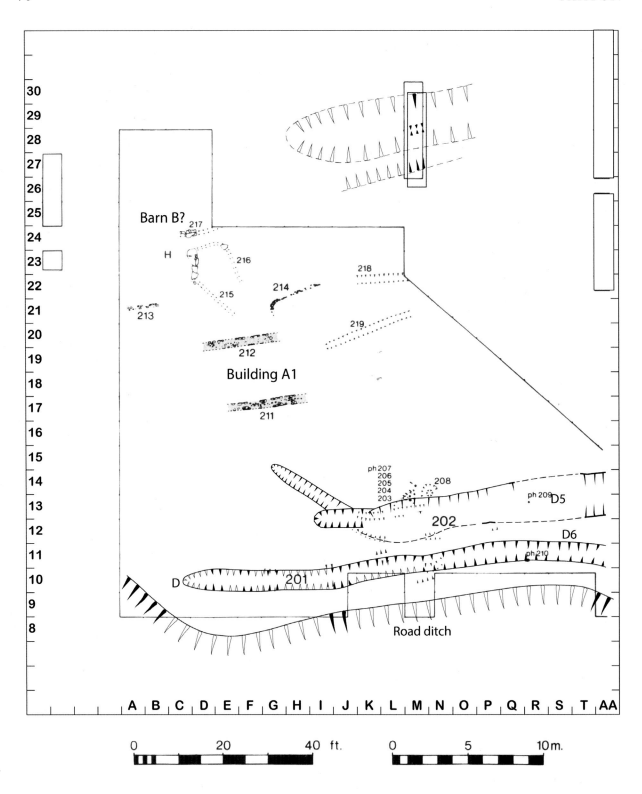

FIGURE 4.7
Croft 29 1966. Phase 1 features showing Building A1. Dated to c.1200–1250 by the excavator

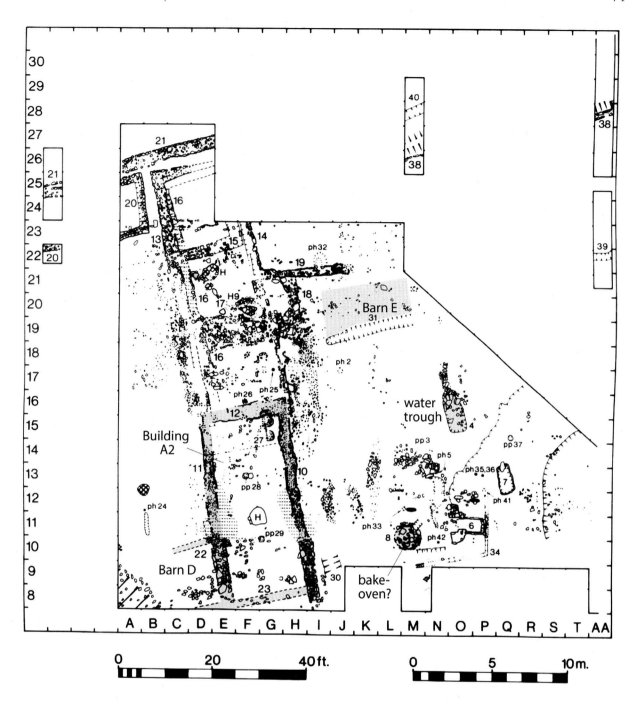

FIGURE 4.8

Croft 29 1966. Phase 2 with Building A2, Barn D and associated water trough (F4) and 'bake-oven' (F8), as originally interpreted by Lawrence Butler. Dated to c.1250–1300 by the excavator

5.25m, was later divided into a three-unit house by constructing an additional interior partition wall with a hearth in the central room. To these were added a bake-oven (H9) and a curving annex (18) on its east wall (Figure 4.32). This house had an elaborate provision of internal and external drainage. The lower room, defined by walls 12 and 16, probably had a cross passage but there was no certain evidence that the lower room was used as a byre. The impression gained from the excavation is that in Phase IV, if not earlier, the occupants of this croft were persons of some substance and this was not a peasant dwelling at a low level of subsistence (and see discussion of finds below and in Chapter 8). Features of this phase may have been recorded in section M 26-29 (Figure 4.33).

Barn F, to the north of wall 19, remained in use and Building C (possibly a byre) with stone footings was added west of the house (see Figure 4.31 for locations). Oven F8 fell into disuse and was incorporated into Barn G to the east of which stood a well preserved oven (F6) built for drying corn, peas and seeds (Figures 4.34 and 4.35; for further interpretation of these features, see Chapter 11). The filling of the rubbish area or garden continued with a gradual encroachment southwards toward the east street and its flanking ditch. The expanded eastern boundary was fixed during this phase.

Phase 5 (post-1400)

This phase represents the late medieval decay of the croft and a period of stone robbing to obtain the large ironstone rubble and the well chosen limestone paving slabs. The abandonment of this croft, originally estimated by the excavator to be shortly after AD 1400 but now thought to be significantly later (see Chapter 7), was originally explained as being motivated by the need for a better water supply which led to the gradual concentration of village houses closer to the wells on The Green.

4.3 THE ROAD SECTION

A north–south trench approximately 30m long by 3.5m wide was dug between Croft 29 and Croft 51 across the track leading from The Green towards Old (see Figure 4.1 for location). Several recent drains were identified here (Figures 4.36 and 4.37) cutting through a shallow hollow-way which was itself heavily metalled with fragments of ironstone up to 15cm across.

4.4 THE FINDS

No finds or human bone survive from the Neolithic burial found in 1966. Indeed, the reasoning behind Lawrence Butler's positive attribution of the burial of the Neolithic period is not understood; there is very little material of Neolithic date from north-west Northamptonshire (RCHME 1981). Elsewhere on the site, some 186 worked flints were recovered from this trench and there was also a single undated human tooth in the topsoil (see Chapter 10). The flints were considered to be Bronze Age in date (see Figure 8.1). Other than these, the overwhelming majority of the objects found on the excavation was medieval in date. No evidence was found for more permanent post-medieval occupation of Croft 29 although there was a mid-16th-century coin in the topsoil (coin number 6, Chapter 8) together with a 17th-century rumbler bell and a bridle bell (see Figure 8.5, nos 33 and 34), a fragment of post-medieval whetstone, clay pipes and a 19th-century lead whistle (see Figure 8.6, no. 35). The pattern of conjoining sherds (see Figure 7.33) all indicates some later disturbance.

Three coins were found in significant stratigraphical locations. Two short cross pennies (nos 3 and 4 in the catalogue in Chapter 8) would have circulated in the first half of the 13th century. They were found close together in 'rubbish layers' (grid FF9; Figure 4.4) to the east of the known buildings. The extent of these middens is clearly pinpointed by the distribution plots of pottery across the croft (see Figure 7.32). The coins both relate to Butler's Phase 1 of the site. A third coin, numbered 5 and badly burnt, is later in date and recovered from the hearth of Building A3/A4 (grid F21; Figures 4.23 and 4.31). It is a long cross halfpenny minted in 1335–43 (Figure 8.2). Its date, in the middle of the 14th century, minted before the Black Death and associated with the abandonment of the building and the croft, was highly suggestive to the excavator and key to dating the end of Building A3.

Other medieval objects recovered in 1966 are in many respects what might be expected from an excavation on the site of a later medieval croft, but there are some intriguing differences too. There is the usual range of objects associated with the preparation and serving of food. Other than the ubiquitous pottery, of which more than 11,500 sherds were recovered (see Chapter 7), there is a metal tripod leg (Figure 8.3, no. 3), probably from a cauldron, which was found in the yard west of the medieval buildings. The three stone pot lids (Figure 8.15, no. 106; Figure 8.17, nos 111 and 112) probably kept liquids covered and there was both a flint pestle (Figure 8.15, no. 107) and an imported quern fragment of possible 13th century date (Figure 8.15, no. 110), probably used for grinding. Knives in the later medieval period are multi-functional but the two iron knives (Figure 8.8, nos 54 and 56), three bone knife handles and a knife terminal (Figure 8.12, nos 73, 75, 76 and 78) might all have been found inside the home. They were probably sharpened on one of the whetstones of which a number were recovered in 1966 (Figure 8.15, nos 91, 95, 96, 97,

99, 103). There was also a key (Figure 8.4, no. 16), probably for a chest to store more valuable items and, more unusually, part of a candlestick (Figure 8.10, no. 69).

More personal items include two finger rings (Figure 8.3, nos 6 and 7), a strap end (Figure 8.3, no. 9), three copper-alloy buckle plates (one gilded) and a buckle and plate (Figure 8.5, nos 26, 28, 29, 31), and a pair of tweezers (Figure 8.4, no. 15) found in the fill of F6, the corn drier dated to Phase 4 of the site (c.1350–1400; Figure 4.31). Only the gilded buckle plate in this list hints at something less ordinary, but it is clear the building itself was not wholly utilitarian. A decorative door strap shows that the house fittings were not all merely functional (Figure 8.9, no. 59) and a roof finial (Figure 9.4, no. 155) suggests that the occupants of Croft 29 were of higher social standing. An undated rosary bead (Figure 8.14, no. 88) was also found in the topsoil.

Turning now to the activities which might have been carried out on the croft, there is a range of agricultural tools and equipment in the form of a gouge chisel (Figure 8.10, no. 62), an iron lynch pin (Figure 8.8, no. 52), a flat iron ring (Figure 8.10, no. 63), a bucket mount (Figure 8.10, no. 67) and a nail with its socket (Figure 8.10, no. 68). The presence of sheep is indicated by a spindlewhorl with dot-and-ring decoration (Figure 8.13, no. 84) and a smoother (Figure 8.15, no. 100). One item originally identified as a weaving needle is more likely to be a toggle (Figure 8.12, no. 77). In addition, there were certainly horses frequenting the site and probably stabled nearby. The finding of a curry comb (Figure 8.9, no. 61) suggests this, while three iron buckles may have been harness straps for horses (Figure 8.8, nos 47–49) and there were also two spurs (Figure 8.9, nos 57 and 58) and a bridle bit. Sheep and horses are topics to which we will return again in Chapter 10 when the faunal remains are discussed.

FIGURE 4.9

Croft 29 1966. Building A2, looking north. Dated to c.1250–1300 by the excavator. For plan, see Figure 4.8

FIGURE 4.10

Croft 29 1966. Building A2, looking south with walls 18 and 19 in the foreground. For plan, see Figure 4.8

FIGURE 4.11

Croft 29 1966. Building A2 in the foreground. Trench about to be extended north to catch Building 4. For plan, see Figure 4.8

75

FIGURE 4.12

Croft 29 1966. View from the west with yard in foreground. Building A2, 'bake-oven' (F8) and corn drier (F6) under excavation beyond. For plan, see Figure 4.8

FIGURE 4.13

Croft 29 1966. Circular 'bake-oven' (F8) and corn drier (F6) to the east (right). Looking north-east. For plan, see Figure 4.8; for reconstructions, see Figure 4.35

FIGURE 4.14

Croft 29 1966. Circular 'bake-oven' (F8) and corn drier (F6) behind. Looking east. For plan, see Figure 4.8; for reconstructions, see Figure 4.35

FIGURE 4.15

Croft 29 1966. Circular 'bake-oven' (F8) at an early stage of excavation. For plan, see Figure 4.17

FIGURE 4.16
Croft 29 1966. Circular 'bake-oven' (F8) at an advanced stage of excavation. For plan, see Figure 4.18

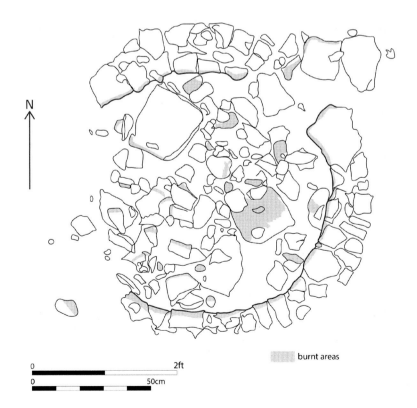

N

2ft

50cm

burnt areas

FIGURE 4.17
Croft 29 1966. Circular 'bake-oven' (F8) at an early stage of excavation. On-site drawing showing burnt stones in the interior. Further consideration is given to this feature in Chapter 11

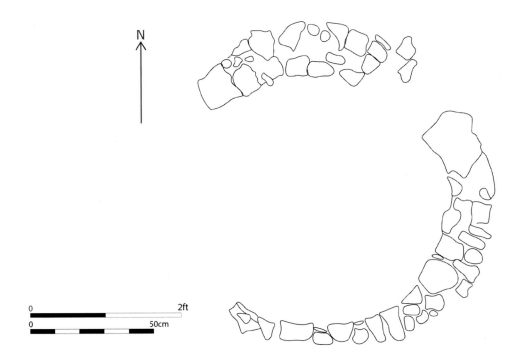

FIGURE 4.18
Croft 29 1966. Circular 'bake-oven' (F8) after excavation. On-site drawing showing structure

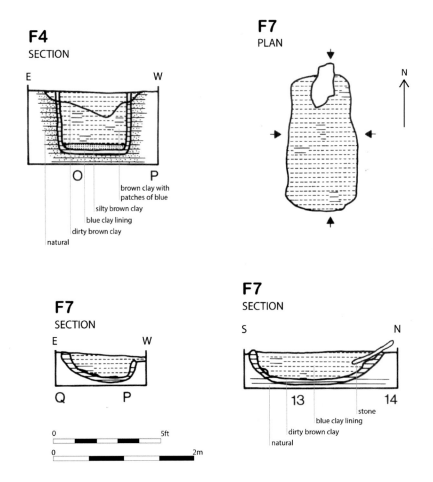

FIGURE 4.19
Croft 29 1966. Water troughs

FIGURE 4.20
Croft 29 1966. Phase 2 water trough/clay-lined pit (F4)

FIGURE 4.21
Croft 29 1966. Looking south along east wall of houses. 'Bake-oven' top left. Area of Barn E in the foreground, north-east corner of Building A2 visible beyond the excavators

HH 8-11
SECTION

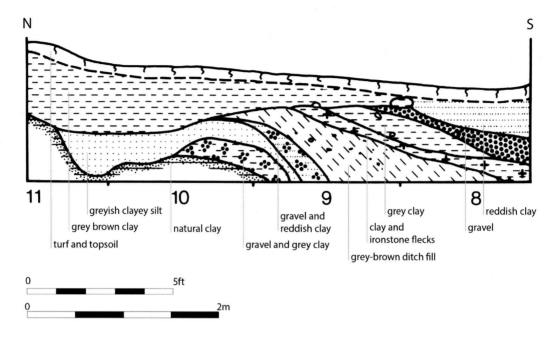

FIGURE 4.22

Croft 29 1966. Section HH 8-11. Note the layering of dumped material in this part of the site

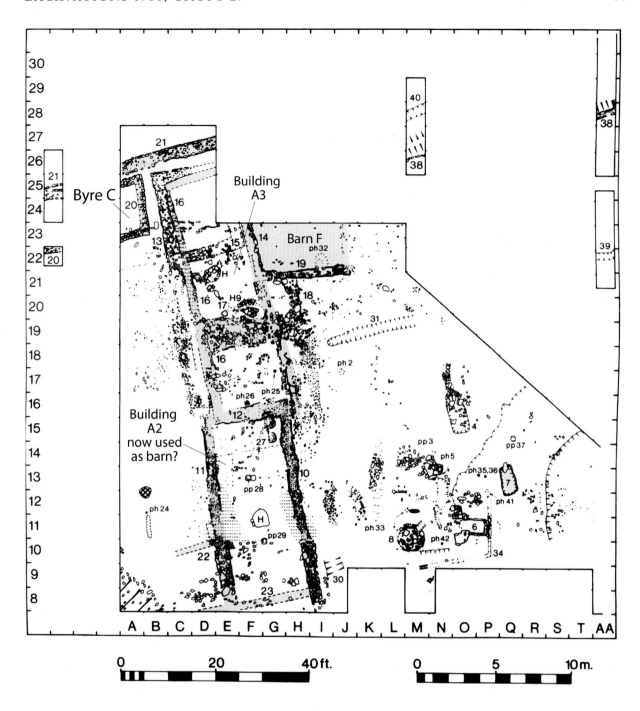

FIGURE 4.23

Croft 29 1966. Phase 3 Building A3 with Barn F and water trough F7. Building A2 was possibly still in use at this time. Dated to c.1300–1350 by the excavator

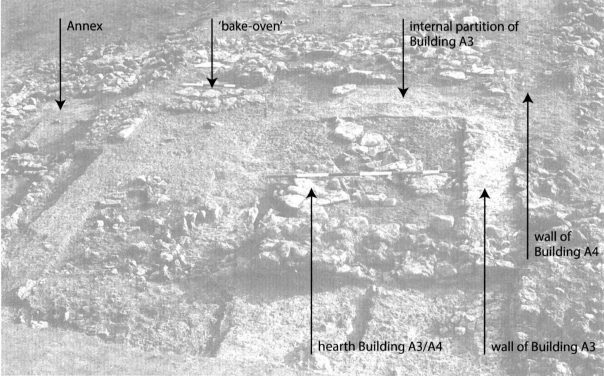

FIGURE 4.24

Croft 29 1966. Detail of walls in Building A3 (c.1300–1350). Coin evidence (Chapter 8) suggested that the hearth ceased to be used before the Black Death

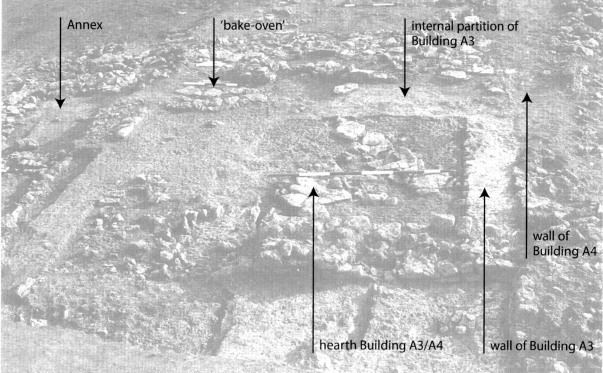

FIGURE 4.25
Croft 29 1966. Wall of Buildings A3 and A4 with Building A2 beyond

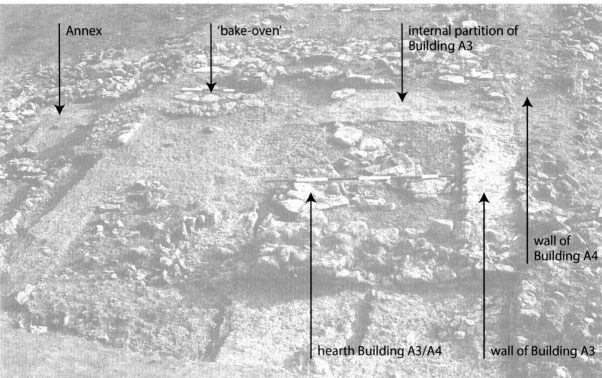

FIGURE 4.26
Croft 29 1966. Walls of Buildings A3 and A4

FIGURE 4.27

Croft 29 1966, looking south-west. Buildings A3 and A4 showing fire-pit, later replaced by the paved hearth area shown in Figure 4.28 and visible here on the left of the photograph

FIGURE 4.28

Croft 29 1966. Buildings A3 and A4 showing paved hearth

AA 21-33
SECTION

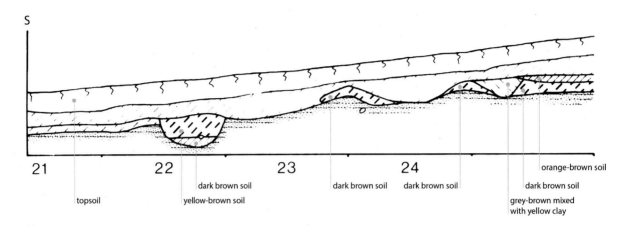

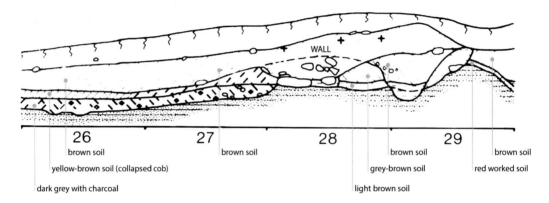

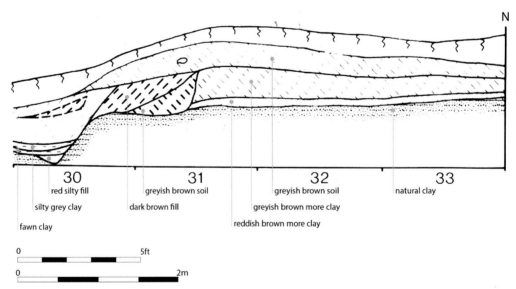

FIGURE 4.29
Croft 29 1966. Section AA 21-33

JJ 29-34
SECTION

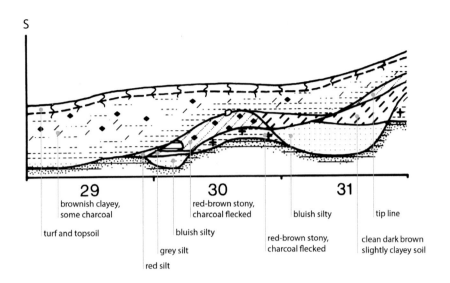

S

29
brownish clayey,
some charcoal

turf and topsoil

30
red-brown stony,
charcoal flecked

bluish silty

grey silt

red silt

bluish silty

red-brown stony,
charcoal flecked

31

tip line

clean dark brown
slightly clayey soil

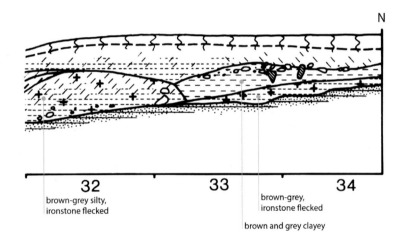

N

32
brown-grey silty,
ironstone flecked

33

brown and grey clayey

brown-grey,
ironstone flecked

34

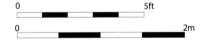

0   5ft

0   2m

FIGURE 4.30
Croft 29 1966. Section JJ 29-34

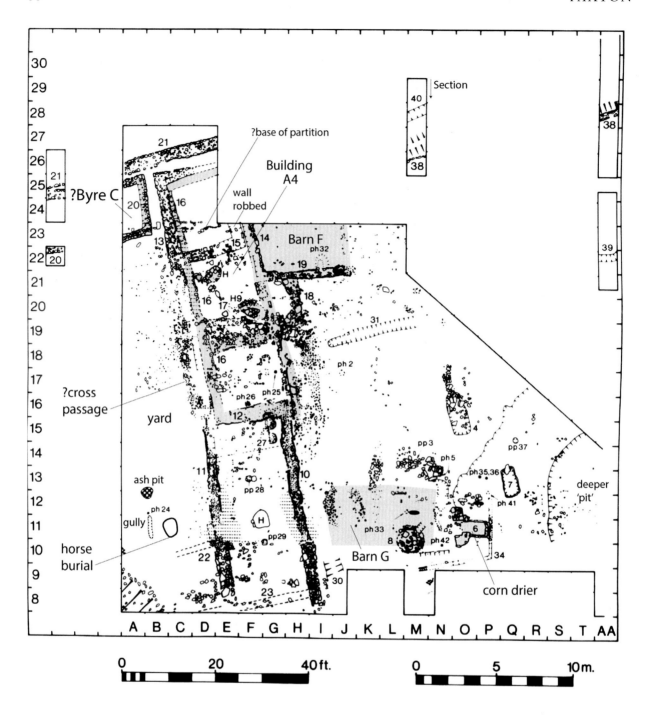

FIGURE 4.31

Croft 29 1966. Phase 4 Building A4 and associated Byre C, Barns F and G and corn drier (F6). Dated to c.1350 by the excavator and thought to be abandoned in the early 15th century. The latest date for Phase 4 is now revised to the mid-late 16th century (see Chapters 11 and 12)

FIGURE 4.32

Photo-montage to show details of interior of Building A3 with hearth centre and bake-oven (H9) under the centre ranging pole. Site in the latter stages of excavation

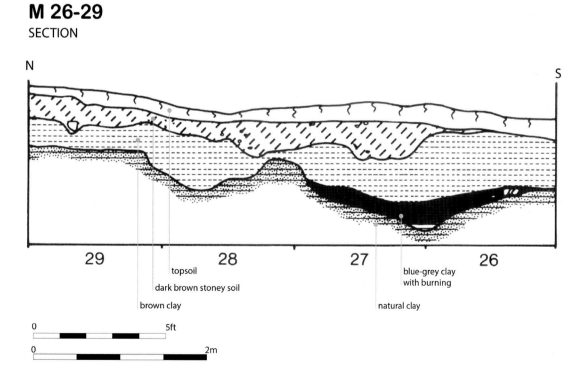

FIGURE 4.33

Croft 29 1966. Section M 26-29

FIGURE 4.34
Croft 29 1966. Corn drier (F6)

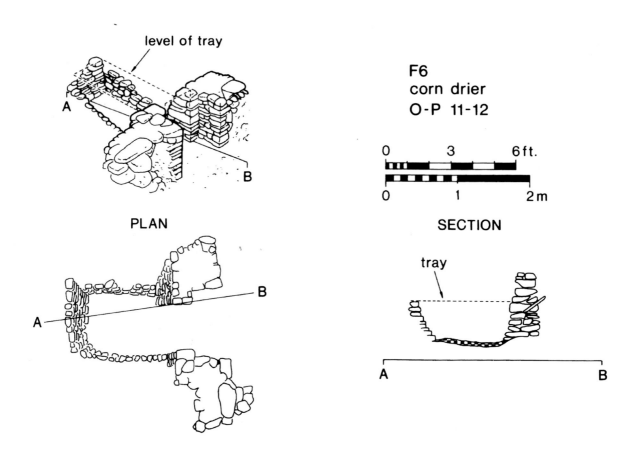

FIGURE 4.35
Corn drier (F6). Plan, section and isometric view

FIGURE 4.36
1966. Road section between Croft 29 and Croft 51, looking north

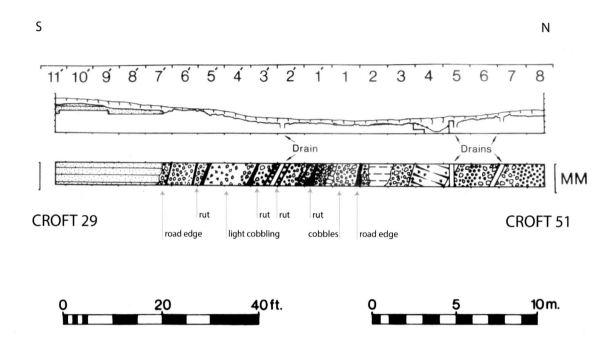

FIGURE 4.37

1966. Section and plan of road between Croft 29 and Croft 51, marked in the 1764 estate map as the 'road to Old'

5

EXCAVATIONS AT THE NORTH-WEST OF THE VILLAGE IN 1967 (CROFTS 6–9)

Christopher Gerrard and Lawrence Butler

This account of the 1967 excavations at Faxton has been assembled from three different sources: handwritten notes left by Lawrence Butler, an interim report to the DMVRG, and the excavator's 1968 Current Archaeology article (Butler 1968b). It is the least satisfactory of the three years of excavation accounts. Only an early list of four stratigraphical 'phases' now survives and all features such as ditches and their fills lack descriptions, though they are numbered on the bromide figures. None of the original on-site plans can now be found but some detail can be rescued by returning to the excavation photographs, which once again provide valuable coverage. For example, the period phase plans can be linked for the most part to the draft stratigraphical listing and from this it is possible to see how the interpretation for Figure 5.23 was arrived at. Features on the excavation photographs can sometimes be matched up and there are also inked-up, but mostly unnumbered, section drawings. In spite of many attempts to do so, it has proved impossible to relate the phased plans to the highly abbreviated text on the 'houses' which Butler wrote for Current Archaeology in 1968.

The choice for the second year of excavation in 1967 was a group of four crofts (6–9) at the north-west edge of the village along 'North Street' leading to Rothwell, Orton and on to Harrington (Figures 5.1A and B). These crofts were selected because they were separated from Crossroads Farm by a green lane to the field's east and another to the south; there was a steep drop into the field called Spinney Lays on its west side but it continued as a plateau into the same field to the north. Winter fieldwalking to the north had found little evidence of medieval pottery in plough soil/mole hills which suggested either that there was no settlement in that field or that it had been ploughed at sufficiently frequent intervals to disperse the material evidence. The chosen field had been under pasture for a considerable time. There was no evidence of housing on the 1746 estate map (Figure 3.1) nor on any OS maps, but the 1955 air photograph (Figure 5.1A) shows evidence of broad-ridge ploughing and indicated five ditches running east–west and deepening to the west. In the initial identification of the crofts it was assumed that four crofts occupied that area (see Figure 3.6 for croft numbering) with Croft 8 being drained by a central ditch and divided on the north by a deeper ditch. However, these surface indications proved an unreliable indicator of sub-surface features and, apart from the southernmost ditch between Crofts 6 and 7, they are best interpreted as field divisions relating to later cultivation or paddocks. Although the ground was slightly higher at the eastern edge, there were no prominent house platforms nor

indeed any satisfactory prior indication of medieval settlement.

The alternative choices for excavation were twofold (Figure 3.6): Crofts 1–5 where it was known that there had been post-medieval housing though there was the probability that the croft layout pre-dated the construction of the moated homestead. Otherwise Crofts 11–16 were likely to provide evidence of the type of housing situated on the north side of The Green. However, there was a strong probability of disturbance by post-medieval house construction and subsequent quarrying for building materials to recycle in housing and road-mending. Crofts 11 and 12 were contour surveyed, but this exercise did not prove particularly informative. The backs of Crofts 10–16, which were in different ownership in 1966, were well preserved and not threatened. This was also the case with the back lane which separated the village crofts from the common field headlands in Cliffesdale furlong and was in 1966 a prominent 'hollow-way' (shown on Figure 3.5).

On this basis, the area of Crofts 6–9 was chosen as the location for the 1967 excavation (Figure 5.1B). Unfortunately, this field was inadvertently ploughed and sown though the unripe wheat crop was taken off part of the field before excavation started in July. A letter in the archive (25 May 1966) states that Butler was:

> surprised to find that the northern part of the site at the west has been bulldozed and sown; this is the whole part of Spinney Lays and prevents any excavation at all on this part of the site, I saw [the

Crofts 6-9

FIGURE 5.1A

This oblique aerial photograph, taken in 1955, looks south-east across Faxton. In the right foreground are Crofts 6–9 and Crossroads Farm. Beyond lie The Green with the church and Rectory on its south side. The light reflects off the water in the moat on the extreme right-hand side of the picture. Reproduced with permission of the Cambridge University Collection of Aerial Photography © Copyright reserved.

landowner] and expressed my disappointment that he had needed to plough this when he promised us in December (1964) that he would leave it. His attitude was that his needs were greater than ours.

This ploughing had disturbed the topsoil to a depth of 9 inches (23cm) and appeared to have penetrated more deeply than any previous cultivation. However, since only this one ploughing had occurred within living memory in this century, it was decided to continue and to record all finds, particularly of pottery, on the assumption that they had not been dragged very far from their original place of deposition. As it turned out, a single ploughing *had* been sufficient to disturb the flimsy house remains at their upper levels and the evidence of structures

from these four crofts is, as a consequence, less satisfactory than the evidence obtained in the 1966 and 1968 seasons. Once more, because of the crop sown on the western half of the field, it was not possible to section the five ditches further west nor to check the profiles of the other ditches that were subsequently discovered, especially those on the northern area of the field (ditches 166, 169, 173 and 174; see Figure 5.6) which did not appear on the air photographs.

5.1 EXCAVATIONS IN CROFTS 6–9

The excavations in 1967 took place between 3 July and 12 August 1967, a six-week period. By contrast with 1966 when one croft had been subjected to

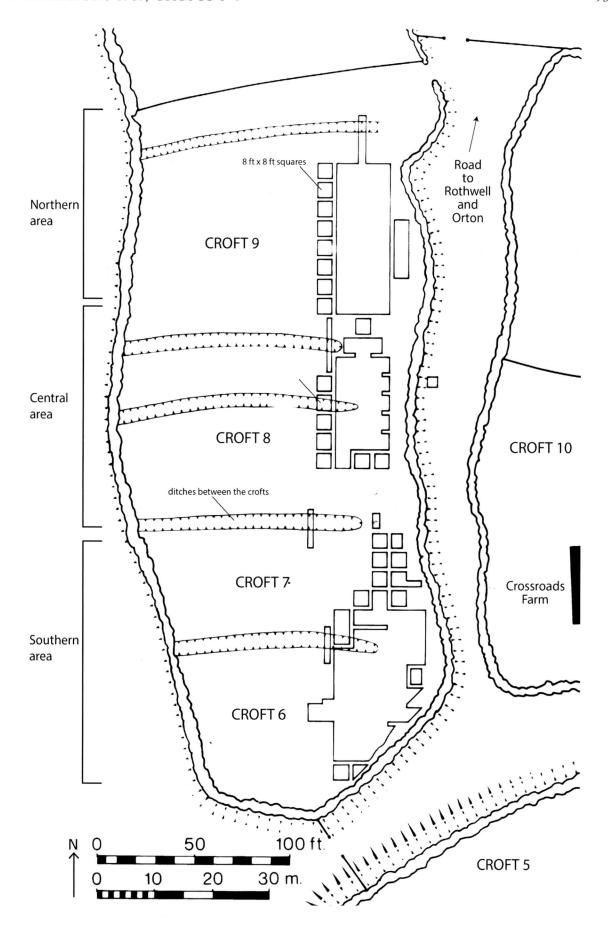

labels within figure:
8 ft x 8 ft squares

Northern area

CROFT 9

Road to Rothwell and Orton

Central area

CROFT 8

CROFT 10

ditches between the crofts

CROFT 7

Crossroads Farm

Southern area

CROFT 6

N   0   50   100 ft.

0   10   20   30 m.

CROFT 5

FIGURE 5.1B

Crofts 6–9 1967 showing location of the excavations at the north-west corner of the village. Note the grid of 8ft sq trenches with 2ft baulks which were then opened out in areas of greatest interest intensive investigation, Lawrence Butler saw 1967 as an opportunity to excavate an entire village street (Faxton tape 1). Originally, after the 1966 season came to end, Butler had not wished to commit himself to returning to Faxton (letter Butler to Hurst, 21 September 1966) and in February 1967 he visited several sites in the Midlands to assess them as alternatives. Two of these were in Leicestershire, at Cotes de Val and Knaptoft, and another two in Warwickshire, at Chapel Ascote and Hodnell. Writing to Hurst on 6 February 1967, Butler concluded that 'none of these sites seem to offer such good opportunities for village study as Faxton'. By now more persuaded of the benefits of a further season, the 1967 excavation at Faxton duly went ahead.

The aim would be to recover house types and examine their relation to the village street and to each other. Four crofts out of a group of six were subsequently stripped down to the natural within an area 320 by 50ft (98 x 15m) (Figure 5.1B). The excavation was tackled entirely by hand. Although the field had been ploughed, manual excavation enabled information to be recovered which would have been lost by mechanical removal of the topsoil (Figures 5.2 and 5.3). The excavated area was the strip closest to the street in the four crofts; the margin of the excavation at the east being taken as close to the hedge line as possible but it was found that recent bulldozing had pushed the earlier hedge bank into the hedge bottom (Figure 5.1B). The hedge bank was formed of house tumble. Therefore the excavation concentrated on the house area in each croft and used the inner garden area for dumping spoil while the outer garden area remained under corn. One test pit (4ft square; 1.2m) was opened on the edge of the green lane leading north to Rothwell, but there was no indication of occupation and only a 2 inch (5cm) layer of road metalling. Two sections cut across the road ditches south of Croft 6 showed that they had been regularly re-cut in recent times; their up-cast included modern pottery assumed to be from the adjacent farms to the east and south-east (no further detail is recorded).

It appears no description of the work on site in 1967 was ever fully written up by the excavator. The following account of the site's phasing has been recovered from a handwritten list of features originally created 'in order to understand better the sequence of occupation', together with a set of phased plans. These include many excavated features which are numbered in a single sequence 1–98 though any clue as to what they might represent has to be deduced by combining the plans with multiple un-labelled slides. Finally, there is a helpful summary figure for the site as a whole (see Figure 5.23), although this was originally un-labelled and less clear, it does now show the major buildings for each of four defined phases (A1, A2, A3, A4–B). In addition, there are 10 labelled section drawings for 1967, labelled S1 to S10 with their locations marked up on the plans. These sections also have layer/context numbers (Figures 5.18–5.22).

5.2   THE EXCAVATED SEQUENCE

The boundary ditches

One of the key questions of the 1967 excavations was how boundary ditches between the crofts might change over time. In every case the east–west ditches between the crofts showed minor variations in their alignments, a feature also noted in 1966 in Croft 29. An east–west section through the house area was extended eastwards to the centre of the ditch separating the house from the street: in three houses this showed a dangerously abrupt dip from the house into the street ditch; this was the result of gradual cutting back of the ditch to drain both house and street area (Butler 1968b; for example, see Section S7, Figure 5.21).

The houses/crofts

In general, all Butler's marginalia imply that he saw closely superimposed sequences of buildings in all the crofts he excavated in 1967. These, he thought, ranged in date from c.1150 to 1300. As he commented in a letter to John Hurst on 21 August 1967, 'it will be very difficult to get internal arrangements absolutely clear for any one house and I suspect that there will be too many phases with only two and not four walls'. Butler also observed that not all houses were parallel to the tracks/streets.

Phase 1 (A4–B) c.1150–1200

In the earliest phases of the site, in the 'southern area' of Crofts 6 and 7, there were three main buildings in c.1150 (Figure 5.4). They were: Buildings 13, 14 and 20. Building 13, in the south-east corner of the site, measured 4 by 8.5m. It comprised walls and post-holes numbered 126, 121, 117, 116, 115, 111, 106, 9, 107, 124 and a hearth (H) with an annex to the west delimited by post-holes 103, 102, 104, 105 and 109. Building 14, orientated north–south, lay immediately to the north-east. This building comprised walls and post-holes 138, 139, 134, 130, 123, 122, 127, 128, 133, 132 and 137 and measured 4 by 6.5m. Both of these structures lay within the bounds of Croft 6. Building 20, which was only partially excavated, was located to the north-west in Croft 7.

Phase 2 (Layer A3) c.1200–1250

In the southern area there was little change 50 years later in Phase 2 (Figure 5.4). The annex to Building 13 was removed, but this structure and Building 14 remained standing on this southern part of the site. Building 20 was removed and two new

FIGURE 5.2
Crofts 6–9 1967, southern area. In the foreground the baulks have been removed

FIGURE 5.3
Crofts 6–9 1967. Looking north. Crofts 6–7 in the foreground, Croft 8 in the middle ground and Croft 9 beyond. The ground slopes away to the east down to the former trackway leading to Orton

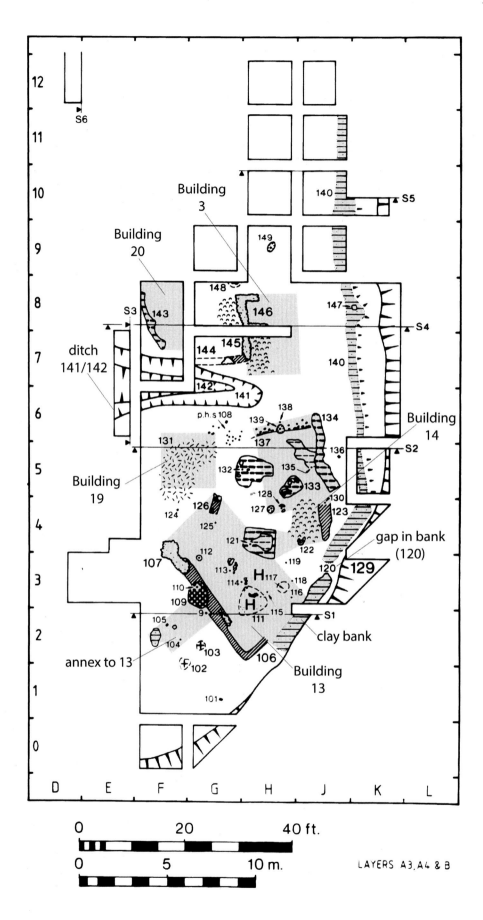

FIGURE 5.4

Crofts 6–9 1967, southern area, Layers A3, A4 and B. The excavator dated Building 20 to c.1150–1200; Buildings 13 and 14 to c.1150–1250; Building 19 to c.1200–1250, and Building 3 to c.1200–1350

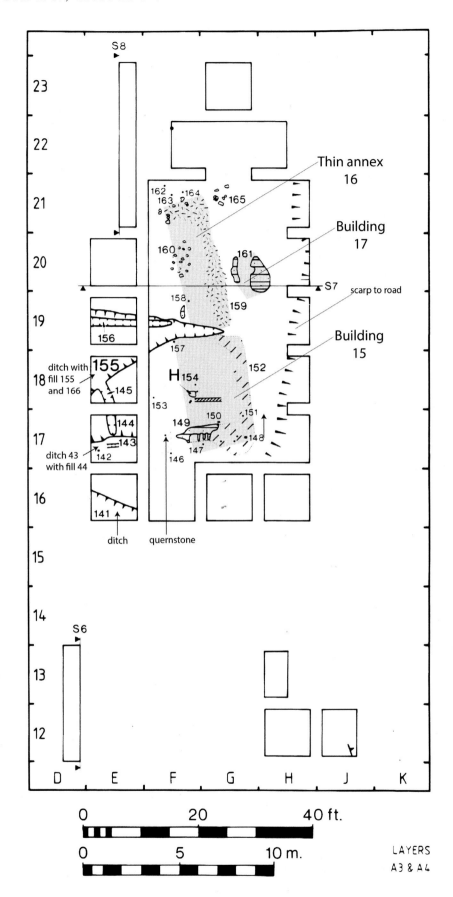

FIGURE 5.5

Crofts 6–9 1967, central area, Layers A3 and A4. Showing Buildings 15, 16 and 17. Dated to c.1200–1250 by the excavator

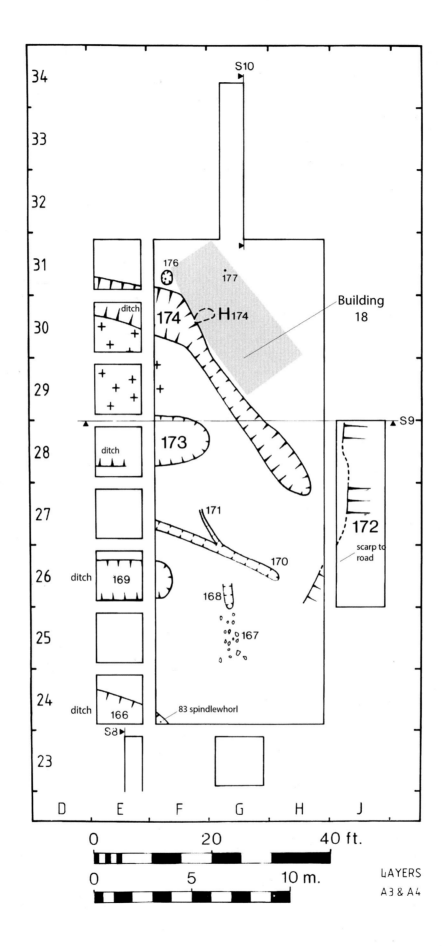

FIGURE 5.6

Crofts 6–9 1967, northern area, Layers A3 and A4. Showing Building 18 and ditches. Dated to c.1200–1250 by the excavator

structures built: Building 19, which had a metalled flooring cut through west–east by a post-medieval ditch or drain (not recorded), and Building 3 which may have had some sort of annex to the west. Only Building 13 had a hearth.

In the central area, the earliest buildings to appear on Croft 8 (Figure 5.5) were Building 15, with its hearth (H) and wall features 152, 151, 148, 147, 149 and 157. This building is very likely that described by Butler as having 'post-holes for timber uprights stuck into the natural clay and walls presumably of mud'. There was a narrow rectangular annex to the north, Building 16, consisting of 163, 164, 159, 158 and 169, with a small building to the east, labelled as a 'shed' and numbered 17. These three buildings measured 3.5 by 5m, 2.5 by 7m, and 2 by 3m respectively and were constructed roughly parallel to the frontage of the road running north out of the village.

In the northern area a single building was identified, Building 18, defined by post-holes 176 and 177 with hearth (H). This structure measured 3 by 7m (Figure 5.6). The rim of an upturned pot (see Figure 7.4, no. 23) was found *in situ* by the hearth here and appears to have been re-used. This standard Shelly Coarseware rim can be dated no more closely than 1100–1400 (Paul Blinkhorn pers. comm.).

Phase 3 (Layer A2) c.1250–1300

In Phase 3 of the site, the southern area presented a very different picture (Figure 5.7). Although Building 3 continued in use until the site was abandoned, with Building 4 at right angles to the west, the principal domestic structure, Building 13, was demolished and replaced by a new building to the north-west, Building 6. This building is defined by its north wall (26) and west wall (21) and a hearth (H) and measured 3.5 by 5.5m. To the south-east lay a smaller structure, Building 5, defined by its east wall (16) and a post-hole along its presumed south side (15). This appears to be on a similar footprint to the south end of Building 14. There is nothing evident on Figure 5.7 to suggest the large unnumbered rectangular building depicted on Figure 5.23 to the north of Building 3. Likewise the narrow Building 7, along the south-east perimeter of the plot (Figure 5.8), seems to comprise features assigned to Phase 1. Its measurements were interpreted as 3 by 11m. In this croft Butler saw evidence of variation in boundaries and what he termed 'a loss in identity' at this phase as buildings crossed between crofts.

In the central area of the site (Figure 5.9), further wall fragments survived to suggest the addition of Building 11, a long rectangular building measuring 3.5 by c.8m which was divided into two cells at its north end (Figure 5.10). This building, and the surviving Building 8 immediately to the north, lay on the same axis within Croft 8 above the scarp down onto the road to Orton (58) and overlapped

with buildings in Phase 2 (Buildings 15 and 16).

In the northern area (Figure 5.11) Building 18 no longer continued and was replaced by two buildings to the south on a different alignment, Buildings 12 and 13 (Figures 5.4). Building 12 was the larger of the two, measuring 3.5 by 5.5m. These structures lay close to the south boundary of Croft 9. Neither contained a hearth.

Phase 4 (Layer A1) c.1300–1350

Structures were recovered across all three of the excavated areas in Phase 1, the final phase of the site. In the southern area a total of four buildings was recovered (see Figure 5.7, where they are numbered 1 to 4), many in a very partial state of survival because of plough damage. Building 1, defined by walls 8, 5, 4 and 11, was orientated north-west to south-east and measured 4 by 8m; its south-east gable lay up against the perimeter wall (17/38) of Croft 6 (Figure 5.8). To the north-east lay Building 2 along the north–south boundary of the croft defined by walls 38, 23 and 34 but with no identified northern gable end. This building was interpreted as a three-cell structure measuring 4.5 by 13m with a heavy metalled floor. Immediately west lay two smaller structures, Buildings 3 and 4, measuring 3 by 4m and 3 by 6m respectively. Buildings 2, 3 and 4 all lie across the alignment suggested by Ditch 27 which separates Croft 6 from Croft 7. In this latest phase no hearths were recorded in the southern area of the excavations.

In the central area, Croft 8, a single building was identified (Figure 5.9). Building 8, made up of walls 61, 60, 64 and 67 and with hearth 65, measured 3 by 6.5m. Orientated north–south and parallel with the 'track to Orton' to the east, the excavator suggested a small annex in its south-east corner including post-hole 62. A wall, comprising 61, 56 and 53 ran along the east side of the building.

Finally, in the northern area of the site another building with a hearth (84) was identified (Figure 5.11). Building 9, comprising walls 83, 87 and 88 extended west out of the trench so its west gable end wall was not recovered. The width of the building was 3.5m by approximately 6m, orientated south-west/north-east up against Building 10 which had been constructed north–south. Its measurements were 4.5 by 6m, defined by walls 89, 81, 82 and 88. Figures 5.12 and 5.13 give a clear impression of how little remained to be excavated of Building 10 in Croft 9 and the difficulties of interpretation. In this case, for example, the tipped and angled stones of wall 82 photographed in Figure 5.14 might be alternatively understood as a drain and certainly bear no resemblance to its partner, wall 81, which was seen to be part of the same structure.

From the account above, there is little doubt that the 1967 excavations were extremely challenging. The area had been more seriously damaged by

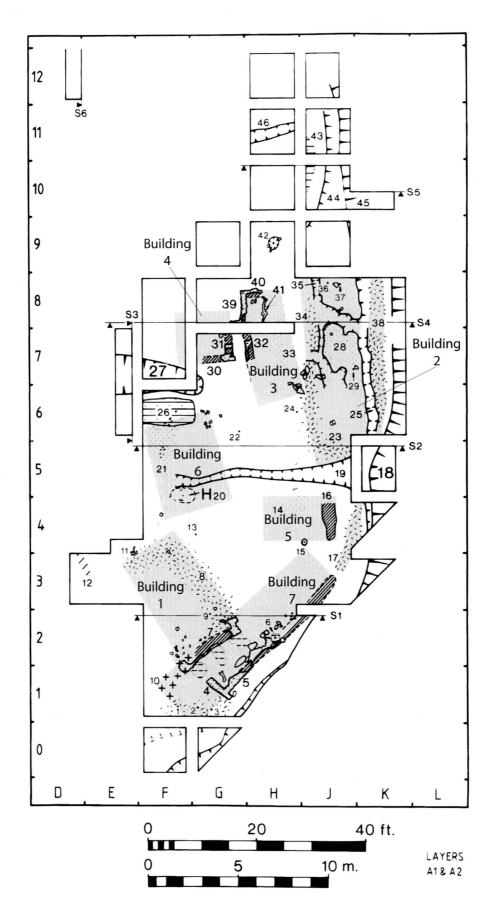

FIGURE 5.7

Crofts 6–9 1967, southern area, Layers A1 and A2. Building 3 was dated c.1200–1350 by the excavator; Buildings 5, 6 and 7 to c.1250–1300; Building 4 to c.1250–1350; and Buildings 1 and 2 to c.1300–1350

FIGURE 5.8

Photo-montage showing the 1967 excavations underway, looking north. In the foreground the southern area including Building 7 (right) and Building 1

ploughing than expected and the stratigraphy was shallow. Figure 5.15, for example, shows the southern area of the site under excavation with the walls of Building 7/13 exposed. The wall to the left of the ranging pole, at the edge of the slope, was interpreted as containing four phases of buildings dating between *c.*1150 and 1300. Yet the remains are ephemeral and many of the stones have been left high on plinths of soil. Although the alignment is certainly there, many of the individual stones have been removed or lifted into the topsoil by the plough. Figures 5.16 and 5.17 demonstrate another of the challenges on this site, the presence of spreads of metalling with closely spaced stones divided by straight lines of blank soil. In Figure 5.16 the photograph has captured the remains of Building 19 in Phase 2 of the site, dated to *c.*1200. Two observations might be made. First, the walls of the building are not visible because they were constructed of cob or 'unshuttered earthen walling'. Second, the stratigraphy is once again very shallow and the difficulties of dating Building 19 to *c.*1200, rather than *c.*1250 or *c.*1150, on the basis of fragmented pottery scatters which have been ploughed through, are evident. That would have been the case no matter how carefully the site was excavated, and there is every indication it was unpicked with great care, even if many of the records have subsequently been lost. Figure 5.17, for example, shows the completed excavation of a 'shallow base pad' which would have been barely visible in these disturbed layers.

Fortunately, a number of sections were also recorded across the site and, in the absence of any other stratigraphical descriptions or explanation behind the sequence of layers, these are essential for further interpretation. Five sections were recorded across the southern area (S1–S5). S1, the southernmost section west–east (Figure 5.18), demonstrates the shallow, largely horizontal, stratigraphy across the site in this area and indicates each of the layers described above, A4 to A1, Phases 1 to 4. This section shows that the west wall of Building 13 (Phases 1 and 2) is earlier than the south wall of Building 7 (Phase 2). S2, a parallel section about 30ft (9m) further north, indicates the metalling inside Building 19, the east wall of Building 14 and the wall running down the east side of the croft; the section indicates that these are contemporary. S2 also shows the fall in the ground surface towards the east and its filling in and building up at a later date. This suggests that the road to Orton has in the past shifted its alignment slightly and that the west side of the road was once terraced down before the wall down the east side of the croft was first constructed. Effectively, Croft 6 has 'gained' ground on its east edge. S4 and S5, east–west sections further to the north, both show a similar profile to the croft edge on the eastern limit of the section (Figure 5.19). S4 also picks up both the west and east wall of Building 2 in Phase 4 and the Building 3 which was only partially excavated and appears, from the section, to represent walls of different date. Thus

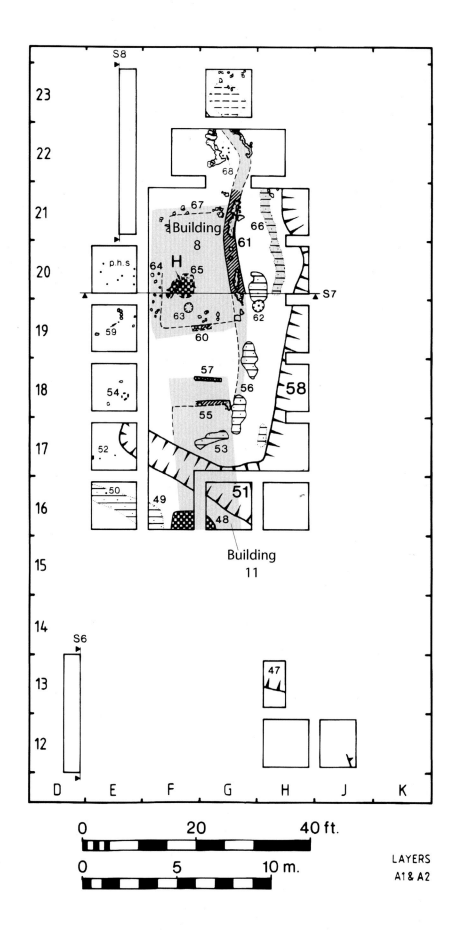

Figure 5.9

Crofts 6–9 1967, central area, Layers A1 and A2. Showing Buildings 8 and 11 dated by the excavator to c.1250–1350 and c.1250–1300+

FIGURE 5.10
Crofts 6–9 1967. Croft 8, central area, looking north, showing features in Layers A1 and A2 including 57, 60, 61, 65. These features are located in Figure 5.9. Building 8 (c.1250–1350) delineated by 60, 61 with hearth 65; Building 11 (c.1250–1300) by 55 and 57

wall 39, which appears in plan on Figure 5.7, post-dates the more substantial wall 146. S3, running north–south to catch the boundary between Crofts 6 and 7, shows a series of at least three re-cuts of the boundary ditch, moving fractionally north on each occasion (Figure 5.20)

In the 'central area' of Croft 8 three more sections were drawn (S6–8). S6 shows little detail except for a boundary ditch with Croft 7 (Figure 5.20). The same alignment appears to be re-cut on several occasions. S7 once again illustrates the ground surface falling away at the eastern edge of the croft and a sequence of fills (Figure 5.21). To the west, the interior surfaces of both Building 17 and Building 16 can be seen to be contemporary in Phase 2 (c.1200) while the east and west walls of Building 8 lie above and higher in the stratigraphy. This again provides support for the phasing as proposed by Lawrence Butler. S8, a north–south section in the north-west corner of the 'central area' only indicates a series of features, including a substantial boundary ditch at the northern edge of the Croft 8 dividing with Croft 9 (Figure 5.20).

Finally, there are two sections in the 'northern area' (S9–10). S9 runs east–west across Croft 9 (Figure 5.22). It shows a considerable falling away of the ground surface at the east edge of the croft and its subsequent infilling. These fills are not mentioned elsewhere, nor were they photographed. To the west, the shallow V-shaped profile of the early ditch (174) can be seen together with various structural elements of Building 10 in Phase 4 such as the west

wall and an internal partition. The stratigraphy in this northern part of the site remained very shallow. Section S10 is recorded on the plans but does not appear to have been inked up.

5.3 THE HOUSES

In his summary of the results from 1967, Lawrence Butler tackled the change from clay-and-timber building to stone construction and questioned whether this was a uniform sequence across the site (Butler 1968b). He concluded that 'the sequence of events in the four crofts was (a) a building with post-holes for timber uprights sunk into the natural clay and walls presumably of mud; (b) a building with a timber framework resting on a horizontal sill beam for which the sleeper trench still remained; (c) a building either timber-framed or mud-walled standing on a low foundation of boulders, pebbles and ironstone; (d) a building similar to (c) but standing on a more substantial foundation of well chosen ironstone and limestone slabs. Although this sequence occurs in full or in part in all four crofts there is no certainty that stage (c) in one croft is contemporary with stage (c) in others. What was true for one house was not necessarily true for its neighbour'. These buildings of different construction were not discussed further nor identified on any plans.

Figure 5.23 is the excavator's phased plan, here re-drawn and enlarged, which aims to summarise the information for the plots by phase. All the houses identified in 1967 were rectangular in plan, varying in length between 40 and 60ft (13–20m) and in breadth between 15 and 24ft (5–8m); fireplaces were central or only slightly off centre, with a subsidiary hearth in one house and an external hearth area in another. The hypothesis that there were animals living within the house in a byre at a lower end was carefully considered because evidence from nearby Wythemail had previously suggested the existence of 'long-houses'. However, the drains at Faxton could not have served such a purpose and, for that reason, Butler stressed that a variety of house types within a small geographical radius is another feature of medieval village life (Butler 1968b).

Other features noted by the excavator included the presence of metal slag (not collected) which hinted at domestic metal-working nearby though not within the excavated houses. Another was the question of how to recognise fallen or destroyed walls made of clay or cob (Butler 1968b). In all house areas, the spread of mud walls was marked by a more concentrated scatter of flint, ironstone chippings and other strengthening materials (including earlier pottery). As we have seen above in Figure 5.17, minor post-holes were often only ½ inch (1.27cm) deep and were more in the nature of post base pads using compacted gravelly clay upon and earth floor.

5.4 THE FINDS

No prehistoric or Roman finds were recovered during the 1967 excavations, bar a single flint (see Figure 8.1, no. 114) which may have been an inclusion in later mud or cob-walling. There was also only a small handful of post-medieval finds, including two whetstones (Figure 8.15, nos 90 and 101) in the topsoil and occasional clay tobacco pipes (Figure 8.18, nos 125, 128, 129 and 133).

Lawrence Butler felt that the later medieval finds were of a different character to those found in Croft 29 in the previous year. There were no coins, for example, and few metal finds; Butler's suspicion was that they were more limited in their variety. A few dress accessories were found: a ring (Figure 8.3, no. 5), a belt fitting (Figure 8.3, no. 10), a belt end plate (Figure 8.4, no. 25), a buckle (not illustrated), a belt end strap (Figure 8.5, no. 32). There were knives too (Figure 8.8, nos 53 and 55), a bone knife handle (Figure 8.12, no. 74), and three whetstones (Figure 8.15, nos 92, 98 and 104). Indications of household activities included a spindlewhorl (Figure 8.13, no. 83) and a perforated pebble, perhaps a weight of some sort (Figure 8.15, no. 108), a pestle (Figure 8.15, no. 109) and a fragment of quern (not illustrated) for food preparation. Lighting inside the houses was indicated by a hasp with a loop, possibly a support for a candle holder (Figure 8.10, no. 70). A latch key (Figure 8.8, no. 45), two possible latches (one illustrated at Figure 8.8, no. 51), a barrel padlock

(Figure 8.11, no. 72), a barrel padlock key (Figure 8.8, no. 43) and four keys (one illustrated at Figure 8.8, no. 44) all suggest the need for security.

Otherwise, besides the iron-working residues which Butler made little comment upon, the artefacts all confirmed the presence of horses, carts and wagons and the daily bustle of agricultural life. There was, for example, a horse harness plate (Figure 8.3, no. 1), a ring and tag (Figure 8.4, no. 18), an iron buckle (Figure 8.8, no. 46), an awl (not illustrated), a horseshoe calkin (Figure 8.9, no. 60), part of a horseshoe (not illustrated), two joined chain links from a cart or harness (Figure 8.10, no. 64), and a swivel loop for a cart or harness (Figure 8.10, no. 71). Although fewer metal finds were recovered than in 1966, the ceramic assemblage from 1967 was significant, more than 20,000 sherds overall, but as Chapter 7 confirms, there had been a high level of post-depositional disturbance (see Figures 7.38–7.40) with many sherds (and presumably all other categories of artefact) being spread through the soil by the action of the plough. In one case, joining sherds from a single pot were found more than 18m apart; two parts of the barrel padlock were also separated. The excavator noted that the majority of the pottery was from the Lyveden kilns: coarsewares were numerous and glazed wares scarce. Stamford Ware was less frequent than in 1966, but there was a greater range in the coarsewares of non-local fabrics and rim forms (possibly dating from the period before Lyveden was fully operational or before it assumed its 13th-century characteristics).

Taken together, these finds are what might be expected of evidence for rural living in the later medieval period. Notably, smaller tools such as scythes and spades were not found and wooden artefacts have not survived; in 1967 no environmental sampling was undertaken. A possible fragment of chimney pot (Figure 9.4, no. 151) may perhaps be intrusive. Otherwise, the excavations produced fragmentary evidence of the dwellings, the byres and the stables for carts and draught animals such as horses (and presumably oxen), and outlined the boundaries of the crofts in which they had once stood. The overall impression of the excavator was that this was an area of rather poorer dwellings in contrast to Croft 29 and adjacent bulldozed crofts. Certainly its final desertion date was earlier than the majority of houses in 'East Street', but it was not a catastrophic desertion, rather a gradual ebb and flow of settlement along the street during the 13th and 14th centuries. Although no single croft was entirely exposed, the excavation was able to show the modifications of building and rebuilding in three conjoining crofts over a period of approximately 250 years. In spite of Butler's evident pessimism about the disturbance that had been caused by ploughing, the stratigraphy had survived rather well in places and rather better than on many medieval rural sites excavated since.

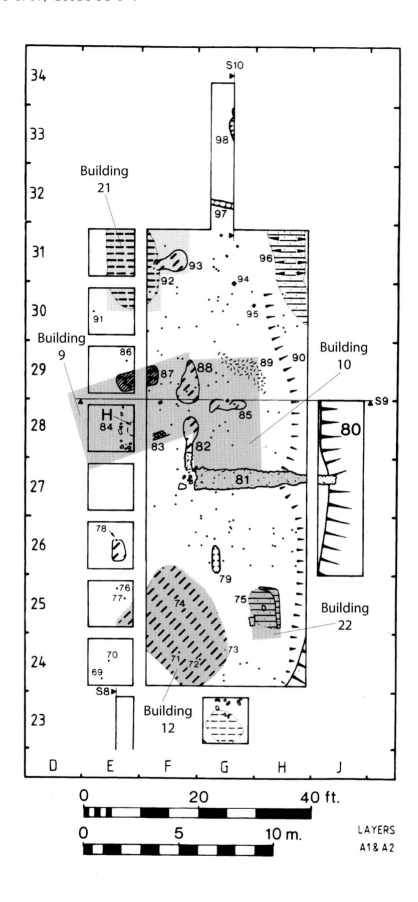

FIGURE 5.11

Crofts 6–9 1967, northern area, Layers A1 and A2. Showing Buildings 9, 10 and 21, dated c.1300–1350 by the excavator, and Buildings 12 and 22 dated c.1250–1300

FIGURE 5.12
Crofts 6–9 1967, northern area, looking north. Wall 81, south wall of Building 10 (c. 1300–1350)

FIGURE 5.13
Crofts 6–9 1967, northern area. Wall 81, south of Building 10 (c. 1300–1350)

FIGURE 5.14

Crofts 6–9 1967, northern area, looking north-east. Wall 82, west wall of Building 10 (c.1300–1350)

FIGURE 5.15

Crofts 6–9 1967, southern area, looking south towards the southern perimeter of the site. In the foreground is the east wall of Building 7 (c.1250–1300)

Figure 5.16
Crofts 6–9 1967, southern area, looking north-west. Building 19 (c.1200–1250) is under the ranging pole

Figure 5.17
Crofts 6–9 1967. A shallow 'post base pad', unrecorded. There were many challenges in 1967 identifying ephemeral features such as this on a plough-damaged site

2 F-J
SECTION 1

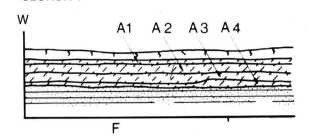

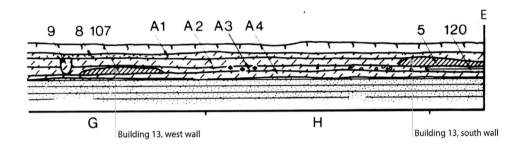

5 F-K
SECTION 2

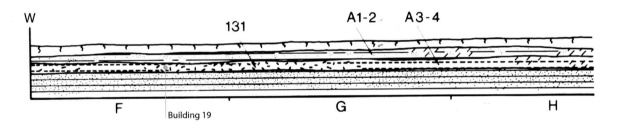

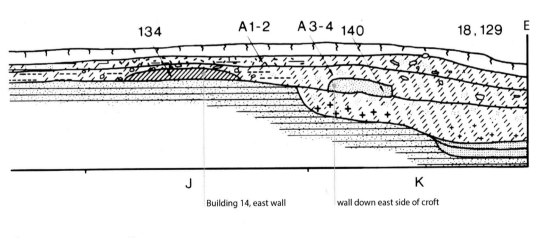

<small>FIGURE 5.18</small>

Crofts 6–9 1967. Sections S1 and S2

10 F-K
SECTION 4

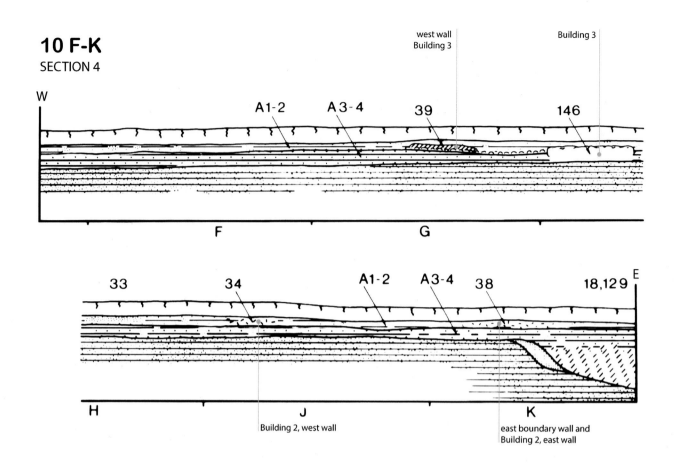

10 H-K
SECTION 5

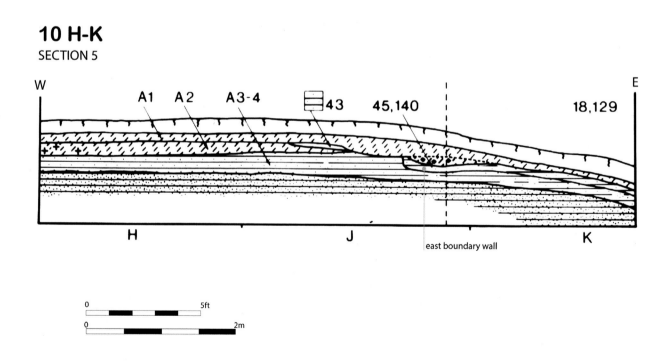

FIGURE 5.19

Crofts 6–9 1967. Sections S4 and S5

E 6-7

SECTION 3

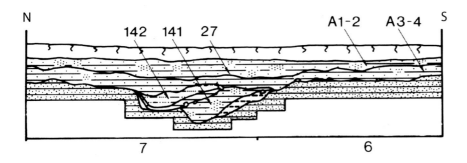

D 12-13

SECTION 6

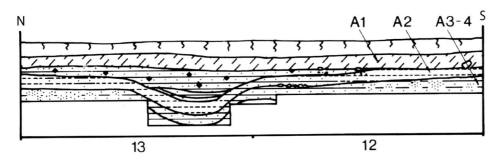

E 21-23

SECTION 8

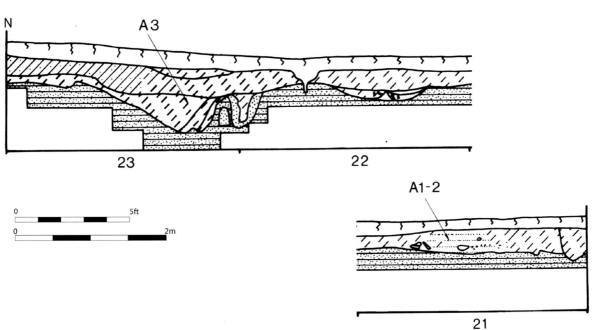

FIGURE 5.20

Crofts 6–9 1967. Sections S3, S6 and S8

20 E-H

SECTION 7

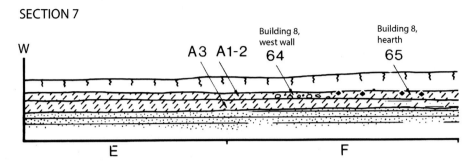

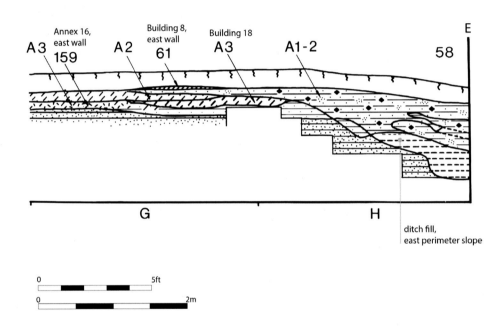

FIGURE 5.21
Crofts 6–9 1967. Section S7

29 E-J

SECTION 9

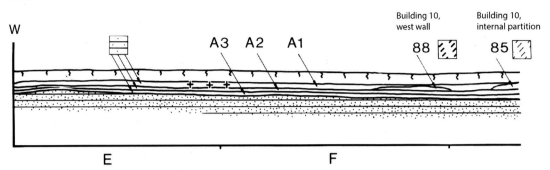

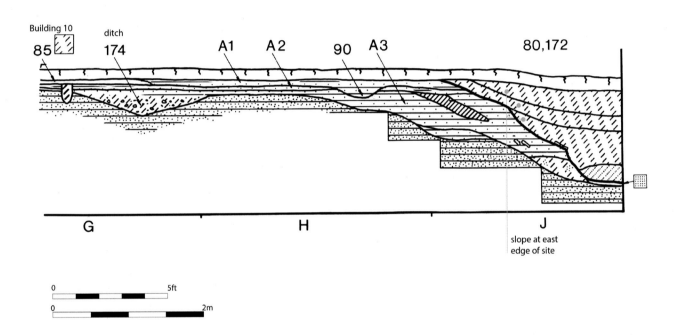

FIGURE 5.22
Crofts 6–9 1967. Section S9

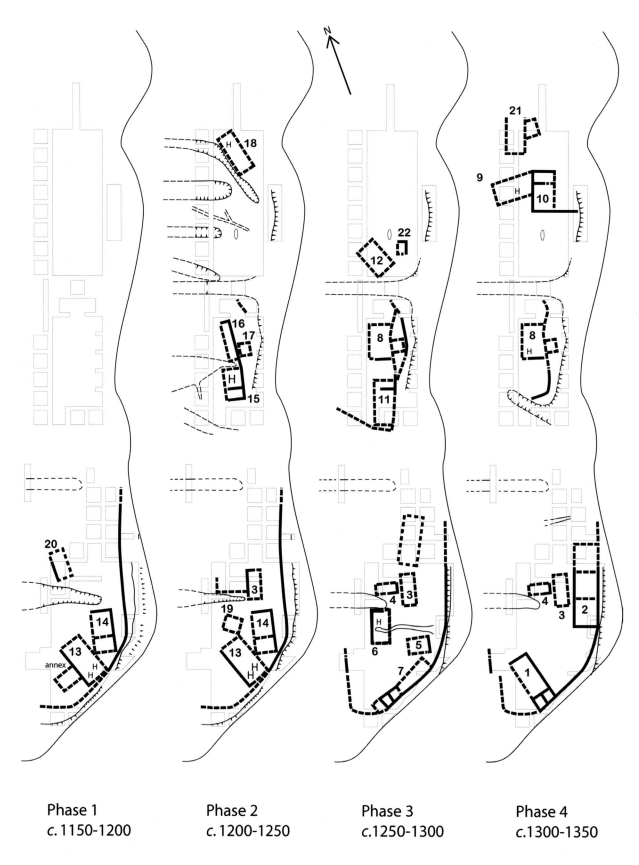

Phase 1
c. 1150-1200

Phase 2
c. 1200-1250

Phase 3
c. 1250-1300

Phase 4
c. 1300-1350

FIGURE 5.23
Summary phasing for Crofts 6–9 1967, Layers A1-B

6

EXCAVATIONS SOUTH OF
THE VILLAGE GREEN IN 1968 (CROFT 52–53)

Lawrence Butler

The most complete write-up of the three years of excavation at Faxton is for Croft 52–53 in 1968. Below Lawrence Butler's text is retained with only minor copy-edits and the addition of an introduction and a conclusion which were written up for other purposes by the excavator. This finalised text evidently supersedes that which circulated as an interim report where some of the detail and phasing is slightly different but no indication of dating is provided. What survives of the recording on site is far less satisfactory. Although there is a site pocket notebook with 26 pages of jottings, it adds little which is new; there are very few photographs of the site, no section drawings and what remains in terms of plans represents only the beginning and end of the recording and publication process. There is a roll of preliminary on-site sketches which lack any precision and final bromides which bear little relation to one another; final on-site plans and the linen-backed plans from which the bromides were taken are all now lost. There is sufficient, however, to add minor details to the phase plans.

In 1965 the village of Faxton was a group of uneven grass fields among the cattle pastures: three years later all the surface indications had been removed and just two ruined cottages on the edge of the cornland remained to show where the village had once stood (Butler 1969a). The only undisturbed area of peasant housing available for a third season of excavation in 1968 was Croft 52–53 which lay on the south side of the village green close to its south-east corner near the church (for location, see Figure 4.1). Since the Rectory Farm provided a terminus to medieval domestic occupation, its front garden was chosen for examination. The siting of this farmhouse implied that any medieval dwelling facing onto the village green had been abandoned previously or at least was no longer considered suitable for domestic use. Not only did the standing structure of the Rectory provide one limit (physical and temporal), but the churchyard's eastern boundary provided another and one aim of the excavation was to show the relationship between the Croft 52–53 and the churchyard. Just as Croft 29, excavated in 1966, stood at the eastern side of The Green, so also Croft 52–53 stood on the south side of The Green and might be regarded as typical for the developments within Crofts 50–53. The good quality of structural preservation in this croft fully justified the decision to excavate. Nevertheless, correspondence between Butler and Hurst reveals that alternative sites remained under discussion (namely Barton Blount in Derbyshire and East Hemsworth in Dorset) before Faxton was once again preferred (letter Butler to Hurst, 26 September 1967).

After 1968, no further excavation was undertaken at Faxton. Resources were not available to examine the medieval moated homestead and, as that site was in any case disturbed by the post-medieval mansion, it was not accorded high priority or protection at the time. By 1989 its interior had been levelled and covered by a conifer plantation, though the moat known as the 'Hall Ponds' still survives today (2019) as a substantial earthwork. Most recently, the Portable Antiquity Scheme records the recovery of a silver hammered cut halfpenny, probably Henry III (*c*.1216–47 AD) from Lamport parish. The coin was found during a metal-detecting rally 'Digging Up the Past: Faxton' on 6 April 2001 on cultivated land (ID NARC-1F8577), but its association with the village site, if any, is not known.

6.1 EXCAVATIONS IN CROFT 52–53

The area chosen for excavation in 1968 (90ft square; approx. 28m square) was bounded on the west by the hedge ditches and banks between Crofts 52 and 53 and on the south by the stone-built Rectory Farm of 16th to 17th century date (see Figure 4.1; and Figures 3.19 and 3.20 for photograph and plan). The total area of Croft 52–53 was 210ft (64m) north–south by 100ft (30m) and the northern half only (100ft square; 30 x 30m) was examined (Butler 1969a). No attempt was made to excavate at the rear (south) of the farmhouse where the croft boundary is visible on the 1956 RAF oblique photograph (Figure 6.1). As well as the main open-area excavation north of the Rectory Farm, there were four extensions from

FIGURE 6.1

Oblique aerial photograph taken in April 1956 showing the location of Croft 52–53 immediately north of the Rectory and the church to the west. By this date the church was roofless but remained standing; it would be demolished two years later (SD73 SP7875/24/06.04.1956 SP784750 CAP). Reproduced with permission of the Cambridge University Collection of Aerial Photography © Copyright reserved.

it: that to the west (at 4 on the grid; Figure 6.2) sectioned the churchyard boundary; that to the east sectioned the croft ditch (also at 4 on the grid); two trenches to the south (F/G and L/M) extended as far as the farmhouse walls to ensure that every substantial medieval structure had been explored. No additional structure was encountered. The boundary on the north between the croft and the village green was never definitely identified. There were no strong surface indications of its alignment and no ditch or depression was encountered at the north of the main area. The entire excavated area was backfilled by machine, levelled, ploughed and sown with mowing grass in spring 1969.

6.2 THE EXCAVATED SEQUENCE

The 1968 stratigraphy was recorded as follows: a dark brown garden soil (0–7 inches; 0–18cm), orange-brown or medium-brown soil (Layer A: 7–19 inches; 18–48cm), red-brown soil, becoming yellow-brown near the natural clay (Layer B: 19–25 inches; 48–64cm), light-brown slightly gritty soil (Layer C: 25–29 inches; 64–74cm), natural yellow clay into which a number of negative features were cut (Layer D: 30–36 inches; 76–92cm). All the features were separately numbered and given internal layer sequences (Layers E, F etc.). All the wall material and wall debris was of local ironstone, varying from orange-brown to a dark chocolate brown in colour. No section drawings were inked up for the 1968 excavation and a note in the file from the mid-1980s reads '1968 – needs section drawings'. The originals drawn on site have never been located.

The various excavated layers are referred to in the finds reports and are noted on the pottery distribution diagrams where the phases (e.g. Layer B2) usually refer to subdivisions within the process of excavation. The sequence of occupation is

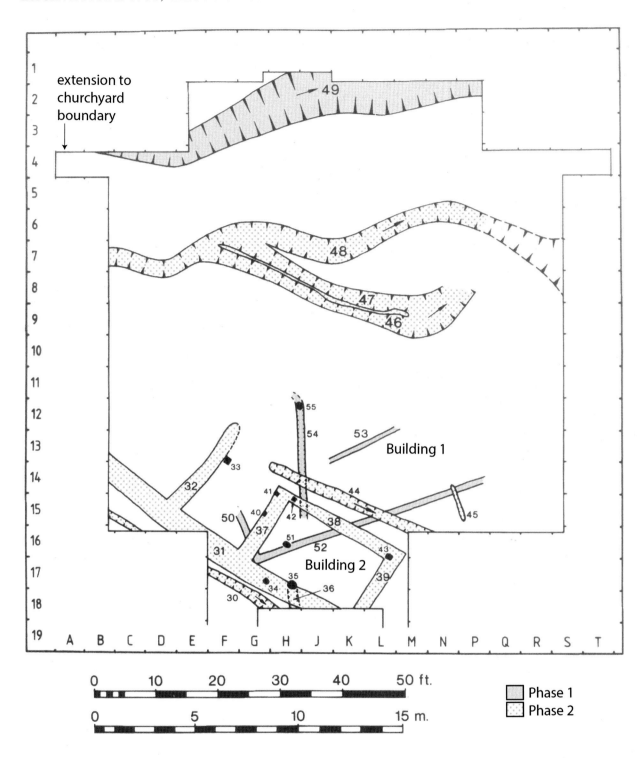

FIGURE 6.2
Croft 52–53 1968. Phases 1 and 2 showing early features (c.1150–1250)

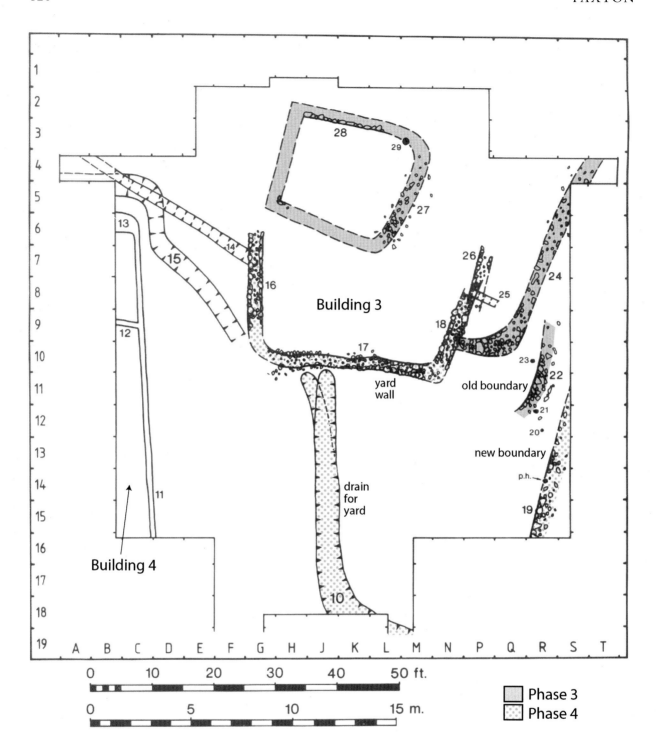

FIGURE 6.3
Croft 52–53 1968. Phases 3 and 4 (c.1250–1350)

best understood by referring to the three phase plans (Figures 6.2 to 6.4) and is described in six phases of occupation beginning with the earliest.

Lawrence Butler did not provide any indication of dates for the phases he defines below. He does say at the end of the text, however, that the six phases he has defined run from the mid-12th century to the mid-15th century, and on the basis of the two previous years at Faxton it seems very likely that the phasing ran in consecutive 50-year blocks. These have been added below.

Phase 1: *c.*1150–1200

The earliest phase was represented by three slots of rounded section (50, 52 and 53) cut into the clay, two post-holes (51 and 55) and a drain or gully (54) (Figure 6.2). The slots, which Butler himself referred to as 'beam slots', represent Building 1 though the east wall was not found; wall 53 was not parallel to wall 52 but it seems likely that both belong to the same structure as their profiles were very similar. To the north of the croft were two major boundary ditches; the more northerly and deeper on (49) ran to join the north-east angle of Croft 52, and may represent the earliest croft boundary although firm proof was lacking. These ditches preceded the present churchyard boundary immediately to the west. Both an arrowhead (Figure 8.8, no. 42) and chain mail (Figure 8.4, no. 13) were recovered from associated contexts.

Phase 2: *c.*1200–1250

This phase was represented by Building 2 whose construction made use of beam slots of rectangular section, with ditches or gullies with U-shaped or V-shaped profiles and post-holes (Figure 6.2). The beam slots indicated a major wall (31) which was also observed in trench L–M 18–25; against this were three walls (32, 37 and 39) and a room enclosed by wall 38. There were post-holes both in the centre of the walls (34, 42 and 43) and set against the outer faces (33, 35, 40 and 41). It is likely that other post positions did not survive or had not penetrated the clay; the excavator thought it probable that they rested on sill beams. Gullies 30 and 44 flanked the house indicated by these beam slots; gully 36 appeared to drain the interior of the house. Gully 45 could not be easily interpreted as part of this complex; it may be secondary within Phase 1 and relate to a later use of beam slot 52 which it cut through.

To the north of the croft the more southerly ditch (46–48) had been re-cut on different alignments gradually moving north. The fill of both the northern ditches was similar with yellow-grey silt as the primary filling sealed by orange-brown clay over which spread the occupation layers of Phase 3; the southerly ditches (46–48) contained burnt grain and

other seeds (not retained). There was no indication which of these two ditches was cut first or whether both were open simultaneously.

Phase 3: *c.*1250–1300

Although Butler thought it likely that the clay-walled houses at the south of the excavated area remained in use (i.e. Building 2), this phase marks a shift to the north of the croft and a change in building technique (Figure 6.3). Building 3 was mud-walled set on a low stone base of one or two courses, using ironstone and field-gathered glacial erratics. This structure is represented by footing 28, wall scatter 27 and two walls to west and south probably lay beneath walls 4 and 7 of the Phase 5 house (Figure 6.4). The construction of these later walls had presumably removed the traces of anything earlier.

Wall 27 in Phase 3 may be a division wall within a larger house indicated by a gable wall 26 (and 6), with drain 25 running outside its southern wall. Two further walls (22 and 24) extended along the eastern croft boundary: it is not clear whether they were boundary walls, or whether they formed part of barns or open-fronted animal sheds of which the other walls were in perishable materials or were displaced by alterations in later phases.

Post positions were visible on or near the inner faces of the footing walls: post 29 within the house, 23 and 21 related to wall 22 and a small post-hole within the later wall 19. Only post 20 was not within a wall. Since this eastern group of four post positions is almost in line they could represent a fence in Phase 4 and their relationship to the wall footings could be quite fortuitous. No ditches were related to these structures though the infilled ditches 46–49 of Phase 2 may well have acted as soakaways.

Phase 4: *c.*1300–1350

The eastern boundary wall 19 seems to belong to this phase, replacing wall 22 (Figure 6.3). A yard wall (16-17-18) encloses an area south of Building 3: the termination of wall 18 is best interpreted as abutting against the south-east corner of a larger northern house (as it later became). The termination of wall 16 may indicate a gate alongside the house or else the rest of the wall may have been removed when Building 5 was constructed. The area south of this inner yard was drained by a major ditch 10, probably serving an outer yard.

The western margin of the site, along the churchyard boundary, was occupied by timber-built structures marked by beam slots (13, 12 and 11). Referred to as Building 4, these structures are described by Butler as 'sheds', but they are extremely large for that. No post-holes were observed in the slots, unlike the earlier Phase 2 walls, and this suggested 'frame-construction' to the excavator.

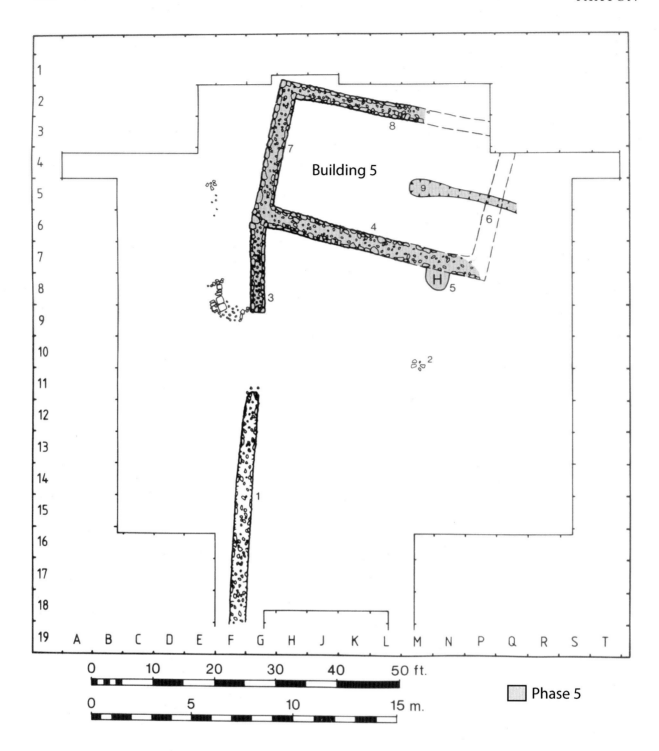

FIGURE 6.4

Croft 52–53 1968. Phases 5 and 6 (originally dated to c.1350–1400 but now revised to the second half of the 16th century)

Drain 15 deepened north-westwards and swung northwards to avoid the building. A later shallow ditch 14 ran south-eastwards and possibly used the infilled ditch 48 as a soakaway.

Phase 5: *c*.1350–1400

Building 5 within this croft was interpreted by Butler as a 'stone-built house' surviving up to nine courses high, represented by walls 4, 7 and 8 and a destroyed wall 6 (Figures 6.5 and 6.6). The floor of the building was composed of a gravelly red-brown soil; and a drain (9), 18 inches (46cm) wide and 7 inches (18cm) deep of U-section, ran centrally down its length from the middle of the building to the eastern wall. There was no evidence of paving, drain capping or of a lintel at the wall junction. There was a distinction between the interior floor of yellow clay, darkening towards the east, and the stony brown clay of the exterior yards. Nothing suggestive of a door was observed, neither a threshold nor a spread of debris around an entrance. This suggests that the building was approached either through the end wall 6 or on the north-east through wall 8. The only hearth (5) was *externally* placed against the south wall and marked by charcoal and burnt stone roughly spread in a semi-circle; the adjacent stones of the house wall were also reddened. This building may originally have used the inner and outer yards of Phase 4, but the ditches gradually silted up and

were filled by soil similar to the surrounding yard surfaces, some probably derived from wall collapse. Although Butler was tempted to think otherwise at the time of its excavation, the function of Building 5 seems more likely to have been a byre with an axial drain (see Chapter 11 for further discussion), even if it is stone-built.

The examination of the churchyard boundary showed a north–south ditch forming its eastern border (not shown or recorded). It was cut at this phase and was flanked by a stone wall on the west side of the ditch. The later wall, now (in 1968) standing up to 3ft (1m) high, was placed west of this first wall partially using it as its base.

Phase 6: *c*.1400–1450

This phase represents the modification of the yard with all its ditches (10, 14 and 15) no longer in use (Figure 6.4). A north–south wall (3, and later 1) now divided the inner croft from an outer area to the west; this wall was 27 inches (68cm) wide and stood two courses high (Figure 6.7). A small area of paving occurred outside the yard entrance. The entrance could be identified by the socket stone on which the gate swung (not recorded). A stone cluster (2) may represent the packing around a post, but it might be no more than the roof capping from a collapsed mud-wall fallen at the wall angle 17–18.

FIGURE 6.5
Croft 52–53 1968. Building 5 from the east (originally dated to c.1350–1400 but now with revised later dates)

FIGURE 6.6

Croft 52–53 1968. Building 5 from the west with junction between walls 3, 4 and 7 in foreground and wall 8 to left (north) of the ladder

FIGURE 6.7

Croft 52–53 1968. Building 5. South wall from the north-east (originally dated to c.1350–1400 but now with revised later dates)

6.3 THE MEDIEVAL FINDS

Other than a handful of flints (see Chapter 8) and two Roman coins from the topsoil (Chapter 8, coins 1 and 2) and a few sherds of Roman pottery, pre-medieval finds were few in 1968. A late medieval jetton (Chapter 7, no. 7, not illustrated) was found in Layer B close to the Rectory. The small items of metal, as analysed by Lawrence Butler, showed an interesting distribution. Taken in general terms by the different metals: the small finds of iron (seven) were in the western and central zones of the excavation; finds of lead (ten) were also in the western and central zones, more numerous in the south than in the north; finds of copper alloy (26) were frequent in the north-west zone, central zone and mid-south zone (dividing the excavated area into nine zones). The five items of worked bone were all found in the south of the excavated area. The seven whetstones were either at the north (two in Phase 5) or at the south (five in Phase 4). The other finds are best considered in relation to their specific location and the period of their deposition or loss. The copper-alloy objects divide between three items in Phase 6 including a buckle pin on the house floor, 14 items in Phase 5 including buckles and lace tags in the yard south of the house, and one item in Phase 4 which was a ring in the south-east yard. There were five items in Phase 3: all lay just outside the house and beneath its wall tumble, including a ring, a buckle and a brooch; and two items from Phase 2: a fragment of a flat plate within the house and a piece of chain mail east of the house (Figure 8.4, no. 13).

Most of the lead came from the destruction or collapse of the house in Phase 4 (from E11 and F15) with one piece of lead sheet in the beam slot (11) of the Phase 3 house. All the worked bone was from Phase 4 or earlier, with a dice (Figure 8.12, no. 82) and a jet bead (Figure 8.14, no. 87) recovered from among the wall stones of the Phase 4 house, and a bone point in the early filling of the Phase 4 ditch (10). A pair of 12th- to 15th-century iron shears was also found in this early deposit within the Phase 4 ditch (not illustrated). An iron arrowhead (Figure 8.8, no. 41) was found in Phase 2 occupation above the clay at north-west in the excavated area, but the other three arrowheads, an iron buckle and a horseshoe were deposited in Phase 5 or 6. The arrowheads suggested to the excavator that archery butts had been set up in the medieval churchyard.

Taken together, the later medieval finds from Croft 52–53 have a different character to those excavated in 1966 or 1967. Dress accessories dominated the assemblage, including various parts of buckles or brooches (Figure 8.3, nos 11 and 12; Figure 8.4, no. 27; Figure 8.5, no. 30; Figure 8.8, no. 50), a dress pin (Figure 8.4, no. 24), studs (Figure 8.4, nos 14 and 23), a ring of twisted wire, probably an eyelet or wire loop fastener (Figure 8.4, no. 17) and a lace tag (Figure 8.4, no. 22). Of the other objects, few could be directly related to agriculture; there were two weights (Figure 8.6, nos 37 and 39), a pin beater (Figure 8.12, no. 81), a tuning peg (Figure 8.12, no. 79), a knife handle (not illustrated), a strainer (Figure 8.6, no. 40), whetstones (e.g. Figure 8.15, nos 93 and 105). There was, however, a horseshoe (Figure 8.10, no. 66).

6.4 POST-MEDIEVAL OCCUPATION

There was no firm evidence for a northern boundary hedge or fence, though the change of direction in the northern boundary of Croft 52 does suggest where it stood. Near the farmhouse, a garden wall enclosed a small area in front of the house and dairy; the footings of this wall remained but the rest had been removed by 1966 to repair potholes in the farm tracks. The soil was noticeably more disturbed within this inner garden, but the whole of the excavated area had been turned over to a depth of 9 inches (23cm) by gardening. Paths, field drains and garden walls of the 19th century were found, together with a rubbish pit of about 1870. These features are not marked on the Phase 6 plans nor otherwise recorded.

6.5 POST-MEDIEVAL FINDS

Coins of post-medieval date or of post-medieval deposition occurred in every area of the excavation, with six coins being found in the northern zone, four in the central zone and five in the southern zone close to the farmhouse. The majority were Stuart (three) or Georgian (seven) in date; small denomination coins ascribed to casual loss. Of the jettons, three were found in the central zone (two in P10, Layer B) and six were in the southern zone (most in L–M 13–15). Both of the trade tokens were found in G15 (see Chapter 8), perhaps suggesting a deliberate deposit in the late 17th century of eight jettons and tokens in 'latitude' 15, later dispersed by gardening.

Twenty-one small items of metal were well scattered: fewest in the central zone and the majority (12) in the southern zone. Domestic and industrial items tended to be nearer the house, as if deliberately discarded and thrown from a door or window. Small personal items such as buckles (Figure 8.3, no. 8), buttons and a ring (Figure 8.3, no. 4) were in the northern zone; two of the three beads and one of the two thimbles were in the central zone. No particular significance need be attached to this distribution which may indicate unintentional loss or gradual dispersal by gardening. The two thimbles, both likely 17th-century in date (Figure 8.4, nos 19 and 20), seem to echo a more general theme on this site of textile-working. For example, there is a seal probably from a bale of linen (Figure 8.6, no. 36; Figure 8.7), also 17th century, and a pair of undated bone pin beaters (Figure 8.12, nos 80 and 81). More recent leisure activities and the presence of children are also suggested by nine clay alleys of probable 18th- to 19th-century date and a button hook or crotchet hook (not illustrated) and among the later dress accessories are a black glass bead from an earring or necklace (Figure 8.14, no. 89), two modern beads of glass and two jet buttons. Clay pipes were plentiful, 178 in all (e.g. Figure 8.18, nos 124, 126, 127, 130, 131, 132).

6.6 SUMMARY

The 1968 excavations demonstrated six main structural phases from the mid-12th to the mid-15th century. There was no continuity between this sequence of medieval houses and the later Rectory Farm: according to the excavator's original analysis, insufficient 16th-century pottery was recovered to suggest that there was any occupation within the croft at the end of the medieval period, though this conclusion might now be doubted (see Chapter 7). There was also no evidence of continuity between the Roman period and the later medieval phase of the site. The presence of Roman sherds at both the crofts at the south-east corner of The Green is best interpreted as hillwash from a substantial building, perhaps a villa, on the level area at the centre of The Green close to the position of the medieval and Elizabethan manor houses.

The sequence of building phases showed increasing sophistication in two directions: that of building techniques and that of farm layout. The former followed the development already observed on the other two crofts at Faxton: first there was a timber structure with large post-holes and with walls presumably of mud or clay; this was partially replaced in the late 12th century or modified internally by a structure using a series of sill beams laid into the floor of the first phase; then followed the first stone phase with a mud-walled building standing on a low foundation wall of ironstone and field-gathered boulders and pebbles. Finally, in the 14th century, there was a substantially built stone structure, standing up to 36 inches (91 cm) high with nine or ten courses surviving.

Three factors seemed to determine the arrangement of the buildings within the croft: the first was the position of the main domestic building in relation to the street. In the first two phases the buildings were placed roughly parallel to the street but 70 ft (21 m) south of it; only in the mid-13th century were buildings brought close to the street and set more exactly parallel to it. This drastic move brought into play the other two factors: the barns, store sheds, byres and kilns were no longer temporary structures quickly replaced, but became fixed in their position in relation to the house. This was particularly seen in Phases 5 and 6 where there was apparently a gradual campaign to rebuild in stone all the sheds to enclose a rectangular courtyard. The final factor was the position of the entrance to the farm unit. When the buildings were set well back from the street and divided from it by only a slight drain, then entry to the croft posed no problem. However, when the buildings were close to the street and occupied nearly all the street frontage, the entrance was at a fixed position with a bridge over the increasingly deepened croft ditch, finally being provided with double-leaf gates into the courtyard, one socket stone remaining *in situ* in 1968 (Butler 1969a).

7

THE POTTERY

Lawrence Butler

with contributions by Brian Hartley and Paul Blinkhorn

This chapter was among the most complete, with several versions left by Lawrence Butler and his colleagues in the archive. In its original form, the Roman report was no more than notes, but by the time the medieval pottery came to be studied in the mid-1980s, the world of the computer had arrived, in this case double-sided quad density discs on a BBC micro-computer. These discs have not been located and parts of the medieval pottery report had become disordered with multiple hand-corrected copies in circulation. Text and illustrations have now been re-united and the chapter re-formatted. Further comment on the medieval pottery from Faxton has kindly been provided by Paul Blinkhorn to bring the report up to date and a new post-medieval pottery section has been added.

7.1 ROMAN POTTERY
by Lawrence Butler, with Brian Hartley

There was a scatter of Roman material from fieldwalking on Crofts 23–28 and excavated material from 12 locations in Croft 29 1966, three locations (including topsoil) in Crofts 6–9 1967 and 2 locations in Croft 52–53 1968. This seems to indicate a general dispersed scatter rather than to pinpoint a specific location though the high ground near the later wells is the most favoured.

Of the Samian wares, nine sherds were found during fieldwalking. These are mostly central Gaulish or east Gaulish with forms represented including Dr. 27, 31, 33 and 77. There were also some indeterminate forms and one sherd is burnt. Dating is 2nd century, mostly Antonine, but one or two sherds could perhaps be Hadrianic. One of these (732) is from the Croft 29 1966 excavation (A-B 11-15 layer B2), recovered while removing stoney yard material from above natural clay, another (96) is from the 1968 excavations (K-L 4-5 A2) and almost certainly redeposited material.

Among the coarsewares, there was a single sherd of amphora, later 3rd–4th century Nene Valley coarse wares including a mortarium and a handled grey ware flagon, late 2nd–4th century Nene Valley colour-coated wares, a single non-local colour-coated ware, an Oxfordshire red colour-coated ware and amorphous grey wares which came from four locations across the excavations and from fieldwalking.

7.2 THE EARLY ANGLO-SAXON POTTERY

When the pottery was first analysed, a small number of Early/Middle Anglo-Saxon (5th–9th century)

sherds were found to be readily distinguishable from the other pottery by their harsh gritty black fabric. They were from hand-made, probably coil-built vessels, and had been completely reduced in firing, and are typical of the tradition in Northamptonshire.

The sherds of this type recovered at Faxton were invariably highly abraded and generally less than 3cm in diameter. Most were worn body sherds, and no rim sherds were identified. One base is illustrated, probably from a small jar (Figure 7.1). It was in a completely reduced fabric with black to light-brown surfaces. Large internal vesicles had probably resulted from the leaching of inclusions.

As with the residual Roman sherds (see above) most of the Early/Middle Anglo-Saxon pottery was recovered from Croft 29 1966. However, it was always found in contexts with much later pottery, and thus cannot be seen as associated with any of the excavated features. Perhaps it is indicative of earlier activity in this area in the village, but outside the area of excavation. There can be no suggestion that it represents a continuous sequence of development from the Anglo-Saxon to later medieval periods since the quantities involved are too small.

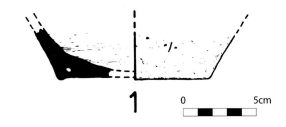

FIGURE 7.1

Pottery illustration 1, Anglo-Saxon sherd from topsoil in G31 (1967)

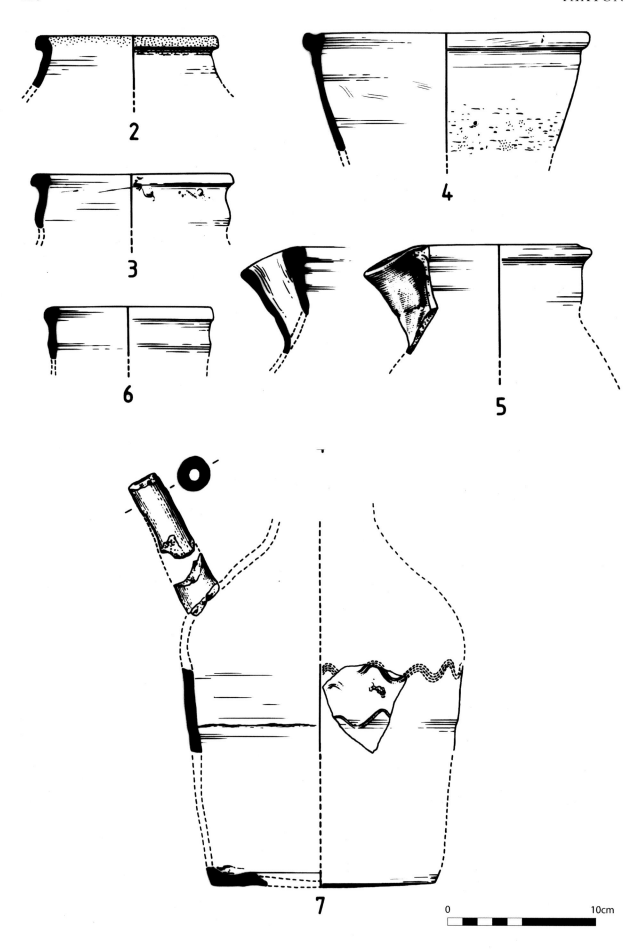

FIGURE 7.2
Pottery illustrations 2–7, Thetford type wares, Stamford ware and Developed Stamford wares

Illustrated sherds:

Figure	Pot	Year	East	North	Layer
7.1	1	67	G	31	Topsoil

7.3 THE LATER MEDIEVAL POTTERY

The later medieval pottery assemblage, totalling some 37,000 sherds, represents the remains of a large number of vessels in use from the 12th to the 15th centuries in rural Northamptonshire. The potential value of this assemblage is not lessened because of the length of time which has elapsed since the excavation of the material, although had the site been dug today then this report would undoubtedly be very different. As it stands, it must be viewed in the context of the excavation of the mid-1960s, combined with some of the research objectives of the 1980s.

The aims of pottery analysis were (a) to define the range of fabrics and forms present at Faxton during the period of occupation, and (b) to use the pottery distribution to examine the presence of activity areas, and from that to study the development of structural phases including croft boundaries, particularly where structural evidence was ephemeral. Since, apart from a small number of features yielding little pottery, a maximum sequence of four stratified layers was recovered throughout the excavations, there appeared to be little potential for detailed vertical stratigraphic analysis. This was confirmed when the highly disturbed nature of the assemblage became apparent (see below). Therefore no detailed quantification by fabric type or number of vessels was undertaken in the limited time available. It was felt that this would only lend a spurious degree of precision to the results.

The preliminary stage of analysis was therefore to separate the medieval pottery from the other excavated material. For each area of the site, the pottery was then laid out according to its original grid square, following the methodology advocated by Moorhouse (1983, 83–84). The number of sherds per square was counted where necessary; for the 1966 excavation they had already been counted by D H Evans, and weighed by M J McCarthy. The squares were then searched for conjoining sherds, and representative types were selected for illustration. The post-medieval pottery, particularly that recovered from Croft 52–53 1968, was intended to be a separate report in the mid-1980s but the assemblage remained unstudied and in store at Daventry until it was retrieved once again for study as part of this final publication project.

The pottery was categorized according to the fabric type using the gazetteer of Northamptonshire ceramic types published by McCarthy (1979). Where each of the pottery types is discussed below, only brief descriptions are given, with references to other more complete published discussions. The Northamptonshire type codes are given where appropriate, for ease of cross-reference to McCarthy. The variety of forms present at Faxton is then described for each type, followed by a list of the illustrated vessels. In these lists the following abbreviations are used to describe the vessel forms: cooking pots (CP), bowls (B), jugs and pitchers (J) and uncertain (U).

Thetford type ware
(McCarthy 1979, W3)

Thetford type ware has been extensively discussed in the literature (see Hurst 1957; 1959; 1976; Wade 1973; 1976). Only one sherd (not illustrated), with characteristic applied and thumbed strip, was identified at Faxton, from Croft 29 1966. This has a hard, slightly rough texture and light grey core and surfaces. In addition, one example of a Late Saxon hand-made vessel of the 10th or 11th centuries was found (2). This was a small cooking pot rim with a harsh sandy fabric and orange surfaces.

Illustrated sherds:

Figure	Pot	Year	East	North	Layer	Form
7.2	2	67	F	3	A2	CP

Stamford Ware and Developed Stamford Ware
(McCarthy 1979, X1)

Stamford Ware has not been well studied (Kilmurry 1980) and it should be sufficient to note points relevant to the small quantities found at Faxton. Stamford Ware had been dated to *c.* AD 850–1150, with Developed Stamford Ware to *c.* AD 1150–1250. None of the forms present at Faxton needs to be earlier than the 12th century.

All the vessels were of the standard fine white or cream fabric, and had clear wheel-throwing marks. The Stamford Ware vessels had a yellow-green mottled glaze (4, 5), whilst the Developed Stamford Ware (3, 6 and 7) was distinguished by a rich dark green glaze. This was frequently accompanied by the use of combed wavy lines, or multiple overlapping chevrons, on the shoulder (7).

The vessels found at Faxton comprise only pitchers, apparently often spouted. One example of a tubular bridge spout was also found (7).

Illustrated sherds:

Figure	Pot	Year	East	North	Layer	Form
7.2	3	68	K-M	13-15	B2	J
7.2	4	68	J-M	13-18	B-B2	J
7.2	5	66	I	9-10	Ditch	J
7.2	6	68	J	10-12	Ditch	J
7.2	7	66	P-AA	10-30	A-CC	J

Saxo-Norman calcite-gritted wares
(McCarthy 1979, T2)

McCarthy classes all Saxo-Norman calcite-gritted wares as 'T2', owing to 'the difficulty which sometimes arises in distinguishing the product of one kiln from those of another' (McCarthy 1979, 156). He notes that the term includes fabrics known as Developed St Neots type wares and fine and coarse, corky and shelly wares. It also includes the products of kilns identified at Olney Hyde, Lyveden and Stanion, and suspected at Harrold. An overall date range of AD 1100–1400 is given for the class.

Since over 90% of the medieval pottery recovered at Faxton falls into this general category it would appear to be useful to attempt to break this down by distinguishing between the products of the different kilns, although a number of residual 'T2' examples must remain. In particular, the transition between Developed St Neots type ware and the true Stanion/Lyveden forms remains a hazy boundary.

Developed St Neots type ware

The most recent synthesis of St Neots type ware is that by Hunter (1979).

The origin of St Neots type ware is placed in the late 9th century. The wares described here as Developed St Neots type ware are a post-Conquest phenomenon. There is no clear-cut end date for these forms as they merge almost imperceptibly into the products of Lyveden, Olney Hyde, Harrold and Stanion in the 12th century.

The fabrics present at Faxton fall within the term 'calcite-gritted', although the major class appeared to be shell-tempered.

The major forms represented at Faxton are the cooking pots and bowls, although a small number of pitchers were also found. Each of these forms was generally manufactured with the use of a wheel, although coil-building was frequently used for the transitional forms.

Cooking pots

The cooking pot forms included a wide variety of flaring and in-turned rims. Some were squared-off (13); some constricted (17, 19); whilst others were straight-sided, widening towards the top (10, 12). A clear carination at the shoulder (15) can be taken as evidence that the cooking pot rims were sometimes formed separately with the use of a template. Many examples showed traces of sooting around the rim. Wipe marks and throwing lines were also visible (12, 14 and 17). Several straight-sided vessels had added vertical applied thumbed strips running down to the base (27, 29 and 30); one large vessel (25) had traces of three applied thumbed strips running almost diagonally around the body.

Illustrated sherds:

Figure	Pot	Year	East	North	Layer	Form
7.3	8	66	G	8-10	C2	CP
7.3	9	67	F-H	2	A3	CP
7.3	10	67	H	3	A1	CP
7.3	11	67	G-H	1-2	A1-2	CP
7.3	12	67	F-G	5	A2	CP
7.3	13	67	F	5	A2	CP
7.3	14	67	G	6	Ditch	CP
7.3	15	67	F	17	A3	CP
7.3	16	66	G	8-10	B2	CP
7.3	17	66	I-K	11-12	Ditch	CP
7.3	18	67	F-J	3	A3-4	CP
7.3	19	66	F-G	11-15	Ditch	CP
7.4	20	67	H	30	TS	CP
7.4	21	68	H-J	10-12	Yard	CP
7.4	22	68	L-N	2	C	CP
7.4	23	67	F	29	A2	CP
7.4	24	68	H-J	6-9	B	CP
7.4	25	67	F-G	24	A4	CP
7.4	26	66	G	8-10	B2	CP
7.4	27	67	F	17	A3-5	CP
7.4	28	67	G	6	A3	CP
7.4	29	67	G	19	A1-5	CP
7.4	30	66	E-G	8-13	A2-B2	CP

Bowls

A wide range of bowls was found at Faxton. These range from those with in-turned rims (31, 33–35), through the 'hammer-head' rim forms (32, 36, 37), to the late 12th-century straight-sided forms (38–42). The range includes some very small examples (35) which could almost be cups, as well as the more massive forms (38, 39). Fragments of the handle of one socketed bowl (54) were found. Many of the bowls are heavily externally sooted (34) and must have been used for cooking. The late 12th-century products are frequently heavily oolite-tempered (e.g. 40, 48). The later rims are often thumbed (37), and begin to merge into the types of the 12th and 13th centuries which may be regarded as truly transitional to the Stanion/Lyveden products (49). Occasionally the thumbing may form part of the attachment of a basket handle (44).

Illustrated sherds:

Figure	Pot	Year	East	North	Layer	Form
7.5	31	66	O-P	11-12	Ditch	B
7.5	32	68	House 2	–	Tumble	B
7.5	33	66	GG	8-10	C	B
7.5	34	66	BB	9-10	B3	B
7.5	35	68	K-L	6-8	C	B
7.5	36	66	P-R	13-14	A2	B
7.5	37	66	Q-T	10	A	B
7.5	38	67	F-G	24	A4	B
7.5	39	67	H-J	4	A3	B
7.5	40	67	J	6	A2	B
7.5	41	68	G-N	9-15	A-B2	B
7.5	42	67	J	8	B2	B

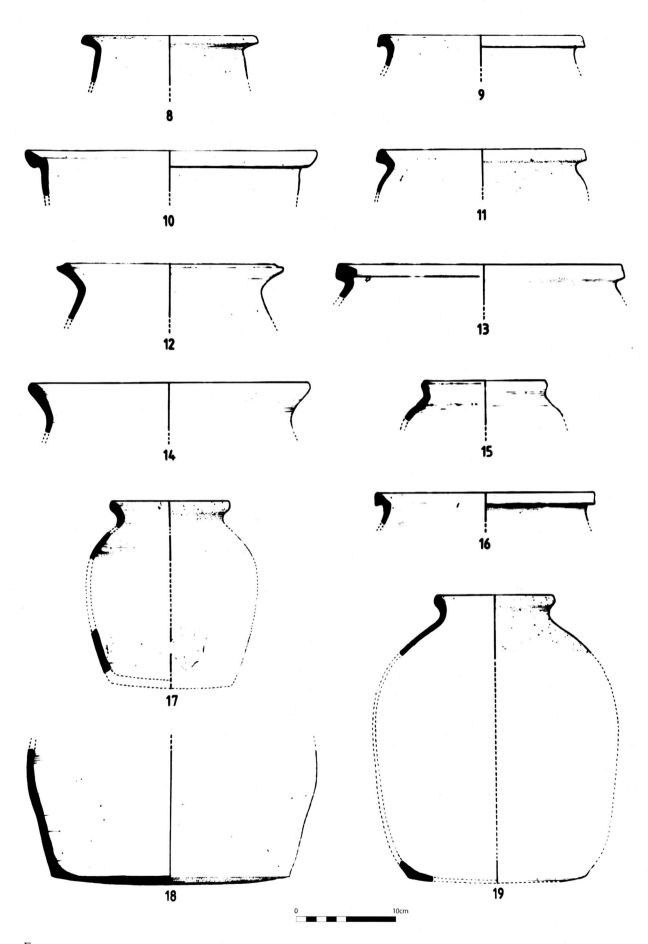

Figure 7.3
Pottery illustrations 8–19, Developed St Neots type wares

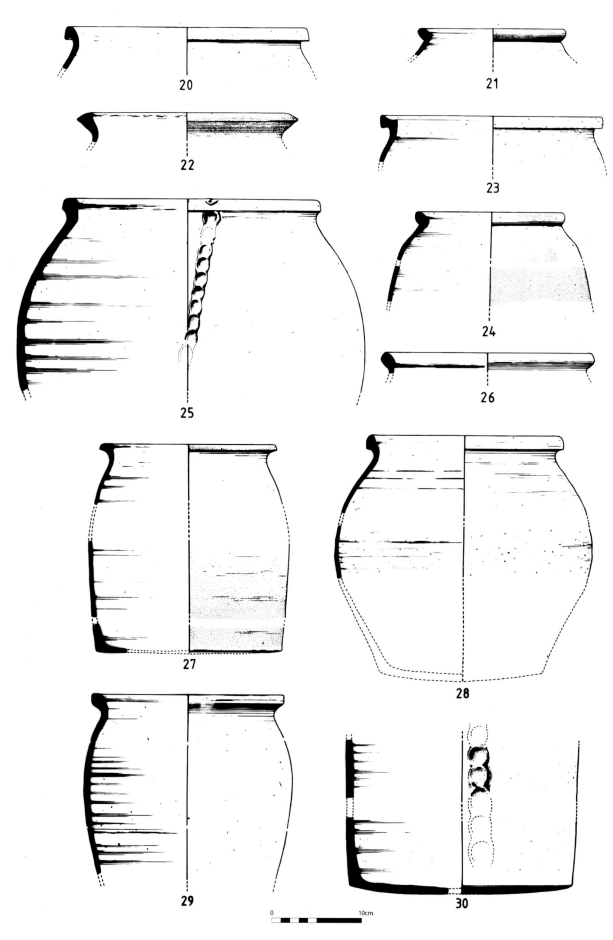

FIGURE 7.4

Pottery illustrations 20–30, Developed St Neots type wares

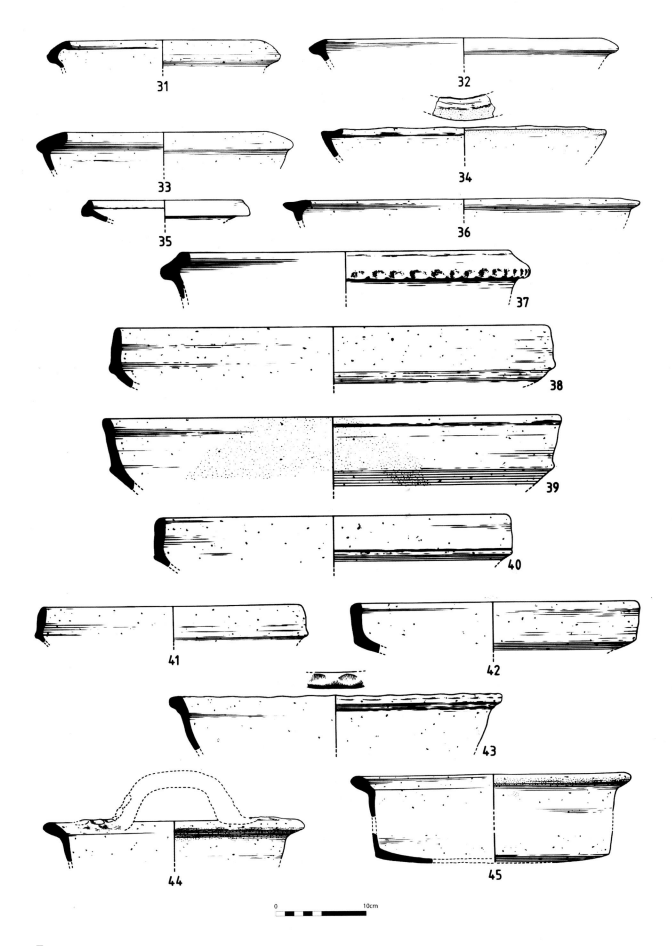

FIGURE 7.5

Pottery illustrations 31–45, Developed St Neots type wares

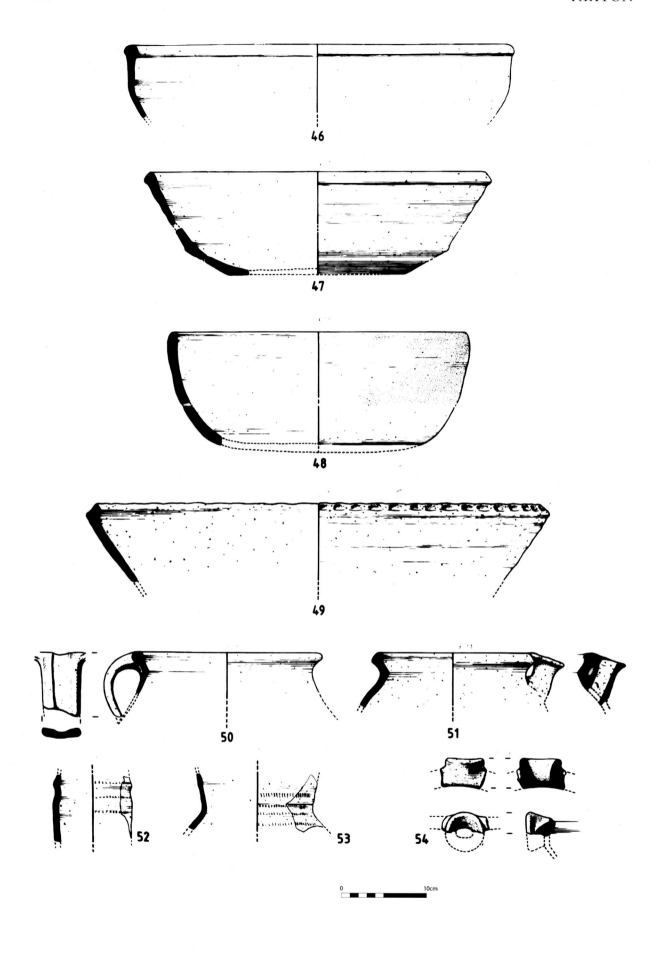

FIGURE 7.6

Pottery illustrations 46–54, Developed St Neots type wares

7.5	43	67	F	16-17	A3	B
7.5	44	68	K-M	13-15	A-B2	B
7.5	45	68	K-M	13-15	B2	B
7.6	46	68	K-L	3-4	C	B
7.6	47	67	G	6	A2	B
7.6	48	67	F-H	1-3	TS-A2	B
7.6	49	67	F-H	17-24	A3	B
7.6	54	66	M	25-30	C	B

Jugs and pitchers

A small number of pitchers were also recovered. In some instances these were clearly copying Stamford Ware spouted pitchers (51); in other cases the roller stamped or rouletted decoration on Late Saxon jars was used on the shoulders and neck (52, 53).

Illustrated sherds:

Figure	Pot	Year	East	North	Layer	Form
7.6	50	67	F-H	17	A3	J
7.6	51	66	AA-BB	9-10	B	J
7.6	52	67	F	18	A3	J
7.6	53	67	J	12	A	J

Olney Hyde/Harrold group

One of the developing forms of St Neots type wares is known to have been manufactured at Olney Hyde, North Buckinghamshire (Mynard 1984). A similar variant is suspected at Harrold, Bedfordshire (Hall 1974). The two groups are difficult to distinguish and will be grouped together here. The number of identifiable Olney Hyde or Harrold products recognised at Faxton was not large; all fall within Mynard's 'A' ware category.

The dating of T2 wares at Olney Hyde is based upon typological considerations to the 13th century [and now thought more likely to be 12th century].

The fabric contains plentiful small calcite grits which may be shell. The surface colour is generally buff-pink with a reduced grey core. The surfaces were often smooth to the touch.

A small number of jugs were the only forms identified at Faxton. Some revealed the use of rouletting on the shoulder (57). Handles were thumb-pressed and stabbed (55), or just with a broad central groove (58).

Illustrated sherds:

Figure	Pot	Year	East	North	Layer	Form
7.7	55	66	A-B	11-15	B2-C	J
7.7	57	67	E-H	26-31	TS-A2	J
7.8	58	67	F	16-17	A3	J

In addition to those clearly Olney Hyde or Harrold products, there was also a group of vessels with similar fabrics which fall into that range, but may be more safely classed as miscellaneous T2 forms. These include a wide variety of jug handles (56, 59–62) and a basket handle (63) with unusual stamped decoration and an applied twisted central spine.

Illustrated sherds:

Figure	Pot	Year	East	North	Layer	Form
7.7	56	67	F-H	1-2	TS	J
7.10	59	67	F-H	2	A3	J
7.9	60	67	F	6	A2	J
7.10	61	67	F	6	-	J
7.10	62	66	DD	11-12	B	J
7.10	63	67	J	5	A3	B
7.9	64	66	House 2	-	-	J

Finally, a distinct class of cooking pots with very shelly fabrics could be identified. The fabric group includes those with thumbed rims (65, 66, 68), as well as examples with a Developed St Neots rim form (69, 70). It also includes early examples of the squat Stanion/Lyveden cooking pot form (67). Most have slightly sagging bases, and some preserve evidence of external sooting (70). One jug (71), with a thumbed handle, also belonged to this fabric group.

Illustrated sherds:

Figure	Pot	Year	East	North	Layer	Form
7.10	65	67	J	11	A	CP
7.9	66	67	E	20	A3	CP
7.11	67	67	F-G	25-28	A4	CP
7.11	68	67	J	28	TS	CP
7.11	69	67	F-H	28-30	A1-3	CP
7.11	70	67	J	26	TS	CP
7.12	71	67	F-G	27-29	TS-A2	J

Stanion/Lyveden ware (T2)

The pottery workshops at Lyveden, Northamptonshire, have been fully published (Steane 1967; Bryant and Steane 1969; 1971; Steane and Bryant 1975; for Stanion, see Hadman 1974). At present it is not altogether clear what was being made at each site, and the degree of overlap between them. In particular, although large numbers of glazed jugs have been found at Lyveden, no kiln wasters have been found, and the jugs may have been exclusively made at Stanion, whilst Lyveden concentrated on the coarseware forms. Because of the variation in fabric between forms, and the different date ranges, the date and fabric of Stanion-Lyveden ware will be considered by each form. A detailed typology has been presented in the Lyveden final report (Steane and Bryant 1975, 61) and that cannot be refined at Faxton, because of the lack of stratified deposits. That typology will, therefore, be used below.

Cooking pots

The range of Stanion-Lyveden cooking pots found at Faxton comprises two major groups. The first consists of oolite-tempered vessels which may be seen as transitional from St Neots type ware; the second comprises the typical Lyveden forms.

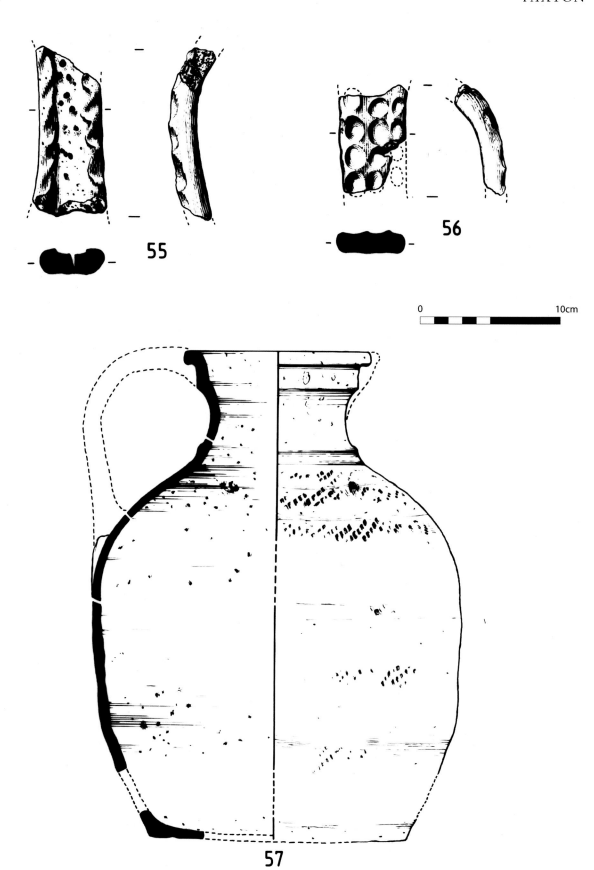

0   10cm

55

56

57

FIGURE 7.7

Pottery illustrations 55–57, Olney Hyde/Harrold group

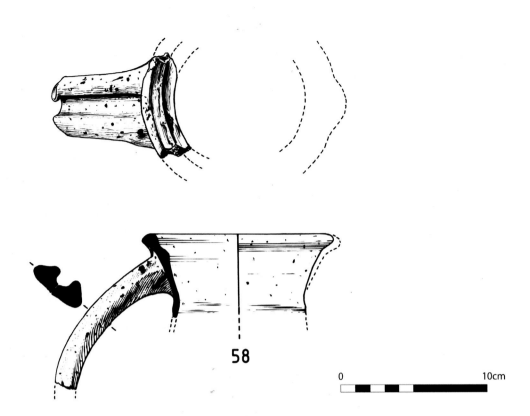

FIGURE 7.8
Pottery illustration 58, Olney Hyde/Harrold group

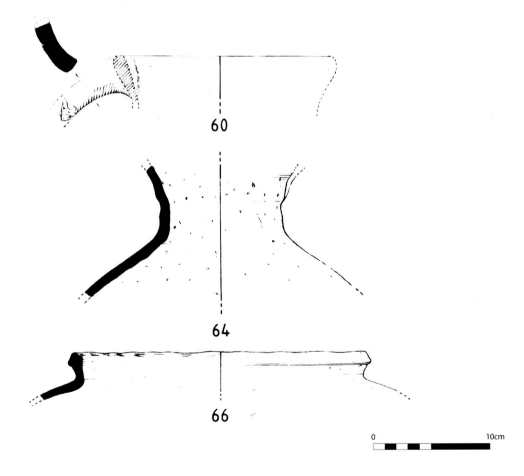

FIGURE 7.9
Pottery illustrations 60, 64, 66, Olney Hyde/Harrold group

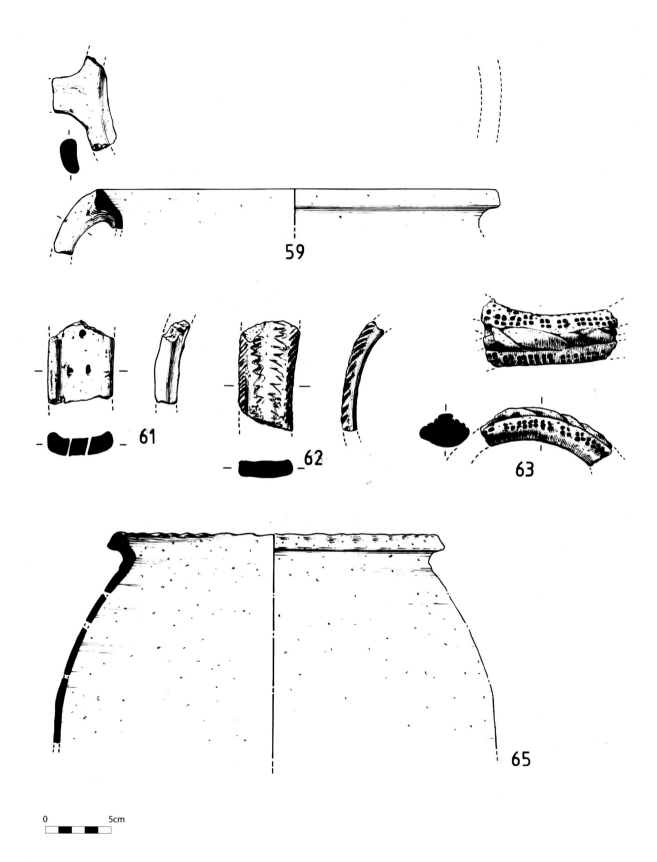

FIGURE 7.10

Pottery illustrations 59, 61–63, 65, Olney Hyde/Harrold group

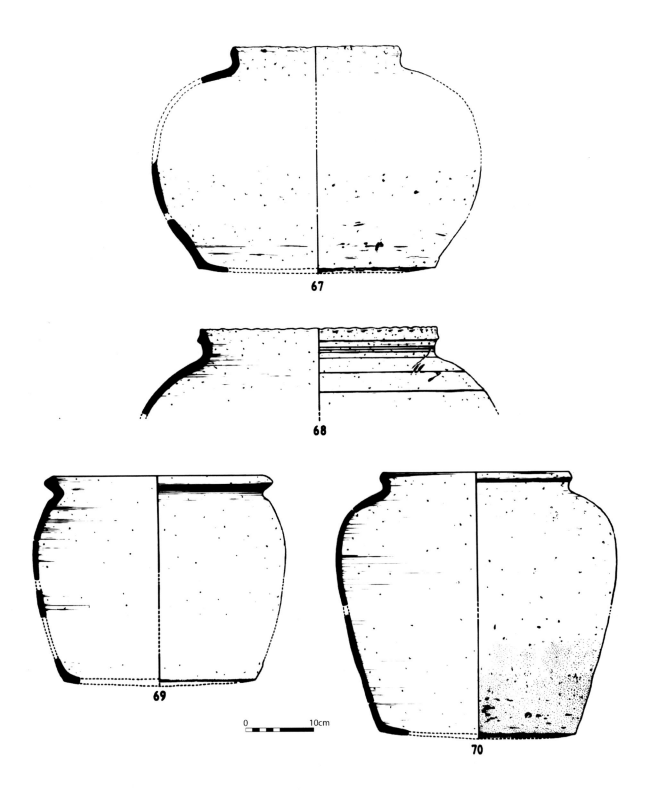

FIGURE 7.11
Pottery illustrations 67–70, Olney Hyde/Harrold group

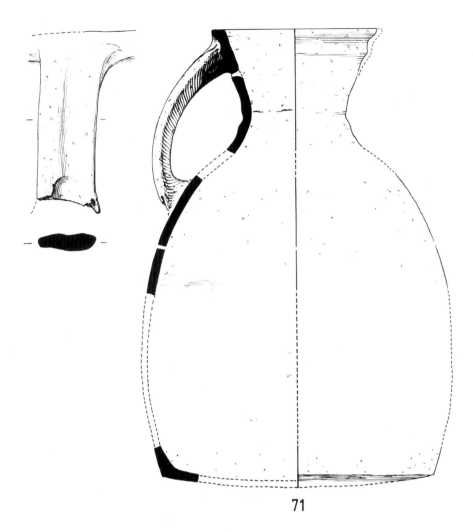

71

FIGURE 7.12

Pottery illustration 71, Olney Hyde/Harrold group

Transitional forms

On typological grounds the transitional forms may be dated from mid-12th to early 13th century.

The group is characterised by extensive oolite-tempering.

The transitional forms generally display an out-turned thumbed rim; bases are rounded and frequently sooted (72). Some are decorated with an incised wavy line around the shoulder (72, 73 and 75). The class includes some rather squat examples (72).

Illustrated sherds:

Figure	Pot	Year	East	North	Layer	Form
7.13	72	67	H	5-6	A3	CP
7.13	73	67	F	1	TS	CP
7.13	74	67	J	5	A2	CP
7.13	75	67	F	17-18	A3	CP
7.13	76	67	H-J	5	A3	CP
7.13	77	66	LL	21-23	TS	CP
7.13	78	67	G	2	A1-2	CP
7.13	79	67	J	8	B2	CP
7.13	80	67	H	3	A1	CP

Cooking pots

The Lyveden cooking pots are dated from the late 13th century *[and now considered to be mid-12th century]*, and continue in production during the 14th century. The earliest types have thumb-impressed rims (86, 87); others have applied thumb-impressed vertical strips (84, 85), copying St Neots forms.

The fabric of this group varies, but fits comfortably within the range identified at Lyveden itself (Steane 1967). Some are dark pink, soft, soapy, shell-filled wares; a number are bright orange with large shelly fragments, but most are a buff ware with crushed shell. A number of these have the shell leached away, leaving a corky surface.

The Lyveden cooking pots are characterised by their angular rims, turned over with a single cordon below. All are clearly coil-built and the coils frequently reveal that the rim and shoulder were manufactured as a separate piece and joined to the body. The line of the join is sometimes clearly visible on the inside of the vessel (81). One miniature example (83) was made in two halves, and joined at the middle. Most have a sagging convex base.

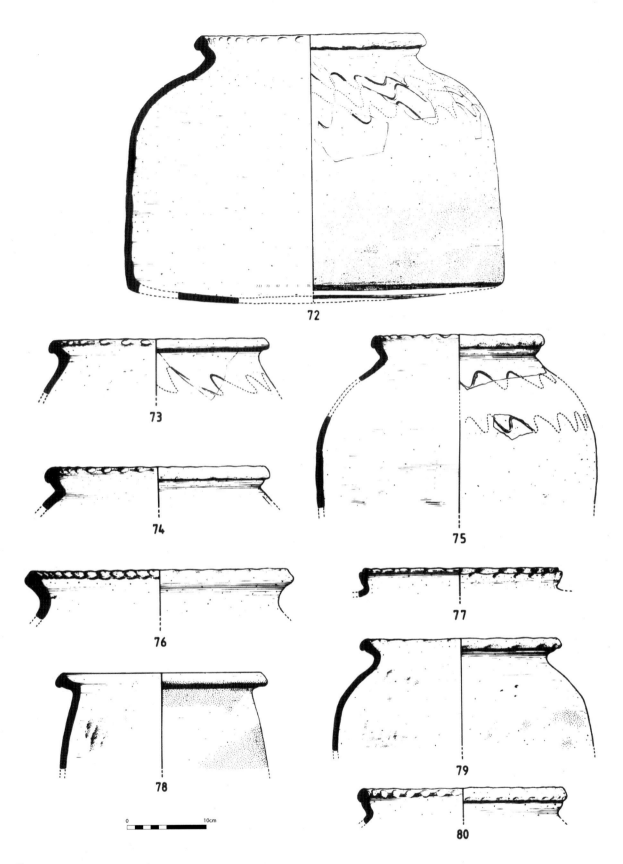

FIGURE 7.13
Pottery illustrations 72–80, Stanion/Lyveden wares

Decoration is fairly limited. In one case (88) two horizontal lines had been incised around the circumference of the vessel. Sometimes applied thumbed vertical strips were added (84, 85). In many cases wipe marks can also be clearly seen. In addition, some vessels appear to have been oxidized in firing as normal, but then deliberately reduced for the final stages to give a thin dark surface to the vessel.

Something can also be said about the use of these vessels. Many were heavily sooted about the base, to a height of about 5cm, indicating that they had been directly exposed to the flames. One very large vessel, of similar profile, was too large to be a cooking pot and could have been used for storage (85). Two unusual forms may be noted: (90) and (91). The former is coil-built but does not have the normal rim; it may be a transitional form.

Illustrated sherds:

Figure	Pot	Year	East	North	Layer	Form
7.14	81	67	F	2-6	TS-A2	CP
7.14	82	67	F	6	-	CP
7.14	83	67	E	27	A3	CP
7.14	84	67	F-G	5-6	A1-2	CP
7.14	85	67	F-J	3-8	A1-3	CP
7.15	86	67	F-J	4	A1	CP
7.15	87	67	E	21-23	A	CP
7.15	88	67	F-J	5	A1-3	CP
7.15	89	67	H	21	A2-4	CP
7.15	90	66	M	11	Oven	CP
7.15	91	66	I-J	21-22	Ditch	CP

Bowls

The Lyveden bowls are introduced during the 13th century [now considered to be mid-12th century] and continue into the 14th and possibly 15th centuries.

The bowl fabric follows the same range as the cooking pots. It also includes orange to light buff surfaces with a grey shelly core.

The range of bowls found at Faxton represents the full range of Lyveden forms. The earliest forms are represented by a few instances of a straight-sided variety, copying St Neots forms (92, 94). The first of these has an unusual rim, thumbed along the upper surface. The pre-14th-century transitional forms are also characterised by the same class of thumb-impressed rim as seen on the cooking pots (93, 95–98). These were mostly shallow bowl forms with gently sloping sides. Finally, two examples of thin-walled vessels with flanged rims (99, 100) may also date to 13th or 14th centuries.

Large quantities of the characteristic Lyveden forms of the 14th century were also recognised. This is the class described by Steane (1967, 24) as having squared-off, expanded, slightly flanged and in-turned rim, as also observed on the Lyveden cooking pots. These were found in a variety of sizes (101–108), including some very large examples (107). Knife paring and wipe marks could also be observed (e.g. 105).

Smaller numbers of the later flanged rims form identified by Steane were also found (109–112). These date to the late 14th century, and include glazed examples (110–112) of the 14th and 15th centuries.

Illustrated sherds:

Figure	Pot	Year	East	North	Layer	Form
7.15	92	66	A-D	11-15	A2-C	B
7.15	93	66	BB	12-13	C2	B
7.15	94	66	H-J	12-15	C	B
7.16	95	67	H	22	A1	B
7.16	96	66	S-T	11-12	A3	B
7.16	97	66	N-O	10	A	B
7.16	98	66	J	19	Ditch	B
7.16	99	67	H	7	A2	B
7.16	100	68	F-G	20-21	Wall	B
7.16	101	67	F	31	A1	B
7.16	102	68	G-H	10-11	Wall	B
7.16	103	67	House 1	-	A2	B
7.17	104	67	F-J	5-6	A1-2	B
7.17	105	67	H-K	3-4	TS-A3	B
7.17	106	67	E	27	A3	B
7.17	107	66	K	19-20	Ditch	B
7.17	108	67	E-G	24	A4	B
7.17	109	66	I-M	19-23	D- ditch	B
7.17	110	66	I-O	18-22	Ditch	B
7.18	111	66	N-O	11	A2	B
7.18	112	66	Unstratified	-	-	B

Jugs

Decorated jugs of the type found at Faxton have elsewhere been dated to the 13th and 14th centuries. A wide range of 13th- and 14th-century forms is illustrated (113–142), plus a smaller number of later 14th- and 15th-century examples (143–147).

The jug fabrics are pink or grey with very finely ground shell. The unglazed surfaces are generally pink or brown. One example of a jug, evidently a product of the Stanion kilns, had an unusual sandy rather than shelly fabric (124).

A wide range of jug forms was identified and has been published in full. The jugs range in size from small examples (120, 122) to larger broad vessels (123, 129), with evidence for tapering bodies joined to a flat disc of clay for the base with thumbed impressions (136). Otherwise bases were generally slightly sagging (122–123; Figure 7.20). Necks ranged from the straight-sided (113–114) to flaring (115–118), with one example of an unusual flared and cordoned rim or collar (119).

Several types of handle were recognised. However, only vessels for which fragments of handle were found have been drawn with handles, although we may assume that all jugs were originally handled. The most common were simple forms, rounded in section, and frequently stabbed (118, 121–122). Occasionally these may have been flattened to an oval cross-section (127), and sometimes may have a rectangular section where they have been joined

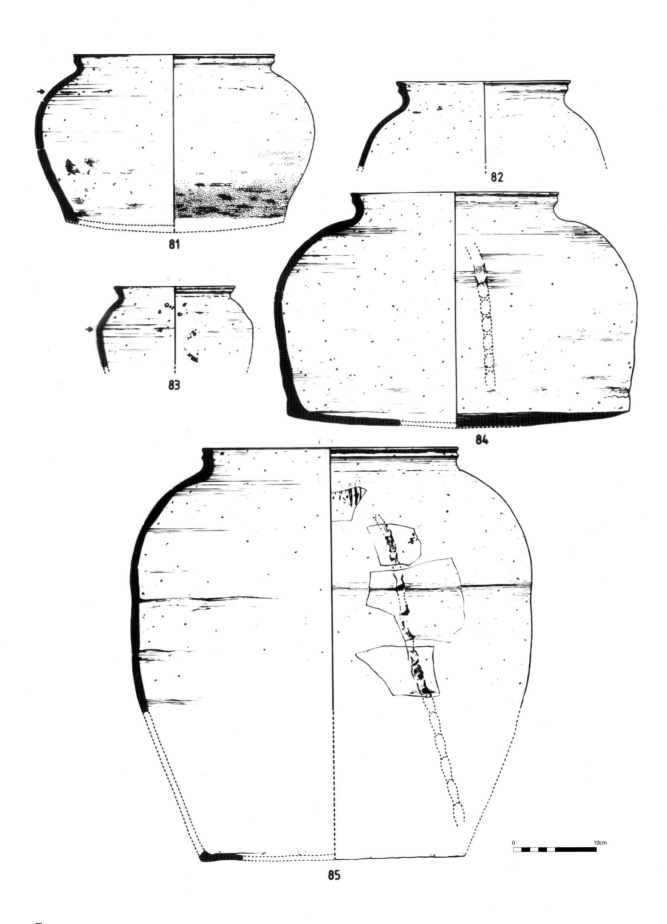

FIGURE 7.14

Pottery illustrations 81–85, Stanion/Lyveden wares

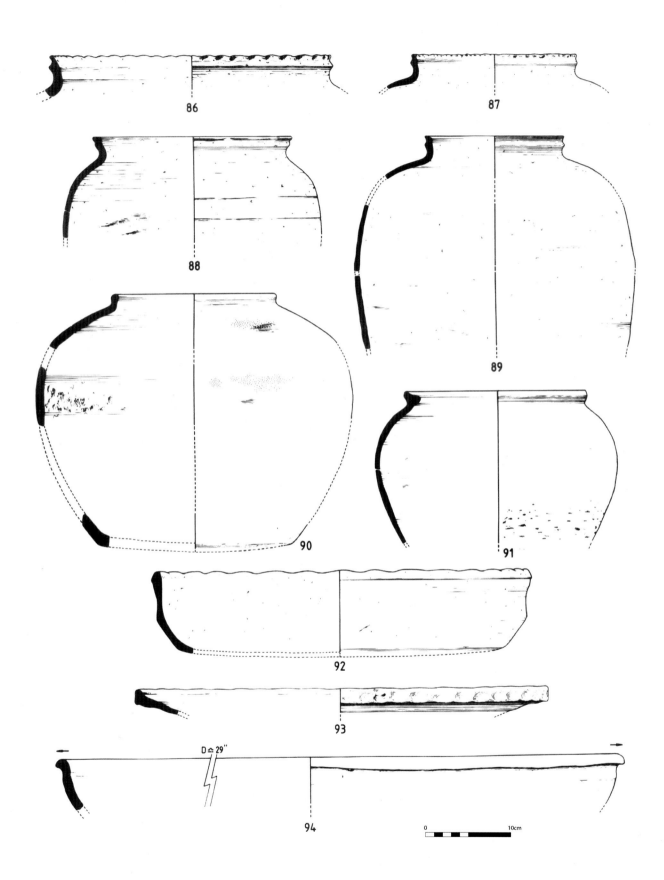

FIGURE 7.15
Pottery illustrations 86–94, Stanion/Lyveden wares

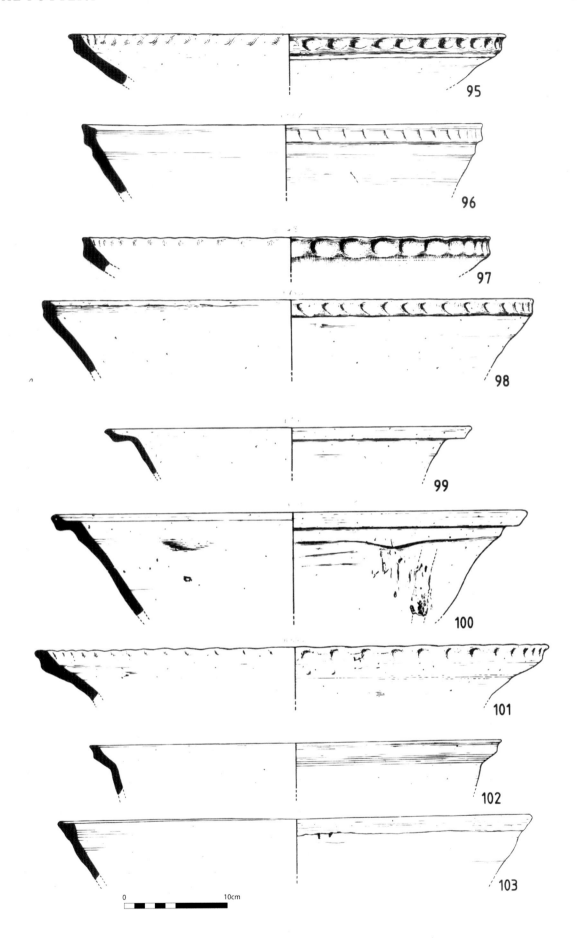

FIGURE 7.16
Pottery illustrations 95–103, Stanion/Lyveden wares

to the neck by thumbing (115). Twisted handles are also common (125), but these usually appear to be glazed. One broad handle was stamped with a rosette design (126), dated to the second half of the 12th century. An oval handle from a later jug was both grooved or ridged and stabbed (143).

The jugs are invariably glazed with a patchy yellow-green or olive-green lead glaze, but there is scope for tremendous individual variation in the ways in which this may be applied. Most jugs are given an all-over glaze on the upper surfaces, although the rim is normally left unglazed (113–114, 119). Below the mid-point the glaze becomes patchy and uneven, but frequently runs down as far as the base (121–122, 136). Occasionally a deliberate pattern is suggested by the criss-cross effect of run lines above the base (137), but this may simply be the result of the various angles at which the jug was held whilst the glaze was painted.

Glazing may sometimes be used over a white slip to produce more elaborate decorative effects with the slip found as a pale yellow-green. These slip-trailed lines may be striped in a combination of horizontal, vertical, or diagonal patterns. The simplest scheme appears to comprise a single horizontal line at the neck or shoulder (123), frequently with the addition of vertical lines trailing from it (113, 115, 130–131). Such vertical patterns may also be defined by a horizontal line below (134), or by a wavy line above (135). The lines may be set closely together (134), or they may be spaced more widely and then towards a sloping pattern (133).

Complex slip-trailed patterns may be built up, such as the criss-cross lattice pattern on a broad jug (128). The slip may be applied thinly with a brush (121), in this case to produce a continuous wavy line around the vessel, or more thickly with a palette knife (135). Sometimes the slip lines appear to follow cordons, or areas of raised clay, beneath (130, 133).

The jugs are frequently also decorated with stamped designs under the glaze, although an unusual example of an unglazed handle with rosette stamps copying a St Neots type (126) has already been noted. The stamps are generally of the grid design and are impressed upon applied pellets of clay which are arranged within panels defined by slip-trailed lines (129, 134–135). Less frequently the pellets may be applied around the neck (119), and sometimes the stamps may be impressed upon horizontal slip-trailed lines around the neck, apparently to give the impression of a rouletted cordon (133). There was one example of a true rouletted cordon (129), and another vessel where rouletted arches were arranged around the shoulder (132).

A number of instances of anthropomorphic decoration were identified. This was generally restricted to the neck and rim, where a combination of applied clay and slip-trailed lines was used to create human features. Several ears were picked out (138, 141), as well as an eye and nose (140). In one case the spout had been extended to form a nose or beak, and an internal partition added (139). Another example conformed more to the traditional 'knight jug' form (142). It comprised a clear human face, again forming the spout. The nose, beard and ears had been pulled out, and the cheeks pushed out from the interior. The eyes were formed in the rim, and the beard had been slashed to give the appearance of hair.

The later jugs (143–147) could be distinguished in a number of ways. The fabric was finer and lighter in colour, and glazes were more even, although still restricted to the upper surfaces (e.g. 143). Changes in the forms of handles have already been noted, and bases tended to become flatter (147). One jug (146) had a flaring neck which was finely corrugated and glazed all over the exterior. Tiny circles of clay had been applied at the shoulder, at the head of vertical cordons; in between were incised vertical wavy lines. Another (147) was decorated with a complex striped pattern of circles and straight lines. A third (144) had stabbed patterns around the shoulder, with traces of a single circular stamp above.

Illustrated sherds:

Figure	Pot	Year	East	North	Layer	Form
7.18	113	67	F-G	25	A3	J
7.18	114	67	F-J	6	A1	J
7.18	115	66	Q-R	11-12	A2	J
7.18	116	66	L-M	19	Ditch	J
7.18	117	66	D	15	A2	J
7.18	118	68	G	2	C	J
7.18	119	66	K	12-15	Ditch	J
7.18	120	67	G-J	5-19	TS-A3	J
7.18	121	67	F-H	25-27	TS-B	J
7.19	122	66	N	15	F4	J
7.19	123	67	F-J	4-6	A1-3	J
7.19	124	67	H	25	A1	J
7.19	125	67	E	12-13	Ditch	J
7.19	126	67	F	5	A1	J
7.19	127	68	L-M	10-11	A2	J
7.19	128	67	F-J	1-4	TS-A2	J
7.19	129	67	G-J	6	A1-3	J
7.19	130	67	F	27	A2	J
7.19	131	67	E	27	A3	J
7.21	132	66	I-J	21-22	Gully	J
7.21	133	67	F-G	19-25	TS-A2	J
7.21	134	67	F	4-6	A2	J
7.21	135	68	H-L	6-15	B-C	J
7.21	136	66	BB	9-10	B3	J
7.21	137	67	G-H	21	A3	J
7.21	138	67	F	19	A4	J
7.21	139	66	J-K	20-21	B2	J
7.21	140	66	S-T	11-12	A3	J
7.21	141	66	L-M	13-16	A2	J
7.22	142	66	CC-FF	10-14	TS	J
7.22	143	66	A-AA	8-23	TS-C	J
7.22	144	66	KK	29-35	C	J
7.22	145	66	K	21	C	J
7.23	146	66	O-T	9-10	A-A2	J
7.23	147	68	F-H	13-20	B	J

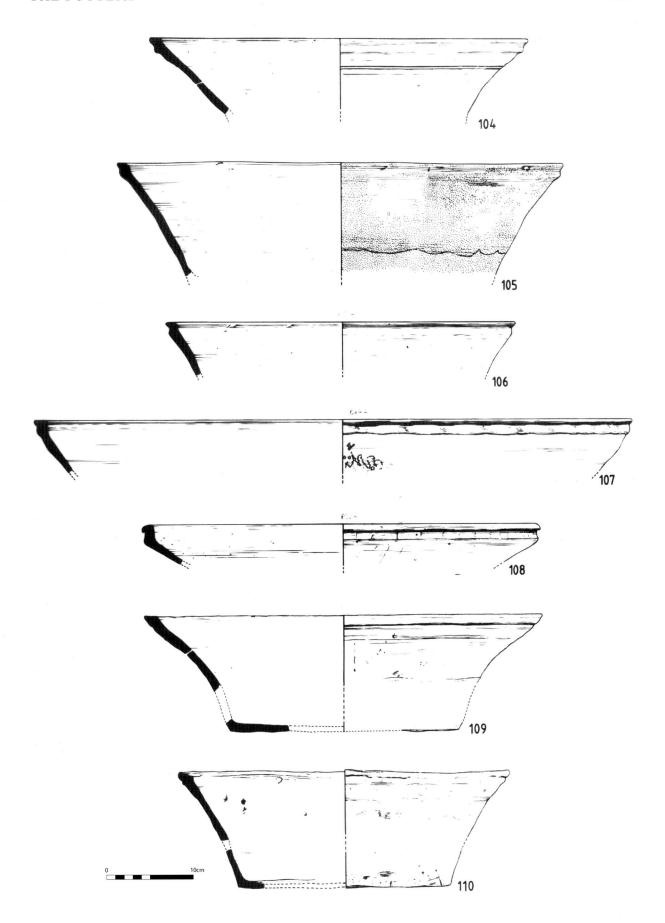

FIGURE 7.17
Pottery illustrations 104–110, Stanion/Lyveden wares

148

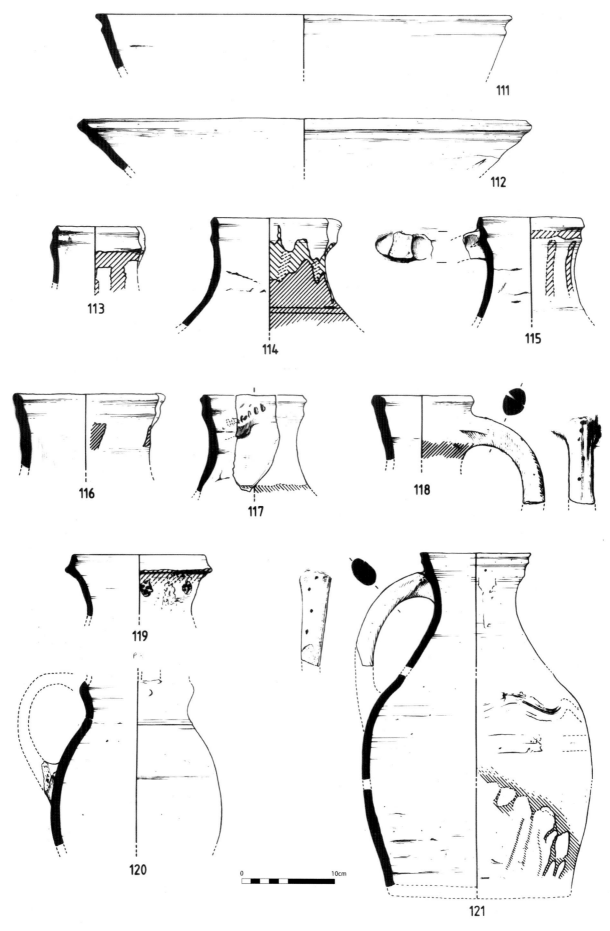

FIGURE 7.18

Pottery illustrations 111–121, Stanion/Lyveden wares

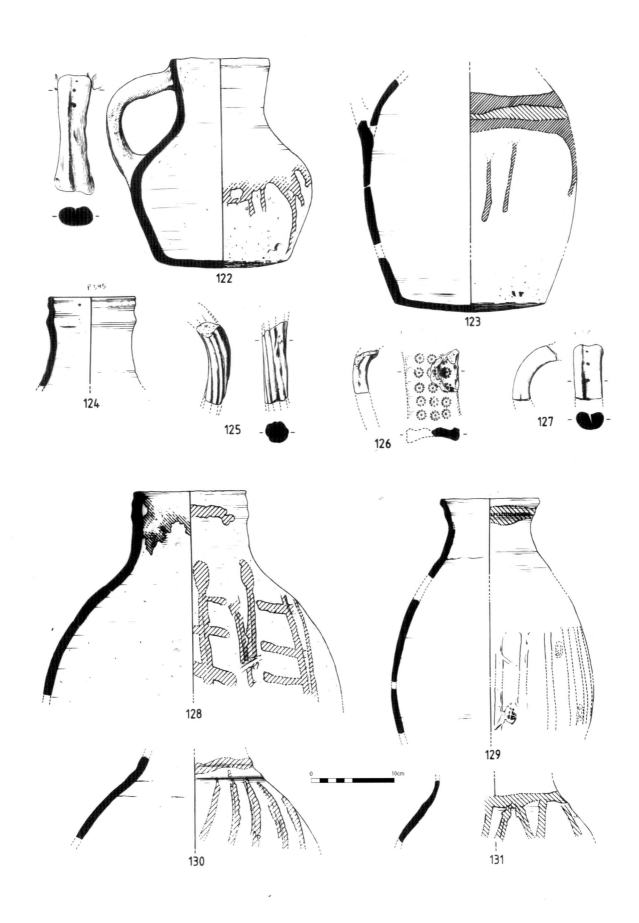

P 3.45

FIGURE 7.19

Pottery illustrations 122–131, Stanion/Lyveden wares

FIGURE 7.20
Jug from F4 (no. 122)

Other kiln products

A limited number of other ceramic forms were found in a Lyveden-Stanion fabric. These included a green-glazed lobed cup (148), probably of the 13th or 14th century *[now considered to be mid-14th to15th century in date]*, and a fragment of a bunghole from a cistern (149). Another sherd (150), with a green glaze on the side and probably from a jug, had been deliberately pierced and shaped for re-use as a spindlewhorl.

Illustrated sherds:

Figure	Pot	Year	East	North	Layer	Form
7.23	148	66	I-T	9-19	A2-C	Lobed cup
7.23	149	66	M	25-30	B-C	Cistern
7.23	150	67	H	4-5	A2	Spindlewhorl

Potterspury Ware
(McCarthy 1979, W18)

The excavation of medieval kilns at Potterspury is recorded by Jope (1950) and Mynard (1972). The range of forms produced is summarised in Mynard (1970). Documentary evidence attests to the presence of an important potting community at Potterspury by the last quarter of the 13th century. The proportion of Potterspury wares increases from the middle of the 14th century, and continues in use throughout the post-medieval life of the village.

The fabric is hard, with a smooth sandy texture, generally 5–7mm thick. The core is normally light grey, and unglazed surfaces may be reddish brown to salmon pink, or cream. Olive glazes occur on bowls or jugs with a cream fabric.

Of the types defined by Mynard (1970), only cooking pots, bowls and jugs are found at Faxton. Throwing lines could generally be seen on all forms.

Cooking pots

A wide range of sizes of cooking pots were represented, ranging from small (157, 168) to large (159, 161). Some examples had rather constricted necks (162). A variety of rims were observed, but most conformed to the distinctive Potterspury out-turned under-cut flange with concave top. Throwing lines could clearly be identified, and some were so exaggerated that the vessels almost appeared to have a corrugated profile (160). The same vessel also showed extensive sooting around the body. Some examples also had vertical applied thumbed strips (166).

An unusual heavy base from a large vessel (156), in a brown sandy fabric, should also be noted. Little attempt had been made to smooth out the coils of its construction and these survived as clear corrugations. The vessel may represent a proto-Potterspury form, possibly from Brackley.

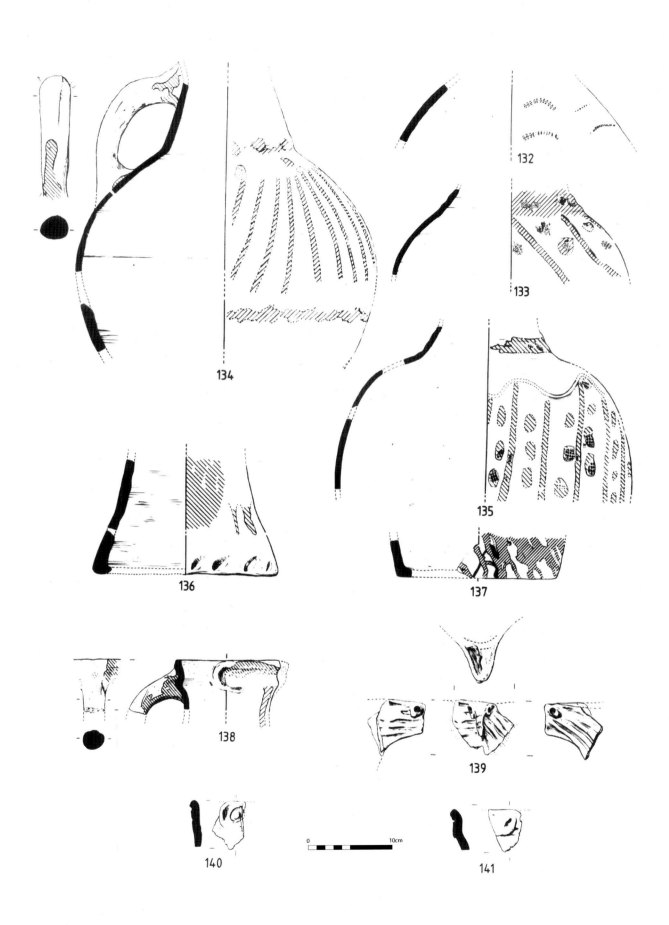

FIGURE 7.21
Pottery illustrations 132–141, Stanion/Lyveden wares

Illustrated sherds:

Figure	Pot	Year	East	North	Layer	Form
7.24	156	66	G	19-23	A	U
7.24	157	67	F-G	2-4	A1-3	CP
7.24	158	67	J	6	A3	CP
7.24	159	67	H	5-6	A3	CP
7.24	160	67	F-H	25-27	TS-A3	CP
7.24	161	66	Q-T	10	A	CP
7.24	162	67	F	3-4	TS-A2	CP
7.24	163	67	F	5	TS	CP
7.24	164	66	GG-HH	8-9	B2	CP
7.24	165	66	MM	0-8	B	CP
7.24	166	66	G	19	C	CP
7.24	167	66	F	11-13	A2	CP
7.24	168	67	H	6	A1	CP
7.24	169	67	G	7	TS-A1	CP
7.24	170	66	L-M	19	Ditch	CP

Bowls

The two main rim types identified by Mynard were both found at Faxton, namely the simple thickened bead rim (176) and the flanged type (174–175). One vessel had a continuous incised wavy line around the inside of the rim (171).

Illustrated sherds:

Figure	Pot	Year	East	North	Layer	Form
7.25	171	67	H	5	A2	B
7.25	172	66	M-N	13-14	A2	B
7.25	173	66	L-M	19	Ditch	B
7.25	174	66	A-B	23	B	B
7.25	175	68	L-N	19-23	A-B	B
7.25	176	66	K	19	Ditch	B

Jugs

Rims may be straight-sided (177, 179), or out-turned (178, 180). Spouts may be pushed out (191) or pinch-formed (180, 184). Bases are frequently thumbed (193). Spots of glaze could be seen on the necks of several jugs (177–178), with more on the shoulders of others (180, 192). Handles appeared to conform to three types:
—broad with slashes parallel to sides (181, 185), sometimes glazed on later examples (183),
—narrower, with diagonal slashes (186–187, 189–190), or stabbed (188),
—broad, with central thumb groove (184), sometimes emphasised to form deep central groove (182).

Illustrated sherds:

Figure	Pot	Year	East	North	Layer	Form
7.25	177	68	J-L	3-5	C	J
7.25	178	66	G-H	19-20	B	J
7.25	179	66	L-M	19	Ditch	J
7.25	180	68	D-E	4-5	Drain	J
7.25	181	66	C	16-20	C	J

7.25	182	66	A-B	17-19	B2	J
7.25	183	66	KK-TT	34	B	J
7.25	184	66	L-M	19	Ditch	J
7.25	185	66	G-H	20	B1	J
7.25	186	66	G	19-23	A	J
7.25	187	68	F-G	17-18	B	J
7.26	188	68	F-G	14-15	A	J
7.26	189	66	surface find	-	-	J
7.26	190	66	L-M	11	Oven	J
7.26	191	66	J	19-20	A2	J
7.26	192	68	F-G	8-18	A-B2	J
7.26	193	67	F	4	A2	J

A number of vessels of 'Potterspury type' were also found. These all had hard smooth sandy frequently micaceous fabric, but could not be matched with known Potterspury products. They included a fine tiny cooking pot (194), a jug with a corrugated neck (195), a large bowl with an in-turned rim (196), and two bowl forms with the more usual Potterspury rim (197–198). A few bases from small 'drinking jugs' were also noted among the late medieval material.

Illustrated sherds:

Figure	Pot	Year	East	North	Layer	Form
7.26	194	67	F-J	6	A1	CP
7.26	195	68	L-N	19-23	A-B	J
7.26	196	66	M-N	19-20	Ditch	B
7.26	197	66	RR-SS	14-15	TS	B
7.26	198	68	D-E	9-10	B	B

Brill and Boarstall wares
(McCarthy 1979, W14)

The kilns of the Brill potters, south Buckinghamshire, were partially excavated by Jope (1953–54), and more recently by Ivens (1981; 1982). The products of the neighbouring Boarstall kilns, from which they are virtually indistinguishable, have been published by Farley (1982).

In Oxford, Brill products are believed to commence in the mid-13th century, and continue through the medieval period [now considered to be early 13th century]. The near-complete baluster jug (199) was found in a ditch sealed with glazed Potterspury bowls of the late 14th century.

The fabric is hard, with a smooth texture, 4–5mm thick. Sherds are fully oxidized with a core and unglazed surfaces reddish yellow to very pale brown. The surfaces may be treated with vertical strips of a dark slip sometimes impressed with square-notched rouletting. Glazes are olive or green yellow.

Of the wide range of products known to have been made at Brill, only wheel-thrown jugs are found at Faxton. Where the form is distinguishable, it would appear to be of the baluster type, although one handle was found (201) copying a Rouen cup form (see Barton 1966). Two examples (200, 203) may have been made at either Brill or Boarstall.

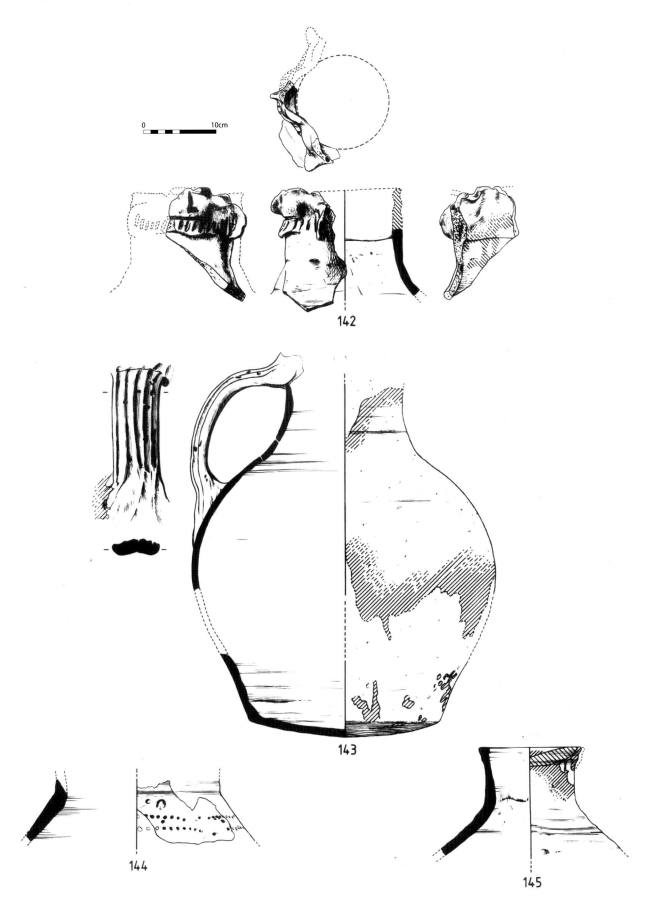

FIGURE 7.22
Pottery illustrations 142–145, Stanion/Lyveden wares

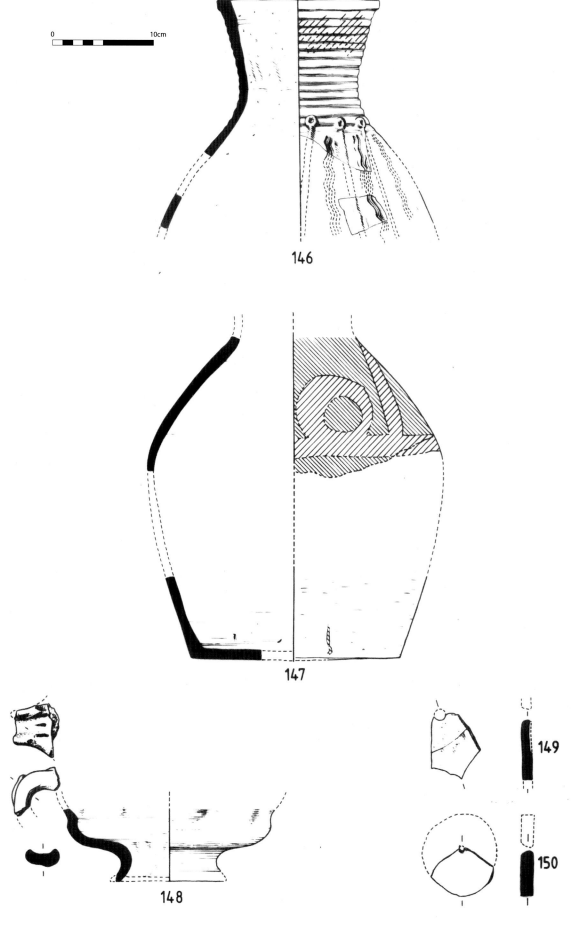

FIGURE 7.23

Pottery illustrations 146–150, Stanion/Lyveden wares

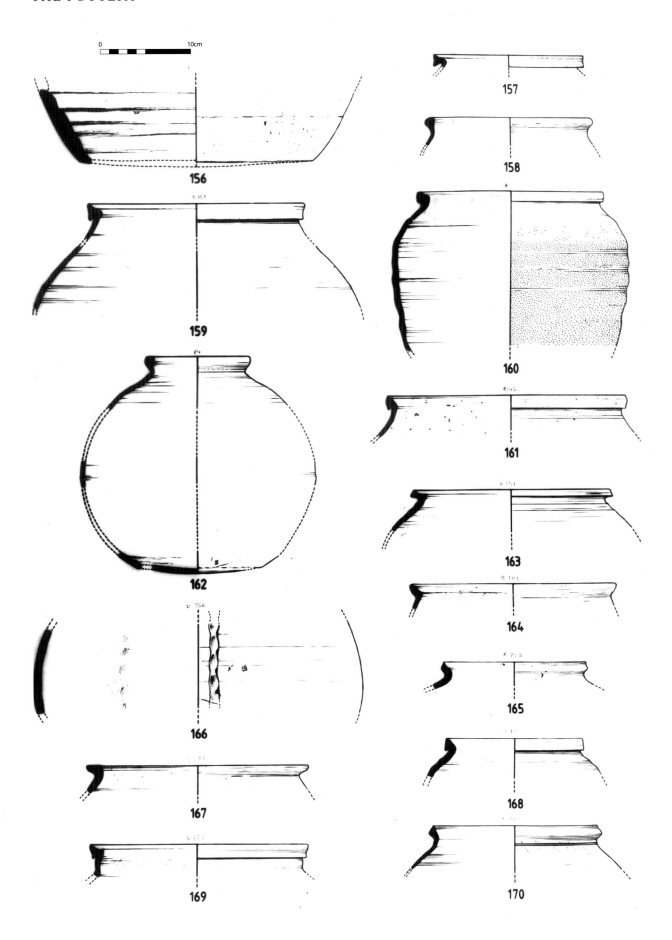

FIGURE 7.24
Pottery illustrations 156–170, Potterspury wares

Illustrated sherds:

Figure	Pot	Year	East	North	Layer	Form
7.27	199	66	I-J	21-22	Ditch	J
7.27	200	68	K-P	2-6	TS-B	J
7.27	201	67	J	8	A	J
7.27	202	67	F-G	3-6	A2-3	J
7.27	203	67	F-G	24	A4	J

Coventry white ware
(McCarthy 1979, W11)

This group is generally dated to the 13th or 14th century, although finds from Northampton suggest a continuation into the last half of the 15th century (McCarthy 1979, 160).

The fabric is hard, rough, white-firing and sandy.

Only two sherds of Coventry white ware were identified at Faxton, and their form confirms that these were rather fine imports. One (212) was a fragment of a slashed jug handle with a thick lustrous green glaze; the other (212A) was a pierced jug from a costrel, with a similar rich glaze.

Illustrated sherds:

Figure	Pot	Year	East	North	Layer	Form
7.28	212	68	H-J	14-15	A2	Jug
7.28	212A	68	F-G	4-6	B2	Costrel

Surrey White Ware 'Tudor Green'
(McCarthy 1979, W21)

The type has been the subject of extensive literature (see, for the example Moorhouse 1971a; 1971b); comments will be confined to the small amount of material recovered from Faxton.

The ware is generally dated from the mid-14th century to the end of the 15th century.

The fabric is hard, with smooth texture, and about 3mm thick. The core and unglazed surfaces are pale brown to white. The glaze is a rich mottled green yellow, only partially covering the body.

Only two examples of Surrey White Ware were found at Faxton; each was of an unusual form, possibly representing a type locally unobtainable. The first (210) may be a small jug; the second (211) the top of a large money-box (though it may also be a lid knob). The former is glazed from below the shoulder, and is also sooted internally; thus its use must also have been unusual.

Illustrated sherds:

Figure	Pot	Year	East	North	Layer	Form
7.28	210	68	L-N	19-23	A-B	Jug
7.28	211	68	G-H	2-6	Wall	Money-box

Miscellaneous Oxfordshire/Coventry region imports

Finally, there were a number of wheel-thrown vessels with unusual fabrics which may have been imported from the Oxford or Coventry region, but which cannot be tied down to a specific kiln. These include two cooking pots (204, 208) with light grey surfaces and a cream to light grey core, and plentiful calcite grits; two cooking pots in a coarse sandy, orange-red fabric (206–207), and a fragment of a thin-walled jug neck in a fine orange-red fabric (209) (these could be Coventry ware from Chilvers Coton).

Illustrated sherds:

Figure	Pot	Year	East	North	Layer	Form
7.28	204	67	E	6	A1	CP
7.28	205	67	E-G	17-18	A2-A3	CP
7.28	206	68	D-F	9-10	B	CP
7.28	207	68	F-G	20-21	Wall	CP
7.28	208	67	G-H	20-21	TS-A2	CP
7.28	209	67	F-H	25-26	A1-3	J

Great Brickhill

These wares are known from 13th- and 14th-century contexts, but it is uncertain how long they persisted. The earliest example from Faxton (215) could date from the 12th or 13th centuries; the majority are 13th century, with one 14th- or 15th-century example (220) [see commentary below by Paul Blinkhorn].

All the examples were in a very coarse, gritty fabric with grey core and orange-red to light-brown surfaces.

A number of unusual forms were identified, suggesting that these were types unavailable locally. These included a number of large cooking pots (213–216), a bowl with a thumbed in-turned rim (217), a jug with an oval handle (220), and sherds from other forms, comprising the flanged base and raised bunghole of a cistern (219), and the raised circular hole from a curfew (218) [now identified as the bunghole from a cistern].

Illustrated sherds:

Figure	Pot	Year	East	North	Layer	Form
7.29	213	66	C	19	B	CP
7.29	214	66	N-O	20-21	B	CP
7.29	215	67	G	6	A2	CP
7.29	216	66	BB-HH	9-12	B-C1	CP
7.29	217	68	H-J	9-10	B	B
7.29	218	68	H	14-15	A2	Curfew
7.29	219	68	D-E	11-13	A	Cistern
7.29	220	68	K-Q	6-13	B	J

East Midland Late Medieval Reduced Ware
(McCarthy 1979, W20)

This type was first identified by Moorhouse (1974), and named from its occurrence on a number of sites in the East Midlands. Brickhill (North Buckinghamshire) was suggested as a possible kiln site, but this is presently doubted (Terry Pearson pers. comm.). Moorhouse concludes that the type was introduced in the early 15th century.

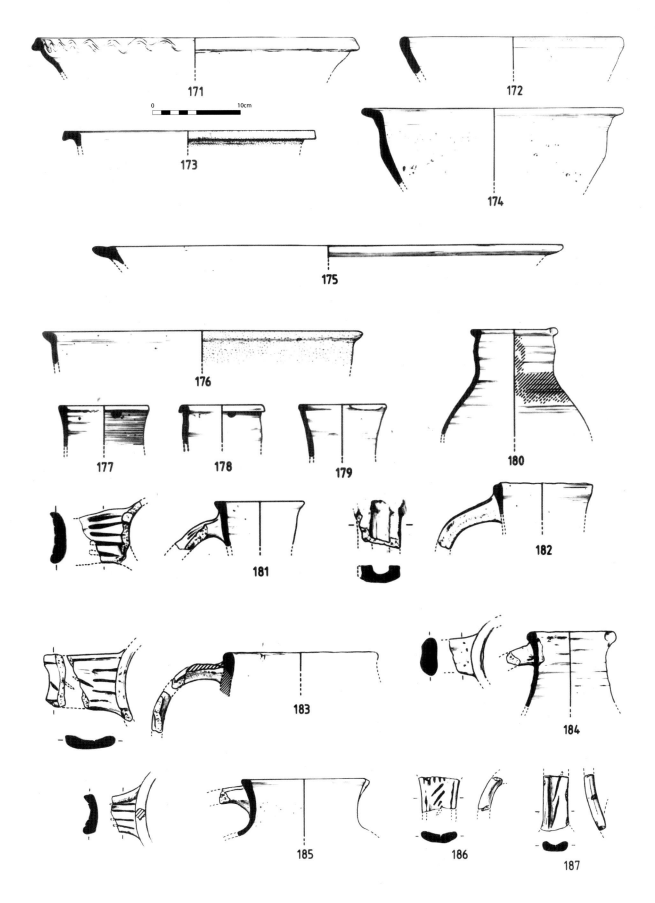

FIGURE 7.25
Pottery illustrations 171–187, Potterspury wares

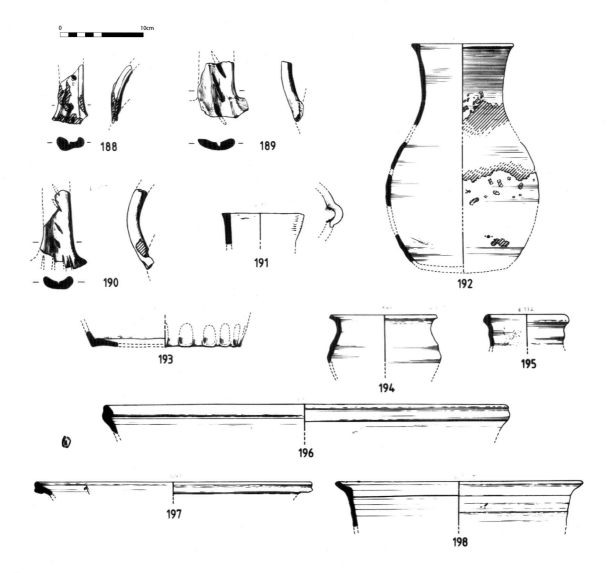

FIGURE 7.26
Pottery illustrations 188–198, Potterspury wares

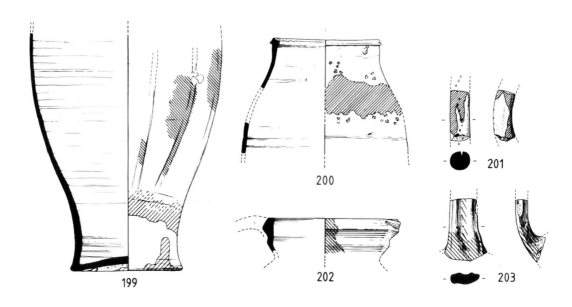

FIGURE 7.27
Pottery illustrations 199–203, Brill and Boarstall wares

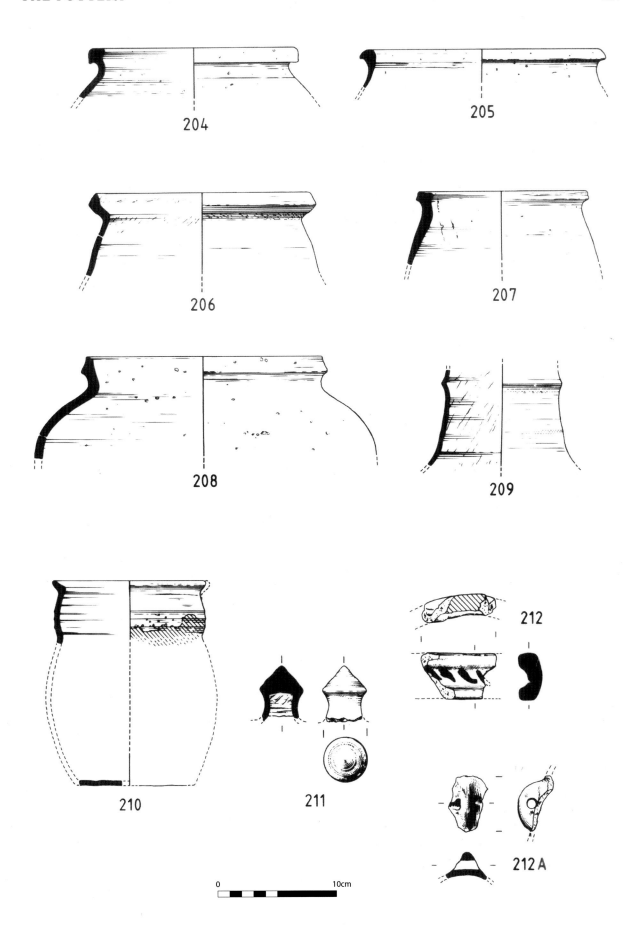

FIGURE 7.28
Pottery illustrations 204–212a, Brill and Boarstall wares, Surrey White Ware, and others

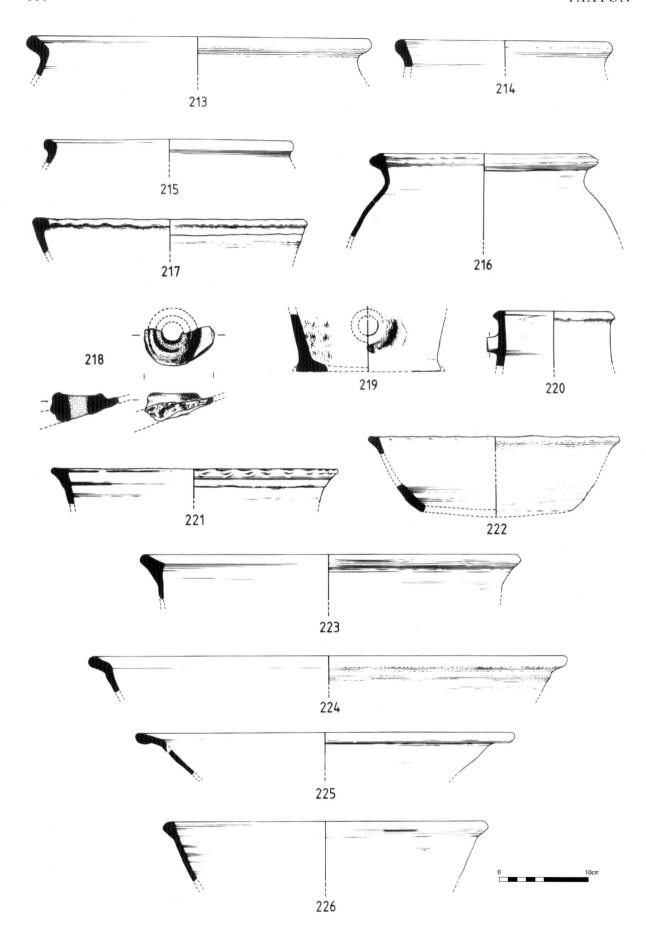

FIGURE 7.29

Pottery illustrations 213–226, Great Brickhill wares, East Midland Late Medieval Reduced wares

The fabric is hard, with a rough sandy texture, and 5–8mm thick. The core and surfaces are usually grey to light grey, sometimes with a brown margin. One vessel (226) of Late Medieval Reduced Ware type had a light grey fabric with dark grey surfaces and core, and a coarse gritty micaceous fabric.

The forms identified at Faxton comprise a variety of wheel-thrown bowls. The smaller examples have thumbed out-turned rims (221–222); the larger types have flanged rims (224–226); but some have vertical sides and must be deeper (223).

Illustrated sherds:

Figure	Pot	Year	East	North	Layer	Form
7.29	221	68	L-N	19-23	A-B	B
7.29	222	68	K-N	13-15	A-B2	B
7.29	223	68	H-J	4-7	A4	B
7.29	224	66	G-H	20	B	B
7.29	225	68	G-J	10-14	Wall-B2	B
7.29	226	68	J-L	3-5	C	B

Repairs

Sherds from 15 vessels which showed evidence of attempted repair were identified. This took the form of a small hole drilled through the body. In one case (238) binding of fine copper wire survived in position looped through the hole. The hole was never more than 15mm from the edge of the sherd, and in only two cases was it more than 30mm from the rim. Presumable a fine crack had developed during the vessel's life, generally from the rim. In order to strengthen the vessel two holes had been drilled either side of the crack, for the insertion of the binding. The vessels had subsequently fractured along the original line of weakness; hence it was normal to find only one half of the repair. In one case (236) both sides were recovered, although sherds were found at least 15m apart.

Flaking around the drill holes, and narrowing of the hole at one end, provided evidence for the direction of drilling for 14 of the repairs. In six cases the hole had been drilled from the inside surface of the vessel; in two cases from the outside; and six holes had been drilled from both sides, producing narrowing towards the centre. In two of the latter examples (240–241) the drill holes did not meet, and in one of these cases (241), the repair had apparently given up once this had been realised, as the holes did not penetrate through the vessel.

The drill holes showed a range of diameters, ranging from 1.5mm to 6mm, but it was not possible to identify holes made by the same drill, although the variation in diameters demonstrated that several tools must have been used.

Apart from the one example of 'botched' repair (241), which had a pouring lip, probably of a jug, all the repairs were to bowls. Presumably these vessels could not have subsequently been used as containers for liquids, but were nevertheless thought

to be worth retaining for some other function. All the repaired vessels except two (236, 241) were in the common Stanion/Lyveden fabric types. These two were of a Potterspury fabric. The fact that it was felt to be worthwhile to repair these damaged vessels must be taken as evidence for a period of impoverishment in the development of Faxton, or at least for a period of disruption of pottery shortage at Raunds during the middle to late 14th century, and it could be that this was a more widespread phenomenon (see Conclusions below).

Certainly the distribution of the repaired sherds appears to show that repairing may have been restricted to certain areas of the village, although they were recovered from all levels. The repairs from the 1966 excavations were found in two areas: I-J/21-22 and N-CC/11-13 within Croft 29 1966; those found in 1967 were all confined to the area of Croft 6 (as also another sherd from fieldwalking).

Illustrated sherds:

Figure	Pot	Year	East	North	Layer	Form
7.30	227	66	S-T	11-13	A2	B
7.30	228	66	O-P	11-12	C	B
7.30	229	66	I-J	21-22	Low levels	B
7.30	230	66	I	21-22	E-W wall	B
7.30	231	66	CC	11-12	F1	B
7.30	232	66	N-O	11-12	B2	B
7.30	233	67	F	6	-	B
7.30	234	67	F-J	5	A1	B
7.30	235	67	F-H	1-2	TS	B
7.30	236	67	E-H	1-7	TS	B
7.30	237	67	G-H	21	A3	B
7.30	238	67	H-J	4	A3	B
7.30	239	67	G	5	TS	B
7.31	240	66	House 2	-	TS	B
7.31	241	67	F	2	A3	J

7.4 POTTERY DISTRIBUTIONS

The following model is proposed for the pottery sequence observed at Faxton. Both the general outline and dates were based upon work by Terry Pearson on the Raunds Furnells ceramic sequence. Paul Blinkhorn makes further [comments] below on a revised chronology:

Date	Pottery types	Comments
c.1150–1200/25 [now considered to be 1150–1200]	Later Developed St Neots Ware Earlier medieval shell/ oolite-tempered wares Stamford Ware Some Developed Stamford Ware	

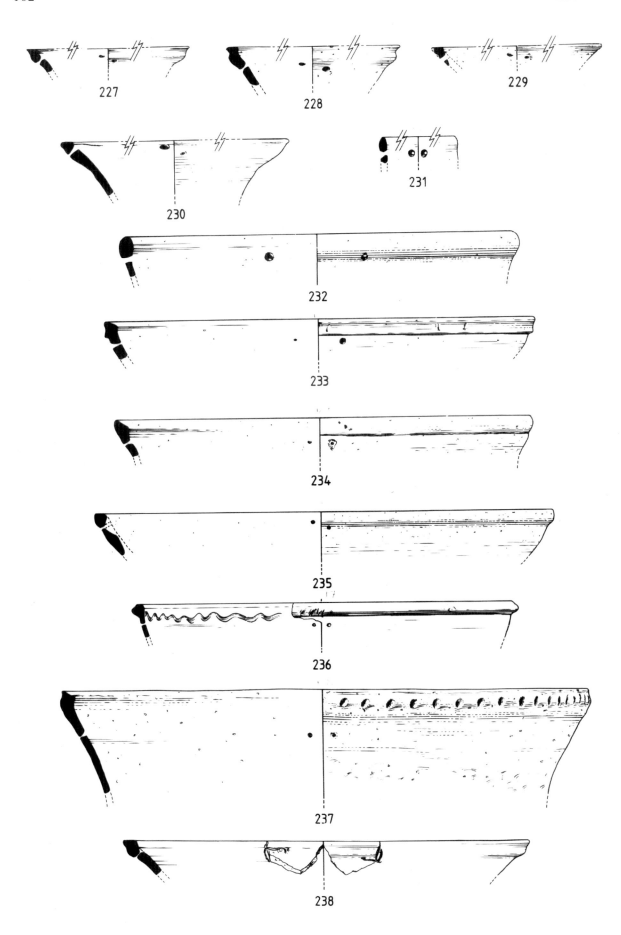

FIGURE 7.30
Pottery illustrations 227–238, repairs in pots

c.1225/50–1325 [now considered to be 1200–1250]	Lyveden hand-made coarse wares Stanion hand-made glazed jugs Brill/Boarstall no clear/Oxon jugs	Everted rimmed jars
c.1325–1390 [now considered to be 1250–1350]	Potterspury jugs Stanion/Lyveden wares continue Late Brill wares	Proportion in c.1350+ Repairer active in late 14thC?
c.1390–1410/20 [now considered to be mid- to late 14th century]	Lyveden wheel-thrown jugs Potterspury wares continue	
c.1425–75 [now considered to be late 14th to mid-15th century]	Late Medieval Reduced Ware Potterspury wares continue	
Post-medieval		Only on Croft 52–53 1968

Croft 29 1966 excavations

A total of 11,564 sherds of medieval pottery were recovered during the 1966 season. The total weight of this pottery exceeded 90kg, with an average sherd weight of 7.5g. The distribution of the pottery is shown in Figure 7.32, plotted by 5ft grid square (1.5 x 1.5m). The quantity of pottery per excavated layer was as follows:

	No. of sherds
Topsoil	698
A1-2	5,602
B1-3	3,615
C-D	1,649

The density plots indicate a general spread of material but with some marked concentrations. In the A layers the greatest density is in the area O-T/11-16, having shifted westwards from the concentration on the B layers at AA-HH/9-13. Both these clusters are on the edge of the yard area, and may represent midden deposits. Again the assemblages seem to have been heavily disturbed, with a high proportion of small abraded sherds, probably reflecting the longer life span of the croft. The high degree of disturbance can also be seen in the proportion of conjoining sherds, which is far smaller than for Crofts 6–8:

	No. of conjoins	Percentage of conjoins
Topsoil	8	1.1
A1-2	105	1.9
B1-3	136	3.8
C-D	79	4.8

Once more it is notable that the proportion of conjoins slightly increases in the lower levels, as these are less mixed. The average sherd weight also increases from 6.8g in the A layers to 8.1g in C-D. Heavy post-depositional disturbance is also attested by plots of the distribution of conjoining sherds from individual vessels (Figure 7.33). One vessel, a cooking pot from Great Brickhill (216) is restricted to the easterly end of the yard, where it is found in layers B and C. The other four vessels (80, 82, 79, 88: not illustrated), representing a Lyveden cooking pot and Stanion-Lyveden jugs respectively, were found distributed in the area of the houses and westerly end of the yard. In some cases (e.g. 79) the disturbance seemed mainly to be horizontal; in others (e.g. 88) there was considerable vertical movement as well.

One vessel in particular, a late Stanion jug (143), appears to have been almost systematically spread

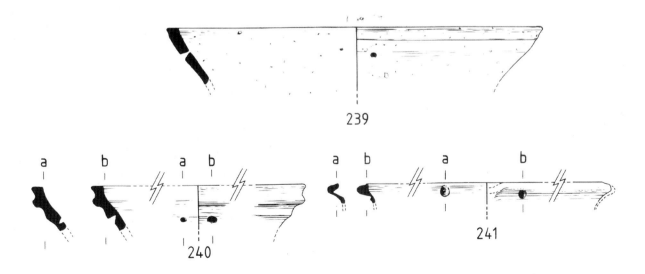

FIGURE 7.31

Pottery illustrations 240–241, repairs in pots

throughout the limits of the croft, with sherds from almost every square and level (Figure 7.34). At the lowest levels two concentrations of sherds from this vessel may be identified, at A-C/18-22 and I-K/15-21, which may be either side of the first phase building. In layer B the main concentration moves south, perhaps representing disturbance of the earlier westerly cluster, so much that none is left in the original area at this level. One sherd is also carried east to AA11-14. Finally, in layer A and the topsoil levels the densest area is once again in the north-east, over the original easterly concentration, in yard areas dug or churned up.

Some of the features appeared to promise sealed assemblages of pottery in contemporary use. However, most only yielded fragmentary and heavily abraded sherds. The only significant group was a number of near-complete vessels recovered from the ditch at I-J/21-22. This included a Lyveden cooking pot (91), a baluster jug from Brill (199) and Lyveden bowls (109–110). In addition, a Stanion jug, complete except for a broken spout (122) was found at the south end of F4, the clay-lined water hole, with its base resting on the bottom. The jug was badly worn, and must have been continuously rocked on its base at the front. Finally, the clearance of the oven at M11 yielded a transitional early Lyveden cooking pot (90), which must provide a *terminus post quem* for the use of the oven.

Pottery sequence in Croft 29 1966

Most phases of the medieval pottery are represented in the assemblage from Croft 29 1966. As noted above, however, the earliest pottery from the area consists of residual Roman and Early/Middle Anglo-Saxon sherds. A few Late Saxon sherds, as well as fragments of Thetford Ware are also represented.

Stamford Ware and Developed Stamford Ware pitchers were found on this croft and by the 12th century occupation was well established, with large quantities of Developed St Neots Ware vessels. The transition between St Neots and Stanion/Lyveden is well represented, followed by true Stanion/Lyveden forms. Vessels were also brought from Olney Hyde, along with quantities of cooking pots from Great Brickhill. Later occupation is represented by a wide range of Potterspury forms, including glazed and unglazed jugs and cooking pots. However, the products of the Stanion/Lyveden kilns continued to be the most extensively used pottery throughout the 14th and into the 15th century. The latest datable vessel in a Lyveden fabric is probably the 16th- or possibly 15th-century copy of a lobed cup (148). Some 15th-century occupation is also represented by quantities of Late Medieval Reduced Ware, and later Potterspury forms *[further data on the later medieval and post-medieval fabrics is provided by Paul Blinkhorn below]*.

Crofts 6–9 1967 excavations

The pottery from Crofts 6–9 represents material from three similar crofts on the periphery of the village. It will first be considered as a single assemblage before differences between the crofts are discussed.

A total of 20,357 medieval sherds was recovered from the three crofts. The distribution of the material is shown in Figures 7.35–7.37, plotted by 10ft grid square (3 x 3m). The total number of sherds per excavated layer was as follows:

	No. of sherds
Topsoil	2,353
A1	4,723
A2	5,247
A3	4,037
A4/5	1,474
B1/2	413

The density distribution plots reveal a general spread of material in the topsoil, bearing little relation to underlying features, apart from an increased density around G2, relating to the higher density in the same area in lower levels (Figure 7.35). Throughout Layer A most of the pottery comes from two major concentrations: F-J/2-6 and F-G/17-20. The density plots indicate some clusters which continue through several layers, as at F18, with a general fall-off around them. Two areas show concentrations of material in the lower levels which are not reflected in the layers above: F-G/25-25 in Layers A4/5 and F-J/7-8 in B1/2.

This distribution is consistent with deposits which have been disturbed, but not to such an extent that any real concentrations have become totally dissipated. The lower degree of disturbance in A4/5 and B1/2 (Figure 7.37) is corroborated by the figures for the numbers of conjoining sherds. These indicate the proportion of sherds from each layer which can be identified as coming from those vessels for which more than one sherd can be found:

	No. of conjoins	Percentage of conjoins
Topsoil	184	7.8
A1	375	7.9
A2	279	5.3
A3	289	7.2
A4/5	182	12.4
B1/2	92	22.3

However, the degree of disturbance throughout most layers is only confirmed when the distribution of conjoining sherds for particular vessels is plotted (Figures 7.38–7.40). This high level of post-depositional disturbance was one of the main factors indicating that a higher level of quantification was unwarranted, and that no sealed assemblage could be identified.

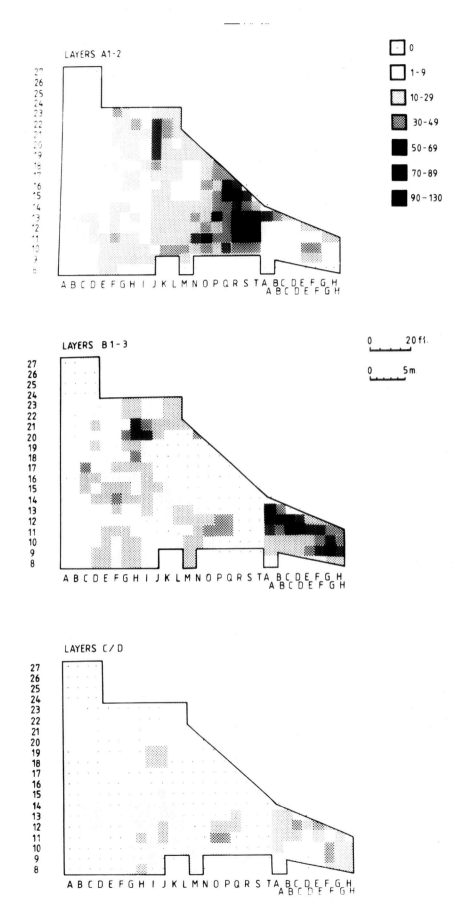

FIGURE 7.32
Croft 29 1966. Pottery distributions across Layers A1-2, B1-3 and C-D

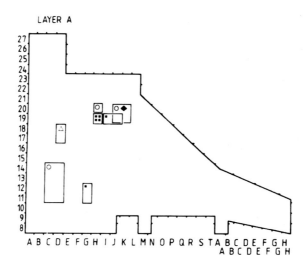

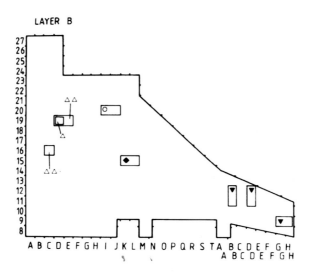

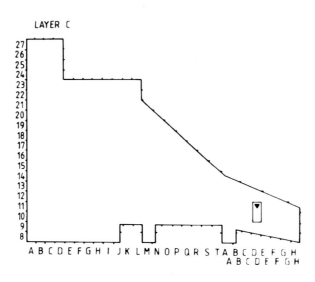

1 sherd of Pot   216 ▼   p80 △   p82 ◆   p79 ▪   p88 ○

FIGURE 7.33
Croft 29 1966. Sherd links

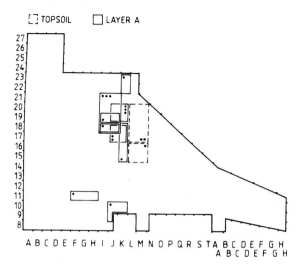

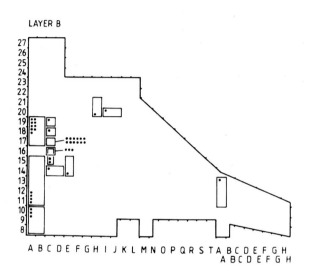

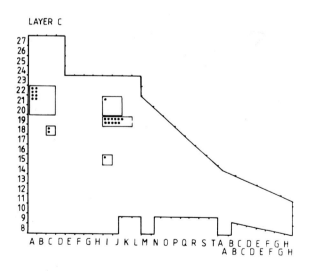

Pot 143 (1 Sherd) •

FIGURE 7.34
Croft 29 1966. Pottery distributions across Layers A1-2, B1-3 and C-D

Figure 7.38 shows the spread of material within the yard area of Croft 6. This was a badly disturbed area with a high proportion of small abraded sherds and the remains of only three or four relatively complete vessels. Within the croft area there was an uneven distribution. The sherds from several vessels are distributed in a north–south direction, perhaps reflecting the predominant direction of later ploughing. These include sherds from two vessels (81, 17: not drawn) which have been carried across a possible earlier croft boundary. The distribution of a third vessel (128) is restricted to the south side of this boundary, whilst a fourth (120) is concentrated to the north. Sherds from this latter jug, however, were found extremely widely dispersed, with one conjoining sherd located in the topsoil over 18m from its nearest join.

Figure 7.39 shows that the spread of material in Croft 7 is again principally in a north–south direction, but that it is less pronounced than for Croft 6. In general, the pottery from this croft was even more disturbed than that from Croft 6. One 13th-century import from the Oxford/Coventry region (205) was found restricted to the south of the internal ditch. Three other unillustrated vessels (210, 212, 226), representing a shelly St Neots Ware cooking pot and two Stanion-Lyveden jugs respectively, were also disturbed both vertically and horizontally. For instance, one sherd of 212 was recovered from layer B, whilst a second was found in the topsoil on the other side of the ditch. Sherds from several Stanion-Lyveden jugs with a white residue adhering to the interior surface were also found in this croft.

Finally, Figure 7.40 shows that for Croft 8, vessels had again become widely dispersed, but with the emphasis upon movement in a north–south direction. From the pottery, this croft appeared to be the least disturbed of those excavated at this end of the village. Once more, one or two sherds from individual vessels were recovered from the lower levels, but the majority of sherds were found disturbed in higher levels (e.g. 57, 69, 71, and 160). In two cases (209 and 307: an unillustrated cooking pot of Lyveden type) north–south movement was restricted, and the spread was more in an east–west direction.

By contrast, one vessel from Croft 8 (23) had practically survived *in situ*. The rim of this large Developed St Neots cooking pot was found inverted, resting in burnt material. It was backed up on the north side by yellow natural clay which contained charcoal, and there were some burnt stone fragments in association. This would apparently seem to represent the re-use of a vessel which had already lost its base, as a means of restricting a fire to one area, or as a container for something which was to be burnt.

Pottery sequence from Crofts 6–9 1967

The pottery assemblage from each of these crofts was noteworthy for consisting almost entirely of local calcite-gritted wares, mainly Developed St Neots wares, transitional St Neots–Stanion/Lyveden vessels, and true Stanion/Lyveden forms. Each croft was also marked by the small proportion of regional imports, although quantities of Potterspury Ware were recovered from Crofts 6 and 8. It is the presence or absence of Potterspury Ware which may apparently be used to date the end of occupation on individual crofts in this area. Some consideration of the pottery sequence for each croft is therefore in order.

Croft 6

The earliest pottery is Developed St Neots Ware and some Stamford Ware, which need not date the beginning of medieval occupation to before the 12th century. One hand-made Late Saxon sherd stands out as the only vessel from the area earlier than the 12th century, and may have been redeposited from elsewhere *[but see below for a new analysis]*. There is a large amount of transitional St Neots–Stanion/Lyveden material, dating to the 12th and 13th centuries. This is followed by similarly large quantities of typical Lyveden bowls and cooking pots of the 13th and 14th centuries. A number of unglazed Potterspury cooking pots also probably belong to the 14th century, continuing into the 15th. The latest pottery from this croft is represented by a few examples of imported Brill jugs of the late 14th century, and a few sherds of Late Medieval Reduced Ware.

Croft 7

The pottery from Croft 7 again commences with 12th-century Developed St Neots wares; forms belong to the St Neots–Stanion/Lyveden transition, including very shelly wares of the late 12th century. There are some Stanion/Lyveden 13th-century forms, but the rarity of later Lyveden cooking pots, and the total absence of Potterspury wares or later types would seem to indicate that occupation of this croft ceased sometime before the early 14th century.

Croft 8

Occupation of Croft 8 may begin later than that of Crofts 6 and 7 as there are few Developed St Neots vessels and only small quantities of Stamford Ware. Much of the pottery belongs to the transitional St Neots–Stanion/Lyveden phase, including oolite-tempered and shelly wares. Again there are few later Lyveden cooking pot forms, although the presence of some Potterspury forms indicates that occupation of this croft continued later than Croft 7, and into the 14th century.

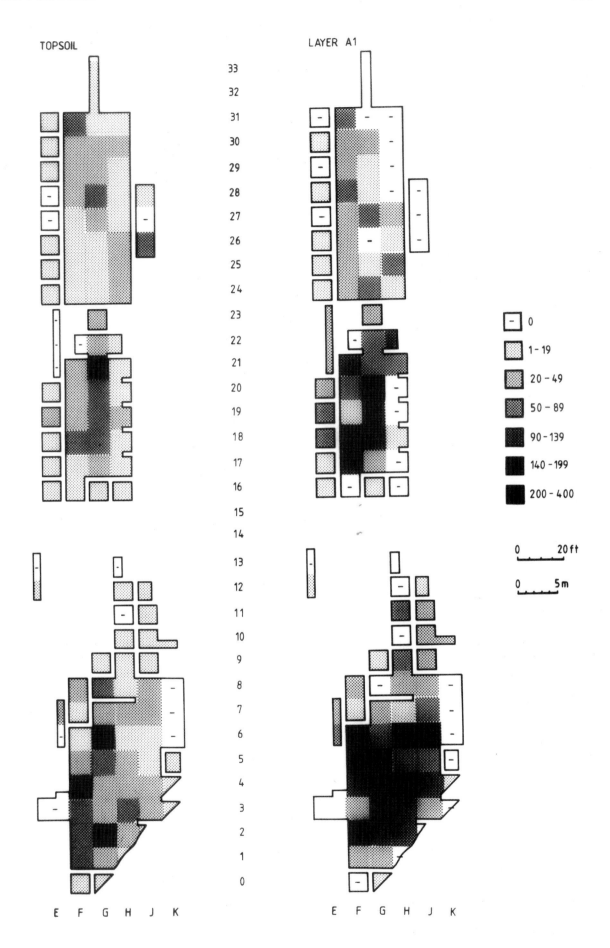

FIGURE 7.35
Crofts 6–9 1967. Pottery distribution. Layers topsoil (left) and A1 (right)

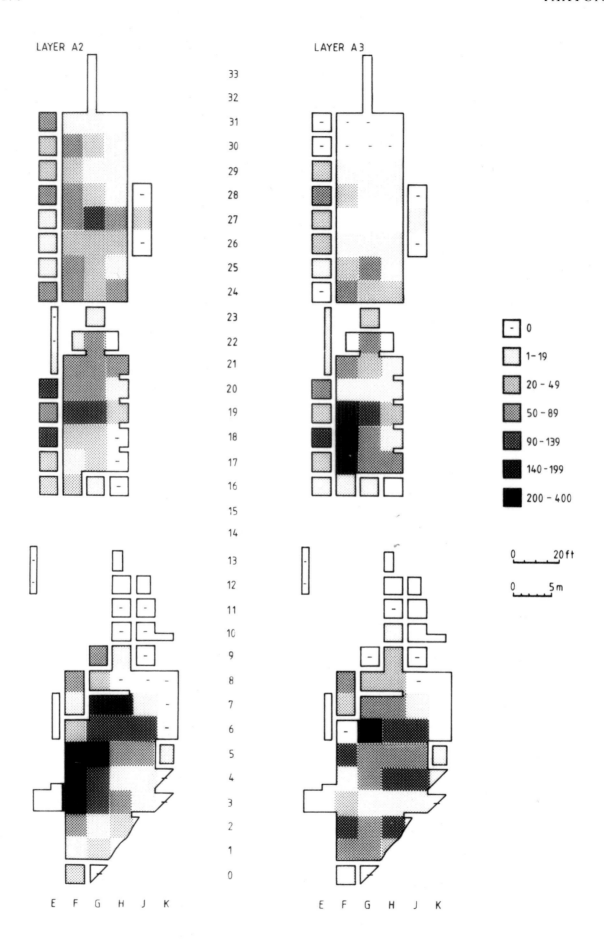

FIGURE 7.36
Crofts 6–9 1967. Pottery distribution. Layers A2 (left) and A3 (right)

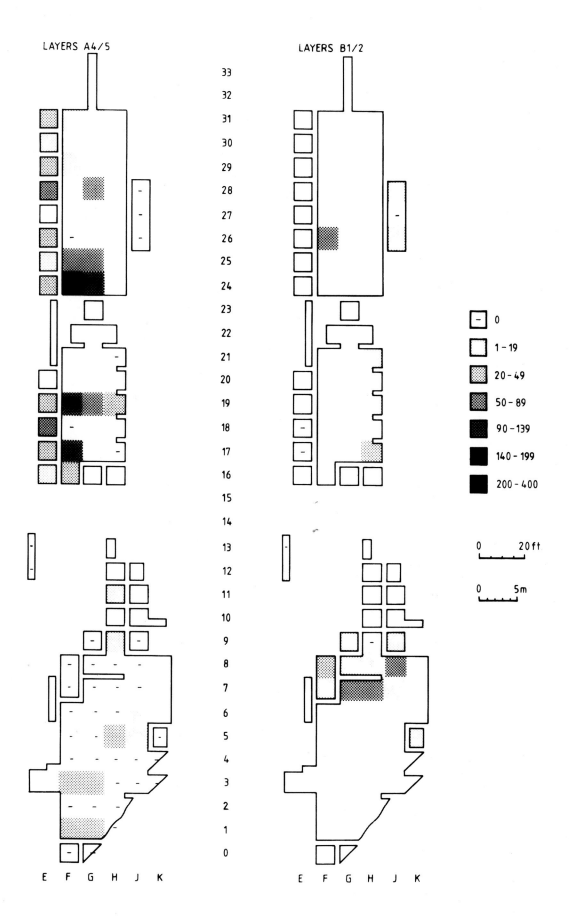

FIGURE 7.37
Crofts 6–9 1967. Pottery distribution. Layers A4/5 (left) and B1/2 (right)

Croft 52–53 1968 excavations

A much smaller total of 2,657 later medieval sherds was recovered from the excavation of Croft 52–53 in 1968, although this was augmented by a similar quantity of post-medieval pottery (see below). The medieval pottery distribution is shown in Figure 7.41, plotted by 5ft grid square (1.5 x 1.5m). This reveals some excavated areas with little or no medieval pottery, as well as some concentrations of material. The number of medieval sherds recovered from each layer was as follows:

	No. of sherds
A1-4	441
B1-3	1,169
C	360

Whereas in the other crofts most of the pottery had been recovered from the A layers, in Croft 52-53 1968 it was found lower down in B1-3. In this case A1-4 would appear to represent post-medieval levels, containing only residual medieval pottery.

Once again, the pottery was highly abraded and appeared to have been heavily disturbed, although the proportion of conjoining sherds was comparable with that from Crofts 6–8. The lower levels again comprised the least disturbed assemblages:

	No. of conjoins	Percentage of conjoins
Topsoil	6	8.8
A1-4	26	5.9
B1-3	100	8.6
C	46	12.8

The high level of both vertical and horizontal mixing can also be seen in the distribution of conjoining sherds of selected vessels (Figure 7.42). The spread of sherds from ten representative vessels is illustrated. Sherds of three vessels (152–153, 45: not illustrated) were found only in layer A, whilst fragments of another (28: not illustrated) were found in adjoining areas in layers A and B. Four vessels (16, 18, 46, all not illustrated) were found spread within layer B, whilst one vessel (15: not illustrated) was confined to C. One sherd (18) in particular appeared to be distributed fairly widely, but within the area of the house. Finally, one Brill jug (200) was remarkable for comprising one sherd from B, 3 from A and 6 from topsoil.

Pottery sequence in Croft 52–53 1968

The ceramic sequence represented in Croft 52–53 1968 is entirely in keeping with its long structural sequence, and continuation of occupation to the end of its medieval period. The earliest vessels, however, represent a similar starting date to the other crofts examined. Although sherds of Stamford Ware jugs were found, none need be earlier than the 12th century. There are also relatively large quantities of 12th-century Developed St Neots Ware. The later 12th and 13th centuries are under-represented, however. There are no transitional St Neots–Stanion/Lyveden wares, and few Stanion/Lyveden cooking pots of the 13th century. There is more material from the 14th century, with products of Brill and Boarstall, and other Oxfordshire and Buckinghamshire kilns, such as Great Brickhill. There is also a full range of 14th- and 15th-century Potterspury products, including a large number of glazed wares. Potterspury continued to supply Faxton into the post-medieval period. In the 15th century, glazed jugs from Stanion were also in use on this croft, as well as Late Medieval Reduced Ware. The Oxfordshire kilns continued to fill most needs through the 15th century, and into the 16th century. Examples of Coventry W11 and Surrey White Ware were also found on this croft.

7.5 CONCLUSIONS

The range of pottery excavated at Faxton compares closely with that recovered from the medieval village excavations at Wythemail (Mynard 1969b). On each croft the majority of the pottery belonged to a broad class of fine or coarse, calcite-gritted or corky wares, corresponding to McCarthy's T2 (1979). This mainly includes Developed St Neots type wares, vessels known to have been made at Stanion and Lyveden, and to a lesser extent, those made at Olney Hyde and Harrold. In the 14th century *[in 2019 considered to be mid-13th century]* this was supplemented by Pottersbury wares. Together, these kilns provided the bowls, cooking pots and jugs which form over 99% of the pottery assemblage. Throughout the existence of the village however, these wares were also supplemented by regional imports of Stamford Ware, and products from the Oxford and Coventry regions, which also supplied the more unusual requirements. Differences between the crofts suggest use of fewer regional imports by those living on the fringe of the village, in Crofts 6 to 9. This is supported by the other evidence: only a small number of small finds and no coins was found on these crofts.

It is also hoped, however, that this report has demonstrated the value of studying the pottery for the light it throws upon the archaeology, rather than as a separate study. In particular, the method proposed by Moorhouse (1983) has indicated that the stratigraphy was highly disturbed, and that further detailed quantification would have been unwarranted, if not misleading. This study demonstrates the high degree of both vertical and horizontal movement of sherds which may be encountered.

Nevertheless, we are able to come to a number of conclusions about the sequence and length of occupation on the individual crofts. Occupation

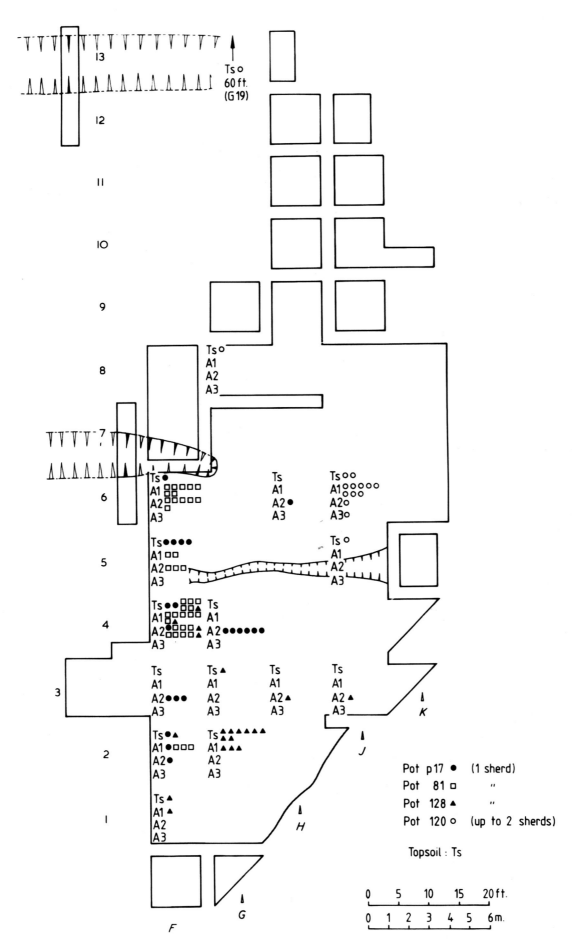

FIGURE 7.38
Crofts 6 1967. Sherd links in the southern area

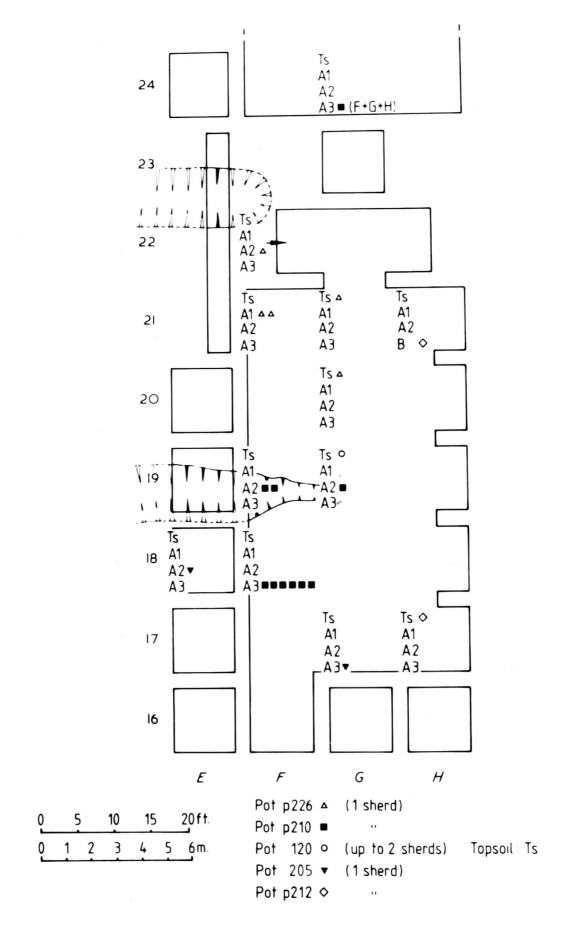

FIGURE 7.39
Crofts 7 1967. Sherd links in the central area

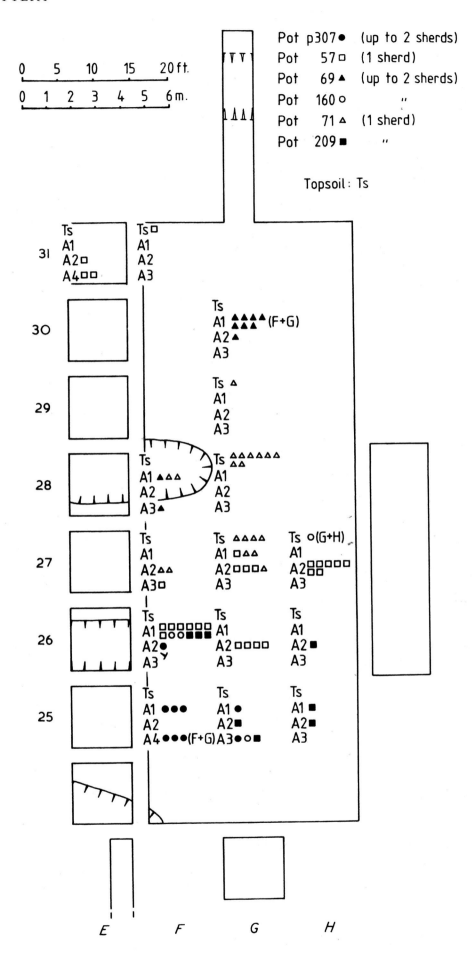

FIGURE 7.40
Crofts 8 1967. Sherd links in the northern area

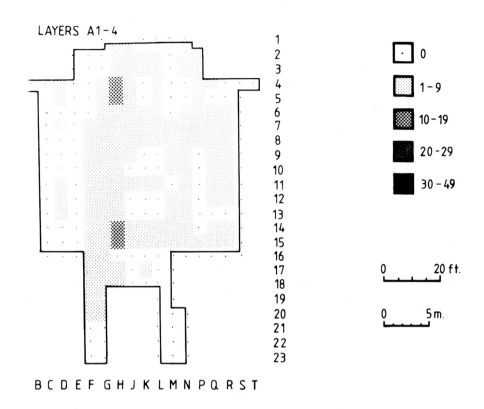

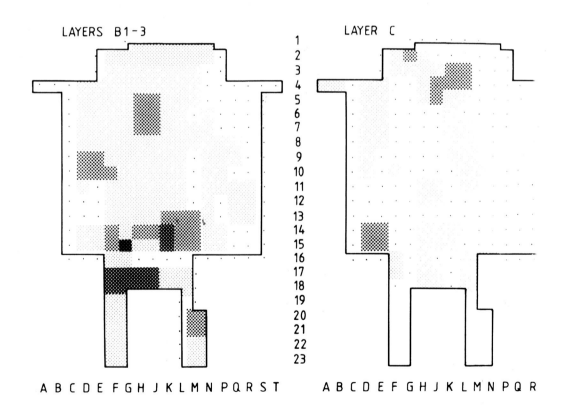

FIGURE 7.41

Croft 52–53 1968. Pottery distributions in Layers A1-4, B1-3 and C

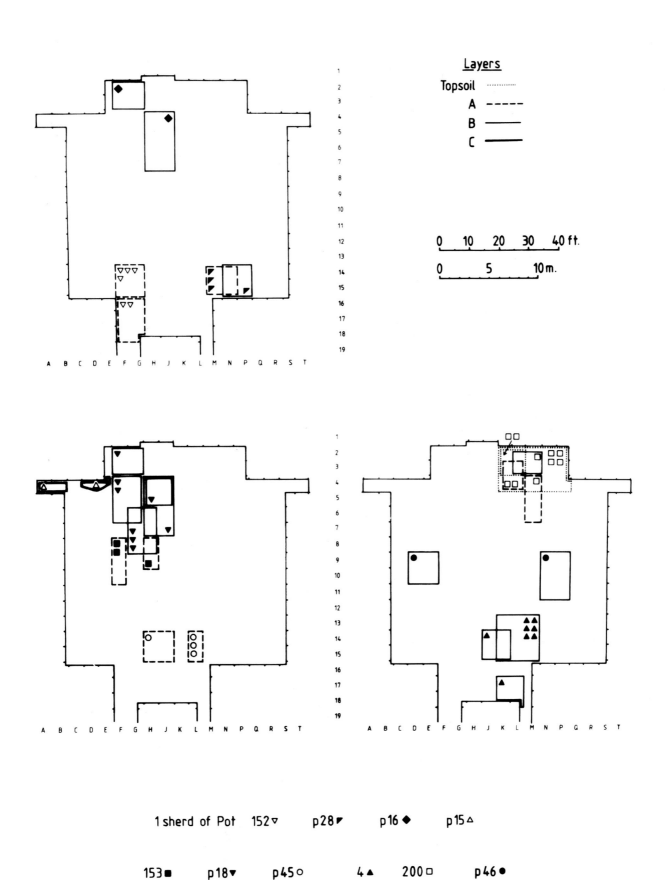

FIGURE 7.42
Croft 52–53 1968. Sherd links

on each of the crofts sampled commenced roughly contemporaneously, and need not be earlier than the mid-12th century. On the periphery of the village, occupation of Croft 8 may commence slightly later, towards the late 12th century. Throughout the village there seems to be considerable activity in the late 12th and 13th centuries, although lower proportions of 13th-century wares on Croft 52–53 1968 may indicate a lapse in occupation here, or later clearance of these levels. Occupation at the edge of the village begins to decline towards the end of the 13th century. Croft 7 goes out of habitation at this time, and Croft 8 ceases to be used during the 14th century. Croft 6 survives into the 15th century, but then declines, and is deserted by the 16th century. By this time, the whole village was waning. Croft 29, at the centre, was also disused by the end of the 16th century. Of the crofts excavated, only Croft 52–53 was still occupied at a later date.

7.6   THE FAXTON MEDIEVAL POTTERY REVISITED
by Paul Blinkhorn

The original medieval pottery report for Faxton was completed in the late 1980s, with most of the dating and fabric categories based on the result of the preliminary analysis of the material from Furnells in Northamptonshire (Pearson 2009), which at the time was the subject of on-going analysis as part of the Raunds Area Project (RAP). The view of the medieval pottery gained from Furnells was superseded before the site was published due to findings from other sites in Raunds, such as Langham Road and Burystead (Blinkhorn 2009) which identified problems in the dating of the Furnells assemblages (Denham 2009). The definitive analysis of medieval pottery came with the publication of the large assemblage from West Cotton (Blinkhorn 2010), and it was this, combined with the type-series for Northampton (McCarthy 1979) which led to the creation of the Northamptonshire County Type-Series (CTS) in the late 1990s. This has been the basis of medieval pottery work in the county ever since. West Cotton was also the last large-scale excavation of a medieval rural settlement to take place in the county, meaning little refinement of the CTS has been possible, but the evidence from smaller, more recent sites suggests that it is basically sound.

With these facts in mind, it was clear that the basic chronology of the original medieval pottery report for Faxton was likely to be in need of adjustment, although this is in no way the fault of the original analyst, but simply that of the state of knowledge at the time. Re-examination of the entire assemblage was not possible due to financial constraints, although it seems likely from the material which has been re-examined that the vast majority of the material was consistently identified, and the basic categories that were created are sound.

Late Anglo Saxon and Saxo Norman

The medieval type-series from Faxton was examined, and each type was correlated to the Northamptonshire County Type-Series (CTS). The results are shown in Figure 7.43. For the most part, the original categories were reliable, with some further subdivision of Lyveden/Stanion Ware, Brill/Boarstall Ware and Potterspury Ware. The only obvious confusion in the type-series is fabric M, which is largely Brill/Boarstall Ware, but the type-series also contains sherds of Potterspury Ware and unglazed Stamford Ware. It is worthy of note that common Late Saxon and Saxo-Norman fabrics such as St Neots Ware (CTS fabric F100) and late St Neots Ware (CTS fabric F200) were entirely absent from the original type-series. Such pottery is always very common at Late Saxon and Saxo-Norman (11th–12th century) sites in the region. For example, at West Cotton, 96.6% of the pottery dated to the 10th century and 85.2% of that from the late 10th–11th century contexts was St Neots types (Blinkhorn 2010, Table 10.14).

However, there does seem to have been some confusion with the categorization of the shelly wares. The fabric described in the pottery report as 'Developed St Neots Ware' is, to judge from the samples in the type-series, CTS fabric F330, shelly coarseware of the 12th–14th centuries (see Figure 7.43). The illustrated material for this type (Figures 7.3–7.6) does however include sherds which are clearly of St Neots Ware type. For example, some of the bowls with in-turned rims (e.g. Figure 7.5, nos 31–37) which are entirely a St Neots Ware form, and unknown amongst the products of the later shelly coarseware industry, are comparable with St Neots Ware from West Cotton. Figure 7.5, no. 37, with thumbing on the carination, is virtually identical to a vessel from West Cotton (Blinkhorn 2010, fig. 10.2, no. 10), which occurred in a deposit dated to AD 1100–1150. Some of the Faxton vessels do appear earlier however, particularly the small vessels which are very typical of the Late Saxon phase of the industry (e.g. Figure 7.5, no. 31). A limited physical re-examination of the illustrated sherds archive confirmed that other St Neots type vessels are present, including some vessels which appear to be of Late Saxon type, such as a near-complete jar rim from context 924.

Some of the Stamford Ware also appears to be Late Saxon. The rim sherds illustrated in Figure 7.2 are largely Kilmurry's late Form 4 (c.1100–1250; Kilmurry 1980, Fig. 29), but Figure 7.2 no. 2 is more typical of her Form 2 group, dateable mainly to c.900–1100. The sherd of a Thetford Ware storage jar noted above may also be Late Saxon, but such vessels seem to have been late arrivals in the region.

Faxton fabric	Comments	Given date	CTS code	CTS code	CTS date
A	Shelly Ware		F330	Shelly Coarseware	12th–14thC
B	Lyveden		F319	Lyveden/Stanion 'A' Ware	mid 12th–14thC
C	Developed St Neots Ware		F209	South Lincs Oolitic Ware	late 10th–13thC
D	Lyveden jugs		F320	Lyveden/Stanion 'B' Ware	13th–mid 14thC
E	Brickhill		F308	Sandy Glazed Ware	?12th–14thC
F	Sandy ware, green glazed		F329	Potterspury Ware	mid 13th–16thC
G	Potterspury		F329	Potterspury Ware	mid 13th–16thC
I		?Roman	F324	Brill/Boarstall Ware	13th–16thC
J	Late Medieval Reduced	15thC	F365	Late Medieval Reduced Ware	late 14th–16thC
K			F320	Lyveden/Stanion 'B' Ware	13th–mid 14thC
L	Oxford		F324	Brill/Boarstall Ware	13th–16thC
M	Brill		F324	Brill/Boarstall Ware	13th–16thC
N			F329	Potterspury Ware	13th–mid 14thC
O	(Old I)		F320	Lyveden/Stanion 'B' Ware	13th–mid 14thC
P	(Old K)	600–650	F345	Oxford Medieval Ware	late 11th–14thC
Q			F324	Brill/Boarstall Ware	13th–16thC
S			F324	Brill/Boarstall Ware	13th–16thC

FIGURE 7.43

Faxton (FAX 67) medieval type-series correlated with the Northamptonshire County Type-Series (CTS)

Sherds of this type were noted at West Cotton, but did not occur in contexts earlier than the 12th century (Blinkhorn 2010, 261).

It would therefore appear that there *was* activity at Faxton which pre-dates the 12th century, and some of it appears very likely to be pre-Conquest. Unfortunately, without a complete re-examination of the early pottery groups from the site, it is simply not possible to ascertain the extent and date of this activity and, in any case, the lack of clear stratigraphy from the 1967 and 1968 excavations negates any possibility of a detailed discussion of any association between structures, features and material culture.

Later medieval

The dating of the later medieval pottery in the original report has to some extent been superseded by the results of more recent work. For example, the dating of Potterspury Ware to the early 14th century, based on Pearson's work, must be disregarded. It clearly starts earlier, most likely in the mid-13th century. This has been confirmed elsewhere, for example there are large assemblages of Potterspury Ware from sites in Milton Keynes (e.g. Ivens and Hurman 1995, 257). Elsewhere in the text above, the nomenclature has changed: 'Coventry White Ware' is now more correctly Nuneaton 'A' Ware, dating to 1250–1400 (CTS fabric F347).

One problematic area appears to be the later part of this period (*c*.1350–1550). The only pottery of this date recognised during the original analysis was Late Medieval Reduced Ware (CTS fabric F365),

which is dated to the late 14th–16th centuries. Other late medieval wares are present, however. The type-series material for Lyveden/Stanion 'B' Ware (CTS fabric F320) includes a few sherds of the late medieval 'D' Ware (CTS fabric F322), which can be dated to 1350–1500 (Blinkhorn 2008). The 'wheel-thrown Lyveden/Stanion jugs' referred to would correspond with Lyveden/Stanion 'D' Ware (Lyveden/Stanion 'B' Ware was coil-built while the 'D' Ware was wheel-thrown). The chronology table above mentions 'Lyveden wheel-thrown jugs' in the definition of the 14th-century assemblages, so it seems that they were recognised, although there is clearly some confusion.

Other common late medieval wares appear to have not been recognised at all at the time of writing the original report. Late Medieval Oxidized Ware (CTS fabric F401, *c*.1450–1600) is not mentioned in the type-series, but is present in very large quantities in contexts which were originally classified as 'post-medieval', as are Midland Purple Ware (fabric F403, *c*.1450–1600) and Cistercian Ware (fabric F404, *c*.1450–1600). The same comments apply to other, minor, late medieval pottery types (e.g. CTS fabrics F325, F356, F369, F405 and F408). The fact that some assemblages containing only these and earlier wares were categorized as 'post-medieval' suggests that at least some late medieval activity at the site has not been recognised. One fabric mentioned above, 'Great Brickhill', may in fact be Late Medieval Oxidized Ware (fabric F401). However, while Great Brickhill has produced evidence of late medieval pottery production, it is of Late Medieval Reduced

Wares, not Oxidized Wares (Slowikowski 2011, 14). This material is dated above to the '13th century, with one 14th- or 15th-century example'. This is incorrect; even if the 'Great Brickhill' material is misidentified Late Medieval Reduced Ware, it is no earlier than the mid–late 14th century, and most likely 15th century. This type of pottery is not only given this later date in the Northamptonshire CTS but also in those for Bedfordshire and Milton Keynes. The fact that bunghole cisterns were amongst the vessel types noted at Faxton also throws doubt on the 13th-century date; such vessels are an almost universally late medieval vessel form in this region. Given that 'East Midlands Reduced Ware' is a separate category in the type-series, there again appears to have been a little confusion here. These previously unrecognised late groups are discussed below in a new post-medieval pottery section, which suggests very strongly that there was a more extended life for both Croft 29 1966 and Croft 52–53 1968.

7.7 THE POST-MEDIEVAL POTTERY
by Paul Blinkhorn

The post-medieval pottery assemblage comprised 2,272 sherds with a total weight of 40.6kg. It was recorded using the conventions of the Northamptonshire County Ceramic Type-Series (CTS) (Figure 7.44).

The range of fabric types is typical of sites in the region. It includes some medieval material which was misidentified as post-medieval wares in earlier analyses. As noted above, late medieval wares, particularly F401, F403, F404, were classified as post-medieval in the original analysis, and late medieval Brill and Potterspury wares were not recognised.

The large quantities of late medieval wares, particularly Late Medieval Oxidized Wares (fabric F401) and Midland Purple Ware (F403), and to a lesser extent Cistercian Ware (F404) suggest very strongly that activity continued at Faxton during the 15th and 16th centuries. Pottery of the mid-16th to 17th centuries (fabrics F406, F407, F409 and F410) is perhaps not as common, and may represent dumped material rather than debris resulting from occupation. This will be discussed in more detail below.

The late medieval and early post-medieval wares comprise almost entirely utilitarian forms in the form of jars, bowls and jugs, with none of the specialist late medieval vessel forms associated with the storage, preparation, serving and consumption of food and drink (other than cups), such as cisterns and dripping dishes, being noted, other than fragments of possible colanders or chafing dishes in fabric F369 from layer C, grid A-C 20-22 from the 1966 excavations and an unrecorded location

in the 1967 trench, a few sherds from drinking jugs in fabrics F329, F356 and F369, and a handle from a skillet or frying-pan in F406 from layer B3 in grid H-J 4-5 in 1968. However, cistern bungholes in Lyveden/Stanion and 'Great Brickhill' fabrics were identified in the medieval pottery report, as was a lobed cup in the former fabric. These are very typically late medieval, and usually date to the late 14th/15th century onwards (McCarthy and Brooks 1988, 113). The large quantity of Cistercian Ware is almost exclusively cups/tygs, some of which were decorated with white slip pads and prunts.

The 17th-century pottery consisted largely of mostly large fragments of press-moulded dishes and plates in Staffordshire-type slipware (fabric F409), with only a few sherds of tin-glazed earthenware occurring. Late 17th-century wares such as English stonewares and Manganese Mottled Ware are somewhat scarce.

It was only during the 18th and 19th century when fairly large quantities of pottery were once again deposited on the three Faxton sites, mainly in the form of heavy bowls in utilitarian earthenwares (fabric F426), although some partially complete, high-quality wares in the form of painted creamware tea-service and fragments of a plain dinner service (including a large meat-dish) in the same fabric were noted, accompanied by a red stoneware tea-pot and fragments of chamber-pots in white stoneware. These occurred in grid Q-R 9-10 of the topsoil in the 1968 trench, and probably originated from the Rectory.

Chronology and pottery occurrence

The bulk of the assemblage (2,109 sherds, 37.1kg) came from the soil horizons overlying the crofts. Thus, the vast majority of the pottery is effectively unstratified. The pottery occurrence per layer for the individual crofts is shown in Figure 7.45. The pottery occurrence by number and weight of sherds per fabric type per layer per site is shown in Figures 7.46–7.48.

Croft 29 1966

The late- and post-medieval assemblage from the soil horizons overlying Croft 29 is relatively small (217 sherds, 2.9kg), with most of the pottery coming from the topsoil and layers A and B (Figure 7.46). These produced wares ranging from the medieval to the modern periods, and most points in between, indicating that they are heavily disturbed and reworked. However, other than 18th- and 19th-century material in form of F426, by far the most common pottery types from these layers are late medieval/early post-medieval wares (fabrics F401, F403, F406 and F407), suggesting very strongly that there was extensive disturbance of strata dating to the mid-15th to late 16th century. A large fragment

Fabric	Name	Date	Number of sherds	Weight (g)
F200	T1 (2) type St Neots Ware	1000–1200	1	4
F205	Stamford Ware	850–1250	24	103
F322	Lyveden/Stanion 'D' Ware	1350–1500	2	35
F324	Brill/Boarstall Ware	early 13th–16th century	10	33
F325	Lyveden/Stanion 'E' Ware	1450–1550	2	15
F329	Potterspury Ware	1250–1600	12	237
F330	Shelly coarseware	1100–1400	1	1
F331	Developed Stamford Ware	late 12th–early 13th century	2	10
F356	Late Medieval Potterspury Ware	late 14th–16th century	5	200
F365	Late Medieval Reduced Ware	1400–?1500	14	179
F369	Late Brill/Boarstall Ware	15th–mid 16th century	11	92
F401	Late Medieval Oxidized Ware	1450–1600	162	2367
F403	Midland Purple Ware	1450–1600	413	8145
F404	Cistercian Ware	1450–1600	179	911
F405	Surrey 'Tudor Green' Ware	1400–1600	1	12
F406	Midland Yellow Ware	1550–1700	166	2309
F407	Red earthenwares	1550–1700	50	1046
F408	Raeren stoneware	1450–1600	3	45
F409	Staffordshire slipware	1650–1750	72	1277
F410	Anglo-Dutch tin-glazed earthenware	1600–1800	3	17
F411	Midland blackware	1550–1700	33	328
F412	Chinese porcelain	1750–1900	1	1
F413	Manganese Glazed Ware	1680–1750	56	432
F415	Creamware	1740–1820	42	819
F417	Nottingham/Derby stoneware	1700–1900	34	1240
F421	Frechen/Cologne stoneware	1550–1700	39	406
F424	Metropolitan-type slipware	17th century	1	22
F425	Brill marbled slipware	17th–18th century	16	566
F426	Iron-glazed coarsewares	late 17th–18th century	628	17351
F429	White salt-glazed stoneware	1720–1780	11	86
F438	English stoneware	late 17th–18th century	30	326
F1000	Miscellaneous wares	19th and 20th century	246	1716

FIGURE 7.44
List of pottery fabrics employed by Paul Blinkhorn in 2019

of a late medieval vessel was noted amongst the medieval material from these soil horizons, a lobed cup from A2-C (Figure 7.23, no. 148).

Layer C, the earliest of the soil horizons, seems to represent the latest occupation at the site. The original catalogue reports that it produced 1,649 sherds of medieval pottery, with just six sherds classified as 'post-medieval'. The lack of quantification of the medieval wares means it is impossible to ascertain if that material is redeposited, and if later medieval wares are well represented. However, the illustrated material includes two 'later' Lyveden/Stanion jugs from layer C (Figure 7.22, nos 144 and 145), as did a fragment of a vessel in 'Great Brickhill' fabric (Figure 7.29, no. 213). These are all likely to be post-1350/1400.

The 'post-medieval' pottery comprises a sherd of Stamford Ware, with the others being Late Brill/Boarstall Ware (F369), Midland Purple Ware, and Cistercian Ware, all typical of the mid-15th to 16th century at sites in the region. This trench also included a layer D, the natural, and a single sherd of pottery is recorded as coming from that, presumably off the surface of it. The sherd is a fragment of Frechen stoneware, fabric F421, suggesting a date of the mid–late 16th century. Assuming the sherd is reliably stratified, this would imply that Croft 29 was still in use during this time, as the pattern of pottery occurrence in the upper soil horizons would suggest.

In addition to this, some of the surfaces in Buildings A1 and A2 produced small groups of fairly large sherds of F403 and a few small sherds of F406

	Turf/Topsoil		A		B		C		D	
Year	No.	Wt (g)	No.	Wt (g)	No.	Wt (g)	No.	Wt (g)	No.	Wt (g)
1966	25	226	128	2076	22	585	11	53	1	13
1967	70	1267	73	1161	0	0	0	0	0	0
1968	616	16428	689	9805	451	5241	26	194	0	0
Total	**711**	**17921**	**890**	**13042**	**473**	**5826**	**37**	**247**	**1**	**13**

FIGURE 7.45

Ceramics by phase chronology

from some of their associated surfaces, suggesting that they were still occupied at that time. Fabrics F403, F404 and F406 had a fairly general distribution across the trench, but F401 was largely limited to the south-east corner, in grid A-F 8-10.

Crofts 6–9 1967

It is striking how little post-medieval pottery was recovered from the soils overlying the crofts in this area of the site (143 sherds, 2.4kg), despite over 17,000 sherds of medieval material being present. The soil layers themselves took the form of the topsoil, then a layer A which was removed in four spits, and an underlying B layer. All the late- and post-medieval pottery (F365, F401, F403 and F404) came from the A layers, with the B layer yielding only medieval wares (Figure 7.47). The lack of quantification again makes judging the date and condition of the medieval material somewhat difficult, but the illustrated material from this trench does not include any late Lyveden/Stanion or Late Medieval Reduced Ware, and just a single sherd of 'Great Brickhill' pottery, suggesting that there was little activity in this area of the site during the mid-14th to 15th centuries.

Just ten fairly small late and post-medieval sherds (total weight 110g) were noted, and no obvious late medieval vessel forms were found, such as lobed cups or cisterns, unlike in the 1966 and 1968 trenches. The only layer to produce late medieval/early post-medieval wares and no later pottery was A3, which yielded a single small sherd of F407 and another of F411, suggesting a date in the second half of the 16th century, but the scarcity of pottery of this date does not strongly suggest occupation activity.

Early post-medieval pottery (F406, F407) was scarce, with just three sherds (47g) identified. The only post-medieval wares that were well represented were the 18th-century iron-glazed earthenwares (89 sherds, 1.5kg) and, to a lesser extent, marbled slipware (13 sherds, 0.5kg), although all the sherds of the latter came from a single vessel which was scattered throughout the layers, suggesting that they had been extensively reworked. It would appear therefore that there was very little activity in this area of the site in the late 14th century and beyond until the 18th century.

Croft 52–53 1968

The soil layers from this site produced a very large late- and post-medieval pottery assemblage (1,785 sherds, 31.7kg), with less than 2,000 sherds of earlier medieval material present (Figure 7.48). As before, the lack of quantification makes it difficult to assess its significance. The area had a similar profile to that from 1966, with topsoil lying over three layers, with layer C representing the latest occupation activity at the site. The upper layers produced extremely large quantities of late medieval pottery, suggesting very strongly that there was extensive activity in this area at that time. Midland Purple (fabric F403; 346 sherds, 6.4kg), Late Medieval Oxidized Ware (fabric F401; 141 sherds, 1.9kg) and Cistercian Ware (fabric F404; 160 sherds, 0.8kg) are all extremely well represented, as are the early post-medieval Midland Yellow Ware (fabric F406; 129 sherds, 1.8kg) and red earthenwares (fabric F407; 43 sherds, 0.8kg). These pottery types were fairly evenly spread throughout the topsoil and layers A and B, whereas the later wares, particularly F409 and F426, largely occurred in the topsoil and the upper part of layer A, although smaller quantities were found in the lower part of layer A and the upper of layer B. This suggests that layer B represents late medieval/early post-medieval deposits which were disturbed in the 18th–19th centuries. Two late medieval cistern bungholes were noted during the analysis of the medieval pottery, from layers A and A2 (Figure 7.29, nos 218 and 219).

The pottery from layer C comprises entirely late medieval and early post-medieval wares (fabrics F369, F401, F403, F404 and F406) other than a few small and probably intrusive fragments of later material in the form of F426 (4 sherds, 35g) and a modern sherd (1 sherd, 1g). The illustrated medieval material from layer C includes a sherd of Late Medieval Reduced Ware, and other sherds of this were noted in the upper soil layers, along with late Lyveden/Stanion Wares and 'Great Brickhill' sherds.

This all suggests very strongly that, like Croft 9, occupation of this area of the site went through to the second half of the 16th century.

Layer	MED No	MED Wt	F365 No	F365 Wt	F369 No	F369 Wt	F401 No	F401 Wt	F403 No	F403 Wt	F404 No	F404 Wt	F408 No	F408 Wt	F406 No	F406 Wt
TOP									8	77	1	2			2	22
A	4	87					2	32	8	214	3	19			5	70
A2★	1	2	2	64	1	23	10	150	8	155	7	25	1	22	2	46
A2/3									1	9					1	3
A&B					1	4			1	10					1	15
B									3	110	1	6			7	105
B/C																
C	1	6			1	24			1	35	3	57				
D																
Total	6	95	2	64	3	51	12	182	30	610	15	109	1	22	18	261

Layer	F407 No	F407 Wt	F421 No	F421 Wt	F409 No	F409 Wt	F410 No	F410 Wt	F411 No	F411 Wt	F413 No	F413 Wt	F426 No	F426 Wt	MOD No	MOD Wt
TOP									1	3	1	24	12	98		
A	2	116			6	36	1	8			5	35	18	471	1	9
A2★	3	72	2	44	3	11			2	18	7	21	9	174	1	1
A2/3																
A&B									1	14	1	2	3	75		
B	1	5											5	41	1	1
B/C					2	33							2	284		
C																
D			1	13												
Total	6	193	3	57	11	80	1	8	4	35	14	82	49	1143	3	11

FIGURE 7.46
Pottery occurrence by layer and fabric type, 1966 (weight in grams; A2★ includes 1 sherd, 3g, of residual Roman pottery)

	F365		F401		F403		F404		F406		F407		F424		F409	
	No	Wt	No	Wt	No	Wt	No	Wt	No	Wt	No	Wt	No	Wt	No	Wt
TOP			1	11	2	57	2	3					1	22	3	35
A															1	7
A1			1	1					2	44						
A1/2	1	4	1	2												
A2															2	5
A2/3			1	13	1	19										
A3											1	3				
Total	1	4	4	27	3	76	2	3	2	44	1	3	1	22	6	47

	F411		F413		F417		F425		F426		F438		MOD	
	No	Wt	No	Wt	No	Wt	No	Wt	No	Wt	No	Wt	No	Wt
TOP			2	3			4	183	47	890	1	22	6	27
A	1	37					1	79	14	328				
A1							4	138	8	144			1	8
A1/2	3	30	1	2	1	1	3	77	4	19				
A2			1	7			1	46	6	88			1	15
A2/3									10	32				
A3	1	5												
Total	5	72	4	12	1	1	13	523	89	1501	1	22	8	50

FIGURE 7.47

Pottery occurrence by layer and fabric type, 1967 (weight in grams)

Layer	MED No	MED Wt	F356 No	F356 Wt	F365 No	F365 Wt	F369 No	F369 Wt	F325 No	F325 Wt	F401 No	F401 Wt
TOP											6	75
A	6	92	4	28	3	46	1	1	1	9	57	793
A1	1	3										
A2	3	13			1	7			1	6	25	399
A3												
A/B	2	21					1	4			9	140
B	13	68			5	27	4	25			39	434
B2	1	9									1	5
B3							1	2			1	36
C	1	4					1	9			3	38
Total	27	210	4	28	9	80	8	41	2	15	141	1920

Layer	F403 No	F403 Wt	F404 No	F404 Wt	F405 No	F405 Wt	F408 No	F408 Wt	F406 No	F406 Wt	F407 No	F407 Wt
TOP	43	1346	8	52					17	345	3	74
A	106	2067	43	274					38	508	9	203
A1	1	14							2	8	1	7
A2	61	844	27	113					23	238	4	64
A3									3	32		
A/B	14	333	5	46			1	9	3	119		
B	106	1737	65	285			1	14	40	520	26	502
B2	6	82	8	35	1	12						
B3			1	7					1	32		
C	9	64	3	23					2	17		
Total	346	6487	160	835	1	12	2	23	129	1819	43	850

Layer	F421 No	F421 Wt	F409 No	F409 Wt	F410 No	F410 Wt	F411 No	F411 Wt	F412 No	F412 Wt	F413 No	F413 No
TOP			27	936	1	4	4	55	1	1	21	227
A	13	106	12	67			8	36			5	26
A1			1	2							1	2
A2	3	68	5	34	1	5	4	34			1	21
A3												
A/B	1	13	1	44			1	6			1	3
B	13	99	7	60			6	87			3	26
B2			1	6								
B3												
C												
Total	30	286	54	1149	2	9	23	218	1	1	32	305

Layer	F415 No	F415 Wt	F417 No	F417 Wt	F425 No	F425 Wt	F426 No	F426 Wt	F438 No	F438 Wt	F429 No	F429 Wt	MOD No	MOD Wt
TOP	42	819	29	1096			173	9490	13	202	10	85	217	1000
A			3	6	3	43	109	2059	5	54	1	1	10	36
A1							1	5						
A2							46	686						
A3														
A/B							5	104						
B							79	1004	9	35			3	19
B2							2	9						
B3														
C							4	35					1	1
Total	42	819	32	1102	3	43	419	13392	27	291	11	86	231	1056

FIGURE 7.48
Pottery occurrence by layer and fabric type, 1968 (weight in grams)

8

ARTEFACTS

Lawrence Butler, Geoff Egan, Ian Goodall,

Richard Kelleher and Eleanor Standley

The text below remains much as Lawrence Butler and his collaborators intended it in *c.*1989. Missing figures have been restored, some lost text has been reconstructed from earlier versions, and correspondence and issues around object numbering have been resolved. To help with the dating of features and layers, locational information, much of which was absent, has been retrieved by cross-referral back to on-site notebooks (for all years for small finds), pottery recording forms (for 1966 only) and a 1985 post-excavation report. In this new version, the prehistoric finds have been divided out from medieval and post-medieval finds for greater clarity. Richard Kelleher has consolidated previous commentaries on the coins and jettons, and further analysis of the later medieval objects from Faxton has kindly been provided by Eleanor Standley.

Except for the coins and jettons, all the small finds in this chapter are grouped by material and those illustrated are numbered consecutively within their different sections. Except for coins, jettons and glass, those objects described but not illustrated are unnumbered and distinguished only by their year code, thus '66' is Croft 29 1966, '67' is Crofts 6–9 1967, and '68' is Croft 52–53 1968. Sometimes a small find number is added also, so that '66 SF16' is Croft 29 1966 small find number 16, and where no other identification is possible from the archive there is a 'bag number' e.g. 67 (985) in which the first number indicates the year of excavation and the number in brackets is the 'bag' list. Coins were given their own numerical sequence (Coin 1, 2, etc.). Descriptions have been kept as short as possible and all details that can be seen on the drawings are omitted.

All the material, some 30 boxes not including the medieval pottery, was deposited at Northampton Museum in November 1989, and later moved to Daventry with the exception of 11 groups of items which, according to the site archive, were left by Lawrence Butler with the Beers family in May 1990. They included the statue (see Figure 9.1), some of the more complete Roman and medieval pottery, the jet and glass beads, the spindlewhorls, the lead objects, the bronze objects and the coins. With the exception of the statue, which was not recovered from the excavation trenches, these finds were subsequently returned to Northampton Museum but cannot at present be traced.

8.1 PREHISTORIC FINDS
by Lawrence Butler

Worked flint

Flints (Figure 8.1) were found in all three seasons at Faxton, but mainly in Croft 29 1966 (186 locations); they were found in 27 locations in Crofts 6–9 1967, mainly in layer A3, but in only four locations in 1968 Croft 52–53, well dispersed both vertically and horizontally. There was a wide variation in colour though black and grey predominated in the worked examples, fawn or pale brown in the unworked flint. No worked examples call for special comment; all were residual in the medieval village and none had been used or re-used in the medieval period. All the worked examples, mainly small blades and a few flakes, are typical of local Bronze Age industries. Some blades show use and some are retouched, as are some natural flints. A number are burnt. The presence of patination after manufacture on some of the blades suggests substantial disturbance since they were deposited. The flints may come from a variety of field-gathered sources, from locations prone to frost fracturing. There is a possibility that they were gathered as strengthening material to incorporate in mud-walling. One piece of quartz and one fragment of red ochre were also found.

1.   Black, simple blade with edge tooling (67 G17 A1/2).

2.   Black, broken discoid scraper (66 F-G11-15 ditch).

3.   Black scraper with secondary retouching (66 AA-BB12-13 B2).

4.   Grey flake (66 O-P11-12 A, topsoil).

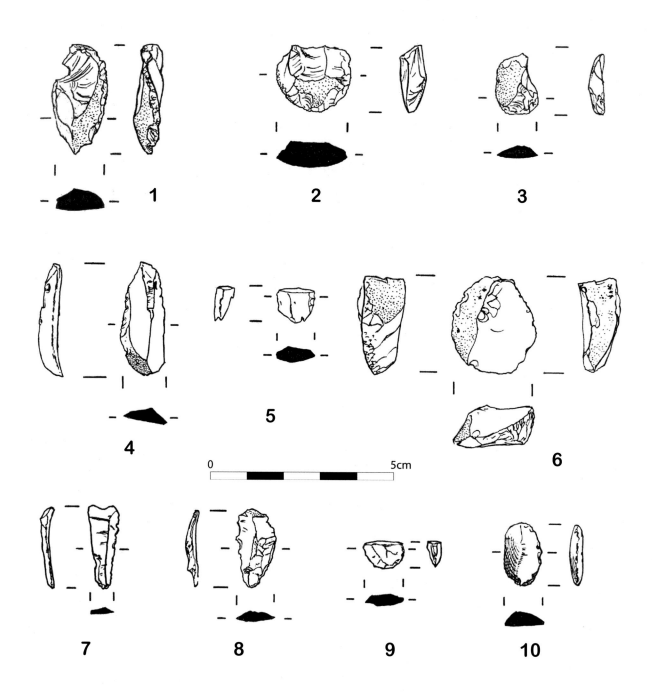

FIGURE 8.1
Prehistoric worked flint

5.   White, broken end of scraper (66 EE9-10 B3).

6.   Grey, discoidal scraper with steep retouching (66 CC12-13 F1 pit fill).

7.   White narrow blade (66 O-P-Q16 A2).

8.   Black blade with a little retouching (66 O-P18-19 A2).

9.   Grey, broken end of scraper (GG8-10 C1).

10.   Pinkish-white flake with retouching (O11 F6).

8.2 ROMAN FINDS
by Lawrence Butler

Coins

The two Roman coins (not illustrated) from topsoil contexts are clearly strays.

1.   The fabric of this piece is almost certainly Roman, but the coin is too worn for exact identification. The reverse is damaged and completely illegible. The obverse shows the faint outline of a bust which may be that of

Maximinus (AD 235–238), who has a very distinctive jowl. The denomination must be either the dupondius or the as (68 coin 21: L4 A, base of topsoil).

2. Constantinian: reduced follis of Constantinus Caesar, *c.* AD 330–335; mint of Treveri. Obv: CONSTANTIN [VSIVN] NOBC, laureate bust to right. Rev: GLOR[IA EXERCITVS], soldier with two standards; mint-mark: wreath over TRS (LRBC I no. 73) (68 coin 23: M10 A, topsoil).

8.3 MEDIEVAL AND LATER FINDS

Coins, jettons and tokens
by Richard Kelleher

The excavations at Faxton produced four 13th- to 16th-century coins which were originally identified and commented upon by Nicholas Mayhew, Michael Metcalf, Jeffrey North and Elizabeth Pirie. The coins can no longer be traced and only one (no. 5) has an accompanying photograph (Figure 8.2).

Three coins and a jetton were found in Croft 29 1966 (nos 3, 4, 5, 6, 16); each coin was in a significant well stratified position. No coins were found in Crofts 6–9 1967 and, taken together with the absence of glass and worked bone and the small quantity of bronze and lead, this absence suggested (to the excavator) a low level of material possessions. Coins, jettons and trade tokens were frequent in Croft 52–53 1968 but only two (7 and 9) were found in late 18th-century deposits. The late medieval contexts contained only two jettons (7 and 9).

Medieval and Tudor coins

3. John or Henry III. Silver penny, Short cross Class VIbi (*c.*1213–15), London, Abel. Circulation possible to 1247 (66 coin 1: FF9 B).

According to a card in the archive, this coin was considered to be significant. 'Its association with rubbish layers in the garden area of the medieval house enables the period of the house's occupation to be dated with a degree of accuracy rare in medieval village excavation'. Coins of the short cross type were struck under four successive kings between 1180 and 1247 and can usually be dated to within a few years of minting. In 1247 the short cross currency was effectively called in and struck into a new type. The process of replacement probably took two to three years and hoard evidence shows that very few coins survived as residue beyond 1250. The overwhelming likelihood therefore is that this coin was lost before 1247.

4. John or Henry III. Short cross silver cut halfpenny, Class V or VI (1204–18). London (66 coin 3: FF9 B).

Prior to a coinage reform under Edward I in 1279, fractional denominations were made by cutting a whole penny into halves and quarters. This coin is one such cut halfpenny. Single find evidence has shown that the use of fractional coins was much more widespread than we could ascertain from the hoard evidence— which tends to favour the highest value and best conditioned coins available to the hoarder. The short cross period (1180–1247) is the first in which rural English and Welsh finds show an

FIGURE 8.2

Coin 5, found in the hearth of Building A3/A4 in 1966

equal division between pennies and fractions (49:51) and are indicative of the extension of monetisation beyond the towns and more economically developed areas into rural zones (Kelleher 2018). In all likelihood, this coin would have been lost before 1247.

5. Edward III (1327–77). Silver halfpenny, second 'star-marked' coinage (1335–43), London. Obv.: [+] EDWARDVS REX A[NG *]. Rev.: CIVITAS * LONDON (66 coin 2: F21 B) (Figure 8.2).

   According to a card in the archive, this coin found in 1966 was considered to be highly important by the excavator. Its location 'is vital to dating the house, Period 3. It lay among the hearth, badly burnt in the ash. This gives a date for this period of occupation'. Nick Mayhew, in a letter to Butler dated 2 September 1988 states 'I believe it to have been lost before the Black Death, though it could have continued in use theoretically well into the 15th century'.

   Site notebook 1967 'small finds' records that this coin 'was shattered by University Photographic Dept when they overheated it during close-up enlargement photography'. More recent coin data would support the assumption that the date of loss of this coin should be before the Black Death. The hoard evidence from this period demonstrates that half-pennies do not tend to survive in circulation for very long.

   The question remains as to why it was found burnt in a domestic hearth. This is unusual and no other examples are known, but in part that might be the result of the coins being reported on without sight of, or interest in, the archaeological context. Most of the coin finds made by detectorists in rural fields are thought to have been moved there as manure from village muck heaps, having been accidentally swept up with other detritus. It is conceivable that a coin could have been accidentally caught up among material to be burnt, but the possibility remains that it was intentionally placed within the hearth for some other purpose.

6. Henry VIII or Edward VI (1544–51), silver penny, Canterbury (66 coin 13: P11A topsoil).

   The original attribution of this coin to either Henry or Edward indicates that it was either from the third coinage of Henry VIII (1544–47) or the early coinage of Edward VI which maintained his father's portrait posthumously. The coins of this period were notoriously debased and as such fell quickly out of circulation when good silver standards were returned from 1550. This coin is highly unlikely to have been a loss after 1560.

Jettons

Jettons were produced in huge numbers in the medieval period, first in France and England and later in Germany, particularly at Nuremberg. They functioned primarily as reckoning counters but the prevalence of jettons on a range of sites right down to small village dwellings suggests a use beyond that for which they were initially made. With the exception of the French or Flemish example (7), all the jettons are of the stock-types made in Nuremberg in the 16th century. The obverse design is of three crowns and three lys, alternately, round a rose, and the reverse depicts the Reichsapfel. The legends vary.

7. Obv.: +AVE MARIA o GRACIA, round heater shield of France-modern. Rev.: A long cross of three strands fleur de lisée, cantoned by four A's; enclosed by a tressure of four arches with .o. in each spandrel.

   The comparatively crude style of the obverse may indicate that the piece is a copy of the French type, from the mint of Tournai, c.1400 (68 coin 26: M/N19 B)

8. Hans Schultes, c.1550–74; the jetton is lightly chipped. Obv.: +HANS : SCHVLTES : GEIT. Rev.: fictitious legend (68 coin 6: L13 A).

9. Hans Schultes, c.1550–74; the flan has a large chip; the centre is pierced. Obv.: +[HANS:] SCHVLTES : NVRNB :. Rev.: +HANS: SCHVLTES : [NVRNB] (68 coin 20: P10 B).

10. Hans Schultes, c.1550–74. Obv.: GLICK: KVMPT : VON : GOT : IST : WAR. Rev.: HANS*SCHVLTES*IN*NVREN (68 coin 5: M15 A2).

11. Hans Schultes, c.1550–74; this jetton has been clipped to a square. Obv.: traces of legend, indecipherable. Rev.:]S SCHV[. (68 coin 19: P10 B).

12. Hans Krauwinckel, c.1580–1610. Obv.: HANNS . KRAVWINCKEL . IN . NV. Rev.: GOTT . ALLEIN . DEINE RESEI (68 coin 24: E14 A, topsoil).

13. Hans Krauwinckel, c.1580–1610. Obv.: HANNS : KRAVWINCKEL : IN : NV. Rev.: +GOTES : SEGEN : MACHT : REICH (from Proverbs x, 22) (68 coin 25: R15 B).

14. Hans Krauwinckel, c.1580–1610; the small flan which is slightly chipped, appears to have been silvered. Obv.: : HANNS : KRA[WINCK]EL : IN : NURE. Rev.: +GOTES : SEEG[EN : M] ACHT : REICH (68 coin 4: L15 A, topsoil).

15. Hans Krauwinckel, c.1580–1610; very worn and indistinct. Obv.: [+GOTES: SEGEN : M] ACHT : REICH. Rev.: Ghost of HANNS KRAVWINCKEL (68 coin 9: L14 A2).

16. Worn jetton of stock-type, with fictitious legends (coin 4: TT21 A topsoil; neither the date of recovery of this jetton nor the site are recorded but the double-lettered grid code suggests Croft 29 1966).

17. Jetton of stock-type, but without legend; each die has a border of wedges (68 coin 16: F7 A, topsoil).

Coins of the 17th century

18. James I (1602–25), copper farthing token (68 coin 10: F10 A2).

19. Charles I (1625–49), silver halfpenny 1625–43 (68 coin 18: K18 A2).

20. William III (1694–1702), copper halfpenny (1695–98). The specimen is worn and only the ghost of the reverse can now be seen to determine attribution to the first issue (68 coin 15: J18 A, topsoil).

Tokens of the 17th century

By the mid-17th century, the farthing tokens of James I and Charles I had become discredited by over-issue and counterfeiting, and had ceased to be produced and used.

Since the Commonwealth did not address the problem of small value coinage, a vast array of tokens was issued by private individuals between 1648 and 1679 for this purpose. The obverse usually names the issuer, with some indication of his or her trade, and the reverse shows the town of manufacture.

Most 17th-century private tokens are found relatively close to the place of issue, as is the case here.

21. Northamptonshire; John Ponder of Rothwell. The token is very worn and detail indistinct. Obv.: IOHN : PONDER : OF : ROWEL; in centre, IDP. Rev.: A : HALF : PENNY : 1664; in centre, OB (abbreviation of obolus or halfpenny). Williamson 1889, Northamptonshire 146 (68 coin 7: G15 B)

22. Buckinghamshire: John Gaynes of Olney. Obv.: IOHN: GAYNE[S]; in centre, a pair of scales. Rev: ★IN: OLNEY: 1652; in centre, G: I: S. Williamson 1889, Buckinghamshire 111 (68 coin 8: G15 B).

Modern coins

23. George I (1714–27): Irish halfpenny. William Wood's coinage, 1772–74 (struck at Bristol); second issue. Obv.: GEORGIUS: DEI: GRATIA: REX, bust to right. Rev.: HIBERNIA: 172-, Hibernia seated left, leaning on harp; last digit of date is uncertain [2, 3 or 4] (Seaby 1970, 4601) (68 coin 22: K3 A, topsoil).

24. George II (1727–60): copper halfpenny 1740 or 1749; second issue (68 coin 14: D4 A, topsoil).

25. George II (1727–60): halfpenny 1754 (68 coin 12: D9 A, topsoil).

26. George III (1760–1820), copper halfpenny, 1775; first issue; now worn so smooth that detail of the date is best accounted uncertain (68 coin 27: F30 A, topsoil).

27. George III (1760–1820), copper halfpenny (68 coin 3: N/P6 A, base of topsoil).

29. George III (1760–1820), copper halfpenny, 1807; Soho mint (68 coin 1: P-Q7-8 A, base of topsoil).

30. ?George III: halfpenny size, but so worn that no detail of issue can be determined (68 coin 17: L17 A, topsoil).

31. Victoria (1837–1901), copper penny, 1862; so worn that virtually only the date can be determined (68 coin 11: C5 A, topsoil).

Medieval village sites have usually not yielded large numbers of coin finds. This is in contrast to the fields surrounding villages, which in Warwickshire account for 50 per cent of all coin finds (Dyer 1997, 35) and is supported by Richard Kelleher's large scale analysis of Portable Antiquities Scheme data in England and Wales (Kelleher 2018). Chris Dyer surveyed 33 excavated rural sites in which at least one house had been completely excavated. Sixteen of these yielded no coins at all, while the remainder produced 60 coins and nine jettons (Dyer 1997, 31–32). Of these sites, just three accounted for more than half of the total and one in particular, Westbury in Buckinghamshire, was responsible for 17 coins. This apparent surfeit was most likely due to the use of metal-detectors on the features and spoil. The low level of coin finds from medieval excavations is not restricted to villages as numismatic material from manors, castles, and monastic sites is often also limited. In terms of chronology, most sites begin with short cross coins as this period saw a huge increase in the quantity of money available in England which then began to find greater use in rural areas. That the coins are all low value pieces is unsurprising given the relative wealth of the inhabitants of a village like Faxton. Another bronze token, described only as being modelled on the Chaise of Louise de Mâle, c.1250, came from the bulldozed Croft 27. No further reference is made to it.

The two 17th-century tokens may each count as having been issued within the general locality of Faxton: Rothwell lies north-west of Kettering and Olney, though in Buckinghamshire, is not far from Northampton itself (being 18km south-east).

These tokens, and the later modern coins, are all of small denomination. The Irish halfpenny (no. 23) is very worn (on the reverse at least), as are many of these site-finds, but for all of them, their period of use and loss may be most closely estimated. Wood's Irish halfpennies and farthings proved to be unacceptable in Ireland. Not only was production stopped in 1724, but the coins were recalled from Ireland and shipped out to America for circulation there. Such as returned to England in circulation before 1724 may only have been tolerated as small change until the Royal Mint resumed striking for George II in 1729.

Copper-alloy objects
by Lawrence Butler

Most of the objects described below are probably bronze but an XRF analysis was performed where the composition was doubtful (Figures 8.3–8.5, nos 1–34). A representative selection only is listed; the unillustrated material includes a number of belt chapes, flat buckle plates and three more sheep's bells.

1. Horse harness with punched decoration; two rivet holes, one rivet in place; back of harness plate suggests it was attached to leather (67 SF18 baulk G/H20 A1).

2. Spoon bowl, silver-plated, Georgian (68 SF2 Q/R11-12 topsoil).

3. Leg of tripod pitcher or ewer (Steane and Bryant 1975, 116, no. 72, Fig. 43). XRF shows major traces of copper, zinc; minor traces of lead; and trace of tin, antimony (66 SF54 C17 B2 from yard west of houses).

4. Ring, possibly from brooch (68 SF26 D/E4-5 B2).

5. Ring, roughly filed surfaces (67 SF24 E16 A2).

6. Finger ring, with decoration of finely incised lines (66 SF37 T11 A2).

7. Finger ring, jewel missing, yellow paste of setting (Steane and Bryant 1975, 114, no. 51,

Fig. 43). XRF shows major traces of copper, tin; minor traces of zinc but no silver (66 SF10 FF10 B, coin nearby).

8. Small buckle or square loop, tongue or attachment missing (68 SF22 F5 B2).

9. Belt or strap end, decoration of interlacing strands, four lobed terminal (66 SF63 11-12 in F6).

10. Belt fitting (Rahtz 1969, Fig. 49, no. 104 in a 15th-century context) (67 SF22 E17 A1).

11. Brooch or buckle, decoration of incised lines on upper surface (68 SF74 Q8 B, above clay and under stones).

12. Buckle, iron tongue, with mount attached by iron rivet (68 SF21 G7 B).

13. Chain links (from mail coat) finely drawn bronze wire infused by iron corrosion (68 SF36 M18 C).

14. Button or stud, six-lobed star set on radiating spokes within a fluted circle; probably Tudor (68 SF57 M17 B).

15. Tweezers made of two flat plates twisted to form a handle and then curled round in decorative terminals; possibly Roman (but see finds from King's Lynn; Clarke and Carter 1977, no. 30 and no. 50, Fig. 43) (66 SF62 P11-12 in Pit F6).

16. Key from small box (66 SF24 T13 A2).

17. Ring of twisted wire (68 SF46 N/P14-15 B1).

18. Ring and tag with bronze rivets. XRF shows major traces of copper; minor traces of tin, zinc; very little silver and trace antimony (67 SF42 F18-19 A1, baulk).

19. Thimble, now crushed but drawn as originally made (68 SF33 M/N11 A, baulk topsoil).

20. Thimble, now a segment but may have been deliberately cut down to present size (Clarke and Carter 1977, no. 31). Both the thimbles from Faxton could well be 17th century (68 SF69 F/G18-20 A, topsoil).

21. Pierced strip (68 SF29 H12 B).

22. Lace end, hollow cylinder (68 SF59 R15 B).

23. Openwork stud, formed of six-armed fleur de lys (68 SF9 L12 A2).

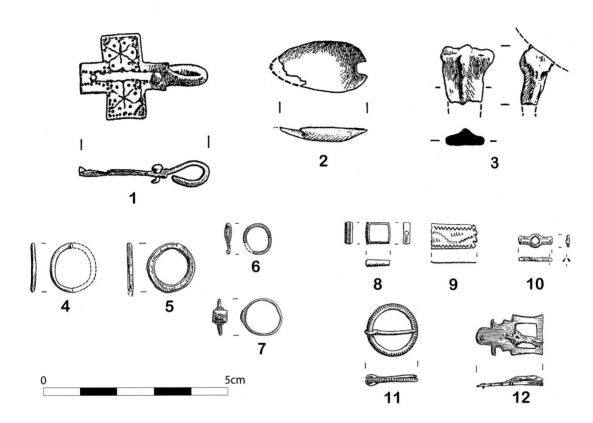

FIGURE 8.3
Copper-alloy objects

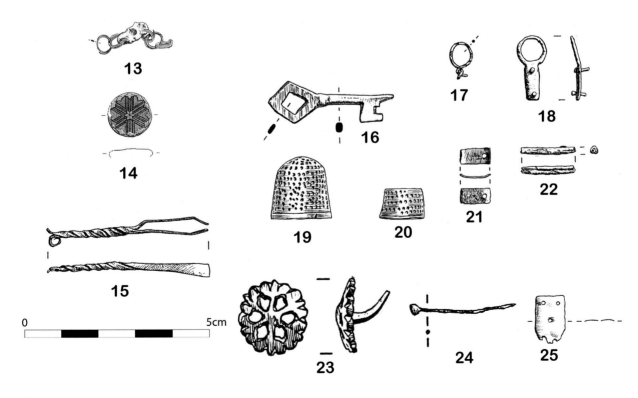

FIGURE 8.4
Copper-alloy objects

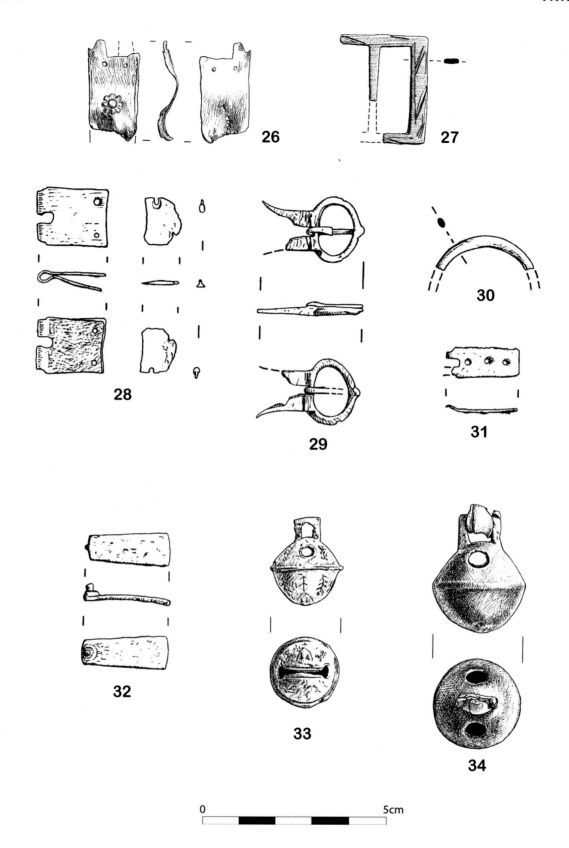

FIGURE 8.5
Copper-alloy objects

24. Pin, twisted wire head (68 SF1 P/Q11-12 A, topsoil).

25. Plate with rivet holes, probably from belt end (67 SF21 H25 A1).

26. Buckle plate with stamped decoration. 0.5mm thick (66 SF41 J/K16 A2 from yard east of house).

27. Buckle with slashed decoration, badly distorted but drawn flat (68 SF3 N/P7-8 A2).

28. Buckle plate with (right) leather fragment within, and stud (66 SF44 010 B).

29. Buckle and plate, tongue now bent; trace of silvering (66 SF3 DD/EE14 topsoil).

30. Flat ring, from brooch or buckle (68 SF53 D15 B).

31. Part of buckle plate, gilded copper, XRF shows very little lead; no tin (66 SF27 GG9 C1).

32. Part of belt strap with rivet (67 SF101 Croft 7 topsoil, house area).

33. Bridle or rumbler bell. Embossed letter T in shield (cf. Northampton with GL in shield; Williams and Farwell 1984, 103, Fig. 13, no. 13). For the Faxton bell a 17th-century date is likely (66 SF8 D10 A, topsoil).

34. Bridle bell for horse or sheep. Post-med. XRF shows copper, tin, iron ('pea'); and minor lead, zinc (66 Croft 29 topsoil).

The relative proportions of copper alloy from the three excavated areas show the poverty of Crofts 6–9. From Croft 29 1966 there were 32 items; from Croft 52–53 1968 there were 37 items, but only 10 items in all were recovered from Crofts 6–9 1967. Once more, apart from the horse harness all the items in the Crofts 6–9 1967 are small items of dress from buckles, belts and rings. The material from the other crofts is much more varied.

Lead objects
by Lawrence Butler, with a contribution by Geoff Egan

Few lead objects were found (Figure 8.6, nos 35–40; Figure 8.7).

35. Lead whistle with an iron suspension ring. Possibly 19th-century Victorian constabulary (from 66 Building A2).

36. Baling seal from Haarlem (68 SF5 L13-14 B1).
    Geoff Egan wrote: This incomplete two-disc seal would originally have been attached to a textile as part of a widespread system of industrial control, which was used in many cloth-producing countries from the medieval period until the Industrial Revolution (Endrei and Egan 1982).

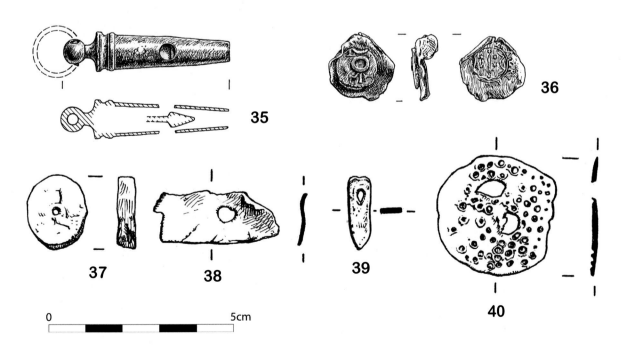

FIGURE 8.6

Lead objects

0   1cm

FIGURE 8.7

Baling seal from Haarlem, probably 17th century

The stamps can be interpreted as: a cross over a sword, with two six-pointed stars to each side, all in an ornately-shaped shield, HAERL (E....O) ET around// (incomplete disc) [2] 0 1/2. The arms are those of the town of Haarlem in the Netherlands. The legend can be restored from several parallels, including one seal which appears to have precisely the same stamp, as HAERLEMS GOET, i.e. 'Haarlem goods'. Twenty and a half is the length, in Flemish ells (equivalent to 27 inches, 68cm), that the particular textile to which the seal was attached was found by measuring. Although most Haarlem seals found in this country are not well stratified, the dating evidence available, for example a seal found in Edinburgh, suggests a 17th-century date is likely.

There is an imprint from the textile on the part of the back of the disc around the rivet. This imprint is an incidental result from the striking of the devices when the seal was attached to the textile (Egan 1985). Frances Pritchard reports that the imprint is of a quite fine, plain-woven fabric, with 22 by 20 threads per 10mm in the two systems.

The water in the coastal area around Haarlem was found to be particularly effective in achieving a brilliant whiteness in the bleaching of linens. An important bleaching industry here from the late 16th to the 18th century processed not only locally woven damasks, but linens woven in France and Germany as well. The 'Haarlem' linen which was sold after finishing included many of these textiles from further afield. As late as 1780 the town of Courtrai complained that 'Haarlem' linens were often Courtrai products which had only been bleached in the area of the eponymous town (Dreissen 1944). The textile imprint on this seal, and on several others found in England, is consistent with a linen, though not a particularly fine one. Haarlem seals are among the most commonly found imported types in Britain and have been found at Bury St Edmunds and Fakenham (Suffolk), Great Yarmouth (Norfolk) and near Waltham Abbey (Essex) as well as London and Edinburgh. Presumably the popular linens they represent were the fabrics known to contemporaries as 'hollands'. Frances Pritchard suggests that the fabric indicated by the Faxton seal imprint may be from the slightly coarser linen cloth than would have been preferred for the purposes described above.

37. Disc or weight, both faces plain (68 SF18 N/ P2-3 A, topsoil).

38. Pierced strip (66 SF60 H20 B2).

39. Threader or weight (68 SF6 J11 B).

40. Strainer, larger holes may indicate position of suspension chain rather than show excessive wear (68 SF32 K2-3 A, topsoil).

Iron objects

by Lawrence Butler with contributions from Ian Goodall

Iron (Figures 8.8–8.11, nos 41–72) occurred frequently throughout the three excavated areas and was usually discarded in the yards. The proportions varied; those items recorded as small finds were 49 in 1966, 31 in 1967, and 9 in 1968. While the items from Croft 29 1966 showed a wide variety of objects, those from Crofts 6–9 1967 were predominantly agricultural and to a lesser extent domestic. The few items from 1968 Croft 52–53 included four arrowheads and a knife, suggesting that archery practice with the butts set up in the churchyard was a common medieval pastime; the other reason for the low total from Croft 52–53 1968 was that relatively little of the yard areas was excavated because the Rectory Farm stood there. According to Ian Goodall (letter 6 September 1974) 'most of the objects are 14th century' and there is little of the 15th century and virtually none of the 16th century.

41.   Arrowhead (68 SF52 D/E14-15 B).

42.   Arrowhead (68 SF70 J/L3-5 C).

43.   Barrel padlock key (67 SF12 F/J5 A1) 12th–15th century (Goodall 2011, 262–263, Fig. 10.15, I201).

44.   Key (wards drawn from X-ray) (67 SF39 E19 A3, beneath stones of wall tumble).

45.   Latch key (67 SF3 F/G6 A1).

46.   Buckle (67 SF41 G20/21 A2).

47.   Buckle (66 (68) EE/FF11-13 A, topsoil from area of garden refuse).

48.   Buckle, rectangular section, circular tongue (66 Building A2 yard).

49.   Loop or slide buckle (66 AA21-22 A, topsoil).

50.   Buckle (68 SF13 K13 A, topsoil).

51.   Latch or binding strip (67 SF20 H5 A2).

52.   Lynch pin (66 Q/T8-10, topsoil).

Knives (Figure 8.8)

53.   Knife, tapering pointed tang (67 SF14 F/J4-5 A1, in stony scatter S of yard)

54.   Knife, slightly bowed back to the blade (66 AA13 A, topsoil)

55.   Knife, bowed back (67 SF17 F0 A2)

56.   Knife, pointed tang, tapering blade (66 SF 23, findspot omitted from both on-site SF notebook and SF filing cards).

Horse furniture (Figure 8.9)

57.   Spur, pin for rowel survives (66 SF57 H19 B2).

58.   Spur (66 SF59 B18 B2).

59.   Terminal of decorative door strap (66 (881) Building A2 yard).

60.   Horseshoe calkin (also see no. 66 below) (67 SF27 F4 A2, to west of yard).

61.   Handle of curry comb (66 O/P18-19 A2).

Domestic (Figures 8.10 and 8.11)

62.   Gouge or scoop chisel (66 D/E20-21 B).

63.   Flat ring (66 O/P11-12 A, topsoil).

64.   Chain links (from cart or harness) (67 SF35 E29 A2).

65.   Hasp with slightly tapering ends (68 E/F20 A2).

66.   Horseshoe, nail holes and fullered groove drawn from X-ray (68 SF48 H11 B).

67.   Bucket mount (66 EE/FF9-10 A2).

68.   Nail within socket (66 J/K9-10 A2).

69.   Tine (which either ends in a point or supported a loop) probably from a candlestick (66 SF56 J12 B2), 12th–15th century (Goodall 2011, 314–315, Fig. 11.7, J89).

70.   Hasp with loop, perhaps support for candle holder (67 SF30 H6 A2).

71.   Swivel loop (from cart or harness) (67 SF37 E31 A2).

72.   Barrel padlock; fin and spring lock remain, outer casing has corroded. Lock (67 SF16 H6 A1) and fin (67 SF28 G5 A2). The type of key needed to open the padlock is shown on the left, 12th–15th century (Goodall 2011, 254–255, Fig. 10.11, I107). Another barrel padlock was found during fieldwalking by John Steane 1971 in Croft 4/5 on 7/2/71 (letter from Steane, 26 May 1972) and another is illustrated in Goodall (2011, 246–247, Fig. 10.7, I42).

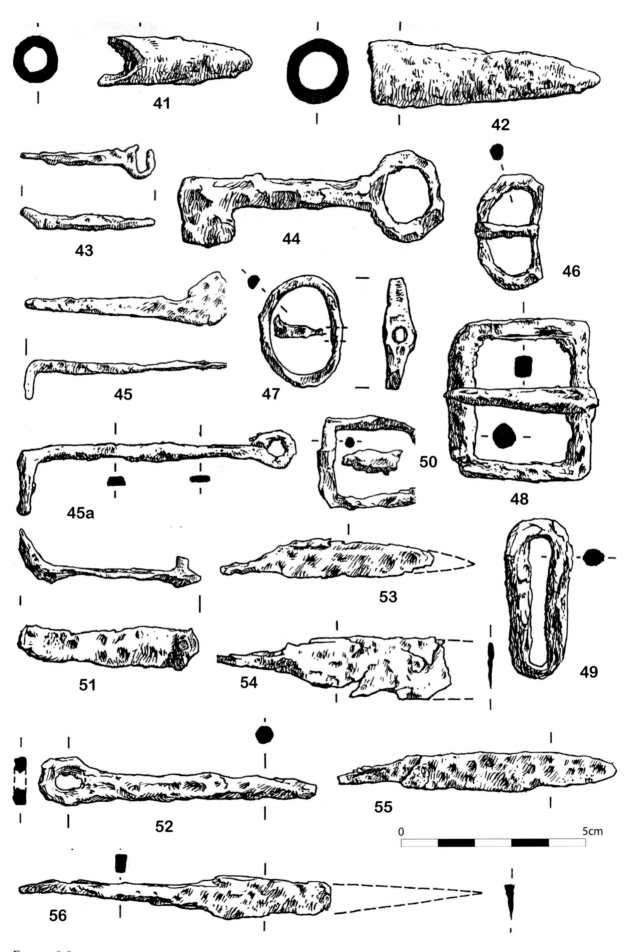

FIGURE 8.8
Iron objects

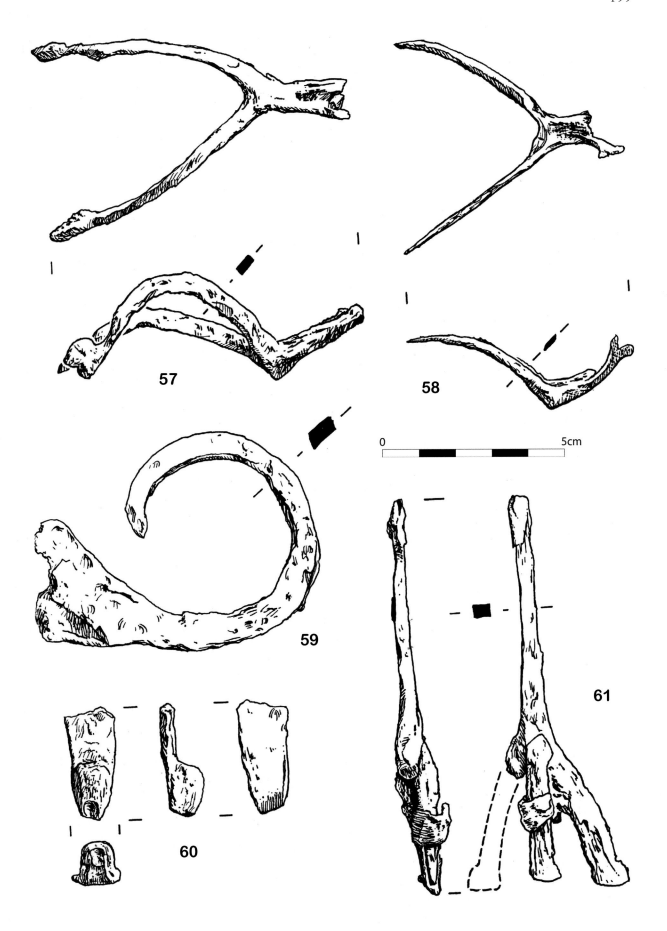

0   5cm

57

58

59

60

61

FIGURE 8.9
Iron objects

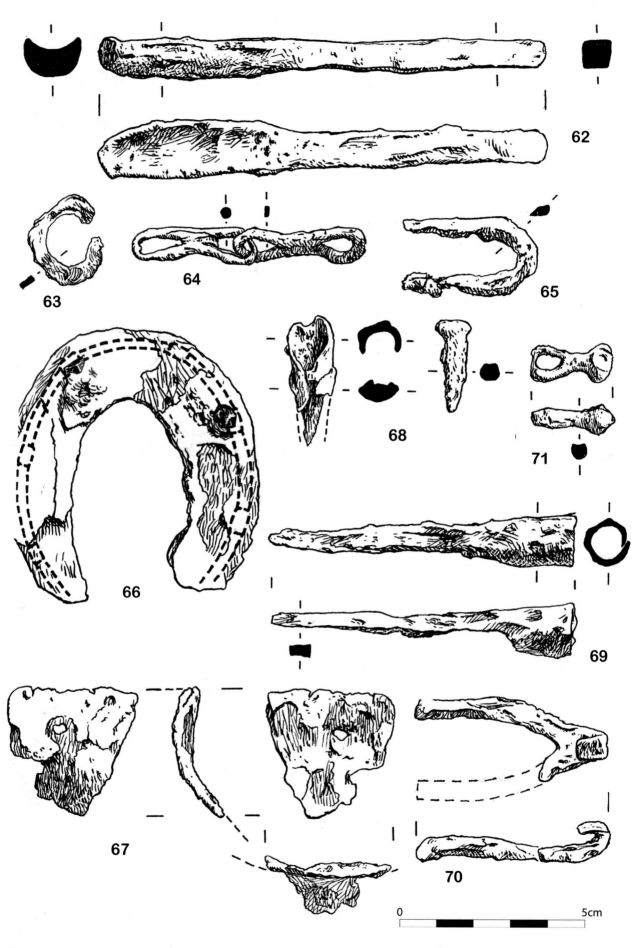

FIGURE 8.10

Iron objects

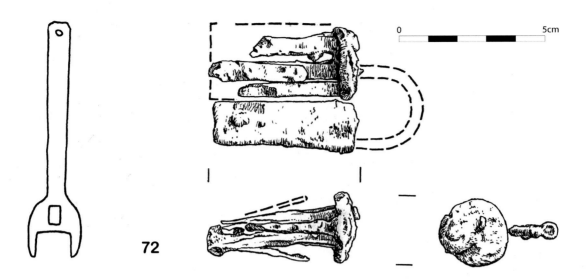

FIGURE 8.11
Iron objects

Other items

Other finds (not illustrated) include:

— Two other arrowheads (68 SF24 D/E9-10 B; 68 SF35 M/N9, from baulk) also probably related to butts in the churchyard.

— Other examples of keys (67 F/G21 topsoil/ baulk; 67 SF8 H6 A topsoil; 67 SF12 F5 A1).

— Buckles: one as no. 50 (66 H17-18 B2), another (as no. 11) diameter 20mm (67 SF43 F6 A3); 12th–15th century (Goodall 2011, 356–357, Fig. 12.9, K228).

— Further examples of latch or strip (66 SF17 JK14 A2; 66 SF22 AA/BB12-13 B; 66 SF29 F21-22 A, topsoil; 66 C/D14-16; 66 P/Q17-18 A, topsoil; 67 SF45 F6 A3).

— Three door hinge plates, 12th–15th century (Goodall 2011, 210–211, Fig. 9.23, H519).

— Large nails and spikes, too numerous to list.

— Knives: six other examples mainly as no. 56 with pointed tang and tapering blade: also one with flat tang and flat blade; also a modern knife with flat tang pierced by rivet holes and flat blade. No knives had any cutlers' marks visible on X-rays. Further Faxton knives are illustrated in Goodall (2011, 136–137, Fig. 8.18, G256, G257).

— Shears: domestic type with curving top to blades (68 SF42 F15, in ditch), 12th–15th century (Goodall 2011, Fig. 8.26, 152–153, G435).

— A further chisel (66 B17-18 A2).

— Awl, of rectangular section, 114mm long (67 SF38 E27 A3), 12th–15th century (Goodall 2011, 72–73, Fig. 6.2, E29).

— Punch: 66 (986) unstratified.

— Bridle bit (66 SF40 K18 A2).

— Horseshoes: all fragmentary (66 SF19 H13 A2; 67 SF44 E28 A3; 68 SF48 H11 baulk).

— Another fork tine (66 M/T15-18 A, topsoil).

— Staple: unknown context. 12th–15th century (Goodall 2011, Fig 9.5, 176-177, H92).

Worked bone objects
by Lawrence Butler

The worked bone objects (Figure 8.12, nos 73–81) include:

73. Knife handle, decorated with dot ornament in groups of four; one iron rivet survives, inner surface hollowed to receive flat tang (66 SF61 C17 B2/C).

74. Handle with knife cuts (67 F/G/H2-3 A2 baulk)

75. Knife handle, plain; one large iron rivet survives, inner surface roughly sawn (66 SF55 K11, ditch fill).

76. Tuning peg or weaving slide, roughly formed handle, central area with three holes and decorative grooves; perhaps second handle now broken (66 SF48 G17 B2). *[More recent study (see below) would identify this object as a scale tang knife handle.]*

77. Weaving needle; chicken leg bone, artificially perforated and smoothed (66 S/T11-13 A2). *[More recent study would identify this as a toggle (see below).]*

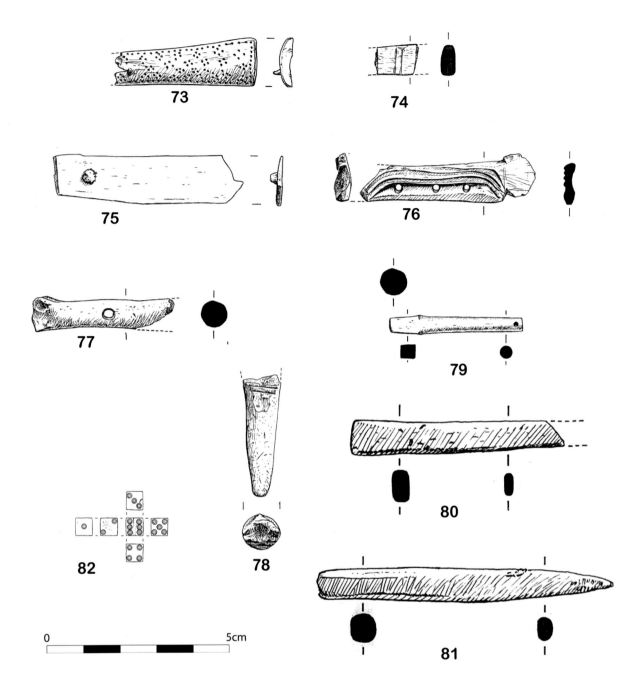

FIGURE 8.12

Worked bone objects

78. Knife handle terminal, roughly cut ?from roe deer antler; unfinished (66 SF16 CC11 B2).

79. Bone punch, well polished circular shaft with eyelet hole, tapering end 4mm square, probably a lace bobbin (68 SF62 S15 A, topsoil).
[More recent study would identify this as a tuning peg (see below).]

80. Rib, highly polished; ?from cow (68 SF51 D/E14-15 B).
[More recent study would identify this as a bone pin beater (see below).]

81. Point, highly polished; from sheep rib (68 SF75 K14, ditch fill). *[Also a pin beater (see below).]*

82. Dice, ring-and-dot ornament (68 SF63 F13, wall collapse).

Not illustrated: Knife handle in two pieces of semi-circular section, flat tang and blade (broken), 3 iron rivets and start of blade. 19th century (68 SF19 G16 A, topsoil).

Not illustrated: Button hook or crochet hook, conical top, turned decoration, post-medieval in date (68 F/G16-17 B).

Stone objects
by Lawrence Butler

Stone objects are illustrated in Figures 8.13–8.17, nos 83–112.

Spindlewhorls (Figure 8.13)

Only one spindlewhorl is of stone; the others are made of baked clay and considered below.

83. White Lias limestone; flat surfaces polished, sides knife-trimmed (67 SF52 F24 C).

Beads (Figure 8.14)

87. Jet bead, evenly pierced hole (68 SF65 F15 B).

88. Melon-shaped black stone bead, broken in half, possibly jet (66 SF35 D8 B; 66 SF38 E8 A2; 66 SF39 A/E21-23, A, topsoil).

Whetstones (Figures 8.15 and 8.16)

Of the 37 whetstones, 15 are of mica-quartz-schist of the type traced to the Eidsborg district of Norway, two of them with suspension holes (Ellis 1969; Moore 1978; and Moore and Oakley 1979 for Northampton). The latter suggests that the sandstones from the Coal Measures or from the Pennines are post-medieval and the stratification at Faxton would support that. Fifteen are of fine micaceous gritstone from the Pennines; these are of tapering rectangular or circular shapes. Less certainly in use as whetstones are five tapering smooth surfaced pieces of dolerite, one of schist and one piece of lava/pumice stone with a smoothed surface.

90. Smooth sandstone, evenly tapering; ?post-medieval (67 F2, topsoil).

91. Coarse grained sandstone, square; ?post-medieval (66 SF1 C11-13 A, topsoil).

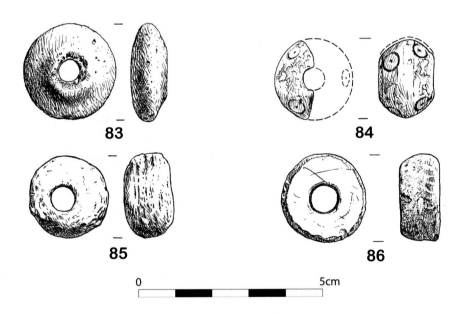

FIGURE 8.13
Spindlewhorls of stone and fired clay

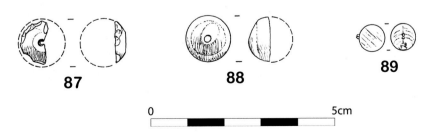

FIGURE 8.14
Stone and glass beads

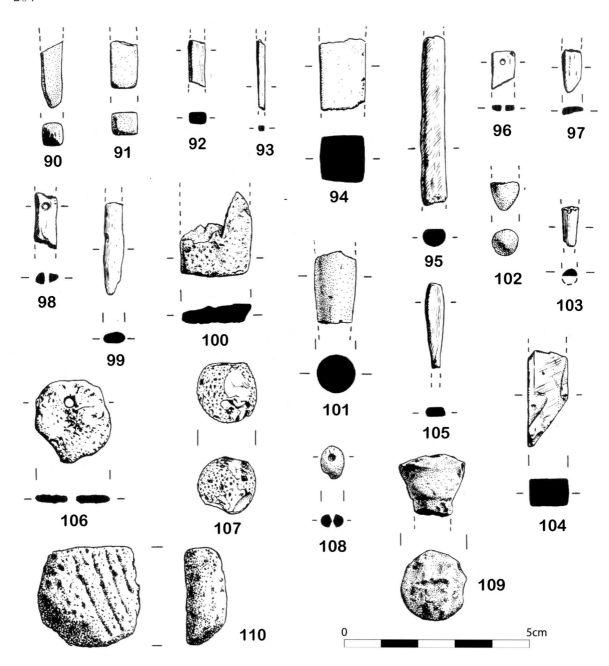

FIGURE 8.15

Stone objects

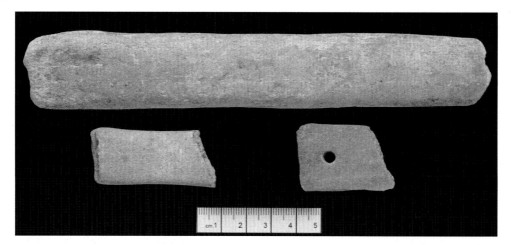

FIGURE 8.16

Whetstones: (92) fine grained schist, (95) grey schist, (96) medium grey schist with drilled hole

92. Fine-grained schist, worn surfaces; ?medieval (67 SF7 F0 A, base of topsoil) (Figure 8.16).

93. Slate/schist, smooth surfaces (68 SF58 unlocated B).

94. Coarse grained sandstone, only worn on two surfaces; ?post-medieval (68 SF7 A-D 20 A, topsoil).

95. Grey schist, worn on broad faces, broken at both ends. ?medieval (66 unstratified surface) (Figure 8.16).

96. Medium grey schist, quartz along edge, well-drilled hole; ?medieval (66 SF14 H8 B) (Figure 8.16).

97. Similar to 96 but separate stone; ?medieval (66 SF15 D8 B).

98. Pale grey schist, laminating surfaces, well formed hole; ?medieval (67 SF102 F18 A, topsoil).

99. Pale grey schist, heavily worn; ?medieval (66 SF50 G19 B).

100. See 'Smoothers' below.

101. Dull grey fine-grained gritstone; ?post-medieval (67 stray surface material/ploughsoil).

102. Fine-grained grit, end of tapering cylinder; ?post-medieval (66 I/J18-21 A2).

103. Dull grey slate, not certainly a whetstone (66 SF46 L/M 20 ditch lower fill).

104. Slate, smooth surfaces, two sharpening grooves (67 SF34 E18 A3) (see 'Smoothers' below).

105. Brown grey schist, worn surfaces. ?medieval (68 SF64 F13 B).

Smoothers (Figure 8.15)

Two stones have smoothed surfaces which seem to be the product of human activity rather than the result of natural causes such as water action.

100. Amphibole, now badly fragmented but with a smooth bottom edge (66 I/J17-20 A2).

Weights (Figure 8.15)

106. Near circular thin slab of oolitic limestone, probably from Barnack, with well formed circular hole. Perhaps originally a roof slate but now has smooth edges. This object could be a weaving weight, but is too light for a loom-weight or thatch-weight, but may have been used as a pot lid when an air hole was needed (66 (573) F/H11 A2).

108. Small slate pebble with hourglass perforation; perhaps a plumb-bob weight. The hole is too small for use as a spindlewhorl unless the hole is unfinished (67 (2) G2, topsoil).

Pestles (Figure 8.15)

107. Globular nodule of flint, surfaces pecked to make them smooth and to fit easily into the hand. Base is flat with exposed flint worn smooth (66 SF33 J21 A2).

109. Lias limestone, carved with slight waist, smooth sides, rough convex base. For use as a pestle with a stone mortar (67 E18 A3).

Quern (Figure 8.15)

110. Fragment of Niedermendig lava, broken, with edges abraded from use as yard material. Later incorporated as building stone in Building A3, west wall (66 G/H16-20 A, topsoil). Another fragment (not illustrated) came from a ditch fill (67 SF47 F17 A5) and from fieldwalking in Crofts 4–5 (Steane 1971). Querns made from Mayen Lava and traded through Niedermendig are relatively plentiful on rural sites in eastern England, particularly in the 13th century. They indicate North Sea trade with secondary distribution via the Fenland river system.

Stone lids (Figure 8.17)

Fine-grained sandstone was shaped to use as lids to cover pottery jars or cooking pots. Two are illustrated.

111. Roughly pecked edges (66 SF53 J15, tumble).

112. Smoothed edge, hint of central perforation (66 I/J20-23 A, topsoil); stone tumble Building A4, west wall. See also no. 106 above.

Glass objects (Figure 8.14, no. 89)
by Lawrence Butler

89. Black glass, bronze suspension loop; from necklace or earring; ?post-medieval (68 SF55 S16 A, topsoil).

Not illustrated: Two modern beads of glass and two jet buttons (68 SF16 K/L11-13 B); nine clay alleys (or marbles) of 18th–19th century date; normal diameter of 15mm but range from 12 to 17mm (68 SF39 D/E11 B); one clay alley painted with fine blue crossed lines.

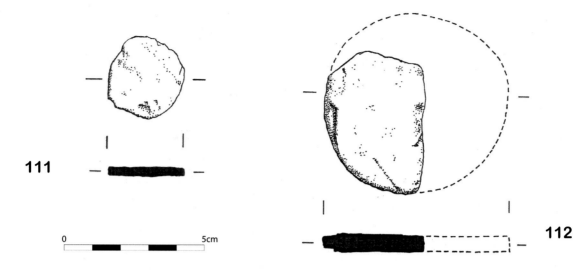

111

0   5cm

112

FIGURE 8.17
Stone objects

Fired clay objects (Figure 8.13, nos 84–86; Figure 8.18, nos 124–133)
by Lawrence Butler

Four types of object were found: floor and roof tiles (see Chapter 9), clay spindlewhorls, clay alleys or 'marbles' and clay tobacco pipes. A spindlewhorl made from re-used pottery fragments is considered in Chapter 7 (Figure 7.23, no. 150).

Spindlewhorls (Figure 8.13)

84. Soft grey clay with ring-and-dot ornament; powdery surface, fire blackened after fracture (66 SF36 HH11 C2).

85. Hard grey fabric, probably fashioned from Roman pottery (67 SF9 F8 A1).

86. Grey slightly micaceous fabric; worn around hole; possibly re-used bunghole from narrow-necked pitcher (67 SF2 F3 A3).

Clay tobacco pipes (Figure 8.18)

All clay pipe fragments were retained, partly to ascertain the range of material, partly to assess the relative density of the post-medieval occupation and land use across the site.

In terms of range of material there were pipe stems in a wide variety of bore diameters, but relatively few bowls. One bowl (132) and one stem (133) were stamped by their makers. There were few decorated bowls: two had fluting, a few had rilling. There were no examples of coloured clays or of glazed mouthpieces.

The sample range of bowl shapes and foot profiles is illustrated; all lie within the London or the Midland traditions. The date range appears to be 1660–1850.

There is far more material from Croft 52–53 1968 (85 locations, 178 items), especially alongside the occupied Rectory (Farm); there was no particularly dense concentration in Croft 29 1966 (31 locations, 36 items) adjacent to the almshouses, but in Crofts 6–9 1967 (24 locations, 35 items) the material was usually near the hedge and adjacent field track.

124. 68 D/E9-10 A topsoil.

125. 67 topsoil; also 68 K/L2-3 A topsoil.

126. 68 H/J11-13 A2.

127. 68 L/M2-3 B.

128. 67 E12, topsoil/ditch section.

129. 67 H7 topsoil; also 67 H9, topsoil, also 68 D/E9-10, topsoil.

130. 68 H/J11-13 A2.

131. 68 F/G14-15 A, topsoil.

132. 68 Q/R9-10, topsoil. This pipe carried the maker's mark RR. There are five makers in Northamptonshire with these initials. On grounds of style, Robert Richards of Northampton (active 1795–1834) is the most probable maker here (Oswald 1975; Moore 1980).

133. 67H7, topsoil. The SV mark is common in Lincolnshire and the northern Midlands in the period 1660–1710 (Oswald 1975, 88, Figures 16 and 20, Map 5).

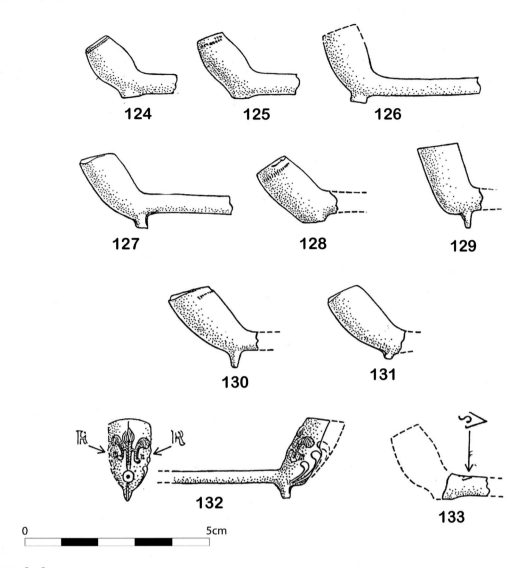

FIGURE 8.18
Clay tobacco pipes

8.4 THE FAXTON FINDS REVISITED
by Eleanor Standley

Due to their relatively simple nature and lack of stratigraphy, medieval village house sites are unlikely to produce much securely dated evidence (Mynard 1991, 245), and with only a few stratified contexts at Faxton there is a limit to the amount of information that can be garnered from the small finds. Comparison with other excavated villages does, however, reveal the widespread occurrence of certain find types, and many objects recovered from Faxton are typical for rural medieval settlements. However, there are some interesting and unusual finds that deserve further comment.

The items of personal adornment, including copper-alloy buckles, buckle plates, and strap fittings, found on all crofts at Faxton, are quite simple and of standard designs. A couple of finger rings and brooches were identified, but none that speak of particular wealth. The pair of tweezers reveals something of the personal grooming habits of the occupants in Croft 29 1966. A small number of beads were found, which may have been from a paternoster, necklace, or decorative adornment; the jet would have been sourced from Spain or Whitby (Yorkshire). The only other religious item recovered was the piece of 14th-century sculpture that had been re-used in the Rectory.

Other personal items found were knives of general use, and knife handles. Both whittle tang and scale tang knives were present at Faxton, with bone handles of scale tangs being most common. The scale tangs were more time consuming and costly to produce, but less practical, and were more common from the 14th century onwards (Goodall 2011, 108). Another iron object of domestic use was a socketed candlestick from Croft 29 1966, a common form from the 13th century onwards.

A range of finds reveals some of the day-to-day activities and manufacturing that would have taken place at medieval Faxton. There is slight evidence for textile production. The few spindlewhorls of re-used ceramic, baked clay and stone were used for processing raw material into yarn. Unusually one of the baked clay whorls was decorated with a ring-and-dot motif. The bone pin beaters may suggest that a two-beam loom was in use for the production of fine works or tapestry. A pair of domestic shears, for cutting of yarn or cloth, and thimbles also indicates the habitual activity of sewing. A notable find, as discussed by Egan above, is the Haarlem baling seal demonstrating the presence of imported linen cloth in Faxton in the 17th century.

Other craft production evidence is limited to the small amount of metal-working at Croft 29, and small-scale bone- and antler-working. An abundance of animal bone would have been available; perhaps residents of the village produced their own knife handles. One incomplete antler knife handle terminal was found; the antler could easily have been acquired after natural loss, rather than from the hunting of the animal.

Two animal crotal bells were excavated, and the spindlewhorls also suggest the presence of flocks of sheep for wool working. At excavations at Wythemail, cow, pig, sheep, and dog were found—and would be expected at Faxton. Horses could be expected too, but there were very few horseshoes when compared with other deserted settlements, such as Great Linford. There were other items of horse furniture at Faxton, including spurs, a bridle bit, and swivel loop. Iron buckles recovered may also have been used on harness straps.

Cooking and storage vessels of local manufacture were abundant with regional imports featuring in the assemblage (see also Chapter 7). Alongside the ceramics other evidence for cooking was a quernstone and pestle fragments, and the oven at Croft 29 1966. The pestles are of interest, as it is more usually the stone mortars that are found in settlement excavations. At Faxton, these pestles would have been used to grind spices and herbs for cooking, and perhaps even for medicinal use. Notably a pestle fragment was excavated from Croft 29 1966, but the second came from Crofts 6–9 1967. The quernstone fragments were made of Niedermendig lava, and along with Norwegian sourced schist whetstones, are further evidence of North Sea imports at Faxton. The schists were relatively small in size, suggesting they were used for the sharpening of smaller blades of personal use, and two of them had suspension holes for carrying on the person.

In the post-medieval period, the cloth seal and mainland European jettons also suggest indirect international contacts. In contrast, there was a lack of English jettons, but the low number of coins at Faxton is not unexpected. From the larger finds assemblage at Great Linford, for example, only 3 or 4 coins on average were found in each croft (Mynard and Zeepvat 1991).

As at other medieval sites, leisure activities were represented in the finds from Faxton. A bone dice, tuning peg, and clay alleys or 'marbles' were excavated. Details of the alleys/marbles are not available, but it is probable that they were post-medieval in date. The bone dice and tuning peg are more likely to be medieval—the latter is comparable to other examples from England dating from the late 12th to 15th centuries. It would have been used with a metal turning key that fitted over the square end, to tune a stringed instrument such as a harp, lyre or fiddle. The dice is decorated with ring-and-dot motif, and the regular layout of sides.

Arrowheads were the only weapons found, with the suggestion that they were used at the butts on The Green or churchyard. A further weapon-related item is the chain links from mail coat that came from Croft 52–53 1968.

The most unexpected find at the settlement is the zoomorphic finial or ridge tile of 13th- or 14th-century date from Croft 29 1966. Such ornamental roof furniture has usually been found at sites of seignorial or higher status (Moorhouse 1988, 43). The suggestion in Figure 9.4 (no. 155) is that the fragment is the body of a wild boar, missing its legs, head and tail. The animal motif on roof finials has been found elsewhere, for example at nearby Lyveden, and is identified as a 'Group VI' form (Dunning 1975; Hurman and Nenk 2000, 68; see also discussion in Chapter 9). A horse and rider and other 13th/14th-century fragments of zoomorphic and human figures were found at the manor house of Faccombe Netherton in Hampshire (Fairbrother 1990, 202–210). It seems that hunting was a common decorative scheme on roof furniture (Jones 1998–99). From the limited documentary evidence, Moorhouse (1988, 46) suggests that ornamental roof furniture would have appeared on all manner of buildings regardless of use or status, whereas much of the archaeological evidence that has been studied indicates the finds are more often associated with wealthier buildings (for example, Jones 1998–99). The Faxton piece (and that from Lyveden) may, therefore, either support the case for occupants of some wealth in Croft 29 1966, or be physical evidence of low status buildings decorated with ornate roof fittings as suggested in contemporary documents. A local production source at Lyveden may be the reason that such an item is present at Faxton.

It was suggested by Butler that the medieval occupants of Croft 29 1966 enjoyed a higher standard of living compared with those of Crofts 6–9 1967 and Croft 52–53 1968. Comparisons between crofts are difficult at Faxton, because of the history of occupation and lack of stratigraphic details. It must be remembered that Crofts 6–9 1967 were occupied from c.1150 to 1300 and were disturbed by ploughing; relatively little of the medieval yard areas were excavated at 1968

ARTEFACTS

209

Croft 52–53 because the Rectory Farm stood on them; whereas a greater number of features were excavated at Croft 29 1966, and occupation was from *c*.1200–1450. The later, post-medieval activity on Croft 52–53 1968 is reflected not only by the pottery recovered there (see Chapter 7), but also by the finds, such as a Georgian spoon bowl, the 17th-century cloth seal, jettons, and larger numbers of clay pipe fragments.

There is some evidence that suggests minor differences between the crofts. A greater total number of finds were excavated from Croft 29 1966 compared with Crofts 6–9 1967 and Croft 52–53 1968. There were personal possessions of a slightly more decorative nature found at the former. They could also afford metal vessels, alongside ceramics, as shown by the small fragment of a copper-alloy vessel leg. A small key from the house also suggests that there were precious articles that required securing in a small box or casket. This was, however, the only key found at the croft, while at Crofts 6–9 1967, there were seven finds related to security: iron keys, latch keys, a barrel padlock key, and a barrel padlock. Iron objects in general indicated that a small amount of craft-working was taking place at Croft 29 1966: residues of iron-working and 'casual smithing', and a punch and two chisels were found. At Crofts 6–9 1967 Butler suggested that the evidence revealed activity of a more agricultural nature, but this evidence seems to be limited to a horseshoe and two elements that may have come from harnesses/carts, a swivel loop and chain links, which is not conclusive.

The structural finds do not help us to definitively distinguish any difference in status at Croft 29 1966. It was fitted with window glass and the unique decorative roof finial—which may or may not be associated with wealth; but then the chimney pots were found on Crofts 6–9 1967 and Croft 52–53 1968, and window glass, in small amounts, was also found at all the croft sites.

9

BUILDING MATERIALS

Lawrence Butler

The contents of this chapter have been extracted, re-ordered and edited from a lengthy 'finds section' which originally combined information for all the Faxton artefacts. Here structural evidence such as window glass and lead came is placed together. No analysis of mortar or plaster materials was undertaken during the post-excavation process nor was there any further analysis of the fabrics of the floor tiles or roofing material. No brick was recorded.

9.1 SCULPTURE OR CARVED ORNAMENT

A statue (no. 113) carved from oolitic limestone, probably quarried from Weldon (Figures 9.1 and 9.2) is of a civilian, his right hand resting on a broad-bladed sword, his left holding the loop of his neck chain. The style of carving, the type of sword and the treatment of the hair all suggest a date in the third quarter of the 14th century. The figure is placed in a niche of which only the sides and base remain. At a later date, probably in the early 17th century, the rear of the statue has been trimmed back to re-use the stone as a window mullion.

The statue was found by Lawrence Butler embedded in a farm track whose rubble core had just been brought from the partly demolished Rectory so it is most likely that it had been incorporated into a window there (Figures 3.19 and 3.20). The Rectory was built in about 1560. It is possible that this statue was part of a tomb chest, presumably a 'weeper', and that this tomb was ejected from the church after the Reformation or when Sir Augustine Nicholls repaired the chancel early in the 17th century (see Chapter 3 for more detail on the church at Faxton).

9.2 WORKED STONE

The underlying bedrock at Faxton is Northamptonshire sandstone with the occasional band of ironstone. These stones were used in the house foundations though other sources, presumably glacial material in the Boulder Clay, were also encountered. All 'foreign' stones that had been worked were retained for study (none are illustrated), as were all flints whether worked or not.

9.3 DAUB

Daub (not illustrated) was found in 32 different locations (1966 in 25 locations; 1967 in 3; 1968 in 4).

Generally it was recognisable as a red-brown brick-like mixture, sometimes pale yellow-brown at lower levels. There was some evidence of burnt surfaces which might represent an oven of hearth canopy at 66 L11-12 B, 67 F-G31 A4, and 68 A-B4 A.

Two specimens showed the imprint of planking, either structural or the result of shuttering when the wall was erected (66 CC8-12 pit fill; 66 CC-FF12 D); another showed the imprint of wattles (66 D-H11-15 B2) and one had a plastered surface (66 D9 B). The locations favourable to the survival of daub were in pits and ditch fills where the daub had avoided attrition from animal and human feet, and would not suffer from frost damage. The other well preserved location was where wall tumble had occurred onto a flat surface and the underside of the daub wall surface had survived, for example in Croft 29 1966 where the tumble had not been cleared away.

9.4 GLASS AND WINDOW CAME

Medieval glass (not illustrated), almost certainly from windows, was rarely found at Faxton; it was either clear or opaque green. In Croft 52–53 1968, it tended to be decayed and friable, but in other locations it was well preserved. It occurred in seven different locations as follows:

—66 SF68 F12 B2, on floor surface, bronzed edge,

—66 X24-25 A/B,

—66 M25-30 B/C,

—67 E17 A2, opaque green,

—67 G17 A2, clear white,

—68 A-B4 C,

—68 Q-R9-10 C, clear white,

Post-medieval glass was more varied and included window glass, wine bottle glass and parts of small cylindrical bottles. One rolled rim came from a

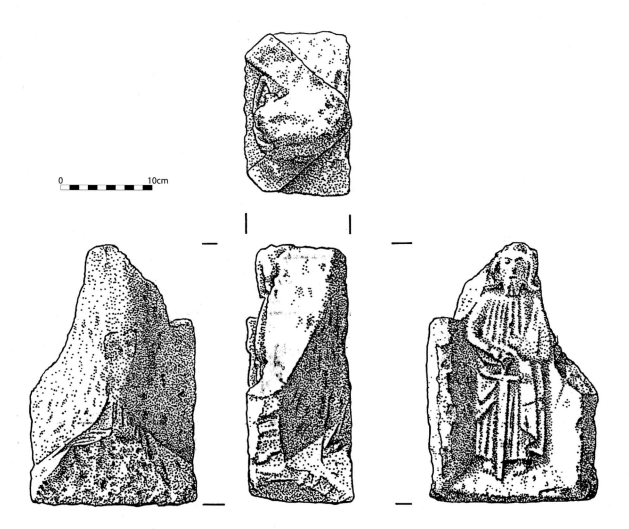

0   10cm

FIGURE 9.1

A statue carved from oolitic limestone (no. 113), late 14th century

FIGURE 9.2

Stone statue (no. 113), late 14th century

bowl (68 F-G16-17 B) and a small fragment of a beaker rim in dark blue glass was decorated with pale blue trails (68 Q-R4-5 B). Much of the glass came from upper contexts, for example from 17 different locations in Layer A in Croft 29 1966, and from 20 locations in Layer A and 16 more in Layer B from Croft 52–53 1968. Four window cames were recovered from Croft 53 1968.

9.5 NAILS

Large nails and spikes were described as 'too numerous to list'. Only one nail in a socket is illustrated (Figure 8.10, no. 68).

9.6 FLOOR TILES

Floor tiles (Figure 9.3) were found in all three areas of excavation, but only one example was recovered from Crofts 6–9 1967. The majority were glazed floor tiles either plain or with an inlaid pattern: four examples came from Croft 29 1966 and 135 from Croft 52–53 1968.

Two main periods are represented. The first is 14th-century tile (thickness 17–21mm) with glazes in orange, yellow and green; the second is a late medieval tile (thickness 23–25mm) with a thinly applied glaze in yellow or bright green. The majority of the tiles occurred in the upper levels of the site (layers A1-A3 and B1). It is tempting to see these as material ejected from the church in a programme of re-flooring in the 17th century. However, as some tiles occur incorporated in wall material or sealed within floors, they must represent debris from earlier re-flooring in the church. Only a selection of patterned tiles is illustrated. Both square and triangular tiles are present; the majority are so heavily worn that the thinly inlaid pattern is completely worn away and the colour is only indicated by glaze spills along the tile edge and base. Many tiles show evidence of kiln stacking obliquely on the edge. A few have mortar adhering to edge and base.

242. Red fabric, well fired sandy surfaces; sharply knife-trimmed edges, 20mm thick; worn floral pattern, white inlay under orange glaze (only visible on tile edge). Pattern lies within range of Leicestershire-Warwickshire designs (68 M4-6 A/B). A tile from 68 D-E14-15 (topsoil) is similar.

243. Hard red fabric, under-fired, smooth surfaces; straight knife-trimmed edges, 19mm thick; broad and deep inlay, white under reddish-orange glaze. This pattern of a fabulous beast with a floral tail is a Warwickshire design (Eames 1980 II, 1397–99) (68 D-E11-13 A). Another tile in similar style is 68 N-P2-3 B.

244. Red fabric, poorly fired, smooth surfaces; sharp edges but evidence of glaze spill and kiln stacking, 20mm thick; clean-cut geometric pattern, yellow inlay under orange-red glaze. Pattern could be a simple cross in a circle with external trefoils at corners, as drawn, or could be a circular shield with a heraldic bar, as at Bordesley (Eames 1980 II, 1606, 1617) (68 F-G2-3 B).

245. Red fabric, poorly mixed, sandy surfaces; under-cut knife-trimmed edge; 19mm thick; white inlay under dull red glaze. The pattern may be heraldic, as shown with arms of Earl of Cornwall, cf. Polesworth (Eames 1980 II, 1527) and Greyfriars in Northampton (Williams 1978, 122, Fig. 16, nos 5 and 5b). An alternative reconstruction is a design where four tiles make a complete pattern of a pelleted circle enclosing foliage and with more foliage in the angles of the tiles as at Pipewell and Ulverscroft (Eames 1980 II, 2704, 2706) (68 L/M11-12, topsoil).

9.7 ROOF TILES

A Roman tegula with a heavy lug and a flue tile with combed treatment were found during fieldwalking in an unspecified location. Three fragments from Croft 29 1966 and three from Croft 52–53 1968 appeared to be medieval roof tiles (Figure 9.4, nos 153 and 154).

All that can be suggested on this evidence is that the houses normally had thatched roofs, but that smaller buildings with hearths and ridges would have had ceramic ridge tiles to protect from flying sparks that part of the roof nearest the heat source. No stone slates were found in any of the medieval layers.

A few items of roof furniture were also found, including two possible chimney pots (Figure 9.4, nos 151 and 152). The most unusual item, however, was a large fragment of a glazed zoomorphic roof ridge tile (Figure 9.4, no. 155), of the type discussed by Dunning (1975; see also Chapter 8.4).

This consisted of the body section of an animal, possibly a wild boar, hollowed underneath, giving a 'U' cross-section. The clay was raised towards the peak where it had been pinched to form a 'mane' or 'back-bone'. This had been finely slashed to give the impression of fur or hair, and further diagonal slashed lines decorated each side. Towards the rear, or haunches, were a number of stabbed holes. The sides were shaped upwards at each end, and clear unglazed breaks indicated where the rear limbs and front limbs and head had been attached. A further break marked the position of a possible tail. This decorated ridge tile was probably made at Stanion, and must have embellished a medieval roof.

FIGURE 9.3
Inlaid floor tiles

151. Chimney pot (67 F2, layer A).

152. Chimney pot (68 F-G 14-18, layer A).

153. Ridge tile (68 F-H 8-10, layer A).

154. Ridge tile (68 F-H 8-10, layer A).

155. Zoomorphic roof ridge tile (66 A-C 20-22, layer C).

9.8 ROOFING LEAD

From Croft 29 1966 there were seven items of scrap sheet lead, from Crofts 6–9 1967 there was just one item (lead sheet 67 SF10), and from Croft 52–53 1968 there were nine pieces of sheet or scrap.

Much of the latter probably represents episodes of re-roofing at the church. The majority of this material came from area E/H11-15, closest to the churchyard.

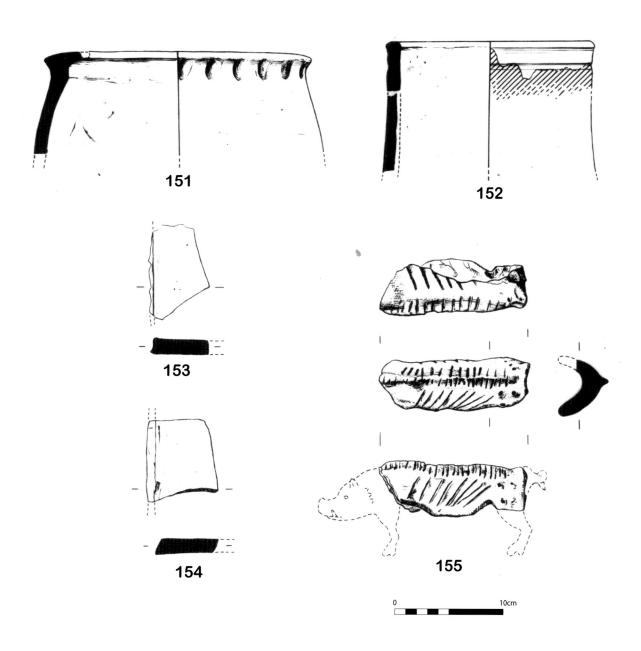

0   10cm

FIGURE 9.4
Roof furniture

10

ENVIRONMENTAL EVIDENCE AND METALLURGICAL RESIDUES

Lawrence Butler

with contributions by Louisa Gidney

In 1966 the analysis of mollusca, charcoal and industrial residues was not yet well established in later medieval archaeology. Although material was recovered by the excavator, the samples taken on site for palaeoenvironmental study were very small by comparison with sample sizes considered to be good practice today and they were not proposed for further study in the 1980s when the main post-excavation programme was underway. Their existence is cursorily noted below by Lawrence Butler. On the other hand, faunal remains were recovered in quantity, but remained unwashed and unstudied. For this chapter the assemblage from Croft 29 1966 has been examined for the first time by Louisa Gidney and she contributes a section on her findings. Only the remains from the 1966 excavations were studied as part of this publication project because the stratigraphy and dating evidence from the other sites had been found to be less secure.

10.1 SHELL

Both shellfish and land mollusc remains were retained from the three seasons of excavation; shellfish as evidence of diet, and land molluscs as a means of locating hedges and fences or in confirming the presence of walls. The method of collection was weighted heavily to large species and visibly spiral species. However, smaller specimens were found. Soil samples of ditch fills and drain fills are available for further laboratory analysis.

Shellfish occurred in three species:

—cockle (one location in Crofts 6–9 67 E20 A3);

—mussel (two locations: Crofts 6–9 67 F-G19 A4; Croft 52–53 68, F-G4-6 B2);

—and oyster, both smooth-shelled and rough-coated in 20 locations.

From the Croft 29 1966 excavations there were four shells in ditch fill F7-8 (one was an oyster), in Crofts 6–9 1967 one shell came from J4 (topsoil), in Croft 52–53 1968 shells were recovered from 18 locations, mainly from Layers B and C, but on two occasions inside houses and on two occasions in drain fills of the medieval period.

Land molluscs were only retained as a matter of policy in Crofts 6–9 1967; on the other occasions soil samples were taken to recover minute mollusc remains. Snail remains occurred in 125 locations in Crofts 6–9 1967 but the methods of hand collection were weighted towards the larger species and banded specimens. Some smaller specimens were recovered. According to the excavator 'the general impression is that there has been little change in flora and habitat between 1200 and 1900'.

10.2 CHARCOAL

Evidence of charcoal was recovered widely disbursed at all levels and periods of occupation on all sites. It occurred at 95 locations in Croft 29 1966 and with similar frequency in Crofts 6–9 1967 and Croft 52–53 1968. No material was identified, but it is likely that about one-third would be capable of determination.

10.3 CHARRED GRAIN AND SEEDS

Evidence of charred grain was recovered in Croft 29 1966 at the corn-drying kiln (F6) and in the ditch fill (CC11 B). A hazelnut shell occurred in Croft 52–53 1968 (M-N18-19 B) with no evidence of an animal burrow nearby.

10.4 SOIL SAMPLES

Samples were taken of ditch fills, kiln material, charcoal areas, pit fills and from collapsed mud-walling in Northamptonshire and Leicestershire to examine for inclusions. It was noticeable how much flint and small stone was mixed with the mud, and in a few instances pottery was included in the grogging material.

10.5 INDUSTRIAL RESIDUES

Evidence of metal-working was found by the presence of slags on a number of locations in Croft 29 1966 and on Croft 52–53 1968. By visual examination, all appeared to be the residues of iron-working and casual smithing. There was no evidence of copper-working slag, no crucible material and no metal-working hearths. All the slag was retained.

10.6 FAUNAL REMAINS

All mammalian bone was retained from all contexts of the excavations and was bagged according to 5 foot squares (1.5 x 1.5m). This has resulted in more than 1,500 locations in the three seasons: Croft 29 1966, 506 fragments (4 boxes, but see below where 12 were studied); Crofts 6–9 1967, 810 fragments (5 boxes); Croft 52–53 1968, 243 fragments (3 boxes). Most animal bone was found in the yard areas between the houses, with relatively little in the boundary ditch fills, even less within roofed structures and none within post-pits and water-pits. In consequence, most is abraded and fragmentary with only those specimens from the ditch fills being in good condition and capable of giving evidence upon butchery, knife cuts and teeth marks. The study of the faunal remains was costed in the 1980s at £1,600, representing 30-40 days 'benchwork' and 20 days writing up. As there was no post-excavation funding for environmental work, examination of the animal bone by student practical classes sorted the material between the species of cow, horse, sheep and pig. This proved to be an unsatisfactory procedure, and any statistics based upon this work were felt by the excavator to be unreliable. Since it was therefore felt that the bone should be studied in its entirety, no further work was done and the collection remained in storage in 2017.

Burnt bone

This occurred at one location in Croft 29 1966, 31 locations in Crofts 6–9 1967 and 9 locations in Croft 52–53 1968. Nearly all the specimens were small and abraded; for only a few was the species easily recognisable. The locations were mainly in ditches or among yard material. In Crofts 6–9 1967 the concentration was at the southern end in Croft 6 and 7; in Croft 52–53 1968 the greater proportion was at the south-west of the site.

10.7 THE ANIMAL BONE FROM THE 1966 EXCAVATIONS
by Louisa Gidney

As Lawrence Butler explains above, the animal bone from Faxton was not studied as part of the original post-excavation programme in the 1980s. Re-evaluation of this position for the current project in 2017 suggested that only the 12 surviving standard archive boxes of animal bones from the 1966 excavation merited detailed analysis. As explained in previous chapters, the excavation pre-dated the adoption of recording systems using numerical codes for archaeological contexts and individual context recording sheets. Instead, the finds bags were given individual numbers linked to the on-site area co-ordinates and the broad divisions into A codes for the upper soil levels, B codes for the underlying destruction and collapse levels of the medieval buildings, and C codes for the latest medieval occupation deposits. Bones were also recovered from discrete medieval features and structures. Some of the numbered bags of bones now stored at Daventry have no site information and are therefore counted as unstratified here, together with fragments from baulks and sections, and bone fragments loose in boxes. The concordance of bag codes with site location is based on the finds of medieval pottery (Chapter 7), with supplementary information written on some bags.

Preservation and recovery

The greater part of the assemblage had not been washed and this has impacted on the observation and recording of, for example, butchery and gnawing marks. The overall assemblage is characterised by high proportions of loose teeth, indicative of the decay of the surrounding bone. Some damage has inevitably occurred during excavation, but this is not excessive. Complete, measurable bones are infrequent and it is clear that breaking of bones for marrow extraction was commonplace. The composition of the assemblage, particularly evidence for unfused epiphysial ends, has been skewed by the extensive evidence for dog gnawing marks observed throughout the assemblage.

Though the bone fragments were hand-collected, the abundance of small fragments, such as loose sheep/goat teeth, indicates a meticulous standard of recovery. The burial environment appears to have been benign in sealed deposits. The paucity of articulating elements and absence of complete skeletons of smaller companion animals and infant mortalities suggests both much contemporary disturbance and subsequent redeposition of faunal remains which may have accelerated fragmentation (for disturbance of the stratigraphy here, see Chapter 7 discussion and Figures 7.33 and 7.44).

Methodology

Bones were identified to species using the author's modern comparative reference collection and published works (Cohen and Serjeantson 1996; Hillson 1986; Schmid 1972). Fragments that required further elucidation were compared with the Durham University Department of Archaeology reference collection. Fragments of cattle, sheep/goat and pig bones were noted as identifiable if they encompassed a 'zone', or discrete diagnostic feature. The zones used are those described by Rackham (1986). This approach reduces multiple recording of fragments potentially from the same bone. Maxillary and mandibular cheek tooth rows which could be reconstructed, but where the surrounding bone had decayed, were recorded as either maxilla or mandible rather than as loose teeth. Given the abundance of loose teeth, no attempt was made to distinguish between loose molars 1 and 2. Teeth identified as either molar 1 or molar 2 were within a tooth row. Ageing from stages of tooth eruption and wear is based on the mandibular teeth, using the Tooth Wear Stages (TWS) and Mandible Wear Stages (MWS) devised by Grant (1982). Incisor teeth of cattle, sheep and pig were not recorded, as these are easily lost from the jaw post-mortem. All identifiable fragments of the remaining species were counted. Unidentifiable fragments were not recorded, but were noted as present if all the fragments from a context were indeterminate. The elements recorded as cattle-size or sheep-size comprise fragments of ribs and vertebrae. While the term sheep/goat is used, no evidence was observed for the presence of goat, whereas skull fragments and a third phalanx diagnostic of sheep were found and the morphology of the metapodials, in particular, was compatible with sheep.

Cattle withers heights are calculated using the average of Zalkin's factors for cows and steers (Driesch and Boessneck 1974, 336), sheep withers heights from the factors of Teichert (Driesch and Boessneck 1974, 339) and horse withers heights from the factors of Kiesewalter (Driesch and Boessneck 1974, 333).

Species

The species represented from layers and contexts/features in the 1966 excavations at Faxton are listed in Figure 10.1. The assemblage is dominated by fragments of cattle, sheep, pig and horse bones, with widespread representation of dog. Over a third of the identifiable fragments were recovered from the upper soil levels, in particular layer A2. Layer B is exceptional for the diverse range of species represented, particularly domestic and wild birds. Game animals and birds are otherwise rare. The occupation deposits of layers C-G and the individual features produced only about a quarter of the assemblage, less than the finds recovered from the destruction and collapse deposits of Layer B. This suggests that little faunal refuse was allowed to accumulate while the houses were occupied but rubbish dumping and incorporation of faunal waste in manure spreading were subsequently acceptable. There was no evidence that the fragments from the corn drier or oven, for example, were related to the primary use of these features. Though the medieval occupation spans the period 1200–1400,

there are insufficient fragments and dating evidence to subdivide the stratified finds chronologically for analysis.

Figure 10.2 shows the relative proportions of the four principal domestic species represented. The smaller medieval groups from Layer C and the other medieval features are sufficiently close in species composition that these may be treated as one unit for analysis. The proportions of pig and horse bones are comparable in Layers B, C and the medieval features but decline in Layer A. The proportion of sheep/goat to cattle fragments increases in Layer B compared to the underlying contexts, with a super-abundance of sheep/goat remains in Layer A. This indubitably reflects greater fragmentation of sheep skulls and mandibles in the upper levels, resulting in an increase in loose teeth.

Cattle

Figure 10.3 demonstrates the effect of taphonomic factors on body part representation. Nearly half the cattle fragments from the A Layer are loose teeth, dropping to over a third in the B Layer but less than a quarter in the medieval contexts. Fragments of the porous axial skeleton, ribs and vertebrae, are infrequent compared to the dense appendicular limb bones. The medieval contexts show the most even representation of body parts, indicative of utilisation of whole carcases on site.

The epiphysial fusion evidence in Figure 10.4 is sparse in all three groups. The same pattern is apparent throughout, probably reflecting continuity in the factors degrading the assemblage rather than genuine patterns of husbandry and consumption. The unfused epiphyses indicate both culling of cattle less than five years old and survival beyond this age. A metacarpal shaft from the medieval layers has been extensively chewed at both ends but is clearly from a young animal, though not an infant calf. A radius shaft from the A layer is from an animal of similar age. Dog gnawing has obliterated much of the evidence for juvenile animals with unfused epiphysial ends.

Given the super-abundance of loose teeth, particularly in Layers A and B, only the data from the mandibular teeth are considered in detail in Figure 10.5 for ageing information. There are no decidu-ous premolars (dp) 4 at early wear stages from infant calves. However, very limited evidence for calf mortality is provided by single examples of maxillary dp4 in Layer B and medieval at such early wear stages. One dp4 from Layer A had been shed, also a maxillary dp4 from medieval contexts. The permanent premolar 4 erupts by roughly 3 years of age. The pattern of wear distribution in Figure 10.5 is similar in all three groups, with a minority of permanent teeth at early wear stages a–f and good representation of advanced wear stages j-m. These data complement the fusion evidence for some culling of

Layers	A1	A2	A/B, A2/ A3? A2/B, A4–B	B	B2	B3	B/B2, B/C, B+ B2/3, B2/C	C	C1	C2	C3	C/D, C+	D	E	F	G	Lower leves	u/s	Topsoil	Total
Cattle	41	91	11	48	43	14	11	31	26	16	2	10	11	8	2		2	10	13	390
Cattle size	1	5		4	2	3		1	6	2			2							26
Sheep/goat	82	232	19	97	74	34	10	31	24	10	6	6	14	1	2	1	1	20	31	695
Sheep		1		1							1									3
Sheep size	1	3		6	2		1				1		1					1		16
Pig	10	35	3	32	16	5		10	7	4		3	3					1	1	4	134
Horse	8	22	4	13	12	10	3	3	6	1		8	3	4	1			2	3	103
Dog	8	10	5	8	9	5	1	8	6	2		1	2					1	2	68
Cat		4	1				1													6
Red deer		2		1														1	1	5
Fallow deer				1																1
Hare													1							1
Rabbit																			2	2
Mustelid				1																1
Domestic fowl	1	3		10	2	1	1	1	1									2	1	23
Goose				3	1							1								5
Rook/crow		1				2												1		4
Jackdaw				3																3
Buzzard				1					2											1
Bird sp.				1																1
Frog/toad		1		1				1	1											4
Human				1																1
Total	152	410	43	232	161	74	28	88	77	35	10	29	37	13	5	1	5	39	56	1495

Features	Corn drier	Ditch fills	All gullies	Houses	Oven	F1	(F6) B3	F7	Pit fills	Trench	Walls	Yard	Drain fill	Total
Cattle		22		1	1	2	2		5	4	2		1	40
Cattle size		2		1							1			4
Sheep/goat	2	13	6	3	3	4	3	1	5	1	5			46
Sheep							1							1
Sheep size							1							1
Pig	1	1	1	1	1	2	1	1	1		1			11
Horse		10					1		1		3	1	1	17
Dog	1	1			2		1		1				1	7
Cat		2												2
Hare			1											1
Domestic fowl		2	1											3
Fish			1											1
Total	4	53	10	6	7	8	10	2	13	5	12	1	3	134

FIGURE 10.1

Fragment count for the species present for layers (above) and contexts/features (below)

	Layer A		Layer B		Layer C		Medieval contexts	
Cattle and cattle-size	149	26%	125	28%	64	34%	69	38%
Sheep/goat and sheep-size	338	59%	225	51%	79	43%	79	43%
Pig	48	8%	53	12%	24	13%	21	11%
Horse	34	6%	38	8%	18	10%	15	8%
N	569		441		185		184	

FIGURE 10.2

Relative proportions of the domestic species

	Layer A				Layer B				Medieval contexts			
	Cattle	Sheep/ goat	Pig	Horse	Cattle	Sheep/ goat	Pig	Horse	Cattle	Sheep/ goat	Pig	Horse
Head: skull, jaw	11	30	12	3	19	29	12	3	22	23	6	7
Loose teeth	67	216	19	20	43	102	16	17	38	47	10	13
Forelimb: scapula, humerus, radius, carpals	13	26	6	3	15	36	15	5	30	22	10	6
Vertebrae and ribs	12	4	2	1	10	10	1	2	15	4	1	4
Hindlimb: pelvis, femur, patella, tibia, tarsals	32	44	6	2	17	24	8	4	41	34	9	9
Feet: metapodials	8	15	1	3	9	10	1	3	19	11	2	3
Toes: phalanges	6	2	2	3	5	4		3	6	4	1	

FIGURE 10.3

Body part representation for the domestic species

young adults but most slaughtered as mature adult or aged animals. Only four tooth rows could be reconstructed for MWS. A juvenile, over 6 months old, at MWS 9 is represented in Layer B. A young adult at MWS 19 and a mature adult at MWS 41 are represented in the medieval contexts. The teeth at MWS 41 had the occluding maxillary teeth also present and may indicate original deposition of a partial skull. A further tooth row at MWS 41 was found in Layer A.

The few fragments with morphological sex characteristics are all from females, with two examples of pubis bones from Layer A and single examples from Layer B and medieval contexts. In addition, there is a frontal with horn cores from the medieval contexts.

Measurable bones were infrequent, with most recovered from the medieval contexts. There are too few examples of any one element for analysis. Three complete metapodials from the medieval contexts indicate withers heights of 1.12m, 1.15m and 1.18m.

The pathological conditions are all indicative of age-related degeneration. Four examples of maxillary molar 3 with malocclusion resulting in an elongated, or hooked, posterior cusp were found, one in Layer A and three in Layer B. This impairment is a contributory cause of mortality in Chillingham

cattle (Ingham 2002). Two mandibles from the medieval contexts display pitting and resorption of the bone along the gum line. A fragment of sacrum from the medieval contexts exhibits the extended anterior process seen on aged Dexter cows with advanced arthropathies (for example, Gidney 2013, Plate 5: 15d–e). One first phalanx from Layer A shows expansion and lipping on the proximal lateral articulation. This condition has been observed in modern draught oxen (Bartosiewicz *et al.* 1997) and adult Dexter bulls (Gidney 2013, Plate 2: 14a and c). The female pubis from Layer A exhibits eburnation indicative of joint degeneration.

Sheep/goat

Fragments identified specifically as sheep comprise a third phalanx from Layer A, a fragment of male horn core from Layer B and, from the medieval contexts, a horn core and a frontal with base of horn core, both female.

The taphonomic bias in the survival of sheep/goat fragments in Figure 10.3 is even more marked than the pattern seen for the cattle remains, with over two-thirds of the elements in the A Layer being loose teeth that could not be re-assembled into

	Layer A			Layer B			Medieval contexts		
	U	JF	F	U	JF	F	U	JF	F
by 18 months									
Scap tub			1						
Acet symph						1			2
Prox rad			3			3			
Dist hum			1	1		2			2
Prox Ph 2			1			3			1
Prox Ph 1			5			1			4
by 2–3 years									
Dist tib	1		3	1			1		4
Dist mc			1			1	2		2
Dist mt			1			1			2
by 3.5–4 years									
Prox cal									
Prox fem	1		2	1			1		2
Dist rad			1				2		
Prox hum							1		
Prox tib	1								1
Dist fem	1		1	1		1			
Prox uln									
by >5 years									
Ant vert ep	2		1	4			5		2
Post vert ep	2		1	2		1	4		3

FIGURE 10.4

Cattle epiphyses in approximate order of fusion (ages of fusion after Silver 1969).
U=Unfused, JF=Just Fused, F=Fused

		Tooth wear stages											
		a	b	c	d	e	f	g	h	j	k	l	m
Layers A	dlp4							1	1	2	1		
	P4			1	1		1						
	M1				1						1		
	M1/M2		1				1	4	1	2		1	1
	M2									2			
	M3						1	2		2			
Layers B	dlp4							2		1			
	P4					2							
	M1				1				1				1
	M1/M2		1					1			1		
	M2			2									
	M3	1		1				1		1	1		
Medieval contexts	dlp4									1			
	P4					2							
	M1							1		1			
	M1/M2				1			5		2	1		
	M2		1							1			1
	M3							1					

FIGURE 10.5

Cattle tooth wear stages (after Grant 1982)

tooth rows, compared to only a third in the medieval deposits. Representation of ribs and vertebrae is poor throughout. Otherwise the numbers of fragments from heads and feet compared to those from fore and hind limbs indicate refuse from whole carcases.

The ubiquity of sheep remains is not reflected in the surviving epiphysial evidence in Figure 10.6. More fused bones from older animals were recovered but this may not reflect the original age distribution of the slaughter population. A tibia shaft from an infant lamb was found in Layer A.

To avoid duplication of evidence, only the ageing data from the mandibular teeth is considered in detail in Figure 10.7. While all three groups show a preponderance of permanent teeth in full attrition, TWS g, there is a suggestion of a chronological change with more teeth from older animals, TWS h–m, in the medieval contexts compared to more teeth from younger animals, TWS a–f, in Layer A. Only one infant lamb is represented by dp4 at TWS a in Layer A. More sheep/goat than cattle mandibular tooth rows have survived. Figure 10.8 shows the distribution of MWS, with a total absence of very young animals in all three groups and only one second year animal, at MWS 17, in Layer B. Layer B also has the greatest range of wear stages represented, with an aged specimen at MWS 44. The mandibles from Layer A are all at MWS 30–36, younger adults, while the medieval mandibles are

older adults at MWS 38–43. This is very tenuous evidence but hints at a shift in preference from older to younger mutton.

Variation in burial environment and bone loss is indicated by single finds of matching maxillary tooth rows, indicative of decayed skulls, in Layer B and medieval contexts,

Despite the high proportion of sheep/goat fragments, there are fewer measurable elements, 11, than of cattle, 16. One complete medieval metatarsal gives a withers height of 0.53m.

Although the ageing data indicate a preponderance of adult to elderly animals, the only age-related arthropathy seen was on a proximal radius from Layer B, which has a lateral exostosis.

Pig

Though there are far fewer pig remains than those of cattle and sheep in Figure 10.2, the proportions of loose teeth in Figure 10.3 are lower than those of cattle and sheep in the A and B Layer. In the medieval contexts, loose pig teeth are intermediate in frequency between that seen for cattle and sheep. While the small numbers of pig fragments recovered are not necessarily representative, the body part distribution of pig, excluding teeth, in all three groups suggests the remains of whole carcases.

There are insufficient pig bones with surviving epiphysial ends for analysis. Dog gnawing has

		\multicolumn{13}{c}{Tooth wear stages}
		a	b	c	d	e	f	g	h	j	k	l	m	n
Layers A	dlp4	1						3						
	P4	1				1		3						
	M1							10						
	M1/M2		1	2	1	7	10	34	2	1	2	1		
	M2					1	3	6	1					
	M3	4	5	2	6	2	17							
Layers B	dlp4							2			1			1
	P4							2						
	M1	1					1	4				1		
	M1/M2			2	1	3	2	10	3	1				
	M2	1					1	4			1		1	
	M3		1	1		3		9				1		
Medieval contexts	dlp4							1						
	P4							3	2	1				
	M1							3	1	2	2	1	1	
	M1/M2		1		1	2	2	5	2		1			
	M2				1	1		3	2	1				
	M3							9						

FIGURE 10.6

Sheep/goat epiphyses in approximate order of fusion (ages of fusion after Silver 1969).
U=Unfused, JF=Just Fused, F=Fused

		Tooth wear stages												
		a	b	c	d	e	f	g	h	j	k	l	m	n
Layers A	dlp4	1						3						
	P4	1				1		3						
	M1							10						
	M1/M2		1	2	1	7	10	34	2	1	2	1		
	M2					1	3	6	1					
	M3		4	5	2	6	2	17						
Layers B	dlp4							2			1			1
	P4							2						
	M1		1				1	4					1	
	M1/M2			2	1	3	2	10	3	1				
	M2	1					1	4			1		1	
	M3		1	1		3		9				1		
Medieval contexts	dlp4							1						
	P4							3	2	1				
	M1							3	1	2	2	1	1	
	M1/M2		1		1	2	2	5	2		1			
	M2				1	1		3	2	1				
	M3							9						

FIGURE 10.7

Sheep/goat tooth wear stages (after Grant 1982)

		Tooth wear stages												
		a	b	c	d	e	f	g	h	j	k	l	m	n
Layers A	dlp4													
	P4		1											
	M1	2			1	1	1	3						
	M1/M2	1		1	3									
	M2	1												
	M3													
Layers B	dlp4													
	P4	1												
	M1			1		1		1						
	M1/M2	1				1								
	M2													
	M3													
Medieval contexts	dlp4													
	P4													
	M1			1	1		1							
	M1/M2	1												
	M2													
	M3													

FIGURE 10.8

Pig tooth wear stages (after Grant 1982)

obliterated much of the potential evidence. The few fused bones seen are those that fuse early in life. Two bones from the medieval contexts lack epiphysial ends but are clearly from piglets, though older than newborn.

Figure 10.8 shows that no dlp4 were recovered and in fact there are no deciduous pig teeth at all in this assemblage. It can be seen that the majority of the pig teeth are molars 1 and 2 in early stages of wear, with only one molar 3 present in Layer A. This indicates slaughter of animals between one and two years old. Two tooth rows from Layer A have MWS of 16 and 27, indicating the lower and upper ends of this age range.

The canine teeth are sexually dimorphic and, though not abundant, suggest equal numbers of males and females with two examples of each sex in Layer A, three examples of each in medieval contexts and five female to three male examples in Layer B.

Horse

Figure 10.2 suggests that the representation of horse is related to that of pig in a comparable way to that seen for cattle to sheep/goat. The abundance of loose teeth and paucity of ribs and vertebrae in Figure 10.3 suggest that the factors causing loss of bone in the other domestic farm animals have influenced the horse remains too. Enhanced survival in the medieval contexts is suggested by remains of two skulls, one represented by teeth from both maxillae and one with parts of the cranium and maxilla surviving.

There is some evidence for young stock, particularly in Layer A where there are two unerupted permanent teeth, a mandibular tooth row of deciduous teeth, two shed deciduous teeth and an unfused distal humerus. In Layer B there is a foal scapula and a shed deciduous tooth and two deciduous teeth in the medieval contexts. One complete metacarpal from Layer B indicates a withers height of 1.35m.

A first phalanx from Layer B exhibits exostoses round the distal articulation and degeneration of the articular surface. The bone has been extensively modified by dog gnawing, which has totally destroyed the proximal end. This appears to be a long-standing condition, as the bone proliferation does not appear to have been active at death, and the horse must have been lame in life.

Dog

Dog remains are the most numerous of the minor species represented and occur in similar proportions throughout. The comparatively small number of actual dog bones belies the impact of this species on the overall assemblage. For example, the general lack of unfused epiphysial ends seen for the domestic farm animals may be primarily attributed to the

destruction of these soft and fragile bones by dog gnawing. The find of one medieval sheep/goat first phalanx with the acid etching characteristic of passage through the canine gut suggests that the low numbers of sheep and pig phalanges in Figure 10.3 may be a result of total consumption by dogs rather than merely bias in hand recovery of fragments. The dogs were not fussy eaters as gnawing marks were observed on dog bones too. Feeding of deceased hounds to their kennel mates is indicated at Witney Palace (Wilson and Edwards 1993).

No complete dog skeleton was recovered though a probable disturbed skeleton, comprising skull and mandible fragments, lumbar vertebrae and sacrum, was found in Layer C. Front paws are indicated by single sets of articulating metacarpals in Layers A and B. No complete bones were recovered from which the stature of the dogs present might be calculated. Examples of particularly large ulnae were seen in Layer A and medieval. A very small dog is represented by a tibia of cat size in Layer A. No evidence for juvenile animals was recovered. Two skulls were found, one from Layer B and one medieval. Both have disintegrated on lifting but clearly derive from elderly animals with fused sutures and robust soft tissue attachments. A premaxilla from the medieval contexts is also from an elderly animal, with exostoses and pitting round the socket for the canine, indicative of gum inflammation.

Cat

Cat is principally represented by mandibles in Layers A and B. Two animals are represented in the medieval ditch fills, one older with a fused femur and one younger with an unfused femur.

Deer

Red deer is represented by two bones from the hind foot in Layer A and one bone from the hind leg in Layer B. A shed antler coronet base with brow tine was found in the medieval contexts and a further fragment of antler beam from a section.

The only find of fallow deer is a tibia from Layer B.

Lagomorphs

Two hare bones from the hind limb were found in medieval contexts.

Rabbit bones were only found in the topsoil, indicating that there has been minimal disturbance of the stratigraphy by this species.

Mustelid

A single tibia intermediate in size between reference specimens of weasel and stoat was recovered from Layer B.

Domestic birds

Domestic fowl are the most numerous bird bones recovered, with a relative concentration in Layer B. One femur from Layer A has rodent gnaw marks and a humerus from Layer B has canid gnaw marks. Again, dogs have probably totally destroyed many of the domestic fowl bones originally present. One juvenile bird is represented by a femur in Layer B. One probably female bird is indicated by an unspurred tarso-metatarsus in Layer A.

Goose bones are rare with only three examples from Layer B and one medieval find. One juvenile bird in Layer B is indicated by a tarso-metatarsus and a further tarso-metatarsus has been burnt.

Wild birds

The most common wild bird bones are corvids, with rook or crow represented in Layer A and B and three bones of jackdaw, probably from one bird, in Layer B. Buzzard remains were found in Layers B and C. The finds from Layer C are an articulating humerus and coracoid from the wing. The distal humerus has been cleanly cut off and the proximal coracoid has been cut through.

A large passerine is also represented by one bone in Layer B.

Amphibian

Bones of frog or toad were found in Layers A, B and C. These indicate excellent recovery during excavation and a burial environment conducive to the survival of such small and fragile bones.

Fish

Small fragments of fish bone were found in the N–S gully in D 21-22.

Human

The only human fragment was a single tooth in Layer B. This has been kindly identified by Dr Tina Jakob as a right maxillary premolar 1.

Discussion

The faunal economy, as indicated by the discard of bone fragments, appears to have centred on sheep and cattle with a second focus on pig and horse and with dog as the main companion animal. The body part representation suggests slaughter or death on site and utilisation of whole carcases. However horn cores of both cattle and sheep are very infrequent, compared to the ubiquity of loose teeth, and may indicate that horns were traded off site.

The faunal assemblage would seem to reflect the low social status of the settlement, with no wastage of any animal parts that could be utilised. The high proportions of loose teeth from the domestic farm animals may indicate that heads were cooked, hastening decay of the bone and tooth loss. Limb bones were fragmented for marrow extraction. All faunal refuse, including the dogs themselves, appears to have been made accessible to the resident dog population.

Although the burial environment has preserved small and fragile bones, there is very little evidence for mortality of infant and juvenile domestic animals. In this respect, the evidence for foals in both medieval and later deposits is of particular interest. Certainly more physical evidence for foals has been found at Faxton compared to Shapwick (Gidney 2007, 907), where there is documentary evidence for foals on the manor. Claridge (2017) observes that the documentary sources indicate the economic importance of demesne horse breeding in the Midlands. While there is not equivalent documentary evidence for the peasantry, Claridge (2017, 19) suggests they had both the potential and incentive to produce a surplus of work horses, in excess of their own draught needs, for cash sale. The foal bones and teeth from Faxton may support this contention. Further, Langdon (1986) emphasises that horses were popular at the lower end of the socio-economic scale as they were valued for their versatility at tasks other than ploughing. This preference for horses is explicitly noted by Langdon (1986, 259) for the peasantry in counties like Northamptonshire. The continuing post-medieval importance of horses within the Faxton economy may be suggested by the provision of a military light horse[-man] by the Nicolls family (see Chapter 2).

Though some of the dog bones are certainly large enough to derive from the more robust types of hunting hounds, as depicted in the Hunting Book of Gaston Phoebus (d'Anthenaise 2002), the general lack of evidence for hunting suggests that these were more probably working farm dogs. The late 13th-century text Fleta (Cripps-Day 1931, 77) explicitly states that each shepherd should provide himself with a good barking dog. Such dogs were an essential part of the shepherd's trade but more to guard the flock against potential predators, either human or animal, than to herd the sheep. The two hare bones from medieval contexts might possibly indicate opportunistic poaching of noble quarry on the sheep-walks. Another possibility may be suggested from documentary evidence in Boldon Book (Austin 1982), relating to tenure under the Bishops of Durham, where settlements further from the Weardale hunting grounds provided the dogs, nets and horses needed (Randerson and Gidney 2011).

The presence of a wider range of species, particularly the domestic fowl, goose and deer bones, in Layer B may indicate either a brief period of relative affluence or deposition of refuse originating from the manor house. Certainly access to both hunted and managed game species appears to have been highly restricted. Red deer might have been sourced from the ancient woodlands still extant to the north and west of the parish and fallow deer from the parks which incorporated deserted neighbouring settlements (see Chapter 2).

There are few remains of commensal species. Either there was too little food available to attract them or they were routinely killed off as a potential threat to crops, infant livestock and poultry. The latter may be the fate of the corvids and buzzards found. The cut marks on the buzzard wing bones from Layer C suggest that the wing feathers may have been of value. Although frog/toad bones were recovered by hand, no bones of mouse, vole or rat were found. Rodent nibbled bones were rare and only seen in Layer A. The rarity of cat bones may indicate that few were needed to control such pests.

Faxton is an important addition to the faunal evidence from medieval rural settlements, for example Shapwick in Somerset. Cattle and sheep/goat fragments provide the bulk of both assemblages. Some of the trends noted at Faxton have also been observed at Shapwick, such as a high proportion of loose teeth but paucity of horn cores (Gidney 2007). The MWS data for sheep/goat are broadly comparable with most jaws at MWS 30 and beyond and little evidence for younger animals, though Shapwick does have jaws at MWS 8–9 from first year lambs (Gidney 2007, Fig. 22.12), which are not represented at Faxton. The rather drier countryside of Faxton may be reflected in a higher proportion of horse remains but fewer of pig compared to Shapwick. Most noticeable is the greater number of dog bones recovered from Faxton compared to Shapwick. Overall, both sites show patterns of continuity in the consumption and discard of faunal waste from the principle farm animals.

11

THE BUILDINGS AND THEIR PLOTS

Christopher Gerrard

with contributions by Peter Brown and Stuart Wrathmell

Lawrence Butler did not summarise the evidence for the medieval buildings he had excavated at Faxton, but given the importance of some of his findings and the prominent place they often find in regional and national reviews, some re-consideration seems appropriate here. In particular, Butler found ample confirmation for what he preferred to call 'mud buildings', a rather imprecise term for a type of construction which he had himself read about and photographed across Northamptonshire in post-medieval structures, but one which has barely been documented by medieval archaeologists even today. At the same time, Butler also saw structures which we now might interpret differently.

Lawrence Butler's ambitions and interpretations at Faxton must be seen in the context of medieval settlement studies as they were developing during the 1960s. Between 1840 and 1968 there had been 209 excavations on medieval house and village sites across Britain (that is, AD 1066–1570), but only on 88 of these had one or more domestic buildings been recorded (Beresford and Hurst 1971, 147). With few exceptions, these excavations were limited in scale and in only a few cases had useful building plans been retrieved. As we have seen in Chapter 1, medieval settlement studies in the mid-1960s were also still very much in their infancy. How then did John Hurst and others imagine the medieval house in 1966 when the first turves were cut at Faxton? What were the key narratives which would influence the excavator Lawrence Butler when he came to interpret his findings?

11.1 THE SHORT-LIVED PEASANT HOUSE

The site phasing at Faxton, as set out in Chapters 4 to 6, might be described as 'characteristically 1960s'. That is to say, the chronology of the site is broken down very simply and evenly into 50-year blocks; structural changes are taken to equate to different building phases and the precise dating of these phases is largely independent of any interpretation placed on finds, or indeed the stratigraphy. There are good reasons for this. First, the Faxton finds were not studied in detail for another 35 years, long after the stratigraphical accounts had been completed and, in the case of the metal artefacts for example, their identification and dating by Ian Goodall depended upon evidence derived from other excavations which were yet to happen or whose materials were yet to

be studied. The crucial reference publication which illustrated and dated the many hundreds of objects from excavations in Winchester between 1962 and 1971 did not emerge until 1990, for example (Biddle 1990; a review of non-ceramic finds studies can be found in Egan 2009). Although his on-site 'finds cards' demonstrate that Butler did correctly identify the finds such as querns, whetstones and knives for what they were at the time of their excavation—he had seen them before at Thuxton and elsewhere and taught medieval material culture at Leeds—in 1966 the accurate dating of ironwork and other finds was still in its earliest stages and in no way informed the interpretation of the site. Second, as excavator Bob Carr recalls, 'the pottery was mostly local stuff, including Lyveden wares which I was familiar with through fieldwalking the kiln site, but it was poorly understood and only dated by generalised form and appearance at the time; this made it difficult when asked to show it to John Hurst'. This is an important observation; the pottery from Faxton could not be classified or precisely dated as it came out of the ground (like the bone, much of it was not washed in any case). In addition, John Hurst, perhaps the person best placed to provide an informed overview of the medieval pottery and other finds, visited Faxton only very rarely because the calendar dates for the excavation overlapped with those at Wharram Percy.[1]

Effectively, the study of the finds and the interpretation of structures were de-coupled from the very start. Third, the stratigraphy at Faxton was shallow and often disturbed by later activity, something which Butler realised perfectly well at

---

1 I am grateful to Paul Stamper and Bob Croft for searching out information from John Hurst's personal diaries.

the time and which the study of pottery sherd links was later to confirm (see Chapter 7).

If there was no effective dating of finds on site and little in the way of stratigraphy, how then did Butler 'phase' his structures so precisely? The answer lies largely with his observations about the different types of medieval construction on the site and the phasing of those buildings. Here again the state of research in the mid-1960s was extremely influential in his thinking. First, in terms of construction, peasant houses were believed to be short-lived and continually being replaced in varying positions and on diverse alignments. Mercer (1975, 8) thought peasant buildings to be of 'uniformly poor quality' or, as John Hurst put it, 'peasant houses were very flimsy and were unlikely to last more than a generation without either repair or even complete rebuilding. It is a very striking fact that on many village sites rebuilding took place once a generation on completely new foundations and often on a new alignment' (Beresford and Hurst 1971, 122). 'Flimsy' was a favourite word of John Hurst's in this context (Hurst 1965, 190; Smith 2006, 61, 63; Dyer 2012, 312) and Guy Beresford, a leading excavator of later medieval sites at the time, felt confident enough to comment that 'the life of a peasant house is generally accepted to have been approximately twenty years' (Beresford 1975, 38). This point was persistently illustrated by examples from Wharram Percy (Yorkshire), Hangleton (Sussex), Hound Tor (Devon), and Milton (Hampshire), among others.

Today, it is no longer accepted that later medieval village houses were so impermanent (Astill 1988, 54–56; Grenville 1997, 123–133). One of the last occasions this interpretation was committed to print was in 1986 in a review of archaeological research since the Second World War (Hurst 1986, 223–225), thereafter the longevity of the peasant house was entirely reconsidered in the late 1980s and it is now understood that peasant houses lasted far longer (Currie 1989; Dyer 1986; Wrathmell 1984; 1989). Nonetheless, Lawrence Butler knew no different when he came to phase the buildings he saw at Faxton. Indeed, what he observed there indicated nothing to contradict the prevailing point of view.

Plan forms

What kind of medieval building plans might Lawrence Butler have expected to see? Three main groups of houses had been defined in 1965 by John Hurst (1965; 1971, 104–114). In brief, these were: the peasant cot, the long-house, and the farm. The peasant cot was described as a one-roomed house while the long-house was divided into two by a cross passage with one end for living and the other for animals or some alternative agricultural function. The long-house was considered to be 'the typical house of the medieval villein... [with] cattle to stall or grain to store' (Hurst 1965, 192). Finally, the farm-

complex placed living and farm accommodation at right angles to one another and, according to the logic of the day, these would have been inhabited by 'emerging yeoman farmers who were working for themselves and therefore would need more storage space' (Hurst 1965, 192). Excavated examples of these three types of house plan (as they were understood to be at the time) were well documented (Hurst 1971, 104–117).

Given that a long-house had been identified at Muscott in 1958 and Gillian Hurst, John Hurst's wife, had also excavated what was thought to be a long-house at Wythemail in 1954, neither site being far from Faxton, Butler would surely have concluded that long-houses were both early and universal and very likely to be found on his site. Today, of course, we would once again see matters very differently. Many of the interpretations taken for granted by John Hurst and other site excavators have since been called into question, among them those for Hangleton (Sussex), Gomeldon (Wiltshire) and Upton (Gloucestershire), all considered to be key reference sites in 1966. The arguments in favour of the Wythemail period III house as a long-house must also be viewed with great caution and more plausible explanations have now been offered (Gardiner 2000).

Techniques of construction

If the typical length of life of peasant buildings was already thought to have been established by 1966, and if Butler had a clear idea of the sorts of building plans he might discover at Faxton, this might be taken to imply that he himself brought little of his own experience and judgement to the project. That, however, would be unfair. The excavations at Thuxton in Norfolk in particular were both formative and recent in Lawrence Butler's mind (Butler and Wade-Martins 1989).

Excavated in 1963 and 1964, the deserted medieval village at Thuxton had produced evidence for four house sites dating between the 13th and the 15th centuries. Among the features identified were flint-cobbled yard areas, toft ditches and pits, as well as chalk clay floors and trodden surfaces, internal dividing walls or partitions, hearths of burnt clay and charcoal, and post-pads. Butler was therefore familiar with the full range of features to be expected from the excavation of a medieval house. Once more, at Thuxton he had excavated collapsed and dissolved 'mud' or clay-lump walls which he had been able to identify from the rows of flints which served as their foundation courses (also seen at Grenstein; Wade-Martins 1980, Fig. 64) (for location see Figure 11.1). Although some of these footings had been dragged out of position by the plough, through patient excavation they were still distinguishable by their many inclusions of chalk and small flints and by the remaining lengths of foundation which consisted

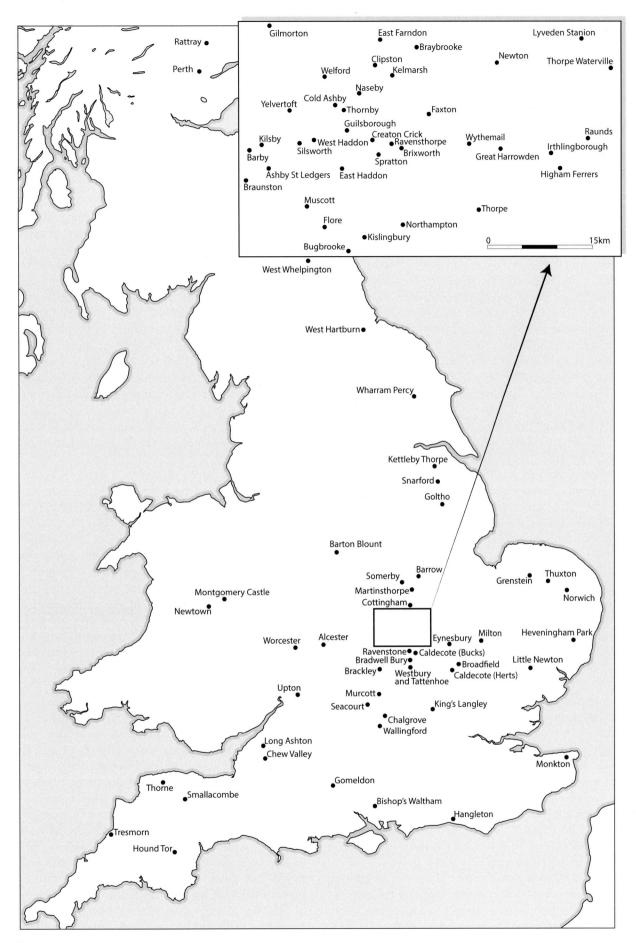

FIGURE II.I
Map showing sites and places mentioned in this chapter

of flints and glacial erratics laid out *directly* on the ground surface. At Thuxton, it might also be noted, he had found no evidence for cruck frames placed at regular bay intervals and none for posts set into a timber ground sill.

To summarise, Butler was an experienced excavator with a track record of excavation at deserted settlement sites. This he combined with his interest in standing buildings and, given his experience at Thuxton, it should be no surprise that a key mission of his work at Faxton was to learn more about earthen construction. In fact, medieval buildings assembled in this way had first been recognised nearly 100 years previously at Smallacombe in Cornwall (Blight 1868), but in 1966 a rash of new sites had only recently begun to produce evidence: at Snarford (Lincolnshire, dug 1957; West 1969), Thorne (Devon, dug 1959–62; DMVRG 1961, 12–13), Eynesbury (Cambridgeshire, dug 1960; Tebbutt 1960), Caldecote (now identified as Bedgrove) (Buckinghamshire, dug 1964–66; Mac-Donald and Gowing 1989) and Grenstein (Norfolk, dug 1965–66; Wade-Martins 1980). In particular, Guy Beresford's contemporary excavations at the shrunken village at Tresmorn in north Cornwall in 1964–67 would also have been uppermost in Butler's mind. The evidence there suggested turf buildings from the mid-10th century, followed by a switch to cob construction in 1150–1200 and finally to stone in the mid-13th century (Beresford 1971).

At the same time, Butler also recognised earthen construction as being typical of parts of Northamptonshire and Leicestershire. In his 1967 BBC interview he named the villages of Ravenstone, Guilsborough and Gilmorton, which provided 'examples of mud-walled construction which continued to be practised, continued to provide the less permanent farmyard features, right until the First World War' (Faxton tape 1). His reels of photographic negatives demonstrate that he visited these places, even if he did not mark up his slides and their locations cannot be precisely identified today. Looking at his bibliographies and notes, it is very likely that a recently published article by M V J Seaborne on 'cob cottages' in Northamptonshire was an important inspiration for him. These structures were described by Seaborne as being 'constructed of solid mud, usually up to 2 feet thick, and always built up on a stone base or plinth, normally about 18 inches high' (Seaborne 1964, 215). The terms 'mud-wall' and 'claywall' are most commonly used to describe mass earth structures in many parts of Britain.

Second, Butler recognised from the beginning that there were both earthfast buildings *and* ground-set buildings at Faxton. The first rectangular houses he understood to be of timber with post-hole constructions and mud walls. These were followed by timber-framed buildings with horizontal sill beams for which the 'sleeper trench' or 'beam slots' still remained, and finally by houses with foundations of boulders, pebbles and limestone. These changes in the form of construction did not happen simultaneously across the village; as Butler commented, 'what was true for one house was not necessarily true for its neighbour'.

On this basis, to create a relative phasing for the site was a straight-forward matter. The number of refurbishments of a building could be multiplied by 50 years to provide the full length of the sequence, so that four refurbishments might indicate a total length of chronology of 200 years. Without any further 'anchors' to help with the dating, this chronology might have floated free, but the occasional 'small find' or coin (on which the correspondence with specialists was understandably more voluminous given their importance) then allowed for a greater degree of precision. To take one example, in Croft 29 1966, the coin dating to before 1350 which was found in the hearth of Building A3 provided not only an end date for that building (Phase 3) but a *terminus ante quem* for Building A4 which, given the predicted 50-year life for a medieval building, logically brought Phase 4 to an end *c*.1400. Subsequent re-analysis of the phasing and dating of the site has now significantly extended the occupancy and life of the Phase 4 building (see Chapter 7).

11.2 THE PEASANT BUILDINGS AT FAXTON

Re-visiting the 50-year-old archive, it is possible to think again about the nature of the vernacular buildings which were excavated at Faxton. Of course, this is not a process without difficulty because of the imprecision of the dating and the damaged quality of the excavation records as we find them today. Nevertheless, two main categories of construction are described and discussed below: earthfast buildings and ground-set buildings.

Earthfast buildings

The evidence for earthfast buildings at Faxton is fragmentary. Butler described Building A1 in 1966 Croft 29 1966 as 'earthfast building with timber uprights' (see Figure 4.7). It is, however, no more than a fragment of a building consisting of two east–west parallel lines of stones each about 5m long; no post-holes or pad-stones are located, hearths and doorways are absent and there is no further mention in the excavator's notes to indicate how the walls might have been constructed. There is certainly a higher density of stone at this location in later phases of the site (see Figure 11.5A), but Building A1 was presumably robbed out and damaged by later construction for Building A3/A4 and, as a result, it is hard now to understand the basis for Butler's conviction.

CROFT 52-53
Building 1

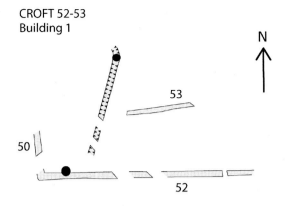

CROFT 52-53
Building 2

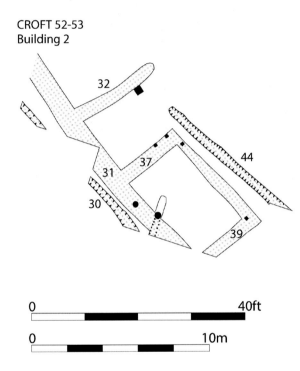

FIGURE 11.2

Earthfast buildings at Faxton with a wall trench from Croft 52–53, excavated in 1968. The upper building is Building 1, the lower is Building 2. Dated to c.1150–1200 and c.1200–1250 by the excavator

Two years later in Croft 52–53 1968 (Figure 11.2) Lawrence Butler identified what he thought were superimposed 'sleeper trenches' or 'beam slots' for the horizontal sills or baseplates/soleplates of timber-framed buildings (Buildings 1 and 2) in the south part of the trench in Phases 1 and 2. These features were dated by the excavator to the mid-12th century.

Building 1 is around 3.5m wide with a minimum length of 11.5m; it lacks its east wall and the two long walls (50, 52 and 53) are not parallel to each other. The 'beam slots' are described as having a rounded section. Building 2 immediately to the south had 'beam slots' of rectangular section, parallel side ditches or gullies with U-shaped or V-shaped profiles and post-holes, both in the centre of the

walls and set against the outer faces (Figure 11.2). The only measurable space has dimensions of 5.5 by 3.3m. The excavator thought it likely that other post positions had not survived or else had not penetrated the clay.

What Butler observed in Croft 52–53 are what is best described as 'wall trenches' which would have had vertical posts set at intervals, perhaps 1m or more apart. There is no evidence of planking along the wall line which might indicate stave-building techniques (as at Raunds Burystead BSP20; Audouy and Chapman 2009, 129–130, for example) nor is there any evidence for pad-stones or stylobates under the feet of the vertical timbers posts. This kind of construction is now familiar to us from excavations at other medieval settlements which have taken place through the intervening decades (Gardiner 2014). Structures of this type have been recognised in the region at, among others, Wythemail Period 1 (Northamptonshire; Hurst and Hurst 1969, 173), Goltho, Lincolnshire (House 1; Beresford 1975, 37), Tattenhoe, Buckinghamshire (Area C, Period 1, Building 3; Ivens *et al.* 1995, Fig. 13), Caldecote, Hertfordshire (Houses 1–3; Beresford 2009, 59–63), Bradwell Bury, Buckinghamshire (Building 1, Phase 1; Mynard 1994, 7–8) and Higham Ferrers, Northamptonshire (Building 9528 (Site 7), Phase 4; Hardy *et al.* 2007, 65–67), the latter probably a barn or outbuilding. While it may be unusual for timber uprights posts to be set against the outer face of the wall trench, as Butler found them, and more common for them to be set against the inner face, it should not worry us that more 'ghosts' of posts were not identified during the excavation. The recognition of post-settings depends on the posts not having been dug out at abandonment and traces of the post-ghost surviving in the soil.

Elsewhere, describing the earliest phase of houses in Crofts 6–9 which he dug in 1967, Butler saw 'mud-walled buildings with timber post-holes, timber uprights where one can see in the excavated plan the clay patten to give support for the posts, for the uprights, and the walls would be mud, possibly with wattling strengthening' (Faxton tape 1). One photograph from 1967 shows just such a shallow post-hole for a timber upright but unfortunately this feature cannot be located (see Figure 5.17). Very probably the principal buildings being referred to by Butler in his commentary are Buildings 12, 15, 16, 17, 18 and 22. Some of these structures from 1967 are placed together in Figure 11.3. Only Buildings 15 (5.2 x 3.5m, though its relationship to Annex 16 is uncertain, see below) and 18 (7 x 3.2m, though the plan is very fragmentary) have hearths and, judging by their dimensions, several of the others were minor ancillary buildings, notably Buildings 17 (2 x 3m) and 22 (2 x 1.8m) whose thick walls would make suitable pig sties. None have a stone plinth.

Although it might seem unusual to raise weight-bearing earthen walling directly on top of the

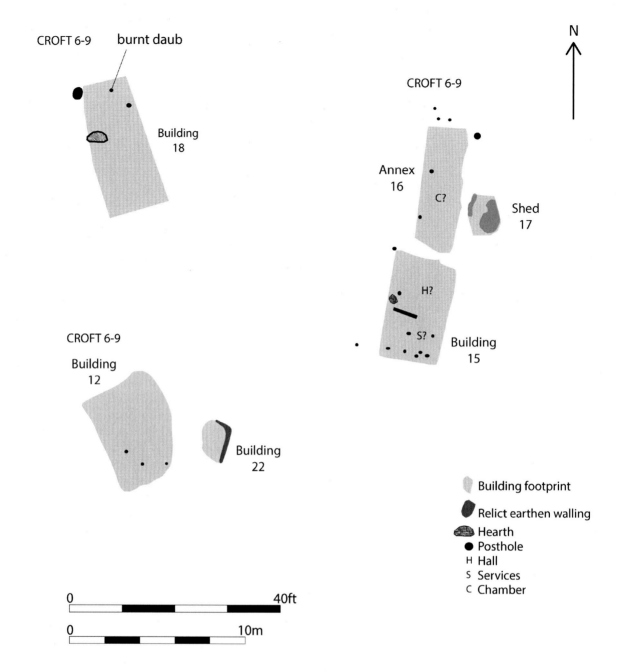

FIGURE 11.3
Earthen wall buildings with timber uprights from Crofts 6–9, excavated in 1967. Mainly dated to c.1150–1250

ground surface without a solid and impermeable stone plinth, Butler had already recorded precisely the same thing at Thuxton. To use his words, the evidence there was 'for structures of mud or clay-lump placed without foundations straight onto the ground surface... there is a further refinement whereby the clay-built structures are strengthened with vertical posts enclosed within the wall but positioned at irregular intervals' (Butler and Wade-Martins 1989, 58). There are also local examples of a much later date (at Ravensthorpe; Seaborne 1964, Fig. 2 where the crucks are raised in the side walls) which, as we have seen, Butler would have been aware of. In his useful review of the archaeological

evidence for 'clay-walled buildings' Longcroft (2006) cites, among a longer list of probable sites, Chalgrove (Oxfordshire; Webster 1979, 270), Long Ashton (Somerset; Webster 1979, 276), King's Langley (Hertfordshire; Neal 1977), Tresmorn (Cornwall; Beresford 1971), Worcester (Dalwood and Edwards 2004, 83), Shanes Castle (Antrim; Wilson and Hurst 1968, 196, 199), West Hartburn (Pallister and Wrathmell 1990), Heveningham Park (Suffolk) and in towns at Newtown (Dyfed; Murphy 1994, 72), Norwich (Atkin et al. 1985, 254 for reconstruction; Atkin 1991), Rattray (Aberdeenshire; Murray and Murray 1993, 141) and Perth (see Figure 11.1 for site locations).

Medieval buildings with earth walls laced by studs have also been identified in London (Horsman *et al.* 1988) where walls were also found to stand directly on the surface of the ground. The same kind of cob-walling was also raised as a possibility at Tattenhoe, Buckinghamshire, after the late 13th century, for example Area B, Period 2, Croft 1, Building 5 (Ivens *et al.* 1995, Fig. 17), just as it was at Caldecote, Hertfordshire, for Period 4, Croft D, Barn 2 (Beresford 2009, 102) for the second half of the 14th century. The remarkable mid-13th century cob buildings discovered inside the middle bailey at Wallingford Castle (Oxfordshire) had survived to a height of 1.8m with walls that were 0.80m thick at the base. Yet there was no plinth nor timbers set within the cob walls there, and had Building 1 not survived in such remarkable condition, it would have been as difficult to recognise what was, without doubt, an extremely substantial structure which measured 8.30 by 15.80m (Christie and Creighton 2013, 190–193). Coincidently, the excavator at Wallingford, Bob Carr, had been one of Lawrence Butler's supervisors at Faxton.

Fifty years later, the difficulty with Lawrence Butler's brief descriptions is not with his insistence on a tradition of earthen wall buildings at Faxton, but rather to understand the role of the timber posts. Guy Beresford has suggested that there was a method of building using mud-encased, poorly aligned timber posts and it is very possible that Butler heard and was influenced by these arguments (Beresford 1981). The post-medieval tradition of 'mud and stud' construction in Lincolnshire was also known to Lawrence Butler and he may have believed that medieval antecedents existed and could be recognised in the archaeological record. Exactly what he saw at Faxton is harder to say—whether the 'mud', 'earth' or 'cob' really stiffened an earthfast timber structure or whether it simply formed a casing around the feet of cruck timbers and acted principally as a weathershield. If the latter then all these buildings might be placed into the category of 'cruck-framed buildings' defined below.

Ground-set buildings

Ground-set buildings with sill beams or soleplates resting on the ground surface

Two ground-set buildings with their sill beams or soleplates resting on the ground surface may be tentatively proposed from the excavation evidence. The first of these is Barn E, excavated in Phase 2 of Croft 29 1966. Only the drip gully on the south side of the building was identified here (Feature 31 on Figure 4.8) and the evidence is slight at best—only one straight length of ditch was excavated rather than a set of gullies around a building as might be expected. The second building is Building 4 identified in Croft 52–53 1968 on the west edge

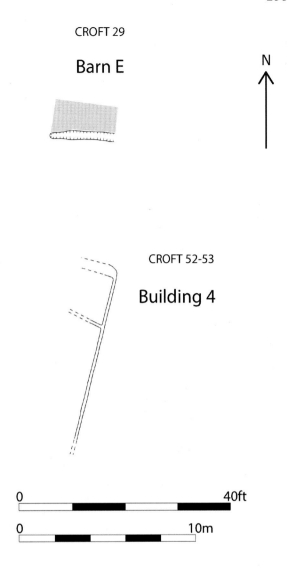

FIGURE 11.4

Ground-set buildings with soleplates resting on the ground surface. Dated to c.1250–1300 (Croft 29) and c.1300–1350 (Croft 53). Tentative identifications only

of the excavated area and defined by ditches 11, 12 and 13 (Figure 11.4). Looking remarkably like field drains on the plan, but described by the excavator as a 'shed', this building was only partially excavated. It is at least 14m long, comprising two units, and by any measure exceptionally large for a 'shed'. No post-holes were recorded nor foundations of any other kind.

Buildings with this form of construction were observed in Period 2 at Goltho (Beresford 1975, 40), dug 1968–70, where 'invisible' walls were marked by eaves trenches or gullies to drain the water away. In these timber-framed buildings the sill is assumed to have run right around the building with the posts mortised into it. Crucially, the sill beam or soleplate was placed on the ground surface. The same excavator, Guy Beresford, saw something similar at Caldecote (Hertfordshire) in 1973–77 such as

Period 3 House 2 (Beresford 2009, 85, 234–235). Among later sites, Area B, Period 2, Croft 2, Building 6 at Tattenhoe (Buckinghamshire) is another example as are the Westbury (Buckinghamshire), Croft 15 and 16 buildings (Ivens *et al.* 1995, Figs 16, 84 and 86). Building 60108 in Croft 16 there is described as a 'vacant rectangle' in which the sill beams of a timber-framed structure lay directly on the natural subsoil (Ivens *et al.* 1995, 155). According to Mark Gardiner's recent analysis (2014, Fig. 2), this type of structure is a characteristic of the first half of the 13th century in some parts of the country, and this is the date at which they appear in London (Milne 1992). The Croft 29 1966 Phase 2 Barn E at Faxton is dated to *c*.1250, that in Croft 52–53 1968 was dated to Phase 4, *c*.1300–1350.

Cruck-framed buildings

Like these possible ground-set buildings with their soleplates resting on the ground surface, cruck-framed buildings were not originally advocated by the excavator at Faxton. One particular building is worthy of further attention, however. Building A2 in Croft 29 1966 was described by Lawrence Butler as 'a house with mud walls on a stone base'. He describes two phases in its construction in which lateral walls of mud or cob are replaced by walls with stone footings and mud or cob above. The end gable walls he identified as being 'stone sleeper walls'. In order to investigate further, Figure 11.5A is a re-drawing of the stone-by-stone on-site plans for the main buildings identified in Croft 29 in 1966, the only one of the three sites for which such an exercise is possible. Although this reveals no evidence for the two phases of construction mentioned by Butler, nor does it clarify how 'stone sleeper walls' might differ from a wall with 'stone base', it does reveal considerably more detail. Specifically, it demonstrates a striking characteristic of its ground plan (11.2 x 4.8m interior dimensions): the long side walls of ironstone rubble are made up of short discontinuous lengths of walling of about 2–3m with slightly differing alignments and stone sizes. The south end of Building A2, for example, has wider lateral walls and a much denser foundation with larger stones. Following Stuart Wrathmell's re-thinking of the peasant houses at Wharram Percy (Wrathmell 1989), this characteristic suggests a type of construction in which the lengths of wall are not integral to the structure of the building and have been replaced at some time, perhaps more than once. Changing alignments like this are much less likely in massive mud-wall constructions or in mud-and-frame buildings, though some unevenness in the line of the faces should be expected. As in the case of the Area 6 farmhouse at Wharram, with its discrete stretches of footings, potentially with trusses at breaks in alignment and successive phases of rebuilding during the life of the house, a more

likely solution is that this is a cruck-framed building, the crucks being set at points of deflection in the wall alignments (Figure 11.5B). Re-examination of the re-drawn site plans confirms that no pad-stones were present for the crucks to rest on, nor was the cruck earthfast, so either the stone base was sufficiently solid not to require one or else the crucks were raised and supported within the wall. While it cannot be *proven* that Building A2 at Faxton was a cruck structure, the excavation record is entirely consistent with a building divided into bays (Wrathmell 2002, 180). This interpretation is pursued further below.

Butler envisaged three phases of north–south buildings in Croft 29 1966. He saw Building A2 as a first phase, followed by Building A3 which made use of the north wall of a now-demolished Building A2, and finally Building A4 which enlarged Building A3 on its west and north sides. This phasing has been simplified on Figure 11.6. Butler did not excavate the north-east corner of Building A3/A4 to investigate the junction of walls there, and he was unable to establish the alignment of the south section of the west wall of Buildings A3/A4 where the wall footings had been badly robbed out (Figure 11.5A). Yet, even with these limitations, there seems no reason not to simplify the sequence in Croft 29 1966 from three into two phases. This only requires for Building A2 to remain standing while Building A3/A4 was built immediately to the north. Given that one building abuts the other, it seems more likely that the two buildings are broadly contemporary. The rectangular north end wall of A2 need not be an issue if A3 is added to the pre-existing Building A2. Possibly an end-fork and hipped roof might have been removed and the wall built up to the first full truss and perhaps this might explain Butler's observation that there was a difference in the construction of the lateral walls of Building A2 and those at the gable ends. Overall, however, cruck forks at the end walls seem the most plausible suggestion, thereby creating a gable and not a hipped end. End-forks would have supported 'end bays' which are half the length of full bays and the space roofed by an end-fork would probably not create much usable space above ground level, unless as extra storage. In Figure 11.5A the north-east corner of Building A2 might be taken to suggest that the gable end is a later insertion.

Butler also described Building A3 in Croft 29 1966 as a 'house with mud walls on a stone base' (Faxton tape 1), dating it to *c*.1300–50, but this interpretation, doubtless influenced by much later buildings he had seen in the local area, must also now be in doubt. The remaining lengths of walling at the north end of the building are not well aligned and it is quite likely that this too was a cruck-framed building (14.5 x 4.5m interior dimensions). Certainly the presence of a hearth set against the east wall of Building A3 (H9 in Figure 4.23) makes

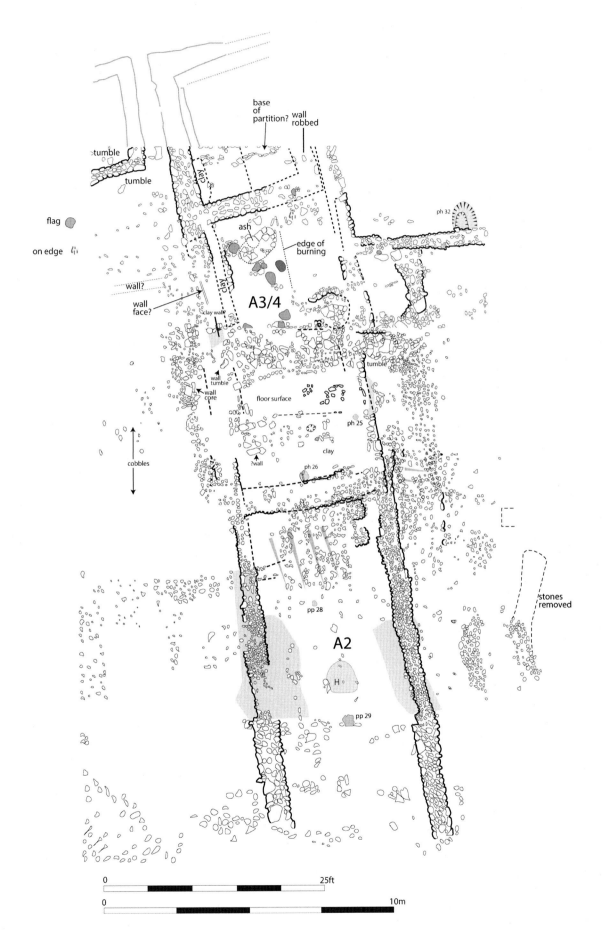

FIGURE 11.5A

Croft 29 1966. Building A2 (c.1250–1300) (see PLATE 3)

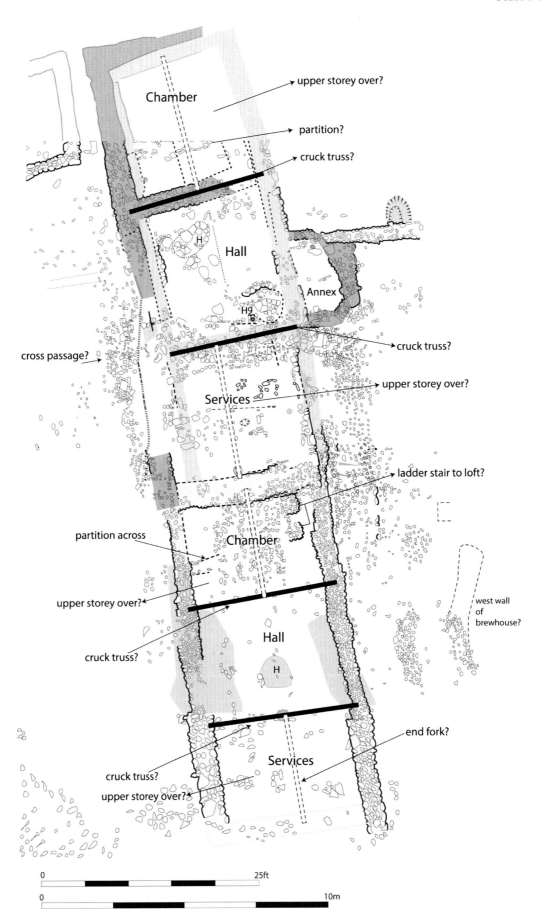

FIGURE 11.5B

Croft 29 1966. Reconstruction of Buildings A2, A3, A4. Re-interpreted as a cruck-framed building with earthen infills and re-dated to c.1250 to mid–late 16th century (see PLATE 4)

it highly unlikely that it was a timber-framed structure. Returning again to the photographic evidence for the walls of Building A3 (Figures 4.25 and 4.26; Figures 11.5A and B), it is clear that the foundations are built up of stone and then smoothed over with clay to create a near horizontal plinth which sits some 10cm above the ground surface. As was the case of Building A2, mud walls would have been constructed on top of this foundation. If, as Butler suggested, the west wall of Building A3 was at sometime replaced (he put a date of *c*.1350 based on the Edward III silver penny recovered from the central hearth, see Chapter 8) then this demolition may have been due to dilapidation; earthen walling is as durable as any other types of walling, but only if it is regularly maintained with a thatch or other covering which sheds the water well away from the base of the wall.

Earthen wall buildings on a continuous stone base or plinth

In 1967 Butler excavated several buildings which he thought might fit this type of construction. In interview he described them as having 'a heavy

packing of flints and small ironstone boulders from the ploughsoil, thrown in to strengthen the walls. A low level of sophistication provides for possibly two courses of stone and on these are placed mud walls. They are apparently occupied at an earlier period and went out of existence by 1350, possibly even earlier judging by the pottery. They were also less wealthy' (Faxton tape 1). The evidence for some of these buildings can be hard to see at times because the remains are far more fragmentary than they had been in the previous year in Croft 29 1966 and paucity of the archaeological record for the 1967 excavation now inevitably complicates their interpretation further. However, by examining them in plan and section we can at least highlight some of the buildings to which Butler wished to draw our attention. These include: Buildings 1, 3, 4, 7, 8, 9, 10, 11, 13 and 14. A selection of the more complete plans is illustrated in Figure 11.7. Of these only Buildings 8 and 9 have hearths (5.5 x 4m and 6 x 3.2m respectively) and, on that basis, the other structures may be ancillary buildings. In 1968 in Croft 52–53 Butler excavated another building which he suggested was 'mud-walled'. This is Building 3 (*c*.10.8 x 5m) which was possibly

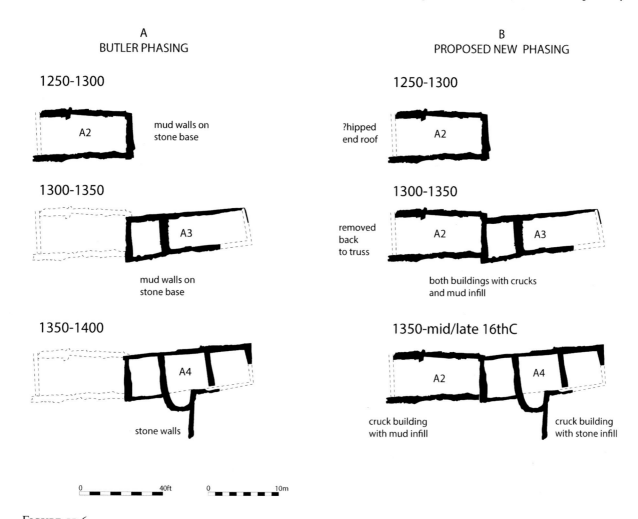

A
BUTLER PHASING

1250-1300

A2   mud walls on stone base

1300-1350

A3   mud walls on stone base

1350-1400

A4   stone walls

B
PROPOSED NEW PHASING

1250-1300

?hipped end roof   A2

1300-1350

removed back to truss   A2   A3

both buildings with crucks and mud infill

1350-mid/late 16thC

A2   A4

cruck building with mud infill   cruck building with stone infill

0 ___ 40ft   0 ___ 10m

FIGURE 11.6

Croft 29. Simplified phasing of Buildings A2, A3, A4 excavated in 1966. A) Phasing as envisaged by Butler B) Proposed new phasing

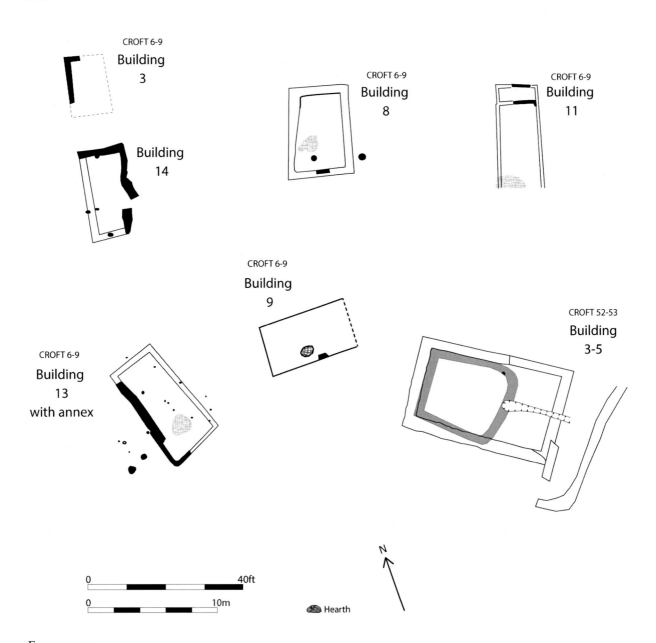

FIGURE 11.7

Earthen wall buildings on a continuous stone base or plinth. Tentative buildings have been omitted. Buildings 3/14, 8, 11, 13 were excavated in 1967 in Crofts 6–9. Building 24–28 is in Croft 52–53, excavated in 1968. In the latter case, features from different phases have been amalgamated

represented by wall 28, stone scatter 27, gable wall 26 with drain 25.

If this evidence from 1967 and 1968 for earthen buildings with a continuous stone plinth can be accepted, then there are few archaeological comparators. Among them are two examples from Westbury (Buckinghamshire), Buildings 53512 and 53513 in Croft 7C, but neither could be said to have such a solid and well constructed plinth as the Faxton examples (Ivens *et al.* 1995, 126, Fig. 72). Building 53513 was suggested to be a workshop. The Westbury examples are also significantly smaller, 4.8 by 2.7m and 8.4 by 4.2m as opposed to 12.19 by 4.57m in the case of the Phase 3 Building A3 in Croft 29 1966. All three of the Westbury examples

were terraced into the slope. These Westbury buildings are more similar in size, and possibly in function, to two other buildings in Phase 3 in Croft 29 1966, 'Byre C' at the north-west corner of the site and 'Barn F'. These too had stone plinths, although the former is not well recorded. The south wall of Barn F is clearest on photograph Figure 4.21 and, like the byre, does not appear to have had right-angled corners. Of the other structures at Faxton, little detail can now be established for Building 5 in Croft 52–53 1968 (see Figure 6.4). It seems possible that building extended further to the east.

In the absence of the kind of detail which might once have been recorded on the lost site plans, it is not easy today to provide confirmation for the buildings which Butler so confidently claimed 50 years ago. The plans show intermittent spreads of walling between 0.5 and 1m wide with post-holes located either within the width of the walling (e.g. Building 13) or at its inner face (e.g. Building 14). Butler had seen very similar archaeology at Thuxton in Norfolk where he identified post-holes both within clay walls and post-pads close to the walls (Butler and Wade-Martins 1989, 26–29). In the case of Faxton, he never states whether the earthen walling was load-bearing (presumably with a wall plate to help spread the weight of the roof) and merely strengthened by the timber uprights or whether the weight was carried by the timbers and the 'mud' walling merely provided infill. Although the post-holes he found were sometimes substantial, there is nothing to suggest the pairing of timbers into trusses, though in Building 14 post-holes do appear centrally in both gable ends as might be expected of an end-fork. On the whole the evidence favours load-bearing earthen walls with a wall plate. Straw thatch is perhaps the most likely roofing material.

Stone-built houses

Butler identified two examples of 'stone-built' houses at Faxton, both interpretations which might now be disputed. The first of these is Building A4 in Croft 29 1966 (Figure 11.5A), measuring 15.25 by 5.25m. The plan of this building is difficult to read because its outline is barely present in its southern half. Its identification by Butler as a 'stone-built house' is based on the heavier ironstone stonework which was present at the north end of the building as well as the thickness and straighter alignment of the walls. With its hearth and partition, this was a three-celled structure.

In his 1967 BBC interview Butler described Building A4 as follows:

a better class of village house, in its last phase, which was round about 1400. It was a stone-built house, probably [with a] stone-built lower storey and then further accommodation under the steeply pitched thatched roof... it would be ambitious to call it a two-storey building... two-storey at the gable ends probably, but it's really a three-roomed one-storey building with extra rooms in the roof. [This] suggests that its occupier, presumably the owner, though one can't be sure of this, had sufficient resources to be able to build [better], and also since this house is a replacement of houses with mud walls, mud walls set upon a low stone base, it is coming up in the world and the house with mud walls on a stone base is in its turn a replacement of one which was entirely mud-walled with massive timber posts at the four corners, along the long walls of the building... we're seeing an increase in sophistication, not in size, but in the provision of more stout walls, [in other words] better accommodation. [This is also reflected in the finds], in the two earliest periods

there were very few finds of metalwork, stone, of any sort of find, [but] in the latter period, in the last period there were finds of bronze, such as a bronze tripod leg, part of a cauldron spout, part of knives with [bone] handles, various indications which suggested that the owner was above the lower strata of society within the village. [That house finally ceased to be occupied] around about 1450, between 1400 and 1450 was the last period of occupation, after nearly 150 to 200 years of life (Faxton tape 1).

A second stone-built structure, measuring 10 by 5.7m, was identified by Butler in the Phase 5 building in Croft 52–53 1968 (walls 4, 6, 7, 8) (Figures 6.5 and 11.7 where its fullest possible reconstruction is labelled Building 3–5). This is Building 5. Here ironstone walling survived up to nine courses high and 0.5–0.7m wide. The coursing was irregular with intermittent thicker blocks (see Figure 6.6). The external corners were typically more substantial stones and facing stones too were larger than those in the core; there was no evidence of rendering. Butler's assumption was that these were not dwarf walls but that they were weight-bearing and stood to the height of the eaves where they would have carried a wall plate. This building, however, has little to recommend it as a domestic dwelling; it is apparently a single room building and, although it has a clay floor, it has no internal hearth, no paving or internal surfaces and must have been entered through its east wall (6) or at its north-east corner. The hearth is awkwardly placed on the exterior south wall of the building, which makes little sense for interior comforts and is presumably a place where things were burnt against the low wall of a demolished building. Little else can be deduced except to note a slight variation in the thickness of the walls; there are no shifts in alignment which might indicate a cruck, for example. It is tempting to see walls 16, 17, 18 as a yard to the south of this structure. The finds from Phase 5 are not especially suggestive for the function of the building and include such things as buckles, lace tags, whetstones and horseshoes—but there was no evidence for a specific craft activity (see Chapter 8). Given the absence of internal fixtures and fittings, the building perhaps originally functioned as a byre with an axial drain. Nevertheless, it is a rare survival. Few stone-walled buildings of this kind still stand, something which is attributed to the use of clay rather than lime mortar as a bonding material (Gardiner 2014).

One final point is worth stressing here. Lawrence Butler consistently suggested throughout his text that the buildings were either built of timber or stone, but they could have been both: stone walls with cruck trusses. It is possible for stone walls to support rafters without trusses, as was clearly the case in post-medieval times, but this would depend on their structural integrity and the strength of the mortar (and for which there is no evidence at Faxton). In

Croft 29 1966 Building A3/A4 might be proposed as a cruck-frame building in which the west wall has been rebuilt in stone. Likewise, Building 5 in Croft 52–53 1968 could have been a raised truss; the width of the building is not exceptional and Alcock and Miles record upper crucks and short curved principals in Northamptonshire as well as true crucks (Alcock and Miles 2013).

Discussion

Earthen buildings

Faxton provides evidence for a number of different building techniques and construction materials in the later Middle Ages. Most strikingly, there was a long tradition of earthen architecture in which 'mud' or earthen walling was successfully combined with other structural materials. Three different uses have been identified. First, there is evidence for earthen wall buildings with timber uprights sitting on clay pattens providing additional strengthening (Figure 11.3). In these buildings, some of which are minor ancillary agricultural buildings and boundary walls, there is no stone plinth. Although their walls sit directly on the ground surface, they are nevertheless load-bearing. In some instances, there is no surviving evidence for timber uprights of any kind. It is assumed that the walls supported the roof, either with rafters bedded into the tops of the mud walls at eaves level in the case of some of the minor ancillary buildings or with rafters on a wall plate supported by the walls but not anchored into timber trusses. The foundations are *not* found in discrete lengths at slightly different angles because, it is argued, this would damage the structural integrity of the walls. The Faxton evidence suggests that most buildings of this type were not large; the largest building in 1967 Crofts 6–9 is Building 18 which measures 7 by 3.2m (Figure 11.3). These buildings were dated by the excavator to 1150–1250. For the most part they pre-date the use of stone foundation walls, but there are at least a couple of examples of later buildings of this type (Buildings 2, 12), both of which might be ancillary farm buildings. This confirms Lawrence Butler's point that there was no universal conversion to stone foundations. Had a visitor walked through Faxton in around AD 1300 they could have seen a variety of construction methods, although these would not have been immediately obvious unless the visitor had stepped inside the houses.

A second use of earthen walling is proposed on the basis of a re-working of the excavation records from Faxton. This suggests that both Building A2 and A3 in Croft 29 are cruck-framed buildings in which the mud-walling sits atop a low stone plinth and provides infill *between* the structural timbers (Figures 11.5A and B). Similarly, it is proposed that Building A4 in Croft A4 is also a cruck-framed

building but this time with stone infills, and it is also likely that A4 is a rebuild of Building A3 rather than being an entirely new build as the excavator originally suggested; in Building 5 in Croft 52–53 the crucks may have been set on the ground wall. In none of these cases does the walling itself take a great structural load; the timber trusses support wall-plates which take the ends of the rafters. The absence of pad-stones in the Faxton building plans presents no concerns: they could have been removed later with the cruck frames, or they may never have been present at all, the feet of the crucks being protected within the stone foundations. Wharram Area 6, Building 1 VI (Wrathmell 1989, 24) did not offer a full suite of pad-stones despite probably being in use until the desertion of the village.

In this context, it is worth highlighting a recent archaeological excavation undertaken in 2016 at Kilsby (Northamptonshire), 37km away from Faxton, as part of a planning condition which revealed three 'probable cob structures' with stone footings constructed on earth and rubble platforms (Kipling 2017). Of these three, Structure 1 was the best preserved: a rectangular building with two principal rooms divided by a cross passage about 10 by 5m with walls 0.6m wide and footings 0.1–0.2m deep. One of the rooms had a central hearth set into a beaten-clay floor, the building as a whole being described as a 'long-house' and compared with that found at Wythemail by John and Gillian Hurst (Hurst and Hurst 1969). While this choice of parallel might require further consideration, the plinth construction is certainly familiar from Faxton and the walls at Kilsby also display the characteristic offsets which might indicate a cruck-framed structure.

The Faxton evidence therefore suggests that crucks are found in combination with earthen and stone walls in successive phases in Crofts 29 and 52–53. In their recent review of medieval peasant houses in Midland England, Alcock and Miles (2013) did not review cruck-built houses in Northamptonshire. However, their national distribution, with its marked eastern boundary, shows Faxton to lie within the clustering of known examples. Recorded cruck-framed buildings with earthen walling now include The Royal George at Cottingham in the north-east of the county (Hill and Miles 2001), a three-bay cruck-built house with an open hall dated by dendrochronology to the summer of 1262. There are also those recorded by Seaborne in Ravensthorpe with raised crucks and another in Braybrooke with upper crucks (Seaborne 1964). Elsewhere in the 'cruck zone', the standard method of infilling between structural timbers is wattle and daub. The suggested dates for Buildings A2 and A3 in Croft 29 1966, 1250 and 1300 respectively, are not out of keeping with this. In general terms, the earliest surviving cruck trusses belong to the second half of the 13th century and their use was widespread in the 14th century (Hill 2005).

There are also significant numbers of earthen buildings at Faxton with a continuous stone plinth (Figure 11.7). Many of these were ancillary buildings, although not all. At Murcott (Northamptonshire), only 32km away from Faxton, documents of 1430–31 studied by Chris Dyer (2008, 64) infer repairs to a three-bay house with stone foundations and mud walls eight perches long (that is, about 132 ft or 40m overall). In this case 44 poles for spars were felled in a nearby wood and the carpenter's wages were probably spent mainly on the roof, so it can be deduced that the house had no major wall timbers and that the earth walls were built up to the eaves. Both thatching and tiles were paid for too, though the latter may have been used to make a hearth. There is also ample later evidence for construction of this type. The Rochefoucauld brothers in 1785, for example, commented that the houses near Northampton 'are small and looked poor; most of them are built only of mud, upon a few lower courses of rough stone... the mud-walling is very compact' (Scarfe 1995, 21). Seaborne (1964) also quotes 18th-century documentation from Spratton and Welford which shows cob-building underway. In the case of the latter, the base for the mud walls at the back of the house was foundation stones in a 'dirt mortar' 18 inches (45cm) deep and 22 inches (55cm) wide. The front of the house was to be of brick.

Overall, the distribution of unshuttered cob structures has been mapped by Brunskill (2000, 202). Over 1,000 buildings are believed to remain (Keefe 2005) and Butler's list of Northamptonshire parishes with them could now be extended to include Ashby St Ledgers, Barby, Bugbrooke, Braunston, Clipston, Creaton, Creaton Crick, Cold Ashby, East Farndon, Flore, East Haddon, West Haddon, Kilsby, Kislingbury, Naseby, Thornby and Yelvertoft (Willatts 2000). Most of these survivals are either ancillary farm buildings or boundary walling which are thought to date from the 18th or 19th century. The tradition seems to have been popular where the supply of timber was limited and 'mud' was abundant on the local Lias geology. Seaborne (1964) was very particular on this point, suggesting that cob-walling survived along the edge of the belt of good building stone. Ironstone of the type local to Faxton 'flakes and crumbles more easily and in many places... it is', he said, 'little better than shale' (Seaborne 1964, 217).

'Mud-walling' of the type described here should be thought of as one particular kind of earthen building to be distinguished from other construction techniques which also make use of unbaked earths such as sods or turf, wichert, clay lump, or 'rammed earth', otherwise known as 'pisé'. The last, for example, makes use of shutter-boards as a mould (Clifton-Taylor 1972, 287–293; Jaquin

and Augarde 2012; Longcroft 2006). There is no evidence at Faxton for any of these construction techniques. Nor is there anything to suggest that earthen walling was used as packing between vertical structural timbers which supported a wall plate, or that earthen materials were used to create plinths for timber-framed walls as was the case in Norwich, for example (Atkin 1991). The type of 'mud-and-frame' construction found in south Leicestershire, in which a timber frame is combined with solid mud lower walling (Finn 2009), has also not been recognised. A characteristic feature in this type of construction is that the main posts in the framing are raised on stone pads, with a rail half way up the walls and a horizontal wall plate which is supported by braces; this timber frame is then exposed externally. The earthen walling itself is raised on a stone plinth one or two courses high, but this plinth is not continuous because it is interrupted by pad-stones on which the wall posts stand; both the plinth and parts of the lower wall can be removed without damaging the building. There are very few surviving examples of earthen buildings anywhere in Britain before 1400 but, in the case of mud-and-frame construction, surviving vernacular buildings date to the second half of the 17th century or the early decades of the 18th. They do not seem to be representative of the medieval housing stock at Faxton.

In summary, it is clear that the clay- or mud-walling tradition was ubiquitous at Faxton before the mid-14th century, and was successfully combined with different modes of construction, acting sometimes as a load-bearing material and elsewhere as an infill between structural timbers. It was probably all produced using a very similar method. To make mud-walling in 19th-century Northamptonshire, for example, soil was thrown into a pile and sprinkled with water-soaked hay and straw. Layers of watered soil were then driven over by oxen or horses to tread the mixture together. Once the foundation of stone had been laid 12–18 inches (30–45cm) above the surface, then 'the labourer takes his fork, and after striking the soil therewith, until it lies like a cake, he takes it up with the fork and lays it on the wall, striking it there repeatedly at top and sides, until he has packed it close... trimming off the sides as he goes along' (Harrison 1984, 157). Tempers such as aggregates and fibres were sometimes added to prevent shrinkage and cracking in the clay mix (McCann 2007). Houses were generally thatched with straw, and the walls very seldom had any covering on the outside (Johnson 1806). This process of construction was still largely unchanged when Seaborne came to describe it in 1964. He emphasised the lack of shuttering as well as the damp state of the layered soil and the addition of chopped straw, together with small pebbles and even pottery and pipe stems (Seaborne 1964). The only difference in the procedure was that new layers were added only when the lower courses had set, thereby slowing down construction. Local knowledge suggested up to six months was needed to build a cottage with walls 2ft (60cm) thick. For the medieval period, Dyer's information for Murcott for 1432–33 suggests that bean haulm (the stalks and leaves left after threshing), and barley straw were purchased in some quantity, perhaps to combine with earth to make the walls (as well as for the thatched roof) (Dyer 2008). In 1587, four villages were before the manorial court 'for that they have digged out and taken upp the manure and gravel lyeing in the streates of Lamporte and in the Quenes highway there' (quoted in Bird 2005, 55) and this too may have been one of the sources for materials.

Butler also reflected on the reasons behind the change in construction materials he had observed at Faxton, and debated both historical circumstances and climatic factors as possible explanations (Butler 1969a). Influenced no doubt by Guy Beresford's work at Barton Blount in Derbyshire, Butler drew attention to the deterioration of the climate in north-west Europe which brought increasingly wetter conditions and as demonstrated by tree-ring analysis. This, it was argued, might be illustrated locally by a change in the course of the Fenland rivers late in the 13th century, the Northamptonshire uplands being drained by tributaries of both the Welland and the Nene. The colonisation of the Forest of Rockingham and the clearance of the tree cover within this royal hunting ground was, in Lawrence Butler's view, a steady process in the first two centuries after the Norman Conquest, but the fines levied during the reigns of King John and Henry III may have deterred further encroachment except by wealthier members of the village community. Although the parish of Faxton retained a considerable acreage of woodland at Mawsley, Fackley and Shortwood, the effective forest boundary was some 9km further north. The logic to Butler's argument was that if the timber available for house repair was now restricted through a harsher enforcement of manorial rights and greater restrictions on taking wood and timber from the forest, then the felling of mature trees for new building could well have been forbidden. The change to stone reflects these same two factors: in a wetter climate any mud-walled building must have a well drained stone footing if it is to survive more than a couple of winters without crumbling to the ground. The replacement of the low footing walls of field boulders by much more substantial walls of quarried stone may reflect easier manorial conditions in the 14th century when lords were eager to retain the services of their peasantry by granting materials for house building free or at minimal dues (Butler 1969a).

If the new interpretations summarised on Figures 11.8A and B are accepted, then parts of this argument can no longer be sustained. Cruck trusses were available, at least in Crofts 29 and 52–53,

for three successive phases of buildings in the former (Buildings A2, A3 and A4), although it is possible that stone could have been introduced in Building A4 in order to provide better protection for timber trusses which were now harder to come by. Quarried stone was never an option in construction for these houses where stones for footings were gathered from field clearance.

11.3 THE BUILDING PLANS AT FAXTON RE-INTERPRETED

Some of the confusion which we see being worked through at Faxton, both during the excavation and afterwards, is due to Butler *not* finding the things that he had expected to find. With reference to John Hurst's most recent thoughts on later medieval house plans (Hurst 1965; see above), Butler was clear in 1967 that what he had seen at Faxton was not a 'peasant cot'. '[The] peasant cot,' he said, 'certainly as far as excavation is concerned, has not yet been traced in this village and it may be difficult to trace it because of the slightness of the building material. [It] may be very difficult to trace in many parts of England because it has been so often rebuilt and so carefully rebuilt, but the farms one finds here... would be recognisable to the present day farmer, with his farmhouse surrounded by barns on three sides of the courtyard' (Faxton tape 1). On the other hand, he could find nothing to substantiate the existence of long-houses either, 'not from the evidence... from Northamptonshire. There is no evidence of byres, of the stone-lined drains or the ditches to take away the animal refuse. As far as we can see, any animals, any stock, which would have been sheltered within the farm area, did have separate accommodation' (Faxton tape 1). While the lack of substantial internal drains usually associated with the house-and-byre homestead (the 'long-house') puzzled him, it also greatly restricted his interpretative options. He would be unable, for example, to show the process of change from the long-house to the farm as at Gomeldon (Wiltshire) and Upton (Gloucestershire) and found the Croft 29 1966 farm with its ancillary buildings around the yard surprisingly early in the sequence given that such well developed complexes were considered to be 'found in many areas from the 13th century onwards' (Hurst 1971, 107). In this respect, as in many others, while he struggled to align his findings with existing concepts, he was perhaps more forward thinking than many.

With hindsight, what kind of building plans *did* Butler see? First, it must be acknowledged, as Butler would wish to have done for himself, that the evidence from Faxton is highly fragmentary. In spite of his best efforts, the excavator was unable to recover fully the plans of many buildings, the functions of rooms were rarely clear, the positions of doorways and their post-settings elusive, and, as

Building	Butler original interpretation	Proposed new interpretation	Date from original phasing	Figure
Croft 29 1966				
A1	Originally identified as a 'long-house', but this was later rejected in favour of a 'living house'	Uncertain	*c.*1200	4.7
A2	'Mud or cob walls laterally with stone sleeper walls at the gable ends'	**Cruck-framed building with earthen infills, probably shortened later to accommodate A3**	*c.*1250	**4.8, 11.5, 11.8**
A3	'House walls were sleeper trenches packed with clay and faced with ironstone'	**Cruck-framed building with earthen infills, probably thatched**	*c.*1300	**4.23, 11.8**
A4	'Stone-built house' for 'persons of some substance'	**Cruck-framed building with stone infills, possibly a modification/repair of A3**	*c.*1350	**4.31, 11.8**
Barn E	'Barn'	Very tentative ground-set building with sill beams resting on the ground surface with drip gully (31)	*c.*1250	4.8
Crofts 6–9 1967				
1	'Mud-walled'	**Tentative unshuttered earthen wall building with continuous stone plinth (7) and post-holes (9, 11). Appears confused with Building 7**	*c.*1300	**5.7, 11.7**
2	Mud-walled buildings with timber post-holes	Very tentative unshuttered earthen wall building, no timber uprights recorded. Maybe confused with the east boundary wall	*c.*1300	5.7
3	'Mud-walled'	**Unshuttered earthen wall building on a continuous stone plinth (145, 146), fragmentary, but possibly related to Building 14**	*c.*1200–1300	**5.7, 11.7**
4	'Mud-walled'	Very tentative unshuttered earthen wall building on a continuous stone plinth (30, 31), fragmentary	*c.*1250–1300	5,7, 11.7
5	'Mud-walled'	Tentative building with one wall (16) and post-hole (15), highly fragmentary and very probably part of Building 14	*c.*1250	5.7, 11.7
6	'Mud-walled'	Very tentative building with hearth (20), highly fragmentary	*c.*1250	5.7
7	'Mud-walled'	Very tentative unshuttered earthen wall building on a continuous stone plinth (4, 7) and post-hole (6). Appears confused with Buildings 1 and 13 and with the east boundary wall	*c.*1250	5.7
8	'Mud-walled'	**Unshuttered earthen wall building on a continuous stone base or plinth (60, 61, 64, 67) and a hearth (65). A more intact plan**	*c.*1250–1300	**5.9, 11.7**
9	'Mud-walled'	Unshuttered earthen wall building on a continuous stone base or plinth (83) and a hearth (84)	*c.*1300	5.11
10	'Mud-walled'	Unshuttered earthen wall building on a continuous stone base or plinth (81, 82, 85, 88). Relationships to Building 9 and wall 81 are uncertain	*c.*1300	5.11
11	'Mud-walled'	**Unshuttered earthen wall building on a continuous stone base or plinth (55, 57), cut by ditch 51**	*c.*1250	**5.9, 11.7**
12	Mud-walled buildings with timber post-holes	**Unshuttered earthen wall building (74) with well defined clay spread and post-hole scatter (71, 72, 73, 76, 77)**	*c.*1250	**5.11, 11.3**
13	Mud-walled buildings with timber post-holes	**Unshuttered earthen wall building on a continuous stone base or plinth, with post-holes (112, 113, 115, 116, 118, 124, 125), with hearth (111) and annex defined by post-holes (9, 102, 103, 104, 105, 110)**	*c.*1150–1200	**5.4, 11.7**
14	'mud-walled'	**Unshuttered earthen wall building on a continuous stone base or plinth (123, 134), post-holes (138, 139, 122, 127, 128). Possibly to be considered with Buildings 3 and 5**	*c.*1150–1250	**5.4, 11.7**
15	Mud-walled buildings with timber post-holes	**Unshuttered earthen wall building (152) with timber uprights (146, 147, 148, 149, 150, 151, 154, 157) and a hearth**	*c.*1200	**5.5, 11.3**

FIGURE 11.8A

Catalogue of the Faxton buildings. Those defined with a high level of confidence are bolded

Building	Butler original interpretation	Proposed new interpretation	Date from original phasing	Figure
Crofts 6–9 1967				
16	**Mud-walled buildings with timber post-holes**	**Suggest pairing with Building 15**	*c.1200*	**5.5, 11.3**
17	**Mud-walled buildings with timber post-holes**	**Minor ancillary building with unshuttered earthen walling to west of Building 15/16.**	*c.1200*	**5.5, 11.3**
18	**Mud-walled buildings with timber post-holes**	**Unshuttered earthen wall building with timber uprights (176, 177) and a hearth (174). Little detail**	*c.1200*	**5.6, 11.3**
19	'Mud-walled'	Unshuttered earthen wall building with no recorded timber uprights, clay spread, very tentative	*c.1200*	5.4
20	'Mud-walled'	Very tentative building, construction unclear	*c.1150*	5.4
21	Mud-walled buildings with timber post-holes	Unshuttered earthen wall building with no recorded timber uprights, tentative only	*c.1300*	5.11
22	**Mud-walled buildings with timber post-holes**	**Minor ancillary building with unshuttered earthen walling (75), no post-holes recorded**	*c.1250*	**5.11, 11.3**
Crofts 52–53 1968				
Phase 1 buildings	Not characterised	Earthfast building with an interrupted sill or baseplate (50, 52, 53), post-holes (51, 55) and drain (54)	1150–1200	6.1, 11.2
Phase 2 buildings	'post position rested on sill beams'	Earthfast building with an interrupted sill or baseplate (31, 32, 37, 38, 39), drip gully (30) and post-holes (33, 34, 35, 40, 41, 42, 43)	1200–1250	6.1, 11.2
Phase 3, features 25, 26, 27, 28	'mud-walled set on a low stone base'	Unshuttered earthen wall building on a continuous stone base or plinth	1250–1300	6.2, 11.7
Phase 4, ditches 11, 12, 13	'timber-built sheds'	Tentative ground-set building with sill beams resting on the ground surface with drip gullies (11, 12, 13)	1300–1350	6.2, 11.4
Phase 5 Building, walls 4, 6, 7, 8	'stone-built house'	?Raised cruck truss on dwarf stone walls	1350–1400	6.3, 11.8

FIGURE 11.8B

Catalogue of the Faxton buildings. Those defined with a high level of confidence are bolded

we have seen, the dating of the remains was always challenging. Fifty years later the task is no easier. However, at least we now have the benefit of a much better understanding of the standard medieval house plan and it is possible to make reference to more complete examples of excavated buildings of the period (Gardiner 2000).

The first buildings which might be reconsidered are Buildings 15 and 16, excavated in 1967 (Figures 5.5 and 11.3). Taken together, they contain elements which might be expected of an unaisled hall with chamber and services such as those found at Monkton (Kent) and Bishops Waltham (Hampshire) (Gardiner 2000) and, on that basis, might be interpreted as an earthen wall building with timber uprights with a two-room unit to the south (5.5 x 3.5m), one with hearth, and a distinctive off-set annex (7 x 2.5m) to the north which forms a continuous wall line on the east. The positions of the entrances were not identified. This layout, however, would conform to a plan with a chamber to the north in the annex, hall in the centre with the hearth (feature 154), cross passage to the south of the

partition with post-hole 151 indicating a doorway on the east side and a small service area on the south side of the cross-entry. The excavator placed a date of *c.*1150–1200 on these buildings and this is not inconsistent with Monkton and Bishops Waltham, although the latter is a higher status building (i.e. manorial or sub-manorial) and the archaeological evidence is more convincing at both those sites than it is at Faxton. A second set of buildings excavated in 1967, deduced by superimposing the excavator's phase plans, is Buildings 3 and 14 (Figures 5.4 and 11.7). If these buildings can also be considered as a single rather than two separate structures, then they take on similar proportions, although in this case no hearth was identified and the identification should be regarded as highly tentative. Both sets of Faxton buildings sit in the lowest part of the stratigraphical sequence (layers A3 and A4).

If these early buildings may cautiously be taken as the first phase of the domestic medieval plan, then the later vernacular buildings present a now familiar layout, although the Faxton evidence is again highly fragmentary. In these buildings, the chamber, hall and services are incorporated into a single building just as Butler described them with 'rectangular and usually of three bays with a central hearth' (Wilson and Hurst 1968, 203). From the 1967 excavations there are several possible examples, including Building 1, 2, 8, 11, 13 and 18. The most convincing of these are Buildings 8 and 13 (Figures 5.4, 5.9 and 11.7), although even here the division between spaces, and the number of spaces, are far from clear. It seems likely that large swathes of medieval buildings, especially in the upper levels of the stratigraphy where these buildings were mostly located, were ploughed out leaving only a series of partial plans. Similarly, Building 3 from the 1968 excavations in Croft 52–53 represented by wall 28, stone scatter 27, possible gable wall 26 with drain 25 may be a fragment of a larger domestic building (Figures 6.3 and 11.7).

The most convincing structural sequence was found in 1966 in Croft 29 and is represented by Buildings A2, A3 and A4 (Figures 11.5A and B). According to both the original and revised phasing of this site, Building A2 is the earliest of these three structures, dated to the mid-13th century (Figure 11.6). Butler described this building only very briefly as having 'a clean, sleeping end at the upper (north) end and a working area with heat supplied by braziers, and opposing doors on the long walls at the lower end' (Wilson and Hurst 1967, 307). Today a tripartite plan seems to be the most straight-forward reading of this building, with a central hall and hearth, services to the south and a chamber to the north of post-pit 28 (Figure 11.5B). Behind partition 27 there may have been a ladder stair to a loft, and this is also suggested by the two concentrations of stones depicted on plans in the north-east corner of the house. The position of the cross-entry in Building A2 presents some difficulties, but this may be because the building doorways were widened and subsequently blocked to accommodate a later change of function when Building A3/A4 was constructed to the north.

Butler made no comment on the plan of Building A3, but described Building A4 in 1966 as a 'three-unit house with a hearth in the central room and a temporary oven... the lower room had a cross passage but no evidence of a byre' (Wilson and Hurst 1967, 308). In fact, Buildings A3 and A4 both suggest similar three-room plans with a central hall and hearth, services to the south and a chamber to the north. These buildings were dated 1300–50 and 1350–1400 respectively and, as we have seen, it is more convincing to see this as a single building with a phase of refurbishment and a longer period of use and occupation for Building A4 than Butler originally suggested. The swathe of stonework across the centre of the floor of Building A3 to the south of the hall almost certainly locates the cross passage, and it may be that the position of the 'temporary oven' in the south-east corner of the central room

(H9) backed on to this passage and had a firehood. Daub fragments from this site may be from a hearth canopy (see Chapter 9). In order to accommodate two phases of Building A3 and A4, Butler saw the hearth and the oven as representing two phases. Given the malting facilities outside (see below), however, it may be one was a furnace to boil water for brewing (Brears 2012, 354). Alternatively, there may have been some advantage in having an oven near the hearth, as burning material from the latter could be placed in the former to heat it up.

In all three buildings there is the likelihood of a partial upper storey, probably over the service room in the case of Building A2 where the weight could have been accommodated on a vertical timber in post-pit 29 and on the west wall perhaps with the door at the east end here, and perhaps also at the north end where post-pit 28 is similarly substantial. Likewise, in Buildings A3 and A4 there is no reason not to suppose an upper storey at either or both ends. The position of hearth H9 in the corner of room, which seems to represent a shift from the hearth in the centre of the hall, might suggest that in the final phase of this building (A4) the living space was also lofted over (cf. Wrathmell 2012, 341). This is not improbable if, as the new pottery evidence suggests, Croft 29 was will in use in the mid–late 16th century (see Chapter 7). In short, rather than envisage anything exceptional, the evidence from Faxton can be comfortably accommodated into our current knowledge of later medieval plans.

11.4   THE LAYOUT OF FAXTON PLOTS

Before the mid-1960s, excavations on medieval village sites had focused largely on house sites, but rather less on the crofts as a whole or the structure of the village. Some excavators such as Philip Rahtz felt that examining boundaries, for example, would provide more detail about site development. As he put it in 1967, writing as editor of the DMVRG annual report: 'small-scale work might well be far more usefully deployed in sectioning toft and croft banks than in uncovering the odd bits of walls, floors and post-holes which have been so prominent in our annual reports' (DMVRG 1967, 2). Over the course of three years of excavation at Faxton, Lawrence Butler did precisely that and began to expand from the excavation of the house, to the croft and then to several crofts, examining exactly the features recommended by Philip Rahtz such as roads and boundaries. The hollow-ways described in Chapter 3, for example, were targeted in 1966 when a long trench was cut across the 'road to Old' in the south-east corner of the village between Crofts 29 and 51.

Faxton medieval boundary walling is best recorded in section AA21-33 in Croft 29 1966 in Figure 4.29. This northern boundary wall had a stone base about 0.76m (2½ft) wide (visible at AA28) with a U-shaped ditch along its north side and had toppled towards the south over the top of charcoal-rich occupation layers (at AA26-27). The ditch was not dated by the excavator, but a number of near-complete vessels including Lyveden bowls and a number of jugs were recovered from another ditch further along its length. The relationship between this length of ditch and that shown in Figure 4.29 was not established during the excavation but it is on the same alignment. All that can be said is that these jugs span the general period 1150–1400; a Brill jug of standard 13th- to 14th-century type probably provides a best estimate for the infilling of the ditch. On the other hand, the earlier east boundary wall in Crofts 6 and 7, if it may be interpreted as such rather than buildings, was also made of earth/mud, but this time laid directly onto the ground surface (Figure 5.18, Sections S1 and S2; Figure 5.19, Section S4). Only in one section (Figure 5.19, Section S5) is there any suggestion of stone rubble packing at the base. The boundaries between the crofts, on the other hand, appear to be shallow ditches about 2.5m wide which silted up and had to be re-cut on multiple occasions (Figure 5.20, Section S3). All of these ditches were dated by the excavator to 1150–1200.

Within these boundaries, the layout of Croft 29 1966 suggests a degree of zoning. On the east side of the plot was a 'garden area', barren of features, with lightly cobbled yard immediately to the west with water troughs, malting ovens and barns (B, E, F, G) behind a range of domestic buildings (Figure 4.23). To the west of the domestic buildings, closer to The Green, was another lightly cobbled yard with further buildings and in some phases this has the appearance of a courtyard arrangement with two further buildings (C and D forming the north and south side of the courtyard respectively). As Butler commented, 'the farms one finds here... would be recognisable to the present day farmer, with his farmhouse surrounded by barns on three sides of the courtyard' (Faxton tape 1). In all cases, these agricultural buildings were either ephemeral (B, E, F, G) or else their full dimensions were not investigated (C, D). For the most part, these buildings also lacked finds, but Butler, in his notes, refers to Building C as a 'byre' and all the other buildings as barns. In all cases these structures were arranged perpendicular to the domestic buildings and, in the case of Barn D, attached at a right angle to the south-west corner of Building A2 (Figure 4.8). On the other hand, a narrow alley was left between Building A3 and Byre C in the north-west corner of the trench (Figure 4.23).

Elsewhere, excavations in 1968 in Croft 52–53 identified a walled enclosure within the plot and up against a building, while in 1967 the four crofts examined produced a range of structures. Some of these, such as Building 2 or 7, are distinctively long and narrow and suggestive of stables while some of the smaller robustly constructed buildings

(e.g. 17, 22) have been identified as possible pig sties, but might equally be outhouses or stores or poultry houses as has been suggested at Wharram (Dyer 2012, 314; 2013, 108). The lack of excavated evidence for them should not be taken to imply that the structures were either poorly built, nor should it be assumed that they were dedicated exclusively to a single function.

Overall, the toft layouts at Faxton were not noticeably similar. Buildings described as 'houses' by the excavator (usually those with hearths) were sometimes positioned at the front of the croft, sometimes parallel with it, at other times at an angle. Indeed, the layouts of the plots at Faxton showed much evidence for re-planning. Buildings changed their alignments frequently and, in the case of Croft 29 1966, involved a rebuilding at right angles over the top of a pre-existing structure. In 1967 Crofts 6–7 there was also clear evidence for the amalgamation of holdings with buildings being constructed across earlier property ditches.

The ancillary buildings
by Peter Brown

The structures identified by Butler in Croft 29 in 1966 as the 'bake-oven' (F8) and 'corn drier' (F6) require further comment in the light of more recent archaeological work. According to Butler's interpretation, structure F8 was constructed in the mid–late 13th century (Period 2) but fell out of use by the early 14th century (Period 3), with structure F6 being constructed immediately to the east during the mid-14th century (Period 4) (see Figure 4.8 for location). Structure F8 is circular, measures 1.52m in diameter internally, and is constructed of rough stone in double-faced walls (Figures 4.17 and 4.18). When excavated, only three courses of stonework survived, the rest being lost through robbing or collapse into the interior, but there is sufficient to understand that this was not a bake-oven but a malting kiln. Another example excavated at Boteler's Castle, Alcester, Warwickshire, bears a strong resemblance in terms of its construction and dimensions. Notably, the Boteler's Castle kiln had an external flue and/or stoke-hole (Jones et al. 1997, 32–34). In a corn drier or malt kiln the fire was usually lit in an external flue from which the warm air would flow inside and then dry the grain. This arrangement prevented the grain from becoming scorched and burnt by direct heat. At Faxton, such a flue might correspond to a depression at the entrance to structure F8 possibly indicated on Figure 4.8, although the scorched stones shown in Figure 4.17 could suggest the fire was internal. In some cases, as at Brackley (Northamptonshire; Atkins et al. 1999, 14), the flue was simply an extension of the kiln's entranceway.

Structure F6 is more distinctive with its rectangular, sloping stone-lined walls and a rectilinear chamber floor which measures about 1 by 0.8m. At the entranceway up to 10 stone courses survived to a height of 0.85m, but robbing had again removed much of the chamber walls. Here again there are well studied parallels in both dimensions and form including the malt kilns encountered at Brackley (Atkins *et al.* 1999, 13–14), Brixworth (Wilson and Hurst 1970, 205–207) and Irthlingborough, all in Northamptonshire (Chapman *et al.* 2003, 81–86), a number of sites in Northampton itself (Williams 1974, 347–348; Brown 2008, 190–191; Miller and Wilson 2005, 30–32) and at Barrow in Rutland (Bolton 1960). The flue would have been positioned at the kiln's entrance from where heated air would enter. In common with the 'malt roasting ovens' encountered at St Peter's Street, Northampton (Williams 1974, 348), the sloping walls facilitated the insertion of trays, probably made up of green branches covered with horsehair sheets (Bolton 1960, 131), on top of which the grains could be spread out to be dried. The process would have been very similar at Faxton and Butler's illustrations of structure F6 (see Figure 4.35) indicate where this tray may have been positioned. There is every possibility that structures F8 and F6 lay inside an outbuilding or brewhouse, but the scatter of post-holes (5, 33, 35, 36, 41, 42), post-pits (3, 37) and wall 34 are insufficient evidence to provide a reconstruction.

In the medieval period, the drying of grains in a kiln was carried out for one of two reasons. Firstly, compared to raw grains, dried grains were easier to mill (Atkins and Webster 2012, 287; Moffett 2006, 52). Secondly, the drying of grains was a key stage in the malting process. This process begins with the steeping of cereal grains in water to begin germination. In theory, any variety of cereal grain can be malted with barley, wheat, oats and dredge (a mixture of barley and oats), all of these being historically documented during the medieval period (Dyer 1989, 57). This could have occurred at Faxton in the clay-lined troughs, features 4 and 7, which were closeby. In the next stage, the steeped grains, while continuing to germinate, are spread out, usually in a dedicated space. At Faxton, Barn F or the sheds erected during Phase 3 would have been convenient spaces well suited to this purpose. The grains are then dried in the kiln which brings germination to a halt, producing the end product, malt, which is then further processed (sieved, cleaned and crushed) before it can be used for brewing (Moffett 2006, 51–52; Beresford 2009, 134–137). The crushing of malted grain could have been accomplished with a quern such as that recovered from Croft 29 (see Chapter 8), although another possibility is that the windmill, historically attested from 1320 (see Chapter 2), may have performed this task. Although, especially in the late 14th century, it was common for mills to specialise, most frequently in either malt or grain, as milling the two using the same grindstones could cause flour

to take on a malty flavour, general-purpose mills handling both products did exist (Langdon 2004, 151–152). Although no systematic archaeobotanical sampling strategy was undertaken at Faxton, the presence of corns, peas and unidentified seed remains was noted in structure F6 (Wilson and Hurst 1967, 308). That peas were present within the kiln presumably relates to their drying in advance of milling. Ground legumes, often mixed with oats, were the main ingredient of 'horse bread', a highly valued animal feed (Campbell 2000, 227; Langdon 2004, 148).

The distinction between corn driers and malt kilns, and the terminology describing both, is poorly defined in the archaeological literature. In many cases it may be a false goal to distinguish between the two as evidence exists to demonstrate that some malt producing kilns were also used to dry other crops. This is indicated by documentary records, as at Cuxham, Oxfordshire, where in addition to malt production, peas and vetch were dried in the kiln (Harvey 1965, 37–38), as well as through archaeobotanical evidence from excavated malt kilns (e.g. Chapman *et al.* 2003, 101). Archaeologically, two principal types of malt kiln are known (Hurst 1988, 874). These are defined by form as, firstly, 'key-hole' shaped kilns which have a circular or sub-circular oven and typically a long, external flue and stoke-hole, and, secondly, kilns with a rectilinear oven, usually sunken into the ground with outward sloping, stone-lined walls. Examples of both types are found, both in isolation as discrete structures as well as within larger structures. The circular variety is found across Britain although it has been suggested that they are predominantly located where conditions were wetter, with their proliferation being seen by some as a human response to the declining climatic conditions which marked the onset of the Little Ice Age (Atkins and Webster 2012, 286–287). Other than an outlier at Montgomery Castle, Powys (Knight 1992, 161–165), known examples of the rectilinear variety are geographically focused in southern Lincolnshire, Rutland and Northamptonshire. This has led to the suggestion that their appearance from the 13th century relates to the diffusion of technology by sea from the Low Countries, although a local development remains a possibility (Mahany *et al.* 1982, 19). The construction date of the Faxton malt kilns was not ascertained, but a badly worn Lyveden-Stanion 'B' jug (Figure 7.19, no. 122; Figure 7.20) found resting on the bottom of the clay-lined water trough (F4) can be dated to 1350–1500 (Paul Blinkhorn pers. comm.) and probably indicates the period when this feature finally went out of use.

All this is persuasive evidence that structure F6 was a malt kiln which was also used at times for drying other crops. It is more difficult to be certain of the function of the earlier structure F8. No grains or seeds were noted here but, even assuming none were present, this does not necessarily mean the oven was not used for drying crops or producing malt. Moffett (2006, 53) suggests careful management and regular cleaning may remove any evidence of charred grains. The fact that structure F6 seems to have replaced structure F8, taken together with its similarity to other circular drying/malt kilns suggests that, prior to the construction of structure F6, structure F8 may have served the same or a similar function. The scorched stones recorded inside the oven, however, may suggest higher than expected temperatures for grain drying, at least on occasions. It is neither unknown nor impossible that structure F8 could have served multiple functions as a bake-oven, a corn drier and a malting kiln (Bailey 1989, 168). It therefore seems likely that first structure F8 and then structure F6 offered a small-scale, but important, facility within the village. As a number of other associated features such as the clay-lined troughs and barns were likely linked to the production of malt, this was probably the main function of both structures, although the drying of other crops also took place. The malt produced presumably fed into local brewing, which may have been domestic or commercial in nature (Bennett 1996, 18), with beer being an important constituent of the medieval diet. The kilns may have been part of the manorial demesne and therefore communal facilities although, as Chris Dyer notes, malt kilns did occasionally belong to wealthier tenants (Dyer 1994, 141) and perhaps in some cases beer was brewed in rotation with the rest of the community.

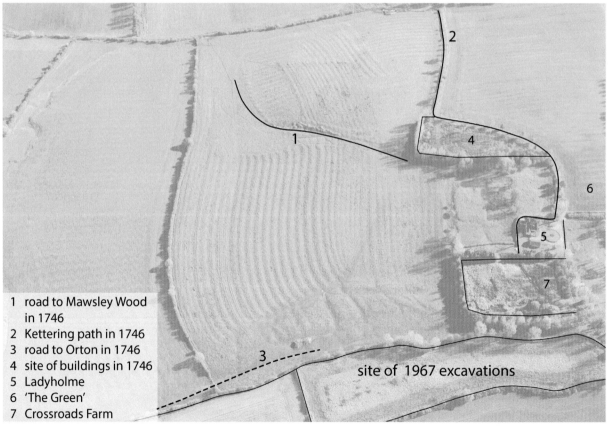

1 road to Mawsley Wood
  in 1746
2 Kettering path in 1746
3 road to Orton in 1746
4 site of buildings in 1746
5 Ladyholme
6 'The Green'
7 Crossroads Farm

site of 1967 excavations

PLATE 2

North end of the deserted village of Faxton today, aerial photograph looking west (EH 27866.04) © Historic England Archive. See Figure 12.5

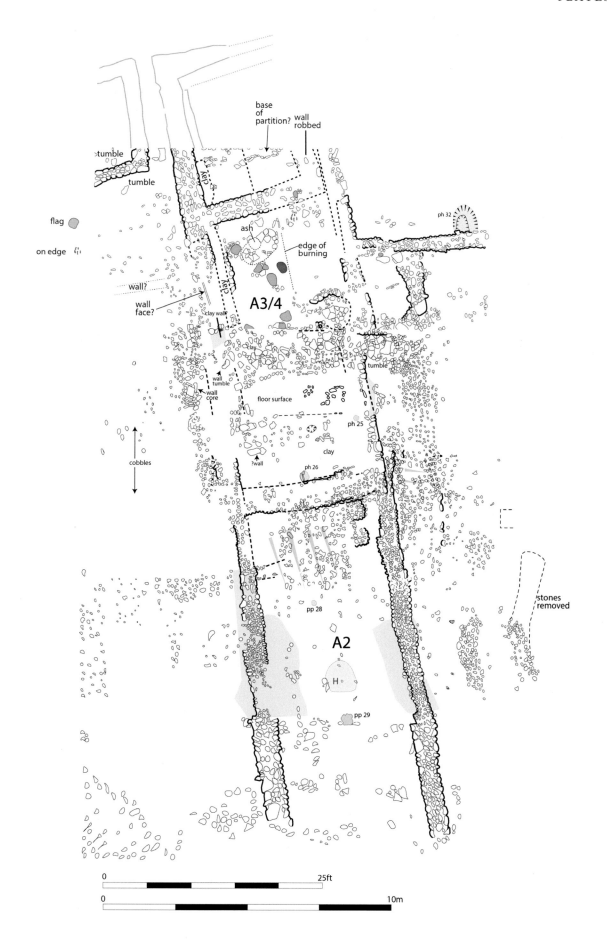

flag

on edge

>tumble

tumble

base
of
partition?

wall
robbed

ph 32

clay

clay

ash

edge of
burning

wall?

wall
face?

clay wall

A3/4

clay

wall
tumble

wall
core

tumble

floor surface

?wall

clay

ph 25

ph 26

cobbles

pp 28

A2

H

stones
removed

pp 29

0   25ft

0   10m

PLATE 3
1966 Croft 29 Building A2 (c.1250–1300). See Figure 11.5A

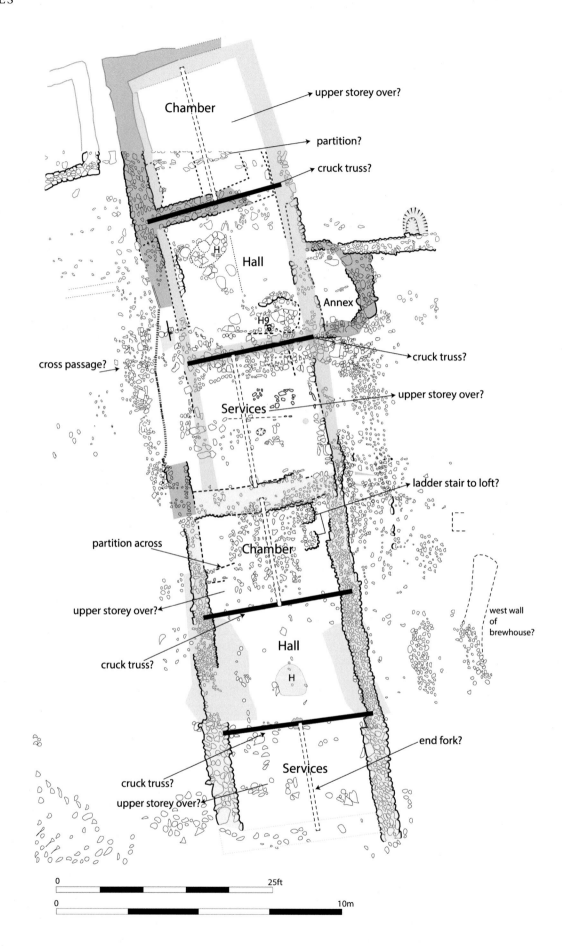

Chamber

upper storey over?

partition?

cruck truss?

H

Hall

Annex

H9

cruck truss?

cross passage?

upper storey over?

Services

ladder stair to loft?

partition across

Chamber

upper storey over?

west wall
of
brewhouse?

cruck truss?

Hall

H

end fork?

cruck truss?

Services

upper storey over?

0   25ft

0   10m

PLATE 4

1966 Croft 29. Reconstruction of Buildings A2, A3, A4. Re-interpreted as a cruck-framed building with earthen infills and re-dated to c.1250 to mid–late 16th century. See Figure 11.5B

12

FAXTON THEN AND NOW

Christopher Gerrard

with contributions by Ronan O'Donnell

The 'rescue' excavations at the village of Faxton in Northamptonshire were undertaken over the course of three summers between 1966 and 1968 under the direction of Lawrence Butler, then of the University of Leeds. This work was funded by the Ministry of Public Buildings and Works at the recommendation of the Deserted Medieval Village Research Group. In its day, Faxton was one of the largest archaeological excavations of a deserted settlement to have been conducted; some 4,000m² were examined here in 140 days over three seasons, compared to Wharram Percy where some 10,000m² were examined over 40 seasons. Although the results were only ever published as interim summaries, Faxton was to have a significant influence on the growing academic and popular literature about village origins and desertion as well as the nature of medieval peasant crofts and their buildings (see Chapter 1). Fifty years on, this volume has drawn on unpublished letters, notes, photographs, on-site notebooks and card indexes, sound recordings, excavators' recollections and partial manuscripts to create the most complete account possible. Every attempt has been made to be faithful to Lawrence's own interpretations, but some gaps in reporting, namely on the animal bone, post-medieval pottery, artefacts and landscape history, have now been filled by newly commissioned work sponsored by Historic England. Even so, more could yet be done; only a small fraction of the finds from Faxton have been re-examined during the course of this project and more could be done to link the archaeological results with historical narratives drawn from medieval documents. Perhaps further excavations records for the site may yet come to light, though that now seems unlikely.

Since the excavation campaigns at Faxton came to an end in 1968, excavations on deserted medieval settlements in the East Midlands have continued. Among those with financial assistance from the, then, Department of the Environment were Barton Blount (Derbyshire) and Goltho (Lincolnshire) (Beresford 1975). Topographical analyses undertaken by the RCHME, including the work at Faxton so extensively cited in this volume (e.g. RCHME 1979; 1981), subsequently became a benchmark of survey and synthesis. The county as a whole has since been fieldwalked on a massive scale resulting in the discovery of many new sites (Hall 1995); there is now an extraordinarily detailed atlas of the medieval county (Partida et al. 2013) as well as new landscape histories (Foard 2004; Hall 2014), not forgetting a regional study of medieval settlement with European implications at Whittlewood (Jones and Page 2006). With regard to medieval rural settlement, Northamptonshire has a strong case for being the best studied English county, not least because the work of the Raunds project after 1977 in the 'champion' landscape of the Nene Valley provided a far larger sample of medieval buildings than Faxton and over a longer time-span (Audouy and Chapman 2009; Cadman 1983; Chapman 2010; Parry 2006). That said, in recent years deserted medieval settlements have received far less archaeological attention across the county. Research has continued into origins and desertions, as at Little Newton (Bellamy 1996–97), and development monitoring in the 1980s and 1990s has also made an important contribution, for example through the watching of a pipe trench which affected the deserted medieval village at Thorpe (Earls Barton; Halpin 1982). Nevertheless, this has generated little work at any scale, exceptions being Bury Dyke at Crick, Churchfield DMV (Finn 2016; a site previously examined in the 1960s), Kilsby (Kipling 2017; and see Chapter 11) and Thrupp DMV (Young and Kay 2015). While documentary and landscape assessments of deserted village sites have continued to make useful contributions (e.g. Hatton 2005 for Onley), one recent assessment found relatively little new to say about medieval peasant buildings in the East Midlands (Lewis 2016; for recent work on rural settlements in counties to the east, see Medlycott 2011, 64–67), and Faxton, for that reason alone, still retains its relevance.

In this chapter we explore the major themes arising from the excavations, in particular the question of origins, the development of Faxton's village plan, its medieval buildings and their plots and what we have learnt about the long decline and final desertion of the village.

12.1 ORIGINS

Prehistoric features from the Faxton excavations amount to little more than a possible Neolithic burial in 1966 Croft 29 and a handful of lithics (see Figure 8.1). That burial was not photographed and, while the rationale behind its dating remains unknown, its attribution must remain insecure. Lawrence Butler thought the flints to be Bronze Age and, although they are likely to be local to Faxton, they were quite possibly incorporated into the medieval earthen walled buildings and should not be assumed to be an *in situ* assemblage. Iron Age settlement archaeology and field boundaries are recorded locally from aerial photographs (Northants HER 1064, 5335, 5336; Williamson 2003, 65 for Iron Age/Romano-British crop marks), but nothing of this date was identified during the excavations. Roman material too was sparse: two coins, a roof tile and hypocaust flue tile, (undated) bronze tweezers and, among a handful of Roman pottery, one fragment which was later re-used to make a spindlewhorl (Figure 8.13, no. 85). Butler speculated on the presence of a nearby Roman site, perhaps under the later mansion at The Green, and such a suggestion would not be incompatible with evidence elsewhere in the county (Foard *et al.* 2009, 46 and Fig. 27; Northants HER 4508). Further Romano-British pottery has since been recorded in the parish by the Portable Antiquities Scheme (Northants HER 8716) and the existence of some sort of pre-existing stock enclosure on The Green can certainly not be excluded, not least given the manner in which many tracks converge at this point in the landscape (Partida *et al.* 2013, 100 for other examples of oval forms with connecting droves). At present, however, and in the absence of any archaeological work on The Green, nothing further can be said. The planting of woodland will inevitably have complicated any future attempts at clarification.

As highlighted in Chapter 1, the early medieval period at Faxton has long been a matter for comment. Lawrence Butler was unequivocal in stating that none of the three sites he had excavated produced evidence for pre-12th-century occupation and this insistence has created its own irresistible logic. Since Faxton is recorded in Domesday Book and the place-name is arguably Scandinavian in origin, it followed that 'Faxton' must lie elsewhere, perhaps close by. How else could the apparent contradiction between documentary and place-name evidence and the archaeological claims be reconciled? While the site remained unpublished, this conclusion could not be subjected to scrutiny and so the claim took on the more solid guise of 'fact' in several prominent publications on the subject (Taylor 1983, 126–128; Pounds 2000, 27; Jones and Lewis 2012, 199). In point of fact, Lawrence Butler must long have suspected this claim to be at best only partially true. One of the referees on his original (very partial)

manuscript commented in 1991 that the haul of pre-12th-century evidence from Faxton had been 'perversely downplayed' by its director, in particular that 'there seems to be a determined effort not to date any of the shelly ware to the 11th century'. It would now appear that judgement was correct. From Paul Blinkhorn's re-assessment of the pottery type-series (Chapter 7), it appears that there *is* Late Saxon pottery from Faxton and, although the lack of detailed stratigraphy prohibits anything more than a general statement, his words are worth re-stating; 'it would therefore appear that there *was* activity at Faxton which pre-dates the 12th century, and some of it appears very likely to be pre-Conquest'.

As we have seen, fieldwork in Northamptonshire has played an important role in national debates concerning the origins and nucleation of medieval villages. However, while Roberts and Wrathmell's study of rural settlement places the county in the Central Province, a region of 'champion' countryside characterised by settlements and their communal field systems (Roberts and Wrathmell 2000; Lewis *et al.* 1997, 67), and while all agree that by the middle and later 12th century Northamptonshire was a landscape of nucleated villages (Williamson 2013, 75), there is still little agreement on precisely when medieval villages came into being.

One influential model, largely driven by evidence from the Nene Valley in Northamptonshire, proposes that village nucleation and the laying out of open fields were completed *by* AD 850, that is, during the Middle Saxon period, by which time earlier scattered farmsteads were abandoned and their inhabitants relocated (Brown and Foard 1998). Fieldwalking has produced evidence for Early and Middle Saxon pottery on these dispersed farmsteads, before wheel-made Late Saxon pottery was in use, principally of St Neots type ware, thereby giving a *terminus ante quem* of *c.* AD 850 for nucleation (e.g. Parry 2006). Plague, rising population and the restructuring of resources within landed estates are all suggested explanations for this re-alignment in settlement (Rippon 2010, 41; Foard *et al.* 2009, 54). The internal arrangement of these settlements has been referred to as 'rather untidy' (Jones and Lewis 2012, 197) and many village cores, it is argued, were later re-organised, perhaps in the 10th century, to produce the regular arrangements of tofts and crofts like the one we see at Faxton. This later reorganisation, sometimes termed 're-planning', has been associated with the rise of local lordship and the development of the manorial system; the implication being that villages *in their later medieval form* originated in the Late Saxon period, several centuries after their initial nucleation. The excavations at Raunds, frequently referred to elsewhere in this volume, were especially important in developing this new hypothesis (Foard *et al.* 2009, 46) and since then there has been significant championing of the 'long 8th century' as a plausible chronological context (Rippon 2008, 8–22 and Rippon 2010 both provide excellent summaries and debate possible causal factors; see also Brown and Foard 1998; Jones and Page 2006, 80–83; Foard *et al.* 2009, 14, 53; Jones and Lewis 2012, 197).

Other researchers take a different view. Whilst accepting the presence of one or two farmsteads at north Raunds during the Middle Saxon period (Audouy and Chapman 2009, 27–28), they find the definition of these sites as 'settlement foci' unconvincing, and see nothing elsewhere to contradict the view that villages are a post-Viking phenomenon unrelated to any pre-existing settlement pattern. Much depends on the imprecise dating of the St Neots type ware as to whether these changes took place under Danish control in the later 9th century or after that date. A second model therefore sees settlement nucleation taking place appreciably later, as a more protracted process between the mid-9th century and the mid-13th century (Lewis *et al.* 1997), while yet another model envisages no single nucleation event but rather 'several centuries of movement, adjustment and failure' (Williamson 2013, 97). According to this third model, settlements stopped drifting and began to grow *in situ* sometime in the 7th or 8th centuries. While many existing settlements expanded from a single settlement, others are fused from two or more sites to create polyfocal villages. The variety noted in settlement form and morphology is therefore to be explained by the density of Saxon settlements and their spatial relationship to each other.

In short, despite a generation of research into medieval settlement, the origins of villages in the Central Province are still unclear. Although there is now better agreement on a date for nucleation between the 8th and 10th centuries, opinions remain divided on the timing of this change and its speed. There is consensus, however, on some important points of principle which are relevant in the case of Faxton. First, the initial layouts of these villages may not be the same as those we see visible as earthworks today (Chapter 3). Second, it is widely understood that villages continued to be added to in a series of blocks (for example at Wharram Percy; Wrathmell 2012, 203–220). Finally, all are agreed that the fullest possible picture of a settlement's biography can only be understood when the pottery assemblage is closely datable and the potential for excavation has been maximised. Faxton does not adequately complete these criteria. While there is currently nothing to suggest an origin for the village in the 8th century and, on that basis, a later date of nucleation in the Late Saxon period fits better with the archaeological evidence, it might still be countered that Lawrence Butler did not excavate in the 'right places' even though excavation was extensive and natural clays were reached in all three sites examined.

On the balance of evidence as it currently stands, a Late Saxon foundation date for Faxton seems the most likely. At the same time, it must be remembered that Faxton never acquired parochial status (see Chapter 3) and its settlement history should not be expected to be typical of one. In terms of a date for the possible restructuring of the village (or at least those rows of housing which were sampled by Lawrence Butler) a post-Conquest date is reasonable (Creighton and Rippon 2017, 74–75). If that is true, then Lawrence Butler's assertion that he was excavating a post-Conquest settlement was, in one sense at least, absolutely correct. Given that barely any sealed contexts were identified in his excavations and all of the Late Saxon pottery appears to be residual, Paul Blinkhorn's findings do not fundamentally undermine the arguments and chronological sequences presented by the excavator. All the structures Lawrence Butler excavated may indeed be post-Conquest even if it must now be suspected that pre-Conquest buildings do lie elsewhere. This hypothetical outline of Faxton's settlement history is also not incompatible with the Scandinavian element in its place-name which must date from later than the last decades of the 9th century (Fox 2000, 54) and a Domesday entry which is now seen to confirm a settlement which was *already in place*. In this context, Faxton would be a Scandinavian name for a new settlement colonising the less favoured wolds of Northamptonshire (Fox 1989, 92–93), part of an intensification of settlement at that time. Previous to that date, in the 7th and 8th centuries, Fox (2000) envisages the wolds here and elsewhere as wood-pasture and exploited at a distance for their summer pastures and woodlands but with few permanent settlements. Notably, a sizeable tract of woodland valued at 100s is recorded as belonging to Faxton manor at Domesday (see Figure 2.2 for reconstruction of its extent).

Nor is this interpretation of Faxton's origins in conflict with current reconstructions of the bounds of the ancient royal estate of Brixworth (Foard 1985, 191–192; Partida *et al.* 2013, 6, Fig. 5) in which the pre-Conquest royal manor of Faxton once lay. Ecclesiastically, as Lawrence Butler and others reveal in Chapter 2, Faxton was one of the northern arc of settlements within the parochia of the Anglo-Saxon minster at All Saints, Brixworth (Parsons and Sutherland 2013), 8km to the south-west. But Faxton had no privileged ecclesiastical status then or later. A dispute of AD 1174 x 1181 makes it clear that Faxton had no burial rights at that time and that this had been the case since 'ancient times'. As Parsons and Sutherland (2013, 224, 228) suggest, it is very likely that Faxton, together with Old and Walgrave, given their manorial dependency on Faxton in 1086, were all subordinate to the church at Lamport. This confused picture with its criss-crossing manorial and ecclesiastical allegiances, in which different 'central place' functions had become dispersed and fragmented, may well have had its origins under Scandinavian rule and can also be seen in other aspects of local territorial administration.

Administratively, for example, Brixworth, the estate centre, together with Faxton, were two of the eight parishes of the hundredal unit of Maleslea or Mawsley which itself lay in the parish of Faxton (Maleslea was later joined with other parishes to create a larger hundredal unit known as Orlingbury; VCH 1937, 149).

12.2 THE MEDIEVAL VILLAGE PLAN
by Christopher Gerrard and Ronan O'Donnell

Lawrence Butler's reconstructed 'medieval village plan', which forms the basis of Figure 12.1, illustrates the village at something close to its presumed maximum extent in the later Middle Ages. It depicts a fairly large settlement centred on a green with its moat, church and rectory and 53 elongated crofts extending along two roads to north and south; the conjunction of roads at this point in the landscape meant that anyone travelling from Scaldwell to Orton or Lamport to Old would have passed through here. Embedded in Figure 12.1 there are some clues to the topographical relationships between the various plan elements of the village which allow us to construct a conjectural sequence of its development.

Bearing in mind that earlier phases of the settlement (e.g. Roman) may have been over-written by later changes, and that Anglo-Saxon pottery is now known from all three of the Faxton sites excavated by Lawrence Butler, the earliest appreciable phases of earthworks at Faxton seem to be the rows of houses to the east and west of The Green. These do not have any stratigraphic relationship to each other, but the block which later contained Crossroads Farm, Ladyholme and Cliffdale Cottage on the north side of The Green appears to overlap the eastern block on the RCHME plan (see Figure 3.5), though Butler did not necessarily agree with this interpretation and saw the east block extending north to include Crofts 18–22. Figures 3.5 and 3.6 are firmly at odds with each other in that respect. Importantly, the western block is certainly overlain by the moat at its north-west corner, which is itself undoubtedly medieval. The Royal Commission omitted the southernmost croft of the western block (Croft 1), as Butler points out in Chapter 3, and so did not observe this critical relationship in the relative sequence (RCHME 1981, 114–125); it is, however, clear from aerial photographs. Finally, it seems likely that the houses along the south-eastern road are later than the eastern row. The junction between old and new crofts here is debatable but has been placed here between Crofts 33 and 34 on the basis of croft size and orientation.

On this basis there are probably three primary units in the medieval village plan: the western row (Crofts 1–9), the eastern row (20–29 or 23–29, Crofts 18 and 23 being a single plot later divided by the road), and the southern row (50–53) (Figure 12.2A). In their original form, these crofts would be of, more or less, regular size and their orientation suggests they were originally laid out *over* pre-existing furlongs on the margins of the former green, in other words, the farms occupied arable land which had already been subdivided (as, for example, at Yardley Hastings; Williamson *et al.* 2013, 84, Plate 26). At a later stage, the crofts in the west block perhaps encroached onto The Green while those in the east block were extended onto the open fields to the east to create more elongated units (Crofts 28–33) leaving vestigial traces of their former dimensions in the boundary between Crofts 27 and 28, and perhaps in the alignment of the eastern boundaries of Crofts 21, 22 and 23. Still later additions include the moat, the plots on the north side of The Green (10–16 or 10–22 depending on which interpretation of the boundaries at the eastern end of the northern block is preferred) with a back lane on their north side (note that these crofts do not respect the alignment of the ridge and furrow to the north), and the crofts in the south-east corner (34–49).

Some specific moments in this relative sequence can be dated, if only approximately, on the basis of the excavation data as well as a suggested historical context for the moat and the architecture recorded in the church. Beginning on the west side of the settlement, the earliest archaeological chronology for the excavated buildings in Crofts 6–9 is 12th century, while the moated site, albeit that its original form is unknown (RCHME 1981), is likely to be of the 'long 13th century'; Butler suggests the tenure of Adam de Periton in the mid-13th century as the probable period of its construction (Chapter 2). The topographical relationships seen in the village boundaries therefore seem to be compatible with this evidence. If the crofts in the west block were extended onto The Green then this encroachment would have taken place between the 12th and mid-13th centuries; the location of any houses in Crofts 1–5 is not known. On the south side of the village, the earliest parts of the church were 12th century (see Figure 3.18) while the excavations immediately to the east in Croft 52–53 produced building plans dating to *c.*1150 (following Butler's phasing). This must make the south-east extension to the village after that date and after the 12th century if the earliest dates for the occupation and laying out of Croft 29 can be relied upon. The plots on the north side of The Green might also be later, but this is less certain and could only be demonstrated through excavation.

In short, by the later 12th century, Faxton had become a nucleated village. Conjecturally, the earliest village plan at Faxton might be a two-row plan (west and east) with church and manor house on the south side of The Green. Excavation suggests that the west and east rows were established at more or less the same time. This plan developed

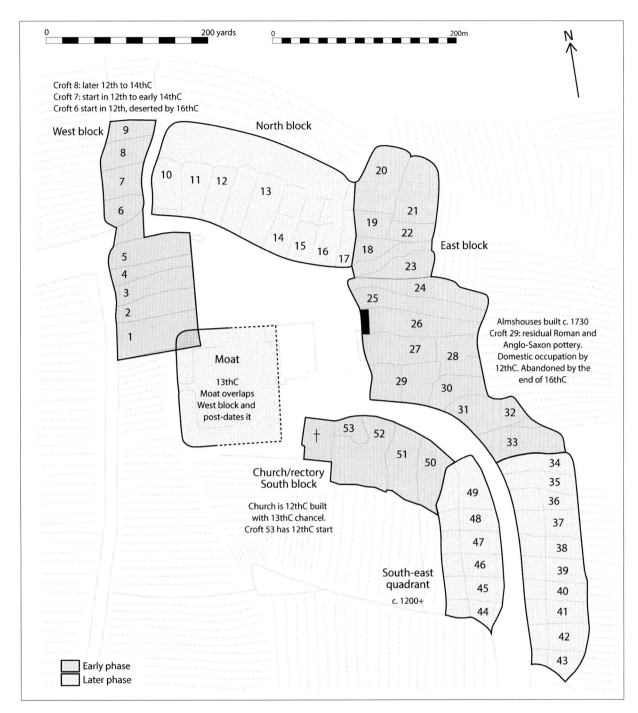

Croft 8: later 12th to 14thC
Croft 7: start in 12th to early 14thC
Croft 6 start in 12th, deserted by 16thC

West block

North block

East block

Moat

13thC
Moat overlaps
West block and
post-dates it

Almshouses built c. 1730
Croft 29: residual Roman and
Anglo-Saxon pottery.
Domestic occupation by
12thC. Abandoned by the
end of 16thC

Church/rectory
South block

Church is 12thC built
with 13thC chancel.
Croft 53 has 12thC start

South-east
quadrant

c. 1200+

Early phase
Later phase

FIGURE 12.1

Faxton medieval village plan with proposed planned units and their dates taken from excavation, topography, architecture and documentary evidence

remarkably during the course of the next 150 years (Figure 12.2B), perhaps beginning with new blocks of housing on the north side of The Green and the digging out of the ditches of the moated site and housing in the south-east corner to follow. The obvious conclusion is that 'planned' elements were introduced on more than one occasion at Faxton. This is, therefore, not a village which came into existence at one date and remained little modified over succeeding centuries; rather, as we shall see, both its growth *and* its decline were incremental.

Indeed, some scholars might argue whether this represents 'planning' at all, favouring a more organic development to the village plan (Williamson *et al.* 2013, 87). Lawrence Butler's excavations do little to resolve this debate, except to infer that Crofts 6, 7 and 8 were not all occupied for the first time at the same date (Chapter 7).

In a wider geographical context, more than 500 medieval settlements have been identified across the county of Northamptonshire, of which there are 430 nucleated villages and hamlets (Foard and Deegan

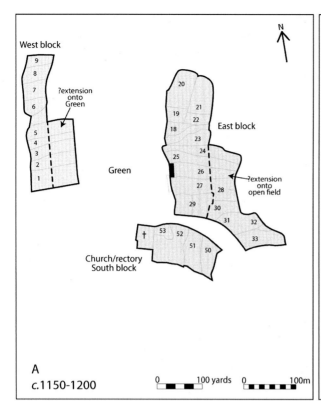
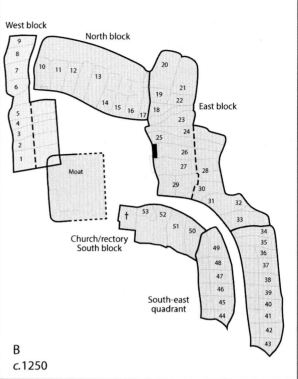
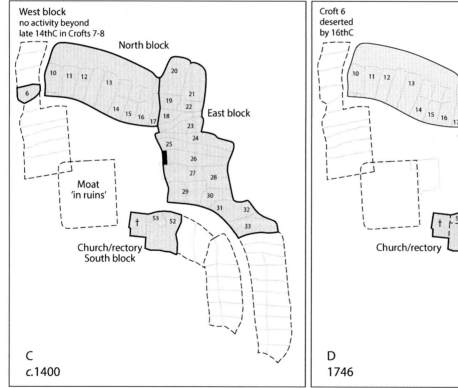
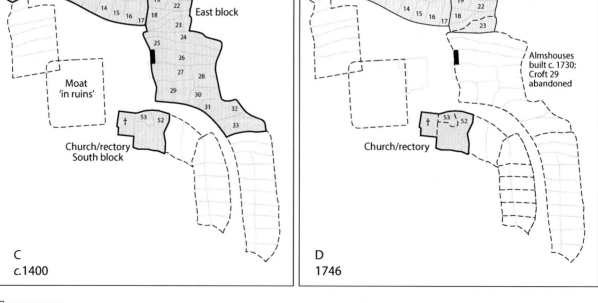

FIGURE 12.2

Conjectural phases in the Faxton village plan. A: c.1150–1200 with a possible Late Saxon nucleus on the south side. B: c.1250 with added units to north and south-east. C: c.1400 after contraction. D: the village in 1746

2008). The early plan type seen at Faxton contains many regularities which might conform to a double-row plan with geometrically similar properties of similar length and width arranged along a north–south axis either side of a green and the road between Old to Orton (for greens in Northamptonshire, see Williamson *et al.* 2013, 81–83). Such a regular plan would not be out of keeping in the 12th century and can be seen elsewhere, for example at Great Weldon, where both the plan and the proposed sequence of development are strikingly similar (Foard *et al.* 2009, 294) and at nearby Isham (RCHME 1979, 99–101; Lewis *et al.* 1997, 124). It might be suggested, purely speculatively, that just as the pre-Conquest settlement at Isham is thought to have been re-planned into a regular row after the Conquest (RCHME 1979, 99–101), so something similar may have occurred at Faxton. In other words, there is a two-phase process of village creation in which settlement coalesces close to the church sometime before the mid-9th century (Figure 12.2A), followed by a phase of re-planning sometime in the early 12th century which created the west and east planned units. This two-stage process fits well with what is being suggested elsewhere in the region at this time (Rippon 2008, 260–253)—and we might go further to propose that the moated site is itself inserted into the 'ovoid' green, perhaps a pre-existing area of common land, around whose margins lay a number of farms (as at Culworth; Williamson *et al.* 2013, 83). Both phases are poorly dated at Faxton and, to resolve the question beyond doubt, further verification would be needed to confirm the dates of its other elements of the village plan. Building on Butler's excavations, trenches might be inserted at very specific locations along boundary earthworks in the village plan such as the north row, the south-west quadrant of the village, and the moated site on The Green, the latter in order to provide a complementary environmental sequence from the wet deposits to be found there.

12.3 THE BUILDINGS

As we observed in Chapter 11, our understanding of later medieval buildings in Britain has changed radically since the 1960s and Lawrence Butler's interpretations on site can only be understood in the national and local context as it was at that time. There is little doubt that Butler struggled to fit what he saw into the accepted model of medieval peasant buildings of the day proposed by John Hurst and the Deserted Medieval Village Research Group (e.g. Hurst 1965; 1971). This is quite possibly one of several reasons why the writing up of the site was so delayed. Two of the main categories of medieval house described by Hurst he could not identify at all: the cot and the long-house. In 1966 Butler did see in Croft 29 a 'farm' with many different ancillary structures, but he did not observe the

expected transition from a long-house. Once more, that 'farm' in Croft 29 with its agricultural buildings arranged around yards to east and west would have seemed unexpectedly early in date to Butler and his contemporaries. In 1966 farms arranged around a yard were thought to be a late feature, though today we understand them to be common throughout the medieval period.

In 1967 and 1968 the fragmentary evidence for buildings was difficult to read and, although Lawrence Butler was innovative in his excavation techniques, he found the experience frustrating (see Chapter 1). With hindsight, he faced three insuperable challenges: shallow disturbed stratigraphy, a lack of finds which hampered both dating (in as far as the dating of medieval finds had developed in 1966) and the definition of room functions and, perhaps crucially, an inherited view that structural changes must represent different building phases. This was commonly accepted at the time, but more recent experience suggests that it is possible to have all kinds of changes at an archaeologically visible level whilst a building continued in use (Wrathmell 1989). With this in mind, what Butler defined sometimes as two phases may simply be the lower parts of foundations or extensions of those foundations (e.g. in Crofts 6–9 1967, Buildings 1 and 13 appear to share a wall on the same line; in Croft 29 Buildings A3 and A4; in Croft 52–53, Buildings 3 and 5 might represent parts of the same structure, as depicted on Figure 11.7). By re-drawing and superimposing plans of the different phases seen at Faxton in Croft 29, we have reached the conclusion that the medieval building plans there conform to the standard domestic arrangement of services, cross passage, hall and chamber (see Figure 11.5B).

Although there are caveats, sufficient survives from the excavation archive to verify some of Butler's conclusions and to propose a re-working of others. Without rehearsing the arguments in Chapter 11, one and possibly two kinds of earthfast building are suggested at Faxton and four kinds of ground-set buildings. Particular attention should be drawn to two aspects of this evidence. First, earthen materials were apparently used in different construction techniques throughout the Middle Ages and across the village, both in the form of load-bearing walls (sometimes with timber reinforcement) and as infill between structural timbers, and in both cases to construct long-lived domestic and ancillary buildings. The archaeological evidence for the use of earthen materials can be extremely difficult to record, but Butler's previous experience at Thuxton (Norfolk) and his interest in vernacular architecture had alerted him to the possibilities of its detection. Taken together, this archaeological evidence makes an important contribution to the debate on 'mud-walling', neatly summarised by Longcroft (2006) and Dyer (2008), which concerns the longevity and regional distribution of earthen materials in medieval housing before AD 1400. Faxton therefore makes an important contribution to our understanding of techniques of building, how they varied from place to place, and the importance of the local availability of construction materials.

Second, Chapter 11 suggests the use of cruck timbers of different types in combination with both earthen and stone walls at Faxton (see Figure 11.5B). Whereas Butler identified what he called 'stone-built houses' and sought to differentiate between houses of timber and houses of stone, it is now proposed that some of the houses were built of both timber and stone. None of Butler's original interpretations proposed the use of cruck timbers, but their presence now provides a much more satisfactory correspondence between the excavated buildings and surviving and demolished vernacular buildings recorded across the region.

Turning now to Faxton's medieval housing as it was experienced by its inhabitants, excavation furnishes very partial detail. As Standley points out (see Chapter 8), to some extent roof lines may have announced that the occupants of the building were, or had pretensions to be, of higher social standing. The buildings (we cannot be sure which one) in Croft 29 not only had some window glass but also a zoomorphic roof ridge tile or finial (Figure 9.4, no. 155). At least one building in or close to Crofts 6–9 and 52–53 also had ceramic chimney pots (Figure 9.4). Once inside, a decorative door strap from Croft 29 shows that house fittings, at least there, were not merely functional. Interiors of heated halls were illuminated in part by hearths (in a corner location in Building A4 in Croft 29 and probably with a canopy to gather and funnel the smoke to the roof), by rush lights which may not have had holders of their own (Brears 2012, 351) and perhaps by candles in unheated chambers, probably of local tallow; parts of two candle-holders were recovered. They lit rooms which variously contained items such as wooden boxes and larger chests for valuables (for which there were keys and padlocks), perhaps tables on trestles, chairs or stools, a cupboard and beds, and housed not only craft activities but also a variety of objects associated with the processing and consumption of food such as pottery bowls (for mixing dough, making cheese, etc.) and jugs for milk and beer, pot lids, perhaps a cauldron (of metal if the house was prosperous), simple pestles of nodular flint (no mortars were found), quern stones from Niedermendig (Germany), knives with bone handles and whetstones from Eidsborg (Norway) for sharpening them. There was neither vessel glass nor pewter, but that is not unusual in medieval villages other than in the manor house. One further interesting domestic detail is that the rim of an upturned pot was found *in situ* adjacent to a hearth in Crofts 6–9 (see Chapter 5). Possibly this acted as a convenient seating or base for cooking vessels taken off the hearth; no medicinal, culinary

or craft use has been identified (e.g. Moorhouse 1981, 114–119).

Textiles such as linens and woollens for clothing, blankets and bedding sheets had all perished, but the metal fittings from leather items do survive in the form of buckles and strap ends. One of the buckle plates from Croft 29 was gilded; other dress accessories included lace tags, studs and a dress pin. With only 23 identified in all from the three Faxton sites, dress accessories were not as numerous as elsewhere; Westbury (Buckinghamshire) produced over 100 such items (Egan 2005, 203). Items of personal grooming such as combs and mirrors were not found, but there was a pair of tweezers. Many other everyday things such as rope, straw matting (the floors are unlikely to have been entirely of cold clay) and wooden tubs are not seen usually through archaeology. The bone dice and a peg to tune an instrument are reminders of the many dimensions of medieval social life, of pageants and seasonal festivals, dancing, singing and music, gaming with dice (quite possibly with the 'stone lids' which might be interpreted as gaming counters; Gilchrist 2012, 152–154) and an appetite for leisure, story-telling and play which otherwise remains hidden.

12.4 THE LAYOUT AND USE OF THE CROFTS

Barns and byres are not commonly found on late medieval farmsteads and, although they do occur, they were a particularly notable feature of Croft 29 in 1966. The function of these structures was largely assumed by Lawrence Butler on the basis of their size and spatial arrangement in relation to the domestic houses; the lack of hearths or partitions probably contributed to his thinking too. In Chapter 6 reference is made to burnt thatch 'in the garden', presumably at the east end of the site, but here is no mention of charred grain in post-holes and wall trenches of the barns and byres; soil samples do not appear to have been taken. If Butler's suspicions can be confirmed, significant expenditure is implied by their construction. The obvious question is who had a particular interest in building and maintaining buildings for crop storage. Was Croft 29 a demesne farmstead perhaps or occupied by a more prosperous tenant? And might this explain the more varied range of finds found on this site and described in Chapter 8, as well as the association with malting?

The byres (e.g. C) and barns (e.g. D) in Croft 29 might have been multi-functional and used for the storage of crops as well as farm equipment including the lynch pins and buckets found on the excavation (see Chapter 4). More specialist functions are also possible. Barn F in Croft 29 would have been a convenient space for spreading out germinating cereals before they were dried in the kiln

(Chapter 11), suggesting that much of the space to the east of the domestic house in Croft 29 could have been dedicated to brewing activities, at least at certain seasons of the year. Other functions for farm buildings are indicated by the animal bone report for 1966 (Chapter 10) which demonstrates the presence of cattle, pig, sheep and farm dogs. In particular the presence of horse bones and of young stock is noted, so animal houses including stables are very likely and confirmed by finds of harness straps, spurs and a bridle bit (Chapter 4). The distribution of these finds of horse gear is focused to the east of the dwelling (Figure 12.3). It is safe to assume

that the daily routines of milking and horse riding dictated that cattle and horses were stabled not far from the living house, but sheep may have been accommodated further away in sheepcotes, at least when the weather closed in.

Artefacts associated with horses, carts and wagons were also found in Crofts 6–9 in 1967 (see Chapter 5) but here the layout of the crofts proved far less clear. On the basis of their morphology both stables and ancillary buildings such as pig sties, stores and chicken houses have been suggested (Chapter 11). The faunal remains from this site have not been studied, but the bones of both chicken and geese are among

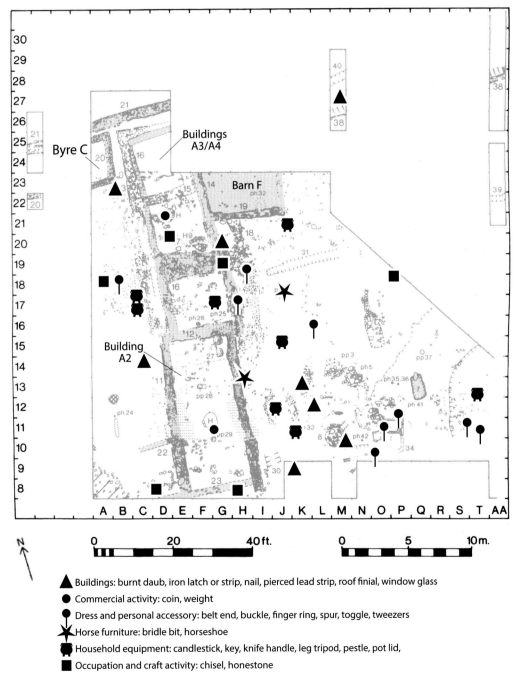

▲ Buildings: burnt daub, iron latch or strip, nail, pierced lead strip, roof finial, window glass
● Commercial activity: coin, weight
● Dress and personal accessory: belt end, buckle, finger ring, spur, toggle, tweezers
★ Horse furniture: bridle bit, horseshoe
■ Household equipment: candlestick, key, knife handle, leg tripod, pestle, pot lid,
■ Occupation and craft activity: chisel, honestone

FIGURE 12.3
The distribution of later medieval finds from Croft 29 at Faxton, not including those recovered from the topsoil

the faunal remains from Croft 29 (Chapter 10). Meanwhile, the function of the buildings excavated in Crofts 52–53 1968 remains unclear, but the fact that so few objects were recovered which could be directly related to agriculture does not preclude the identification of Building 5 as a barn with an adjacent yard (see Figure 6.3). Elsewhere, as we have seen in Chapter 11, croft boundaries were plainly marked by ditches and mud walls. In some cases buildings ran right up the edge of the boundary walls (e.g. wall 21, Figure 4.23), presumably to maximise the available yard space.

As might be expected, there would have been a strong link between activities in the toft and those which must have taken place inside the medieval houses. Among the pottery vessels are large bowls, for example from Lyveden, which might have been used for dairying; the wooden vessels also used to make butter and cheese have not survived. The evidence in Croft 29 for malting is fully discussed in Chapter 11 and, as implied there, there is no reason why a brewhouse should not belong to an individual farmstead as it appears to here (Wrathmell 2012, 342). However, there was nothing here or elsewhere to suggest the baking of bread so presumably there was a common oven for all the Faxton villagers somewhere else, perhaps in a location which was more central or closer to The Green. Likewise, beehives are likely to have been common, but the archaeology does not specifically suggest them. No rubbish pits were identified at Faxton anywhere, but the suggestion from Croft 29 was that waste had accumulated at the east end of the toft, far from the house, which the excavators identified as a garden soil (see Chapter 4). Figure 12.3 shows the findspots of artefacts from Croft 29 and the patterning which might be expected when household material has been collected and dumped at a distance from the house. Everything from spindlewhorls, knives and buckles, to bucket mounts and coins was found here. In the absence of any programme of recovery of botanical remains little can be said about what may have been grown; all the vacant space was probably well used. With a little imagination, what emerges is a medieval table with eggs and onions, bacon and cheese, chicken and goose, honey and bread, not to mention seasonal fruits and ale as well as beef (some from aged cows) and lamb and mutton on occasions. However, while all these ingredients were present from time to time, little went to waste. The large numbers of loose teeth may indicate that heads were cooked and the limb bones were split open to extract the marrow before being fed to the dogs (see Chapter 10). The presence of hare probably indicates that they were hunted with dogs of a greyhound type, and dogs both large and small were found among the animal remains. Venison too added something different to the diet, perhaps being poached illegally in nearby Rockingham Forest to the north-east, in one of the relict stretches of

woodland such as Mawsley Wood, or in a local deer park such as Overstone (see Figure 2.1) where other instances of 'park-breaking' are documented (Steane 1975, 216, 229; and see Chapter 2). In 1248 the parson at nearby Old was convicted of taking a roe deer at Walgrave and men from Faxton were among those who convicted him (Turner 1901, 89). The arrowheads found in Croft 52–53 suggest that the villagers had ample opportunity to practise their shooting skills at the archery butts which may have been set up in the medieval churchyard (Chapter 6), but hunting made very little overall contribution to peasant diet judging by the proportions of animal bones.

The excavations only hint at crafts and industries both at Faxton and off site. Metal slag is mentioned from two of the three sites, but was not recovered in large quantities and not retained. The lack of comment from the excavator suggests it was iron slag from smithying. Tools such as the gouge chisel suggest wood-working skills were in demand and there was doubtless a healthy exchange of services, favours and bartering across the village in the 13th century when the village population was probably at its highest. Dairy produce, meat and brewed ale might have been bartered locally, but there is no reason to suppose that Faxton villagers did not participate in wider markets when they were able to do so. The spindlewhorls from Crofts 6–9 and Croft 29 suggest the spinning of yarn, probably from wool with a drop-spindle, and this would perhaps have been sold on. There was also a pierced weight of Barnack limestone and some bone pin beaters which may have been associated with textile-working at a two-beam loom (see Chapter 8) but no particular concentration of these artefacts (Figure 12.3); they were doubtless discarded once they were no longer useful. Wool and perhaps textiles were not the only products traded off site, however.

As the faunal remains indicate, the slaughtering of animals took place on site and the lack of horn cores of sheep and cattle may indicate that they were sold on, perhaps together with hides, while the cut marks on the buzzard wing bones from Croft 29 suggest that the feathers may have been of value. Perhaps they were used elsewhere to make whistles or flutes for which their long hollow shafts would have been well suited (MacGregor 1985, 148–151). There may have been a modest saleable surplus of grain too, but this seems just as likely to have been put to use for brewing ale. Finds of coins from the excavations are few (Chapter 8), as they typically are on rural settlement sites, but sufficient to show that money was received and spent and doubtless kept safely under lock and key. The French or Flemish jetton of c.1400 might also have circulated as coinage or was used for working out accounts, but besides these occasional exotics there is little to suggest any great diversity of economy, rather more of a sense of isolation and austerity.

12.5 THE LONG PROCESS OF DESERTION
by Ronan O'Donnell and Christopher Gerrard

Although it has often been labelled as such, Faxton is not a deserted medieval village. The story of its decline is at once more complex and interesting. Gathering the evidence from excavation, earthworks and documents together, Figure 12.2C proposes that, by around 1400, a number of the crofts in the village had already been abandoned. In the west block, for example, excavation shows that Crofts 7 and 8 were abandoned in the early 14th century. Evidence elsewhere suggests that Croft 6 was deserted by the 16th century and that Croft 29 followed by the end of the 16th century (this being new data drawn from Chapter 7). Overall, the archaeology indicates substantial abandonment by AD 1400 with continuing contraction during the 16th century, although the extent to which that statement is true admittedly hinges on the archaeological evidence from only a handful of the 53 numbered plots on Butler's village plan. Further clues are provided by some of the topography and the known sequence of buildings within crofts. In the east block, for example, Croft 26 must already have been abandoned by 1730 in order for the almshouses to be constructed there, whereas Croft 53 was not deserted until the 20th century.

The overall impression from this topographical assessment is of a settlement which expanded during the course of the 13th century but then became severely diminished after a peak of population in c.1300. The conventional explanation for this initial pre-mid-14th century contraction is a combination of the famine of 1315–17, poor harvests, cattle plagues like murrain and rinderpest, and warfare. Because of its relative poverty, emigration may also have been a factor. The 'chief messuage' in Faxton is described as having 'buildings in ruins' in 1320 and the archaeology in Crofts 7 and 8 also suggests that these parts of the village too were affected and there must have been many empty houses. As we also saw in Chapter 2, the taxation returns for Faxton and Mawsley in the 1334 Lay Subsidy assessed Faxton with Mawsley at just 38s 8d which was the lowest return across the Hundred (Glasscock 1975, 212); the average Northamptonshire vill paid 93s while the average for villages that would later be deserted was 36s 5d (Bellamy 1996–97, 203). Faxton hovered just above the demographic waterline and this was followed by the disaster of the Black Death in 1348–49 and its successive outbreaks. Nevertheless, when Faxton came to be assessed for the 1377 Poll Tax it had 94 paying tax, a relatively healthy number against an average of 140 persons in Northamptonshire vills and well above the 64 persons of the average vill later to be deserted. The archaeological evidence is consistent with this trajectory, suggesting that many plots remained in use (e.g. Crofts 6, 29, 53). It should not be assumed

automatically that a physical contraction in the topographical footprint of the settlement reflects a dramatic decline in its population because young labourers and living-in servants could have lodged with their employers in farmhouses. There is also the possibility that some of the crofts, for example those in the south-east quadrant of the village, were laid out and never occupied. Whatever the reason, neighbouring settlements were certainly far worse affected and medieval depopulation became a 'very marked feature of the [English] wolds'; some 73% of the villages in the Northamptonshire wolds were involved (Fox 1989, 97 and Fig. 5.4 for a map of deserted villages in the county). These settlements included, for example, Wythemail and other case studies analysed during the Whittlewood project (Jones and Page 2006, 204–209). Faxton though, struggled through, in part because it may have absorbed the population from nearby Mawsley or successfully attracted new tenants from elsewhere to halt the decline in its population (Dyer 2017).

In all, a total of 82 villages in Northamptonshire were fully deserted, the final blow being dealt in the second half of the 15th century when tenants were sometimes evicted and a sheep-rearing monoculture imposed (Allison et al. 1966). In 1491, John Rous deplored the depopulation of Upper Charwelton in the south of the county, and the mid-16th-century pamphlet *The decay of England only by the great multitude of sheep* would find a ready response in a county where the Spencers of Althorp and the Knights of Fawsley had engaged in depopulation for sheep grazing. Great estates such as that of the Montagues at Boughton also had their origins in this process. Of the deserted villages listed by Allison et al. (1966), 41% are thought to have been abandoned between c.1450 and 1700, many of them as a result of imparking or conversion to pasture for sheep (McDonagh 2011). Faxton, albeit noticeably shrunken, clung on, and in this it was typical of many others. Only a minority of villages were totally deserted (Lewis et al. 1997, 152–155) and perhaps the construction of the almshouses in the 1730s was a reflection of an already ageing and impoverished population?

That the village depicted on the 1746 estate map (Figure 12.2D) is so much smaller than that revealed by the earthworks is a tell-tale sign that Faxton was already in an advanced state of decay long before the 18th century. By 1746 only the west ditch of the moated site remained. No manorial buildings are indicated there although they are mentioned in 1720 (see Chapter 2) and all the houses bar one in the south-east quarter along the track to Old had been abandoned as well as many other of the medieval plots. The remaining settlement in 1746 was therefore spread along the north side of The Green and at the north-west corner of the western block with the church and rectory to the south. Within the next 100 years the village contracted further (Williamson *et al.* 2013, 167). By 1840 many of the buildings present on the north of The Green in 1746 had also gone, as had one to the east of the rectory, and by the 1880s the village had reached the form shown on Ordnance Survey maps of the 1960s when the last inhabitants departed. At this point there were only four structures standing. This decline is clear in the census. From a population estimated at around 150 people in 1720, by 1841, shortly after the tithe plan was drawn up, the village had 63 inhabitants; this dropped again to 41 in 1851, but rose to 59 in 1861. From that date it fell continuously, flattening out at 14 in 1901 (Census of England and Wales: parish of Faxton and Lamport 1901; 1861; 1851; 1841). It appears then that while the village entered its terminal decline in the second half of the 19th century, it would only have become visually noticeable by the end of the century, as the number of uninhabited dwellings rose sharply (Census of England and Wales: parish of Faxton and Lamport 1911; 1841). During the same time period, however, the population of the dispersed farmsteads remained steady.

Some of the reasons for this final decline, such as the absence of a resident landlord or rector, are presented in Chapter 2, where Butler also cites the absence of a metalled road. Probably of greater importance, however, is the observation that the substantial tenant farmers did not live in the village; indeed only three lived in the parish at all, and most had probably not done so since at least the 18th century. The 1839 tithe apportionment is the first direct evidence we have for this situation. Of the 18 occupiers of land listed, only five lived in the village (other than the 'sundry tenants' occupying one fairly large cottage about whom we have no further information). Of these five, William Hales was not actually resident in his house in the village, instead living in Shortwood Lodge (Census of England and Wales: parish of Faxton and Lamport 1841). The remaining four, or their relatives, appear in the 1841 census, though one, Thomas Marsh, had moved to Fox Hall as a servant. The others lived in the village and one, William Freeman, is listed as a 'farmer', though his 1839 holdings only amounted to 8 acres, 1 rod and 19 perches in small closes around the village. As noted in Chapter 2, the 1839 tenanted farms are very similar to the 1789 to 1829 farms listed by Patrick King and so it is likely that this situation had pertained at least since the late 18th century.

By 1851 William Freeman had left the village or died and there were no longer any farmers living in the village (Census of England and Wales: parish of Faxton and Lamport 1851). This meant that the village was largely populated by agricultural labourers and their dependents, though 'graziers' are listed twice in 1851 and again in 1901 and 1911. To use Hilton's phrase, the 'coherent organism' of the village was lost (Hilton 1975, 162) and the village

was now vulnerable to the replacement of arable farming with pastoralism which in turn required fewer labourers and may be indicated by a rise in the number of people identified as shepherds in the census of 1851. Arable land on the heavy soils of the wolds was less highly valued and the village was some way from local markets (Fox 1989). Much of this decline occurred during the agricultural depression of the late 19th century, though it does begin prior to the usually accepted start date for the depression of 1873. Either increased mechanisation or a greater emphasis on pastoralism would have been reasonable responses to late 19th-century economic conditions (Hunt and Pam 1997). Faxton certainly had a pastoral economy by the 1930s; Sir Dudley Stamp's *Land utilisation survey* shows nearly the whole of the parish under pasture (Stamp 1931). A reduction in demand for agricultural labour was, however, a feature of the whole south of England during the 19th century and, as noted by Allison (Allison *et al.* 1966, 39–40), Faxton's late desertion is especially unusual. Perhaps the lack of a metalled road dissuaded the influx of commuters which propped up other Midland English villages during the 20th and 21st centuries.

Either way, the desertion of Faxton was no act of gentry aggression, but is better described as a desertion of souls yearning for a better life. As Lawrence Butler noted to himself on one occasion on a scrap of unused exam paper: 'there was no benevolent squire, no humanitarian rector, no inspired schoolteacher and no eccentric publican in the late nineteenth century. It was a village lacking in characters and in leadership. For its supply of amenities Faxton remained reluctantly locked in the time-warp of the 19th century well beyond the middle of the 20th century'. Faxton's inhabitants probably never thought of themselves as living in a dying village. Only quite late in its desertion did the village betray the appearance of abandonment, with large numbers of derelict cottages; prior to that time its inhabitants probably thought of it simply as a shrunken village if they considered its historical development at all. A similar ahistorical pragmatism was probably applied to all the various landscape elements that we have considered as significant here. They must, at least on a daily basis, simply have been the pieces of an entire, coherent, contemporary and useful landscape.

Overall, Faxton's landscape history seems typical of many Midland villages until its very late desertion. Even then, the causes of desertion, settlement dispersal, pastoralism and mechanisation, are familiar from earlier times. Faxton developed through the various eras of landscape history in the usual sequence. It emerges into history as a village with an open-field system. This system changed and developed through the Middle Ages as population fluctuated with assarting, creating new hamlets at the margins. By the early modern period the open-field system began to be enclosed, at first in small pieces and finally through Parliamentary Enclosure. There is evidence that, as this enclosure progressed, so the open fields themselves changed, perhaps with more land being put down to grass. During this period some isolated farmsteads were built as fashion and convenience dictated. It appears that at least some agricultural improvement was conducted by the residents of these farms. The land-holding population eventually left the village entirely, leaving it to decline dangerously once farming demanded less and less labour. War and industry became the most obvious agents in Faxton's 20th-century landscape, but the farming landscape continued to develop as new technologies and agricultural policy wrought their changes. Eventually the last villagers left but the dispersed farmsteads did not decline and some new ones even emerged.

The impression of completeness offered by the text above is illusory. There were doubtless many details and local causative factors which have been overlooked due to the limited documentation available. Among the most significant questions is: how did the open-field system function? It is not known how many people farmed it, whether there were regular cycles of occupants or whether a three-course rotation was always used. Without manorial documents it is unlikely that we will ever answer questions such as this satisfactorily. Similarly, we do not know when the engrossment that led to the situation revealed by the 1744 Enclosure Act occurred, and what other changes to landscape and agriculture accompanied it. There is little documentation for this, but it is possible that glebe terriers and deeds which have not been examined here may offer some hints. A possibly related process is the origin of the dispersed farmsteads. These are assumed to be early modern, which is likely, but there is no concrete reason to rule out an earlier origin. Finally, while map regression has shown some evidence of agricultural improvement, there were doubtless other innovations, such as the introduction of new machines or manuring regimes which have not been apparent to us here.

12.6 FAXTON NOW

LiDAR coverage shows best what now remains of a fragmented but ancient countryside (Figure 12.4),

FIGURE 12.4
LiDAR view of Faxton and its surrounding fields

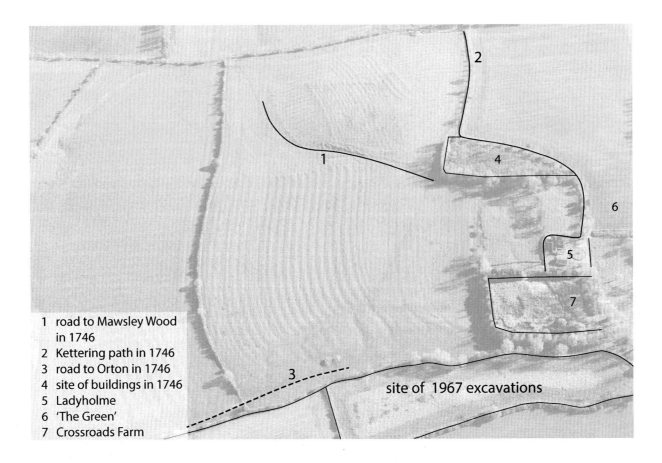

1 road to Mawsley Wood
   in 1746
2 Kettering path in 1746
3 road to Orton in 1746
4 site of buildings in 1746
5 Ladyholme
6 'The Green'
7 Crossroads Farm

site of 1967 excavations

FIGURE 12.5

North end of the deserted village of Faxton today, aerial photograph looking west (EH 27866.04) © Historic England Archive. For a transcription of the 1746 estate map, see Figure 3.1. See also PLATE 2

which would still be recognisable to Lawrence Butler. To the north of the former site of the village, in the field called Cliffes Dale in 1746, ridge and furrow survives in excellent condition (see Figure 2.4B). In fact, many 18th-century field boundaries can also be traced as can some of the ancient roads and tracks in and out of the former village. 'The road to Mawsley Wood', as it was labelled on the 1746 estate map, survives as a hollow-way to a depth of 1.25m with well defined ridge and furrow to either side. A footpath marks the track running north-east out of the village and alongside it the standing remains of Cliffdale Cottage which was still lived in on occasions by Mrs Bamford when Lawrence Butler first arrived at Faxton and which he later used as a home base for the excavations.

Comparison with Figure 3.5 quickly reveals that the main loss of earthworks and historic landscape features is to the east and south of the former village and, of course, within the village itself. Faxton itself now comprises a series of earthworks of building platforms and croft boundaries around the property now known as Ladyholme at the north end of the former settlement (Figure 12.5). To the west of Ladyholme, a converted barn is all that remains of Crossroads Farm and beyond it the site of the 1967 excavations along the west side of North Street.

Closer inspection reveals the banks and ditches of Adam de Periton's mid-13th-century moated site still standing 1m high and 2.5m deep in the conifer wood to the south. The southern and eastern arms of the moat, still visible when they were surveyed by the Royal Commission in the late 1970s (see Figure 3.5), have since been ploughed through and the earthworks of the manor house itself have mainly been levelled; there is a considerable amount of stone in the plough soil.

The site of the Faxton church is today defined by a low wall which stands up to three courses high in places. The churchyard can clearly be picked out on the LiDAR image (Figure 12.4). Within this enclosure a sundial and pedestal have been placed on a stone plinth to mark the position of the former altar; the plinth, sometimes alleged to be part of a medieval font or cross base, is in fact a column drum taken from one of the capitals in the nave (Figure 12.6). The architectural heritage of the church is spread far and wide: the north door arch was re-erected in the garden of Lamport Old Rectory by actor and historian Sir Gyles Isham, where it can still be seen (Figure 12.7). At Lamport Hall there is a wooden door in store which may once have been in the church, as well as sandstone mullions and the base of a pillar, among other stones

FIGURE 12.6

The site of the former altar of Faxton church. Photograph by kind permission of Janice Morris

FIGURE 12.7

The arch taken from the demolished church and re-erected in the garden of The Old Rectory, Lamport. Photograph by kind permission of Janice Morris

very probably rescued from Faxton church by Sir Gyles.[1] The font from Faxton was installed at All Saints' Church in Kettering in 1954, the 1703 bells by Henry Penn were recast for St Lawrence's Church in Stanwick and a fragment of wall plaster can be found among Sir Gyles Isham's papers at Northampton Record Office (NRO I/649; Morris 2016). Many of the church monuments are to be seen in the Victoria and Albert Museum in London (see Chapter 3) and one is in the Isham chapel in Lamport church where the church plate from Faxton can also be found. While a few churchyard memorials have been placed near the site of the former altar, the graves themselves were not lifted. To the east of the church, where Lawrence Butler dug in 1968 near the Rectory Farm, there is now a dense conifer plantation.

When compared with the excellent condition in which Lawrence Butler found the site in 1966, Faxton 'the monument' is painfully damaged, at least in archaeological terms. Indeed, the site continues to be threatened by ploughing and is still considered 'vulnerable' (Natural England 2014, 67). Nevertheless, Faxton has not been completely erased and both the excavated materials in store and the monument itself

still hold potential for further investigation. The site has unusual promise because of its upland setting which contrasts with the better researched landscapes and settlements of the Nene Valley, for example. Today the medieval village is still designated as a scheduled monument, and therefore still regarded as being of national importance (Scheduled Ancient Monument 109) and it is also listed as a 'relict landscape' in a recent Historic Landscape Characterisation exercise for Northamptonshire (Northamptonshire County Council 2015, 57). With awareness of the site being so high, there is every reason to be hopeful for the future.

When Lawrence Butler died early in 2014, an anonymous tribute to him was pinned on the gatepost at Dolforwyn Castle, the Welsh castle site in Montgomeryshire with which Lawrence is most closely associated as an archaeologist (Williams 2014). It was a faded colour photograph of the bearded excavator in his characteristic bobble hat. Above it were the words 'Dr Lawrence Butler. This was his place. "Good"'.

With the publication of this monograph, we hope that Lawrence will also be remembered for his pioneering work at Faxton; this was his place too.

---

1   I am indebted to Paul Stamper and Neil Lyon at the Lamport Estate Office for this information.

APPENDIX 1

Church repairs in the 18th and 19th centuries

Transcribed by Patrick King with corrections by Matt Bazley

An estimate of pulling down and rebuilding the Parish Church of Faxton in the County of Northampton, April 1796

NRO I(L) 3079/BB/1 and 1a

Taking off the lead and old timber, pulling down sorting and moving 530 yards of stone walling, taking down 6 monuments and putting ditto [monuments] up again, digging foundations and laying ditto [foundations] 379 yards of new stone walling to the new church and tower, 160 feet of new paving for the alter and steps (according to plan), 354 feet of old paving different isles in the church, 12 square of stout oak kingpost roofing, finding ironwork framing and putting up complete, 10¼ square of ceiling flooring and brackets for cove ceiling, 3 large window frames circular and Gothick heads 5 feet by 9 – one ditto for the chancel end 7 by 10 with casements, ironwork and crown glass complete, 61 foot of inch and ¾ doors with jambs and casing complete, 80 feet of [?] for lead roof & clock with stout oak boards, joists and ladder, 2 bell frames and new wheels and hanging complete, handrail and banister for the alter and fixing complete, hanging the doors, fixing the locks and joints and hanging complete, 15 square of slating for new building, torching and finishing 114 yards of lath and plaster ceiling coved with the angles, 300 yards of wall plastering to church and tower, leadwork to strips and ridge and covering the tower, painting the window frames and doors, finding scafeling carriage and every other expense

The total amount of this estimate £339 6s 7½d

Estimated by S Brampton

An estimate of repairing the parish church of Faxton in the County of Northampton

For repairing 12 square of roofing in the north isle, 2 new beams, 41 joists, ridge pieces and side plates and new deal boarding, labour and putting up, repairing the south isle, 6 square of roofing, finding new timber and board, labour, nails and work complete, 2 new doors and sundry repairs, plastering and whitewashing the inside of the church, repairing the outward walls, making good the coping, painting and cleaning down.

Repairing the roof of the porch, including scaffolding and carriage

Summ total £121 14s 6d

Recasting the lead and laying down £42 1s 0d

£163 15s 6d

Patrick King, in his accompanying text, notes that Mr Brampton's estimate for repairs mentions a porch which must have been pulled down at a later date, as 'no trace remains' (in the mid-1960s when the church was standing). As he says, the repairs mentioned in the second estimate above were evidently carried out, one of the roof timbers in the nave (the roof being mainly 15th century) is actually inscribed W x A x I x H, 1796, T&B (carved in the centre of the third beam of six from the west end) and in the churchwardens' accounts under 14 August 1797 is an entry of payments of £99 16s 8d to Samuel Brompton, £48 9s 3d to William Cook, £40 0s 11d to John Ball, £2 15s 8d to William Corby, £8 1s 0d to John Davis 'for carridge' and £4 4s 6d for a few smaller items making £203 8s 0d in all.

In the next century the churchwardens paid £14 16s 2d to Mr Brown of Scaldwell and in 1855 and in 1862 the walls of the chancel were taken down and rebuilt. The work was done by a man named Cosford at a cost of £76 4s 1d paid for by the rector, the Revd Robert Isham, whilst the churchwardens paid a further £15 10s 0d to Mr Brown in 1863, £17 4s 9d to Mr Gammage in 1862 and £36 9s 2d to Mr Woods the following year. In 1899 there was a fire which partly burnt the old square pews. The necessary restoration was done under the direction of J A Gotch who also bought some of the panelling from the old pews. F J Kirby's bill for fixing new seating and new stone flooring came to £8 4s 6d.

APPENDIX 2

Monuments in the church

Christopher Gerrard, incorporating notes by Lawrence Butler and Patrick King

The memorials that were once inside Faxton church were dispersed and partly lost after it was demolished in 1953. The last record of the monuments *in situ* was made by architect D Martin on behalf of SPAB in 1950. Thereafter, one monument went to Lamport church (no. 5 below), another group Butler registered as being 'lost' or destroyed (nos 3, 8, 9, 10, 11, 12 and 13 below), one was certainly broken by vandals (no. 6) and the most important part of the collection was kept in a potting shed for over a decade before being given by the Rector and Churchwardens of Lamport with Faxton to the Victoria and Albert Museum in London in 1965. This latter group is the best documented and may be seen on display (Hodgkinson 1971–72; Bilbey with Trusted 2002). Photographs may be found online and the memorials, now fully restored, can be seen on display at the museum.

1. Wall memorial south wall of nave at clerestory level (i.e. over the wall between two arches between nave and south aisle):

    Sir Augustine Nicols d. 1616, Justice of Common Pleas. Perhaps by Nicholas Stone, in alabaster and black marble with central robed kneeling figure, flanked by others (see Figure 3.16). Now in Victoria and Albert Museum, London. Nicolls died on circuit in Kendal where another tablet was erected in the parish church, placed at the west end near the font (Hodgkinson 1971–72, 337–339; Bilbey with Trusted 2002, 16) (Victoria and Albert Museum number: A.9-1965). The architect and sculptor Nicholas Stone was the foremost important English sculptor of the first half of the 17th century.

2. Wall tablet on north wall of chancel:

    Sir Edward Nicols d. 28 February '1682' (i.e. 1683 in Gregorian calendar), aged 63 years 2 months. Now in Victoria and Albert Museum, London. Slate slab in white marble frame (Hodgkinson 1971–72, 339; Bilbey

with Trusted 2002, 39) (Victoria and Albert Museum number: A.10-1965). Great-nephew of the above Augustine Nicolls. The main text of the translated inscription reads:

'This is the monument to Edward Nicolls, Baronet from the illustrious line of the Seymour, whose body is covered by a tombstone nearby. As long as he lived the doors of his house were open to good and civilised men, in which place remain his virtues and those of his uncle Augustine and the religion, honesty and humanity of his father Francis to all his people; and likewise his continual domestic and hereditary splendour'.

Sir Edward (1619–82) was a leading parliamentarian in the English Civil War.

3. Wall tablet on south wall of chancel:

    Dame Susannah d'Anvers, d. 17 June 1730, wife of Sir John d'Anvers, Baronet, and daughter of Sir Edward Nicolls; with information on her charitable gift of 10s a year each to four poor widows or widowers of Faxton charged on Pissford Bridge Close in Brixworth then occupied by John Wittsey. Now lost.

4. Wall tablet on south wall of chancel:

    John Nicols Raynsford, d. 4 Sept 1746, aged 23 leaving only daughter Elizabeth (by John Hunt of Northampton, a well known local carver). Now in Victoria and Albert Museum, London (Hodgkinson 1971–72) (Victoria and Albert Museum number: A.11-1965). Marble memorial slab by John Hunt with gilded and painted wood and incised lettering.

5. Wall tablet by William Cox of Northampton: on north wall of chancel:

    Hester Raynsford (née Isham), widow of Francis Raynsford of Brixworth and daughter of Sir ?Isham Bart of Lamport who died 14

November 1763 aged 68. Now re-erected in Lamport church.

6. Wall tablet at west end of south aisle:

Elizabeth, wife of John Flamwell, d. 8 Feburary 1781, aged 46. In 1966–68 this painted stone memorial slab was recorded to be in Faxton churchyard and broken by vandalism.

7. Wall tablet by John Bacon Junior of London on south wall of chancel:

Elizabeth Raynsford, widow of John Nicolls Raynsford and eldest daughter of the Revd Sir John Dolben, Baronet, 14 February 1810 aged 87. Now in Victoria and Albert Museum, London (Hodgkinson 1971–72). Marble slab with black inset lettering (Victoria and Albert Museum number: A.12-1965).

Memorials now lost or destroyed:

8. Floor slab under altar:

Jane Nicolls, wife of Sir Edmund Nicolls, d. 3 May 1707.

9. Floor slab under altar:

Sir Edward Nicolls d. 1716/7.

10. Floor slab under altar: Jane [Nicolls], wife of John Raynsford, and of William Kemsey of Hill Hampton, Worcestershire, who died on 14 November 1736, aged 68 years.

11. Floor slab under the altar:

Susanna d' Anvers d. 1730 [see no. 3 above]. A thin slate slab with incised lettering.

12. Wooden tablet (in Bridges 1791, II, 96):

Mary wife of Francis Nicolls, d. 16 July 1634, aged 46.

13. Wooden tablet (in Bridges 1791, II, 96):

Anne Nicolls (?nee Purefoy), d. ?1615.

In addition to these, Patrick King in his handwritten text notes that the estimate for rebuilding in 1796 mentions six monuments and that there was at one time a monument to Eusebius Isham as follows:

'Sir Eusebius Isham D D Rector of Lincoln College Oxon and Rector of Lamport unto Faxton Capel died at Tunbridge Wells on the 17th of June and was buried at Lamport on the 24th June 1755 in the 57th year of his age'.

This monument too seems to have disappeared.

BIBLIOGRAPHY

Primary sources

Census of England and Wales: parish of Faxton and Lamport, Northamptonshire, 1841

Census of England and Wales: parish of Faxton and Lamport, Northamptonshire, 1851

Census of England and Wales: parish of Faxton and Lamport, Northamptonshire, 1861

Census of England and Wales: parish of Faxton and Lamport, Northamptonshire, 1901

Census of England and Wales: parish of Faxton and Lamport, Northamptonshire, 1911

Charity Commissioners 1831 Reports from Commissioners, Volume XI

Enclosure map of Faxton, 1746 (NRO map 702)

Faxton tape 1: this BBC tape was recorded as material for the fifth programme in the 'On site' series on 10 September 1967. Narrator's script only for BBC transmission on 10 September 1967 'Amidst thy desert walks, the lapwing flies' for series 'On Site'. The original tape number was: TLN 37 WT 665. There is a transcript of an interview with Lawrence Butler, but the tape itself is lost.

Faxton tape 2: undated and untitled sound recording made in August 1966, about 15 minutes long, containing interviews with local villagers, Lawrence Butler and his excavation team. Possibly an unedited tape made by an independent filming unit supervised by Michel J Holding from Kettering. The associated film has not been located.

Hartshorne, N A, Drawings volume 3, 26a: mid-19th century drawing showing the leper window in Faxton church. Available at Northamptonshire Record Office

Journals of the House of Commons from June the 25th, 1741 to September the 19th 1745, reprinted by Order of the House of Commons, London; JHC 1803

Kelly's Directories of Northamptonshire 1877–1910, Kelly's Directories, Kingston upon Thames

Maxwell Lyte, H C (ed.), 1902 *A descriptive catalogue of ancient deeds, Volume 4. Deeds in the Public Record Office: A.6123–A.10426*, Treasury of the Receipt of the Exchequer, Her Majesty's Stationery Office, London

Nomina Villarum 1316, National Archives, Kew, E370/2/1–9

Ordnance Survey, 1885 County Series 1st edition 6 inches

Ordnance Survey, 1901 County Series 1st revision

Ordnance Survey, 1952 County Series 3rd revision

Ordnance Survey, 1958 National Grid 1st Imperial edition

Ordnance Survey, 1965 National Grid 1st edition

Ordnance Survey, 1969a National Grid 1st revision

Ordnance Survey, 1969b National Grid latest version

Simons, N, 1834 *Reports of cases decided in the High Court of Chancery by The Right Hon. Sir Lancelot Shadwell, Vice-Chancellor of England*, Volume IV, 1830 and 1831, J and W T Clarke, Lincoln's Inn, London

Tithe apportionment for Faxton, 1839

Tithe plan of Faxton and Mawlsey, 1839

Trade Directory 1890

Secondary sources

Adkins, W R D and Serjeantson, R M, 1902 *The Victoria County History of the county of Northampton, Volume One*, Archibald Constable and Company, Westminster

Alcock, N and Miles, D, 2013 *The medieval peasant house in Midland England*, Oxbow Books, Oxford

Algar, D and Musty, J, 1969 'Gomeldon [Wiltshire]', *Current Archaeology* 14, 87–91

Allison, K J, Beresford, M W, and Hurst, J G, 1965 *The deserted villages of Oxfordshire*, Leicester University Press, Leicester

Allison, K J, Hurst, J and Beresford, M W, 1966 *The deserted villages of Northamptonshire*, Leicester University Press, Leicester

Andrews, D D and Milne, G, 1979 *Wharram: A study of settlement on the Yorkshire Wolds I,* The Society for Medieval Archaeology Monograph 8, London

Astill, G, 1988 'Rural settlement: The toft and the croft', in G Astill and A Grant (eds), *The countryside of the medieval England*, Blackwell, Oxford, 36–61

Atkin, M, 1991 'Medieval clay-walled building in Norwich', *Norfolk Archaeology* 41, 176–177

Atkin, M, Carter, A and Evans, D H, 1985 *Excavations in Norwich 1971–1978, part II*, East Anglian Archaeology 26, Gressenhall

Atkins, R, Chapman, A and Holmes, M, 1999 'The excavation of a medieval bake/brewhouse at The Elms, Brackley, Northamptonshire, January 1999', *Northamptonshire Archaeology* 28, 5–24

Atkins, R and Webster, M, 2012 'Medieval corn-driers discovered on land probably once part of Repton Manor, Ashford', *Archaeologia Cantiana* 132, 275–289

Audouy, M and Chapman, A, 2009 *Raunds: The origins and growth of a medieval village AD 450–1500*, Oxbow Books, Oxford

Austin, D (ed.), 1982 *Boldon Book*, Phillimore, Chichester

Bailey, M, 1989 *A marginal economy? East Anglian Breckland in the later Middle Ages*, Cambridge University Press, Cambridge

Bailey, M, 2009 'The form, function and evolution of irregular field systems in Suffolk, *c.*1300 to *c.*1550', *Agricultural History Review* 57, 15–36

Barnwell, P S, 2015 'Dr L A S Butler (1934–2014)', *Yorkshire Archaeological Journal* 87.1, 200–201

Barton, K J, 1966 'The medieval pottery of Paris', *Medieval Archaeology* 10, 59–73

Bartosiewicz, L, van Neer, W and Lentacker, A, 1997 *Draught cattle: Their osteological identification and history*, Annales Sciences Zoologiques 281, Tervuren

Bellamy, B, 1985 'A nineteenth-century bottle kiln at Faxton', *Northamptonshire Archaeology* 20, 141–144

Bellamy, B, 1996–97 'Little Newton: A central Northamptonshire deserted village', *Northamptonshire Archaeology* 27, 200–210

Bennett, J M, 1996 *Ale, beer and brewsters in England: Women's work in a changing world, 1300–1600*, Oxford University Press, Oxford

Bentz, E, 2012 'The Danish connection: Axel Steensberg and Wharram Percy', in S Wrathmell (ed.), *A history of Wharram Percy and its neighbours,* Wharram, a study of settlement on the Yorkshire Wolds 13, York, 10–23

Beresford, G, 1971 'Tresmorn, St Gennys', *Cornish Archaeology* X, 55–73

Beresford, G, 1975 *The medieval clay-land villages: Excavations at Goltho and Barton Blount*, The Society for Medieval Archaeology Monograph 6, London

Beresford, G, 1979 'Three deserted medieval settlements on Dartmoor: A report on the late E Marie Mintner's excavations', *Medieval Archaeology* 23, 98–158

Beresford, G, 1981 'The timber-laced wall in England', in A Detsicas (ed.), *Collectanea historica: Essays in memory of Stuart Rigold*, Kent Archaeological Society, Maidstone, 213–218

Beresford, G, 2009 *Caldecote: The development and desertion of a Hertfordshire village*, The Society for Medieval Archaeology Monograph 28, Leeds

Beresford, M W, 1954 *The lost villages of England*, Lutterworth Press, London

Beresford, M W, 1961 'Habitation versus improvement: The debate on enclosure by agreement', in F J Fisher (ed.), *Essays in the economic and social history of Tudor and Stuart England in honour of R H Tawney*, Cambridge University Press, London, 40–69

Beresford, M W, 1971 'A review of historical research to 1968', in M W Beresford and J G Hurst, *Deserted medieval villages,* Lutterworth Press, 3–75

Beresford, M W, 1983 *The lost villages of England*, Sutton, Stroud

Beresford, M W and Hurst, J G, 1971 *Deserted medieval villages,* Lutterworth Press, London

Biddle, M, 1990 *Object and economy in medieval Winchester: Artefacts from medieval Winchester. Part II*, Winchester Studies 7.ii, Oxford University Press, Oxford

Bilbey, D with Trusted, M, 2002 *British sculpture 1470–2000: A concise catalogue of the collection at the Victoria and Albert Museum*, V&A Publications, London

Bird, H, 2005 'Seaborne re-visited: Cob cottages in Northamptonshire 2004', *Northamptonshire Past and Present* 58, 54–69

Blight, J T, 1868 'Notice of enclosures at Smallacombe, near the Cheesewring, Cornwall', *Journal of the Royal Institution of Cornwall* III (1868–70), 10–16

Blinkhorn, P, 2008 'The pottery', in P Chapman, P Blinkhorn and A Chapman (eds), 'A medieval potters' tenement at Corby Road, Stanion, Northamptonshire', *Northamptonshire Archaeology* 35, 215–271 (215–269)

Blinkhorn, P, 2009 'The pottery from Langham Road and Burystead', in M Audouy and A Chapman, *Raunds: The origins and growth of a Midland village AD 450–1500,* Oxbow Books, Oxford, 172–193

Blinkhorn, P, 2010 'The Saxon and medieval pottery', in A Chapman, *West Cotton, Raunds: A study of medieval settlement dynamics AD 450–1450,* Oxbow Books, Oxford, 259–333

Blunden, J and Curry, N (eds), 1989 *A people's charter? Forty years of the National Parks and Access to the Countryside Act 1949,* Her Majesty's Stationery Office, London

Bolton, E G, 1960 'Excavation of a house and malt kiln at Barrow, Rutland', *Medieval Archaeology* 4, 128–131

Brears, P, 2012 'The interiors of Wharram's farmhouses and their contents: Two artist's impressions and a commentary', in S Wrathmell (ed.), *A history of Wharram Percy and its neighbours,* Wharram, a study of settlement on the Yorkshire Wolds 13, York, 349–356

Bridges, J, 1791 *The history and antiquities of Northamptonshire, compiled from the manuscript collections of the late learned antiquary J Bridges, Esq, by the Rev Peter Whalley,* 2 vols, T Payne, London

Brown, G, 1999 'Post-enclosure farmsteads on Salisbury Plain: A preliminary discussion', in P Pattison (ed.), *Patterns of the past: Essays in landscape archaeology for Christopher Taylor*, Oxbow Books, Oxford, 121–127

Brown, J, 2008 'Excavations at the corner of Kingswell Street and Woolmonger Street, Northampton', *Northamptonshire Archaeology* 35, 173–214

Brown, T and Foard, G, 1998 'The Saxon landscape: A regional perspective', in P Everson and T Williamson (eds), *The archaeology of landscape: Studies presented to Christopher Taylor*, Manchester University Press, Manchester, 67–94

Brunskill, R W, 2000 *Vernacular architecture: An illustrated handbook,* London, Faber, 4th edition

Bryant, G F and Steane, J M, 1969 'Excavations at the deserted medieval settlement of Lyveden', *Journal of the Northampton Museum and Art Gallery* 5, 3–50

Bryant, G F and Steane, J M, 1971 'Excavations at the deserted medieval settlement of Lyveden', *Journal of the Northampton Museum and Art Gallery* 9, 1–94

Butler, L, 1967 'Faxton', *Bulletin of the Northamptonshire Federation of Archaeological Societies* 2, 20–23

Butler, L, 1968a 'Faxton', *Current Archaeology* 2, 48–50

Butler, L, 1968b 'Faxton medieval village', *Current Archaeology* 6, 163–164

Butler, L, 1969a 'Faxton', *Current Archaeology* 16, 144–147

Butler, L, 1969b 'Faxton', *Bulletin of the Northamptonshire Federation of Archaeological Societies* 3, 20–23

Butler, L and Wade-Martins, P, 1989 *The deserted medieval village of Thuxton, Norfolk*, East Anglian Archaeology 46, Dereham, Norfolk

Cadman, G, 1983 'Raunds 1977–1983: An excavation summary', *Medieval Archaeology* 27, 107–122

Campbell, B M S, 2000 *English seigniorial agriculture, 1250–1450,* Cambridge University Press, Cambridge

Carr, J L, 1993 *Churches in retirement: A gazetteer,* Redundant Churches Fund, Her Majesty's Stationery Office, London

Chapman, A, 2010 *West Cotton, Raunds: A study of medieval settlement dynamics AD 450–1450. Excavation of a deserted medieval hamlet in Northamptonshire, 1985–1989,* Oxbow Books, Oxford

Chapman, A, Atkins, R and Lloyd, R, 2003 'A medieval manorial farm at Lime Street Irthlingborough, Northamptonshire', *Northamptonshire Archaeology* 31, 71–104

Cheyette, F L, 1984 'Review of *Village and farmstead: A history of rural settlement in England* by Christopher Taylor', *Speculum* 59.4, 956–961

Christie, N and Creighton, O, 2013 *Transforming townscapes. From burh to borough: The archaeology of Wallingford AD 800–1400,* The Society for Medieval Archaeology Monograph 35, London

Claridge, J, 2017 'The role of demesnes in the trade of agricultural horses in late medieval England', *Agricultural History Review* 65.1, 1–19

Clarke, H and Carter, A, 1977 *Excavations in King's Lynn, 1963–70,* The Society for Medieval Archaeology Monograph 7, London

Clifton-Taylor, A, 1972 *The pattern of English building*, Faber and Faber, London

Cocroft, W D, Thomas, R J C and Barnwell, P S, 2003 *Cold War: Building for nuclear confrontation 1946–1989,* English Heritage, Swindon

Cohen, A and Serjeantson, D, 1996 *A manual for the identification of bird bones from archaeological sites*, Archetype Publications, London

Creighton, O and Rippon, S, 2017 'Conquest, colonisation and the countryside: Archaeology and the mid-11th- to mid-12th-century rural landscape', in D M Hadley and C Dyer (eds), *The archaeology of the 11th century: Continuities and transformations*, The Society for Medieval Archaeology Monograph 38, London, 57–87

Cripps-Day, F H, 1931 *The Manor Farm: to which are added reprint facsimiles of The Boke of Husbandry, an English translation of the XIIIth century tract on husbandry by Walter of Henley and The Boke of Thrift containing English translations of the same tract and the anonymous XIIIth century tract Hosebonderie*, Bernard Quaritch Ltd, London

Currie, C R J, 1989 'Time and chance: Modelling the attrition of old houses', *Vernacular Architecture* 19, 1–9

Dalwood, H and Edwards, R, 2004 *Excavations at Deansway, Worcester, 1988–89: Romano-British small town to late medieval city*, Council for British Archaeology Research Report 139, York

d'Anthenaise, C, 2002 *The hunting book of Gaston Phébus*, Hackberry Press, Texas

Denham, V, 2009 'Introduction: The Saxon and Medieval pottery', in M Audouy and A Chapman, *Raunds: The origin and growth of a midland village AD 450–1500*, Oxbow Books, Oxford, 151

DMVRG, 1954 *The Deserted Medieval Village Research Group Report*, The Deserted Medieval Village Research Group, London

DMVRG, 1960 *The Deserted Medieval Village Research Group 8th annual report*, The Deserted Medieval Village Research Group, London

DMVRG, 1961 *The Deserted Medieval Village Research Group 9th annual report*, The Deserted Medieval Village Research Group, London

DMVRG, 1964 *The Deserted Medieval Village Research Group 12th annual report*, The Deserted Medieval Village Research Group, London

DMVRG, 1965a *The Deserted Medieval Village Research Group 13th annual report,* The Deserted Medieval Village Research Group, London

DMVRG, 1965b 'The preservation of deserted medieval villages. Memorandum to the Chief Inspector of Ancient Monuments to the Ministry of Public Buildings and Works', in *The Deserted Medieval Village Research Group 13th annual report, Appendix*, London

DMVRG, 1966 *The Deserted Medieval Village Research Group 14th annual report*, The Deserted Medieval Village Research Group, London

DMVRG, 1967 *The Deserted Medieval Village Research Group 15th annual report*, The Deserted Medieval Village Research Group, London

DMVRG, 1968 *The Deserted Medieval Village Research Group 16th annual report*, The Deserted Medieval Village Research Group, London

DMVRG, 1970 *The Deserted Medieval Village Research Group 18th annual report*, The Deserted Medieval Village Research Group, London

Dreissen, L A, 1944 'Linen weaving and linen bleaching in Holland', *CIBA Review* 48, 1735–1738

Driesch, A von den and Boessneck, J, 1974 'Kritische Anmerkungen zur Widerristhohenberechnung aus Langenmassen vor- und fruhgeschichtlicher Tierknochen', *Saugetierkundliche Mitteilungen* 22, 325–348

Dry, W, 1932 *Northamptonshire*, Methuen, London

Dunning, G C, 1975 'A zoomorphic roof-finial from Churchfield near Lyveden', in J Steane and G F Bryant, 'Excavations at

the deserted medieval settlement of Lyveden', *Journal of the Northampton Museum Art Gallery* 12, 103–105

Dyer, C, 1986 'English peasant buildings in the later Middle Ages (1200–1500)', *Medieval Archaeology* 30, 18–45

Dyer, C, 1989 *Standards of living in the later Middle Ages: Social change in England c.1200–1520*, Cambridge University Press, Cambridge (revised edn)

Dyer, C, 1994 *Everyday life in medieval England*, Hambledon Press, London

Dyer, C, 1997 'Peasants and coins: The uses of money in the Middle Ages', *British Numismatic Journal* 57, 31–47

Dyer, C, 2008 'Building in earth in late-medieval England', *Vernacular Architecture* 39, 63–70

Dyer, C, 2012 'The late medieval village of Wharram Percy: Farming the land', in S Wrathmell (ed.), *A history of Wharram Percy and its neighbours*, Wharram, a study of settlement on the Yorkshire Wolds 13, York, 312–327

Dyer, C, 2013 'Documentary evidence', in N Alcock and D Miles, *The medieval peasant house in Midland England*, Oxbow Books, Oxford, 105–117

Dyer, C, 2017 'The Midland economy and society, 1314–1348: Insights from changes in the landscape', *Midland History* 242.1, 36–57

Eames, E, 1980 *Catalogue of medieval lead-glazed earthenware tiles in the Department of Medieval and Later Antiquities, British Museum*, British Museum Publications, London

Eastwood, D, 1996 'Communities, protest and police in early nineteenth-century Oxfordshire: The enclosure of Otmoor reconsidered', *Agricultural History Review* 44, 35–46

Egan, G, 1985 *Leaden cloth seals*, Finds Research Group Datasheet 3, Coventry

Egan, G, 2005 'Urban and rural finds: Material culture of country and town, c.1050–1500', in K Giles and C Dyer (eds), *Town and country in the Middle Ages: Contrasts, contacts and interconnections, 1100–1500*, The Society for Medieval Archaeology Monograph 22, Leeds, 187–210

Egan, G, 2009 'Material concerns: Non-ceramic finds c.1050–1500', in R Gilchrist and A Reynolds (eds), *Reflections: 50 years of Medieval Archaeology*, The Society for Medieval Archaeology Monograph 30, Leeds, 289–303

Ekwall, E, 1960 *The concise Oxford dictionary of English place-names*, Clarendon Press, Oxford (4th edn)

Ellis, S E, 1969 'The petrography and provenance of Anglo-Saxon and medieval English honestones, with notes of some other hones', *Bulletin of the British Museum (Natural History) Mineralogy* 2.3, 133–187

Endrei, W and Egan, G, 1982 'The sealing of cloth in Europe, with special reference to the English evidence', *Textile History* 13.1, 47–75

Evans, D H and Jarrett, M G, 1987 'The deserted village of West Whelpington, Northumberland; third report, part one', *Archaeologia Aeliana (series 5)* 15, 199–308

Evans, D H, Jarrett, M G and Wrathmell, S, 1988 'The deserted village of West Whelpington, Northumberland; third report, part two', *Archaeologia Aeliana (series 5)* 16, 139–392

Fairbrother, J R, 1990 *Faccombe Netherton: Excavation of a Saxon and medieval manorial complex*, British Museum Occasional Paper 74, London

Farley, M, 1982 'A medieval pottery industry at Boarstall, Buckinghamshire', *Records of Buckinghamshire* 24, 107–117

Finn, C, 2016 *Archaeological excavation of land at Harley Way, Benefield, Northamptonshire, September–November 2012*, unpublished report MOLA Northampton 16/154

Finn, N, 2009 'Mud and frame construction in South Leicestershire', *Vernacular Architecture* 40.1, 63–74

Fletcher, A, 2010 'The ambition of a young baronet: Sir Thomas Isham of Lamport, 1657–1681', in A McShane and G Walker (eds), *The extraordinary and the everyday in early modern England:*

Essays in celebration of the work of Bernard Capp, Palgrave Macmillan, Basingstoke, 31–47

Foard, G, 1979 *Archaeological priorities: Proposals for Northamptonshire,* Northampton County Council, Northampton

Foard, G, 1985 'The administrative organisation of Northamptonshire in the Saxon period', *Anglo-Saxon Studies in Archaeology and History* 4, 179–222

Foard, G, 2004 'Medieval Northamptonshire', in M E Tingle (ed.), *The archaeology of Northamptonshire,* Northamptonshire Archaeological Society, Northampton, 102–133

Foard, G and Deegan, A, 2008 'The contribution of aerial photography to medieval and post-medieval studies', in A Deegan and G Foard (eds), *Mapping ancient landscapes in Northamptonshire,* English Heritage, London, 136–155

Foard, G, Hall, D, and Partida, T, 2009 *Rockingham Forest,* Northamptonshire Record Society, Northampton

Fox, H S A, 1986 'The alleged transformation from two-field to three-field systems in medieval England', *Economic History Review (2nd series)* 39.4, 526–548

Fox, H S A, 1989 'The people of the wolds in English settlement history', in M Aston, D Austin and C Dyer (eds), *The rural settlements of Medieval England: Studies dedicated to Maurice Beresford and John Hurst,* Blackwell, Oxford, 77–101

Fox, H S A, 2000 'Wolds: The Wolds before c.1500', in J Thirsk (ed.), *Rural England: An illustrated history of the landscape,* Oxford University Press, Oxford, 50–61

French, H R, 2000 'Urban agriculture, commons and commoners in the seventeenth and eighteenth centuries: The case of Sudbury', *Suffolk Agricultural History Review* 48, 171–199

Gardiner, M, 2000 'Vernacular buildings and the development of the later medieval domestic plan in England', *Medieval Archaeology* 44, 159–179

Gardiner, M, 2014 'An archaeological approach to the development of the late medieval peasant house', *Vernacular Architecture* 45.1, 16–28

Gerrard, C M, 2003 *Medieval archaeology: Understanding traditions and contemporary approaches,* Routledge, London

Gerrard, C M, 2007a 'Excavations in Shapwick Park 1992-97', in C M Gerrard with M Aston (eds), *The Shapwick Project, Somerset: A rural landscape explored,* The Society for Medieval Archaeology Monograph 25, Leeds, 503–536

Gerrard, C M, 2007b 'Not all archaeology is rubbish: The elusive life histories of three artefacts from Shapwick, Somerset', in M Costen (ed.), *People and places: Essays in honour of Mick Aston,* Oxbow Books, Oxford, 166–180

Gerrard, C M, 2009 'The study of the deserted medieval village: Caldecote in context', in G Beresford, *Caldecote: The development and desertion of a Hertfordshire village,* The Society for Medieval Archaeology Monograph 28, Leeds, 1–19

Gidney, L J, 2007 'Animal bone', in C M Gerrard with M Aston, *The Shapwick Project, Somerset: A rural landscape explored,* The Society for Medieval Archaeology Monograph 25, Leeds, 895–922

Gidney, L J, 2013 *Offspring of the aurochs: A comparison of a reference collection of Dexter cattle skeletons with archaeological and historical data,* unpublished PhD thesis, Durham University

Gilchrist, R, 2012 *Medieval life: Archaeology and the life course,* Boydell Press, Woodbridge

Glasscock, R E (ed.), 1975 *The Lay Subsidy of 1334,* Oxford University Press, Oxford

Goodall, I, 2011 *Ironwork in medieval Britain: An archaeological study,* The Society for Medieval Archaeology Monograph 31, Leeds

Gover, J E B, Mawer, A and Stenton, F M, 1933 *The place-names of Northamptonshire,* English Place-Name Society 10, Cambridge

Grant, A, 1982 'The use of tooth wear as a guide to the age of domestic ungulates', in B Wilson, C Grigson and S Payne (eds),

Ageing and sexing animal bones from archaeological sites, British Archaeological Reports British Series 109, Oxford, 91–108

Gray, H L, 1915 *English field systems,* Harvard University Press, Cambridge, MA

Green, M, 1805 'Sir A Nicolls of Faxton', *The Gentleman's Magazine,* September 1805, 793–794

Grenville, J, 1997 *Medieval housing,* Leicester University Press, London

Hadman, J, 1974 'Stanion', *Northamptonshire Archaeology* 9, 110

Hall, D, 1973 'A thirteenth-century windmill site at Strixton, Northamptonshire', *Bedfordshire Archaeological Journal* 8, 109–118

Hall, D, 1974 'Medieval pottery from the Higham Ferrers hundred, Northamptonshire', *Journal of the Northamptonshire Museum and Art Gallery* 10, 38–58

Hall, D, 1995 *The open fields of Northamptonshire,* Northamptonshire Record Society 38, Northampton

Hall, D, 2014 *The open fields of England,* Oxford University Press, Oxford

Hall, D and Nickerson, N, 1966 'Sites on the north Bedfordshire and south Northamptonshire border', *Bedfordshire Archaeological Journal* 3, 1–6

Hall, D and Wilson, D R, 1978 'Elm: A field survey', *Proceedings of the Cambridge Antiquarian Society* 68, 21–47

Halpin, C, 1982 'The deserted medieval village of Thorpe, Earls Barton', *Northamptonshire Archaeology* 16, 197–198

Hammond, J L and Hammond, B, 1987 *The village labourer, 1760–1832,* Sutton, Gloucester

Hardy, A, Mair, C B and Williams, R J, 2007 *Death and taxes: The archaeology of a Middle Saxon estate centre at Higham Ferrers, Northamptonshire,* Oxford Archaeology, Oxford

Hargrave, R K, 2013 'John Alfred Gotch (1852–1942)', *Northamptonshire Past and Present* 66, 25–28

Harrison, J R, 1984 'The mud wall in England at the close of the vernacular era', *Transactions of the Ancient Monuments Society* 28, 154–174

Harvey, M, 1980 'Regular field and tenurial arrangements in Holderness, Yorkshire', *Journal of Historical Geography* 6, 3–16

Harvey, M, 1982 'Regular open-field systems on the Yorkshire Wolds', *Landscape History* 4, 29–39

Harvey, M, 1983 'Planned field systems in eastern Yorkshire: Some thoughts on their origin', *Agricultural History Review* 31, 91–103

Harvey, M, 1984 'Open field structure and landholding arrangements in Eastern Yorkshire', *Transactions of the Institute of British Geographers* 9, 60–74

Harvey, N, 1970 *A history of farm buildings in England and Wales,* David & Charles, Newton Abbot

Harvey, P D A, 1965 *A medieval Oxfordshire village: Cuxham 1240 to 1400,* Oxford University Press, London

Hatley, A A (ed.), 1973 *Northamptonshire militia lists 1777,* Northamptonshire Record Series 25, Kettering

Heward, J and Taylor, R, 1996 *The country houses of Northamptonshire,* RCHME, Swindon

Hatton, G W, 2005 *The medieval settlement at Onley, Northamptonshire,* unpublished paper presented to the CRAASH seminar, Cambridge University

Hill, N, 2005 'On the origins of crucks: An innocent notion', *Vernacular Architecture* 36.1, 1–14

Hill, N and Miles, D, 2001 'The Royal George, Cottingham, Northamptonshire: An early cruck building', *Vernacular Architecture* 32.1, 62–67

Hillson, S, 1986 *Teeth,* Cambridge University Press, Cambridge

Hilton, R H, 1975 *The English peasantry in the later Middle Ages,* Clarendon Press, Oxford

Hilton, R H and Rahtz, P A, 1966 'Upton, Gloucestershire, 1959–64', *Transactions of the Bristol and Gloucestershire Archaeological Society* 85, 70–146

Hinton, D A, 2010 'Deserted medieval villages and the objects from them', in C Dyer and R Jones (eds), *Deserted medieval villages revisited*, University of Hertfordshire Press, Hatfield, 85–108

Historic England, nd *Thor missile site at former RAF Harrington including the pyrotechnic store and classified storage building to the west of the three emplacements, 1400809*, unpublished Historic England document, https://historicengland.org.uk/listing/the-list/list-entry/1400809 (accessed September 2016)

Hodgkinson, T, 1971–72 'Monuments from Faxton Church in the Victoria and Albert Museum', *Northamptonshire Past and Present* 4, 335–339

Holden, B, 2008 *Faxton: The lost village*, Roseworld Productions, Solihull

Homans, G C, 1941 *English villagers of the thirteenth century*, Harvard University Press, Cambridge, MA

Horsman, V, Milne, C, Milne, G and Allen, P, 1988 *Aspects of Saxo-Norman London: 1, building and street development*, London and Middlesex Archaeological Society Special Paper 11, 71–84

Hoskins, W G, 1950 'The deserted villages of Leicestershire', in W G Hoskins, *Essays in Leicestershire History*, Liverpool University Press, 67–107

Hunt, E H and Pam, S J, 1997 'Prices and structural response in English agriculture, 1873–1896', *Economic History Review* 50, 477–505

Hunter, R, 1979 'St Neots type ware', in J H Williams, *St Peter's Street, Northampton: Excavations 1973–1976*, Northampton Development Corporation, Archaeological Monograph 2, 230–242

Hurman, B and Nenk, B, 2000 'The Gerald Dunning archive and the study of medieval ceramic roof furniture', *Medieval Ceramics* 24, 63–72

Hurst, D G and Hurst, J G, 1969 'Excavations at the medieval village of Wythemail, Northamptonshire', *Medieval Archaeology* 13, 167–203

Hurst, J G, 1956 'Deserted medieval villages and the excavations at Wharram Percy', in R L S Bruce-Mitford (ed.), *Recent archaeological excavations in Britain*, Routledge and Kegan Paul, London, 251–273

Hurst, J G, 1957 'Saxo-Norman pottery in East Anglia', *Proceedings of the Cambridge Antiquarian Society* 50, 29–60

Hurst, J G, 1959 'Middle Saxon pottery', in G C Dunning, J G Hurst, J N L Myres, and T Tischler, 'Anglo-Saxon pottery: A symposium', *Medieval Archaeology* 3, 13–31 (1–78)

Hurst, J G, 1965 'The medieval peasant house', in A Small (ed.), 'The fourth Viking Congress, 1961', *Aberdeen University Studies* CXLIX, 190–196

Hurst, J G, 1971 'A review of archaeological research to 1968', in M W Beresford and J G Hurst, *Deserted medieval villages*, Lutterworth Press, London, 76–144

Hurst, J G, 1976 'The pottery', in D M Wilson (ed.), *The Archaeology of Anglo-Saxon England*, Methuen, London, 283–348

Hurst, J G, 1986 'The medieval countryside', in I Longworth and J Cherry (eds), *Archaeology in Britain since 1945*, British Museum Publications, London, 202–232

Hurst, J G, 1988 'Rural building in England and Wales', in H E Hallam (ed.), *The agrarian history of England and Wales, Volume II, 1042–1350*, Cambridge University Press, Cambridge, 854–930

Ingham, B, 2002 'Dental anomalies in the Chillingham wild white cattle', *Transactions of the Natural History Society of Northumbria* 62, 169–175

Isham, T, 1971 (repr.) *The diary of Thomas Isham of Lamport (1658–81) kept by him in Latin from 1671 to 1673 at his father's command*, Gregg International, Farnborough

Ivens, R J, 1981 'Medieval pottery kilns at Brill, Buckinghamshire: Preliminary report on excavations in 1978', *Records of Buckinghamshire* 23, 102–106

Ivens, R J, 1982 'Medieval pottery from the 1978 excavations at Temple Farm, Brill', *Records of Buckinghamshire* 24, 144–170

Ivens, R J, Busby, P and Shepherd, N, 1995 *Tattenhoe and Westury: Two deserted medieval settlements in Milton Keynes*, Buckinghamshire Archaeology Society, Aylesbury

Ivens, R J and Hurman, B, 1995 'The medieval pottery', in R Ivens, P Busby and N Shepherd, *Tattenhoe and Westbury: Two deserted medieval settlements in Milton Keynes*, Buckinghamshire Archaeology Society Monograph 8, 241–302

Jaquin, P and Augarde, C, 2012 *Earth building: History, science and conservation*, BRE Press, Bracknell

Jarrett, M G, 1962 'The deserted village of West Whelpington, Northumberland', *Archaeologia Aeliana (series 4)* 40, 189–225

Jarrett, M G, 1970 'The deserted village of West Whelpington, Northumberland, second report', *Archaeologia Aeliana (series 4)* 48, 183–302

Jarrett, M G and Wrathmell, S, 1977 'Sixteenth- and seventeenth-century farmsteads: West Whelpington, Northumberland', *Agricultural History Review* 25.2, 108–119

JHC, 1803 *Journals of the House of Commons from June the 25th, 1741 to September the 19th 1745*, reprinted by Order of the House of Commons, London

Johnson, S W, 1806 *Rural economy: Containing a treatise on pisé building*, I Riley, New Brunswick, NJ

Jones, C, Eyre-Morgan, G, Palmer, S and Palmer, N, 1997 'Excavations in the outer enclosure of Boteler's Castle, Oversley, Alcester, 1992–93', *Transactions of the Birmingham and Warwickshire Archaeological Society* 101, 1–98

Jones, L, 1998–99 'Four zoomorphic roof finials from Worcestershire', *Medieval Ceramics* 22–23, 154–159

Jones, R and Lewis, C, 2012 'The Midlands: Medieval settlement and landscape', in N Christie and P Stamper (eds), *Medieval rural settlement: Britain and Ireland, AD 800–1600*, Windgather, Oxford, 186–205

Jones, R and Page, M, 2006 *Medieval villages in an English landscape: Beginnings and ends*, Windgather Press, Macclesfield

Jope, E M, 1950 'Northamptonshire: A late medieval pottery kiln at Potterspury', *Archaeological Newsletter* 2.10, 156–157

Jope, E M, 1953–54 'Medieval pottery kilns at Brill, Buckinghamshire: Preliminary report on excavations in 1953', *Records of Buckinghamshire* 16, 39–42

Keefe, L, 2005 *Earth building: Methods and materials, repair and conservation*, Taylor and Francis, London

Kelleher, R, 2018 *Money in the medieval town and countryside: Coin finds from England and Wales 1066–1544*, British Numismatic Society Special Publication 14, London

Kilmurry, K, 1980 *The pottery industry of Stamford, Lincolnshire, c. AD 850–1250*, British Archaeological Reports British Series 84, Oxford

Kipling, R, 2017 'Kilsby, Daventry Road', *South Midlands Archaeology* 47, 51

Klingelhofer, E C, 1974 *The deserted medieval village of Broadfield, Hertfordshire*, British Archaeological Reports British Series 2, Oxford

Knight, J, 1992 'Excavations at Montgomery Castle, Part I', *Archaeologia Cambrensis* 141, 97–180

Langdon, J, 1986 *Horses, oxen and technological innovation: The use of draught animals in English farming from 1066 to 1500*, Cambridge University Press, Cambridge

Langdon, J, 2004 *Mills in the medieval economy: England 1300–1540*, Oxford University Press, Oxford

Lewis, C, 2016 'The medieval period (850–1500)', in *East Midlands Historic Environment Research Framework* http://archaeologydataservice.ac.uk/researchframeworks/eastmidlands_v1/wiki/Eastmid8 (accessed May 2017)

Lewis, C, Mitchell-Fox, P and Dyer, C, 1997 *Village, hamlet and field: Changing medieval settlements in Central England*, Manchester University Press, Manchester

Lindley, K, 1982 *Fenland riots and the English Revolution*, Ashgate, London

Longcroft, A, 2006 'Medieval clay-walled houses: A case study from Norfolk', *Vernacular Architecture* 37.1, 61–74

Longden, H I, 1943 *Northamptonshire and Rutland clergy from 1500, volume XV*, Archer & Goodman, Northampton

Loyd, L C and Stenton, D M (eds), 1950 *Sir Christopher Hatton's Book of Seals*, Northamptonshire Record Society 15, Oxford

MacDonald, A and Gowing, C, 1989 'Excavations at the hamlet in Bedgrove, Aylesbury, 1964–66', *Records of Buckinghamshire* 31, 120–136

MacGregor, A, 1985 *Bone, antler, ivory and horn: The technology of skeletal materials since the Roman period*, Croom Helm, London

Macnamara, F N, 1895 *Memorials of the Danvers family (of Dauntsey and Culworth)*, Hardy and Page, London

Mahany, C, Burchard, A and Simpson, G, 1982 *Excavations in Stamford, Lincolnshire 1963–1969*, The Society for Medieval Archaeology Monograph 9, London

May, J, 1973 'Rescue archaeology in the East Midlands', *Midland History* 2.1, 11–17

Mayes, P and Butler, L, 1983 *Sandal Castle excavations, 1964–1973: A detailed archaeological report*, Wakefield Historical Society, Wakefield, West Yorkshire

McCann, J, 2007 'Clay-walled houses in Norfolk: Some comments', *Vernacular Architecture* 38.1, 58–60

McCarthy, M R, 1979 'The pottery', in J H Williams, *St Peter's Street, Northampton: Excavations 1973–1976*, Northampton Development Corporation, Archaeological Monograph 2, 151–242

McCarthy, M R and Brooks, C M, 1988 *Medieval pottery in Britain AD 900–1600*, Leicester University Press, Leicester

McDonagh, B, 2011 'Enclosure, agricultural change and the remaking of the local landscape: The case of Lilford (Northamptonshire)', *Northamptonshire Past & Present* 64, 45–52

McDonagh, B and Daniels, S, 2012 'Enclosure stories: Narratives from Northamptonshire', *Cultural Geography* 19, 107–121

Medlycott, A, 2011 *Research and archaeology revisited: A revised framework for the East of England*, East Anglian Archaeology Occasional Paper 24, ALGAO, Dorset

Mellows, W T (ed.), 1927 *Henry of Pytchley's Book of Fees*, Northamptonshire Record Society Series 2, Kettering

Mercer, E, 1975 *English vernacular houses: A study of traditional farmhouses and cottages*, Her Majesty's Stationery Office, London

Miller, P and Wilson, T, 2005 *Saxon, medieval and post-medieval settlement at Sol Central, Marefair, Northampton: Archaeological excavations 1998–2002*, Museum of London Archaeology Service, London

Milne, G (ed.), 1992 *Timber-building techniques in London c. 900–1400*, London and Middlesex Archaeology Society Special Papers 15, London

Moffett, L, 2006 'The archaeology of medieval plant foods', in C M Woolgar, D Serjeantson and C Waldron (eds), *Food in medieval England: Diet and nutrition*, Oxford University Press, Oxford, 41–55

Moore, D T, 1978 'The petrography and archaeology of English honestones', *Journal of Archaeological Science* 5, 61–73

Moore, D T and Oakley, G E, 1979 'The hones', in J H Williams (ed.), *St Peter's Street, Northampton: Excavations 1973–1976*, East Anglian Archaeology 22, Gressenhall, 280–283

Moore, R 2015 'The development of archaeology in Northamptonshire to 1980', *Northamptonshire Archaeology* 38, 5–21

Moore, W R G, 1980 *Northamptonshire clay tobacco-pipes and pipemakers*, Northampton Museums and Art Gallery, Northampton

Moorhouse, S, 1971a 'Two late and post-medieval pottery groups from Farnham Castle, Surrey', *Surrey Archaeological Collections* 68, 39–55

Moorhouse, S, 1971b 'A sixteenth-century Tudor Green group from Overton, Hampshire', *Post-Medieval Archaeology* 5, 182–185

Moorhouse, S, 1974 'A distinctive type of late medieval pottery in the Eastern Midlands: A definition and preliminary statement', *Proceedings of the Cambridge Antiquarian Society* 65, 46–59

Moorhouse, S, 1981 'The medieval pottery industry', in D W Crossley (ed.), *Medieval Industry*, Council for British Archaeology Research Report 40, London, 96–125

Moorhouse, S, 1983 'The medieval pottery', in P Mayes and L A S Butler, *Sandal Castle excavations 1964–73*, Wakefield Historical Publications, Wakefield, 83–212

Moorhouse, S, 1988 'Documentary evidence for medieval ceramic roofing materials and its archaeological implications: Some thoughts', *Medieval Ceramics* 12, 33–55

Morris, J, 2016 *Torn apart: The lost church of St Denis, Faxton, Northamptonshire*, unpublished typescript report

Muir, R, 1992 *The villages of England*, Thames and Hudson, London

Muir, R and Muir, N, 1987 *Hedgerows: Their history and wildlife*, Michael Joseph, London

Murphy, K, 1994 'Excavations in three burgage plots in the medieval town of Newport, Dyfed', *Medieval Archaeology* 38, 55–82

Murray, H K and Murray, J C, 1993 'Excavations at Rattray, Aberdeenshire: A Scottish deserted burgh', *Medieval Archaeology* 37, 109–218

Musty, J and Algar, D, 1986 'Excavations at the deserted medieval village of Gomeldon, near Salisbury', *Wiltshire Archaeological and Natural History Magazine* 80, 127–169

Mynard, D C, 1969a 'Excavations at Somerby, Lincs, 1957', *Lincolnshire History and Archaeology* 1, 4

Mynard, D C 1969b 'The pottery', in D G Hurst and J G Hurst 'Excavations at the medieval village of Wythemail, Northamptonshire', *Medieval Archaeology* 13, 182–198

Mynard, D C, 1970 'Medieval pottery of the Potterspury type', *Bulletin of the Northamptonshire Federation of Archaeological Societies* 4, 49–55

Mynard, D C, 1972 'A late medieval kiln at Potterspury', *Milton Keynes Journal* 1, 12–13

Mynard, D C, 1984 'A medieval pottery industry at Olney Hyde', *Records of Buckinghamshire* 26, 56–85

Mynard, D C, 1991 'The medieval and post-medieval pottery', in D C Mynard and R J Zeepvat, *Excavations at Great Linford, 1974–80*, Buckinghamshire Archaeological Society, Aylesbury, 245–372

Mynard, D C, 1994 *Excavations on medieval sites in Milton Keynes, Buckinghamshire* Archaeological Society 6, Longdunn Press, Bristol

Mynard, D C and Zeepvat, R J, 1991 *Excavations at Great Linford, 1974–80*, Buckinghamshire Archaeological Society, Aylesbury

Mytum, H 2015 'Obituary: Lawrence Butler (1934–2014)', *Post-Medieval Archaeology* 50.1, 178–180

Natural England, 2014 *National Character Area Profiles*, https://www.gov.uk/government/publications/national-character-area-profiles-data-for-local-decision-making (accessed May 2017)

Neal, D S, 1977 'Excavations at the Palace of King's Langley, Hertfordshire, 1974–1976', *Medieval Archaeology* 21, 127

Northamptonshire County Council, 2015 *Historic Landscape Characterisation*, http://archaeologydataservice.ac.uk/archives/view/northamptonshire_hlc_2015/ (accessed December 2016)

O'Donnell, R, 2011 'Adapting landscapes: The continual modification of Leicestershire's open fields', *Landscapes* 12, 63–83

O'Donnell, R, 2014 'Conflict, agreement and landscape change: Methods of enclosure of the northern English countryside', *Journal of Historical Geography* 44, 109–121

O'Donnell, R, 2015 *Assembling enclosure: Transformations in the rural landscape of post-medieval north-east England,* University of Hertfordshire Press, Hatfield

Oliver, R, 2005 *Ordnance Survey maps: A concise guide for historians,* Charles Close Society, London

Oosthuizen, S, 2006 *Landscapes decoded: The origins and development of Cambridgeshire's medieval fields,* University of Hertfordshire Press, Hatfield

Orwin, C S and Orwin, C S, 1938 *The open fields,* Clarendon Press, Oxford

Oswald, A, 1975 *Clay pipes for the archaeologist,* British Archaeological Report British Series 14, Oxford

Pallister, A F and Wrathmell, S, 1990 'The deserted village of West Hartburn, third report: Excavations of Site D and discussion', in B E Vyner (ed.), *Medieval rural settlement in north-east England,* Architectural and Archaeological Society of Durham and Northumberland Research Report 2, Durham, 59–78

Palmer, A (ed.), 1947 *Recording Britain II,* Oxford University Press, Oxford

Parry, S J, 2006 *Raunds area survey: An archaeological study of the landscape of Raunds, Northamptonshire 1985–94,* Oxbow Books, Oxford

Parsons, D and Sutherland, S, 2013 *The Anglo-Saxon Church of All Saints, Brixworth, Northamptonshire: Survey, excavation and analysis, 1972–2010,* Oxbow Books, Oxford

Partida, T, Hall, D and Foard, G, 2013 *An atlas of Northamptonshire: The medieval and early modern landscape,* Oxbow Books, Oxford

Pearson, T, 2009 'The pottery from Furnells', in M Audouy and A Chapman, *Raunds: The origins and growth of a Midland village AD 450–1500,* Oxbow Books, Oxford, 151–170

Pettit, P A J, 1968 *The royal forests of Northamptonshire: A study in their economy 1558–1714,* Northamptonshire Record Society 23, Gateshead

Phillimore, W P W, Faithful, R C and Longden, H I, 1908 *Northamptonshire parish registers: Marriages, volume I,* Phillimore, London

Phillimore, W P W, Faithful, R C and Longden, H I, 1909 *Northamptonshire parish registers: Marriages, volume II,* Phillimore, London

Posnansky, M, 1956 'The Lamport post mill', *Journal of the Northamptonshire Natural History Field Club* 33, 66–79

Pounds, N J G, 2000 *A history of the English parish: The culture of religion from Augustine to Victoria,* Cambridge University Press, Cambridge

PRO, 1906 *Inquisitions and assessments relating to feudal aids, with other analogous documents preserved in the Public Record Office, AD 1284–1431, Volume IV, Northampton-Somerset,* Her Majesty's Stationery Office, London

Rackham, D J, 1986 'Assessing the relative frequencies of species by the application of a stochastic model to a zooarchaeological database', in L H van Wijngaarden-Bakker (ed.), *Database management and zooarchaeology,* PACT 14, Strasburg, 185–192

Rackham, O, 2000 *History of the countryside,* Phoenix, London

Rahtz, P A, 1969 *Excavations at King John's Hunting Lodge, Writtle, Essex, 1955–57,* The Society for Medieval Archaeology Monograph 3, London

Rahtz, P A, 2003 'John Hurst, 1927–2003', *Antiquity* 77, 880–881

Randerson, M J and Gidney, L J, 2011 *The 'Great Chase' of the Bishops of Durham: Princely power and the hunt,* unpublished report, Archaeological Services Durham University

RCHME, 1979 *An inventory of the historical monuments in the county of Northamptonshire, volume 2,* Royal Commission for Historical Monuments of England, London

RCHME, 1981 *An inventory of the historical monuments in the county of Northamptonshire, volume 3,* Royal Commission for Historical Monuments of England, London

Redundant Churches Fund, 1990 *Churches in retirement,* Her Majesty's Stationery Office, London

Rippon, S, 2008 *Beyond the medieval village: The diversification of landscape character in southern Britain,* Oxford University Press, Oxford

Rippon, S, 2010 'Landscape change in the "Long Eighth Century"', in N Higham and M J Ryan (eds), *The landscape archaeology of Anglo-Saxon England,* Boydell, Woodbridge, 39–64

Roberts, B K and Wrathmell, S, 2000 *An atlas of rural settlement in England,* English Heritage, London

Roberts, B K and Wrathmell, S, 2003 *Region and place: A study of English rural settlement,* English Heritage, London

Rowley, T, 2006 *The English landscape in the twentieth century,* Hambledon Continuum, London

Russell, E, 1974 *Excavations on the site of the deserted medieval village of Kettleby Thorpe, Lincolnshire,* Journal of the Scunthorpe Museum Society Series 3 (Archaeology) Number 2, Scunthorpe

Salzman, L F (ed.), 1943 *Chartulary of Lewes Priory,* Sussex Record Society I, London

Saunders, G (ed.), 2011 *Recording Britain,* V&A Publishing, London

Scarfe, N, 1995 *Innocent espionage: The La Rochefoucauld Brothers' tour of England in 1785,* Boydell, Woodbridge

Schmid, E, 1972 *Atlas of animal bones,* Elsevier Publishing Co, London

Seaborne, M V J, 1964 'Cob cottages in Northamptonshire', *Northamptonshire Past and Present* 3, 215–230

Seaby, P J, 1970 *Coins and tokens of Ireland,* Seaby, London

Serjeantson, R M and Longden, H I, 1913 'The parish churches and religious houses of Northamptonshire: Their dedications, altars, images and lights', *The Archaeological Journal* 70, 105–106

Sharp, B, 2010 *In contempt of all authority, rural artisans and riot in the west of England, 1586–1660,* Breviary Stuff Publications, London

Shaw-Taylor, L, 2001a 'Parliamentary enclosure and the emergence of an English agricultural proletariat', *The Journal of Economic History* 61, 640–662

Shaw-Taylor, L, 2001b 'Labourers, cows, common rights and Parliamentary enclosure: The evidence of contemporary comment c.1760-1810', *Past & Present* 125, 95–126

Silver, I A, 1969 'The ageing of domestic animals', in D Brothwell and E Higgs (eds), *Science in archaeology,* Thames and Hudson, London, 283–302

Slowikowski, A, 2011 *'Genius in a cracked pot'. Late Medieval Reduced Ware: A regional synthesis,* Medieval Pottery Research Group Occasional Paper 4, London

Smith, G, 1998 *Northamptonshire airfields of the Second World War,* Countryside Books, Newbury

Smith, P J, 2006 'Roots and origins: Archaeology and Wharram. An interview with John G. Hurst', *Medieval Settlement Research Group Annual Report* 21, 59–64

Stamp, L D, 1931 *The land utilisation survey of Britain, Northamptonshire and the Soke of Peterborough,* Geographical Publications, London

Steane, J M, 1967 'Excavations at the deserted medieval village of Lyveden', *Journal of Northampton Museum* 2, 1–37

Steane, J M, 1971 'Faxton', *Bulletin of the Northamptonshire Archaeological Society* 7, 43

Steane, J M, 1974 *The Northamptonshire landscape,* Hodder and Stoughton, London

Steane, J M, 1975 'The medieval parks of Northamptonshire', *Northamptonshire Past and Present* 5, 211–233

Steane, J M and Bryant, G F, 1975 'Excavations at the deserted medieval settlement of Lyveden', *Journal of the Northampton Museum and Art Gallery* 12, 1–160

Stenton, F M, 1961 *The first century of English feudalism, 1066–1166,* Clarendon Press, Oxford

Tate, W E, 1978 *Domesday of English enclosure acts and awards,* University of Reading, Reading

Taylor, C C, 1983 *Village and farmstead: A history of rural settlement in England,* George Philip, Over Wallop

Tebbutt, C F, 1960 'An early twelfth century building at Eynesbury, Huntingdonshire', *Proceedings of the Cambridge Antiquarian Society* 54, 85–89

Thirsk, J, 1964 'The common fields', *Past & Present* 29, 3–25

Thirsk, J, 1966 'The origin of the common fields', *Past & Present* 33, 142–147

Thompson, B and Markham, Major, 1929 'Faxton pottery kiln', *Journal of the Northamptonshire Natural History Society and Field Club* 200, 103

Turner, G J, 1901 *Select pleas of the forest,* B Quaritch, London

Turner, M E, 1980 *English parliamentary enclosure: Its historical geography and economic history,* Dawson Publishing, Folkestone

Twigge, S and Scott, L, 2000 'The other missiles of October: The Thor IRBMs and the Cuban missile crisis', *Electronic Journal of International History* 3, 1471–1443

VCH, 1902 *Victoria County History of the county of Northampton Volume 1,* Constable, London

VCH, 1906 *Victoria County History of the county of Northampton Volume 2,* Constable, London

VCH, 1930 *Victoria County History of the county of Northampton Volume 3,* Constable, London

VCH, 1937 *Victoria County History of the county of Northampton Volume 4,* Boydell & Brewer, London

Wacher, J S, 1960 'Excavations at Martinsthorpe, Rutland', *Transactions of the Leicestershire Archaeological and Historical Society* 39, 1–19

Wade, K, 1973 *The Thetford ware tradition with special reference to Norfolk,* unpublished BA Dissertation, University of Southampton

Wade, K, 1976 'Excavations at Langhale, Kirkstead', in P Wade-Martins (ed.), *Norfolk,* East Anglian Archaeology Monograph 2, Gressenhall, 101–129

Wade-Martins, P, 1980 *Norfolk: Village sites in Launditch hundred,* East Anglian Archaeology Monograph 10, Gressenhall

Wailes, R, 1954 *The English windmill,* Routledge and Paul, London

Wake, J (ed.), 1935 *The Montagu Musters Book 1602–1623,* Northamptonshire Record Society 7, Peterborough

Wake, J, 1959 'Churches in trust', *Northamptonshire Past and Present* 2, 294–303

Wake, J, 1962 'The destruction of Faxton church', *Northamptonshire Past and Present* 2 no. 6, 296–301

Watkins Pitchford, D, 1941 *The Countryman's bedside book,* Eyre and Spottiswoode, London

Webster, L, 1979 'Medieval Britain in 1978', *Medieval Archaeology* 23, 234–278

Welles, A, 1876 *History of the Welles family,* Albert Welles, New York

West, S, 1969 'The deserted medieval village of Snarford, Lincs', *Lincolnshire History and Archaeology* 4, 93–97

Whellan, W, 1849 *History of the diocese of Peterborough,* Whittaker and Co, Peterborough

Whetham, E H and Orwin, C S, 1964 *History of British agriculture, 1846–1914,* Longmans, London

Willatts, R M, 2000 'Mud structures in the Harborough area', *The Harborough Historian* 17, 24–28

Williams, H M R, 2014 'Commemorating an archaeologist: Dolforwyn and death', at the blog *Archaeodeath. Archaeology, mortality and material culture* https://howardwilliamsblog.wordpress.com/2016/01/04/commemorating-an-archaeologist-dolforwyn-and-death/ (accessed February 2017)

Williams, J, 1974 'Northampton', *Current Archaeology* 4.45, 340–348

Williams, J H, 1978 'Excavations at Greyfriars, Northampton, 1972', *Northamptonshire Archaeology* 13, 106

Williams, J H and Farwell, C, 1984 'Excavations in the Riding, Northampton, in the area of Gobion Manor, 1981–82', *Northamptonshire Archaeology* 19, 83–106

Williamson, G C, 1889 *Trade tokens issued in the seventeenth century in England, Wales and Ireland,* revised edition, Elliot Stock, London

Williamson, T, 2003 *Shaping Medieval landscapes: Settlement, society, environment,* Windgather Press, Macclesfield

Williamson, T, 2013 *An environmental history of wildlife in England 1650–1950,* Bloomsbury, London

Williamson, T, Liddiard, R and Partida, T, 2013 *Champion: The making and unmaking of the English Midland landscape,* Liverpool University Press, Liverpool

Wilson, B and Edwards, P, 1993 'Butchery of horse and dog at Witney Palace, Oxfordshire, and the knackering and feeding of meat to hounds during the post-medieval period', *Post-Medieval Archaeology* 27, 43–56

Wilson, D and Hurst, D G, 1965 'Medieval Britain in 1964', *Medieval Archaeology* 9, 170–220

Wilson, D and Hurst, D G, 1966 'Medieval Britain in 1965', *Medieval Archaeology* 10, 168–219

Wilson, D and Hurst, D G, 1967 'Medieval Britain in 1966', *Medieval Archaeology* 11, 262–319

Wilson, D and Hurst, D G, 1968 'Medieval Britain in 1967', *Medieval Archaeology* 12, 155–211

Wilson, D M and Hurst, D G, 1969 'Medieval Britain in 1968', *Medieval Archaeology* 13, 155–211

Wilson, D M and Hurst, D G, 1970 'Medieval Britain in 1969', *Medieval Archaeology* 14, 155–208

Wrathmell, S, 1984 'The vernacular threshold of northern peasant houses', *Vernacular Architecture* 15, 29–33

Wrathmell, S, 1989 *Domestic settlement 2: Medieval peasant farmsteads,* Wharram, a study of settlement on the Yorkshire Wolds 6, York

Wrathmell, S, 2002 'Some general hypotheses on English medieval peasant house construction from the 7th to the 17th centuries', in J Klápště (ed.), *The rural house from the migration period to the oldest still standing buildings,* Institute of Archaeology, Academy of Sciences of the Czech Republic, Prague, 175–186

Wrathmell, S, 2012 'Observations on the structure and form of Wharram's late medieval farmhouses', in S Wrathmell (ed.), *A history of Wharram Percy and its neighbours,* Wharram, a study of settlement on the Yorkshire Wolds 13, York, 340–432

Wrightson, K, 2003 *English society: 1580–1680,* Rutgers University Press, New Brunswick, NJ

Yelling, J A, 1977 *Common field and enclosure in England 1450–1850,* Palgrave, London

Young, S and Kay, F, 2015 *Archaeological excavation of a cable trench on the B4036 (Daventry to Long Backby Road) near Thrupp Grounds Farm, Northans,* unpublished typescript report available at OASIS claspi-224802

INDEX

(Page numbers in *italic* refer to illustrations, those in **bold** to tables.
Sites are in Northamptonshire, unless stated otherwise.)